MW00850919

Supply Chain Management
A Learning Perspective
THIRD EDITION

This edition of *Supply Chain Management* (SCM) was revised to appeal to a wider readership besides students taking SCM courses. Global supply chain managers and researchers in the fields of SCM and operations strategy would find it a useful reference. Rather than discuss the technical issues of SCM, the book focuses on the strategic perspectives and approaches of SCM. Students learn to identify SCM issues from the top management's perspective. The book also presents real-world managerial problems and incorporates case studies for connecting theories with practices. By exploring the fundamental issues of SCM, managers acquire a new learning perspective that enables them to solve problems in a more sustainable and innovative manner rather than use short-term, ad hoc solutions. Finally, it distills various theoretical concepts to allow researchers to observe real SCM issues in a managerial context which allows for practical, meaningful, and impactful research to be carried out.

Bowon Kim is Professor of Operations Strategy and Management Science at KAIST Business School in Seoul, Korea. He earned a Doctor of Business Administration in Technology and Operations Management from Harvard University (1995), an MS in Operations Research from Stanford University (1989), and a Bachelor's from Seoul National University (1988). He is teaching and doing research on supply chain management, new product innovation, and value chain sustainability. He has published numerous papers in prestigious academic journals. In 2017, he published a book entitled *Optimal Control Applications for Operations Strategy*, which elaborates on SCM using optimal control theory and differential games.

Supply Chain Management
A Learning Perspective

THIRD EDITION

BOWON KIM
Korea Advanced Institute of Science and Technology (KAIST)

CAMBRIDGE
UNIVERSITY PRESS

CAMBRIDGE
UNIVERSITY PRESS

University Printing House, Cambridge CB2 8BS, United Kingdom

One Liberty Plaza, 20th Floor, New York, NY 10006, USA

477 Williamstown Road, Port Melbourne, VIC 3207, Australia

314–321, 3rd Floor, Plot 3, Splendor Forum, Jasola District Centre, New Delhi – 110025, India

79 Anson Road, #06–04/06, Singapore 079906

Cambridge University Press is part of the University of Cambridge.

It furthers the University's mission by disseminating knowledge in the pursuit of
education, learning, and research at the highest international levels of excellence.

www.cambridge.org
Information on this title: www.cambridge.org/9781107137745
DOI: 10.1017/9781316480984

First edition published in 2005 by John Wiley & Sons
Second edition published in 2014 by Hankyungsa Publishing Co.
Third edition 2018

Printed in the United Kingdom by TJ International Ltd, Padstow, Cornwall

A catalogue record for this publication is available from the British Library.

Library of Congress Cataloging-in-Publication Data
Names: Kim, Bowon, author.
Title: Supply chain management : a learning perspective / Bowon Kim, Korea Advanced
Institute of Science and Technology (KAIST).
Description: Third edition. | Cambridge, United Kingdom ; New York, NY : Cambridge
University Press, 2018. | Includes bibliographical references and index.
Identifiers: LCCN 2017048719| ISBN 9781107137745 (hardback) | ISBN 9781316502761 (paperback)
Subjects: LCSH: Business logistics – Asia.
Classification: LCC HD38.5 .K478 2018 | DDC 658.7–dc23
LC record available at https://lccn.loc.gov/2017048719

ISBN 978-1-107-13774-5 Hardback
ISBN 978-1-316-50276-1 Paperback

Additional resources for this publication are available at www.cambridge.org/LearningSCM

For my parents
부모님께

Contents Summary

Contents

Part V   Analytical Tools (Online)

Online Chapter 12 Analytical Methods for Supply Chain Management[1]

---

[1] This can be downloaded from our companion website: www.cambridge.org/LearningSCM.

Figures

Tables

Case Studies

Preface to the Third Edition

Supply Chain Management: A Learning Perspective is the third edition of my book on supply chain management originally published by John Wiley & Sons in 2005. Supply chain management is about creating value through coordination. In this book, I explore essential issues of supply chain management from the learning perspective – a philosophical prism through which I analyze and understand value and the value creation process.

As we will see, Confucius taught three ways for a human being to obtain wisdom. The first was through reflection, the noblest way. The second was through imitation, the easiest way. Finally, one could get wisdom through one's own experience, the bitterest way! Drawing an analogy with Confucian teaching, I suggest we can learn in three different ways – analyzing, benchmarking, and experiencing. What is the fundamental commonality underlying all these three methodologies? That is the causal relationship, i.e., **cause-and-effect analysis**. For instance, we analyze, benchmark, and experience to understand the cause-and-effect relationship between variables, e.g., key factors in managerial decision-making. Unless the manager understands the complex causal relationship among managerial variables or factors, she is not able to make a decision that can solve real-world managerial problems.

In fact, the cause-and-effect analysis is the fundamental base for a systemic perspective, which is the underlying principle of managerial learning. As such, it is the quintessential perspective for this book – *Supply Chain Management: A Learning Perspective*.

Is there a perfect solution to a managerial problem? Possibly except for some of the most basic problems, we cannot find a definitive solution to a real-world managerial problem. Then, what is the role of a professor in a business school? It should be a kind of coaching. A coach for a chef! Cooking is probably for the most creative people. Suppose there are two chefs, who use the same ingredients and also the same cooking processes. Then, will the two dishes prepared by the two chefs be exactly the same? The answer is an unambiguous "no." Even if the two chefs use the same resources and processes, their foods will be very different. In fact, the chef is a creative director, who finalizes the food. It is the chef's creative capability that determines the food's ultimate taste. What the chef does for her food can never be predetermined completely, since she has to constantly adapt her cooking to the emerging unknowns in the kitchen environment. No one can foretell what those unknowns are and how they will unfold down the road. In a sense, the chef is a self-adapting, self-organizing system. The chef's tasks cannot be programmed a priori.

With this book, I hope to help students to become managers like the chefs, who can self-adapt and self-organize to create value in the global economic ecosystem. The learning capability is the most important competence such managers should master first. In effect, in this book, I would like to teach the future managers the learning capability that enables them to design a highly effective supply chain strategy for maximizing value creation.

Book Structure

This book consists of eleven chapters and one digital (online) chapter on analytical methods and additional five online appendixes that supplement five of the main chapters. The online chapter deals with more advanced or technical subjects that are related with those in the associated chapter. All of the online resources are available on the book's companion website. According to a logical sequence, the chapters can be grouped into four parts as follows:

Part I Basic Principles in Operations and Supply Chain Management

- Chapter 1 Value Chain and Value Creation
- Chapter 2 Learning and Learning Perspective
- **Online Appendix 2A** Learning and Learning Perspective
- Chapter 3 Fundamentals of Operations and Supply Chain Management
- **Online Appendix 3A** Fundamentals of Operations and Supply Chain Management

Part II Structural Dimension of Supply Chain Management

- Chapter 4 Supply Chain Configuration and Connection
- Chapter 5 Strategic Roles of Inventory
- Chapter 6 Logistics, Procurement, and Supplier Relationship

Part III Infrastructural Dimension of Supply Chain Management

- Chapter 7 Supply Chain Coordination
- Chapter 8 Strategic Tools of Supply Chain Capability
- **Online Appendix 8A** Strategic Tools of Supply Chain Capability
- Chapter 9 Innovation and Technology
- **Online Appendix 9A** Case Studies

Part IV Sustainable Value Chain Management

- Chapter 10 Global Supply Chain Management
- **Online Appendix 10A** Application of the Dynamic Research Framework
- Chapter 11 Sustainability and Supply Chain Management

Part V Analytical Tools

- **Online** Chapter 12 Analytical Methods for Supply Chain Management

As Figure P1 shows, we postulate there are three building blocks for value creation in supply chain management, i.e., fundamental foundation, strategic supply chain design, and sustainable implementation. Parts I and V constitute the fundamental foundation,

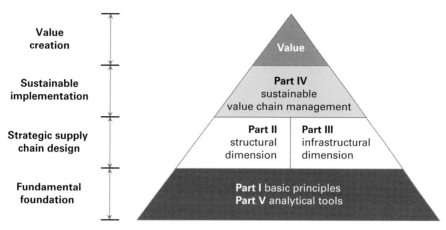

Figure P1 Book Structure

Parts II and III form the strategic supply chain design, and Part IV establishes the sustainable implementation. We provide brief definitions of the five parts in this book.

Part I (Basic Principles in Operations and Supply Chain Management) puts forth fundamental principles that lay the foundation for our theoretical and empirical discussion on supply chain management in the succeeding chapters. In particular, we define value, value creation, and value chain, which enable us to define supply chain management in the context of broader management theory and perspective. We thoroughly focus on learning and learning organization as the most important theoretical underpinning of our discourse on supply chain management. In fact, the learning perspective is the core of our approach to studying essential issues in supply chain management. Based on the value and learning theory, we introduce students to the basics of operations management and supply chain management.

Part II (Structural Dimension of Supply Chain Management) explores the structural dimension of supply chain management, which compares to the computer hardware. That is, it consists of decision factors that are in general physical, tangible, or visibly observable. Supply chain configuration is the decision about physical location or placement of value chain activities across different geographic regions, e.g., where to place the supplier, to build the plant, to construct the warehouse, or to have the target market. It is also concerned with the physical capacity or size of the value chain activities scattered across the global market. To maximize value creation through supply chain management, the company should make a decision on supply chain connection, i.e., how to connect the scattered value chain activities most effectively. It also encompasses which product, service, information, or communication to flow through the supply chain configuration. Once supply chain configuration and connection are structured to a functional extent, the company should develop a mechanism to deal with diverse uncertainties in the market. Inventory is such a mechanism used to buffer against uncertainty. As such, the company should make a decision on where and how much inventory to have. In general, the larger the uncertainty the company should face, the larger the inventory size. Although inventory often accounts for the largest asset or cost elements in the financial statements, it has other more significant strategic implications, two of which we discuss in great detail, i.e., innovation and learning. Finally, the company should plan to actually deliver the various forms of materials through the supply chain, i.e., to make a logistic or transportation decision. In addition, we elaborate two related issues, i.e., procurement and supplier relationship, which are deeply connected with not only another structural element, inventory, but also the infrastructural dimension, coordination. We have to emphasize that although these four elements of the structural dimension have distinctive attributes, they are also intricately linked with each other. For example, once the supply chain configuration is decided, the boundary or extent of the decisions on supply chain connection might be determined at least roughly or loosely. In turn, the supply chain connection once designed can influence the company's decision on inventory to a potentially great extent. Similarly, the decision on logistics or transportation is tightly correlated with the inventory decision. How to design the elements in the structural dimension can also have a lasting effect on how to coordinate supply chain activities, i.e., the infrastructural dimension.

Part III (Infrastructural Dimension of Supply Chain Management) explores essential characteristics of supply chain coordination, the only element in the supply chain infrastructural dimension. Coordination is embodied in actual collaboration and communication between supply chain partner companies for such strategic activities as information-sharing, new product development, R&D, and other joint decision-making such as marketing, finance, procurement, and distribution. Since the practical performance measurement of supply chain management is concerned with the mismatch between demand and supply, one of the most practical objectives of supply chain coordination should be to minimize the mismatch between demand and supply throughout the supply chain. Thus, we deliberate capabilities that underpin the supply chain strategies, which in turn enable the company to achieve the goal of minimizing mismatches. One cannot comprehend capability without perusing creativity, innovation, and technology, whose fundamental characteristics and principles we elaborate.

Part IV (Sustainable Value Chain Management) discusses two subjects for constant value creation, i.e., globalization and sustainability. In order for a small and medium enterprise to grow continuously, it should regard the global market as its target market from the very beginning and design its supply chain on a global scale. We examine key questions the company should ask when it develops its global strategy: *Why should we globalize? Which market is strategically important? Which product should we globalize first? What entry mode should we take? How can we transplant our corporate culture in the global market? How should we localize effectively? How should we grow or expand continuously in the global market?* Then, we look at sustainability. In fact, we define value system sustainability, which emphasizes a firm's effort to make decisions in a way to be sustainable not just from the firm's own perspective, but from the perspectives of the entire value chain participants, including both internal and external stakeholders. Consistent with published research, we suggest that sustainability be approached from three perspectives, i.e., economic, social, and natural (environmental). Sustainable implementation of supply chain strategy enables the company to create value optimally from the three perspectives simultaneously. This should be the ultimate goal of the company.

Part V (Analytical Tools) delineates basic analytical methods, which the decision-maker can utilize to solve problems in supply chain management. Key concepts and methods presented in this part include: uncertainty, probability, mean, standard deviation, and normal distribution; break-even point (BEP) analysis; economies of scale versus learning curve effect; cause-and-effect analysis; mathematical programming; regression analysis; simulation; and balanced scorecards (BSC). We believe these are some of the most important and relevant concepts and theories, which help the decision-maker to answer critical questions in supply chain management. However, our goal is not to explain pure or advanced theories of these concepts and methods, but to underscore how they can be effectively applied to real-world problem solving in value and supply chain management. As Figure P1 indicates, Part V along with Part I constitutes the fundamental foundation for this book.

Highlights of Each Chapter

In order to present the contents effectually, we structure each chapter as follows.

o **Key learning points** – We put forth a structured list of learning points or lessons.
o **Wisdom box** – In the wisdom box, we discuss a conceptual framework for the chapter, which is often historical, philosophical, cultural, norm, or principle-based. We expect the wisdom box to enable the student to fathom supply chain management from a more comprehensive perspective beyond the narrow boundary of business.
o **In-depth concept** – When it is necessary to explain a certain concept in greater detail or in technical terms, we use the box "in-depth concept," which can be skipped without disrupting the flow of logic in the chapter.
o **Discussion questions** – After the main text, we list a set of discussion questions, which can stimulate the student to internalize the learning points by endeavoring to answer them.
o **Case study** – Our goal is to make sure that what the student learns in this book should be relevant to real-world business decision-making. The best way to ensure the goal is to provide case studies that describe the actual business situations, closely related to the specific learning points in the chapter.
o **Bold letters** – New or important concepts or words are highlighted to readers through the use of bold formatting.

Supplementary Resources

In order to help instructors who adopt our books for their courses, we have developed an instructor's companion website (www.cambridge.org/LearningSCM), which will allow instructors to download supplementary materials, such as the online instructor's manual.

The instructor's manual includes suggested answers to discussion questions, teaching notes for the case studies, and extra exercise problems for the chapters. PowerPoint slides for each chapter have also been prepared to allow instructors to adapt the content for their courses.

Unique Features of this Textbook

- Includes **twenty case studies** from a variety of industries and countries for instructors who are keen to use the case method in their courses.
- Introduces difficult concepts through the use of more than **200 illustrations and charts**.
- An online **chapter on analysis methods** provided for students who wish to understand and apply the methods in their managerial problem-solving.
- **Teaching notes** and **PowerPoint slides** (including figures) for each chapter provided for instructors who adopt this textbook for their courses.

Preface to the Second Edition

This book is the revision of *Supply Chain Management*, originally published by Wiley in 2005. Since its first edition, I have successfully used it for MBA courses in operations strategy and supply chain management at KAIST. Over the years, however, I have been able to identify innovative new ideas as well as cases in supply chain management and tried to incorporate them into the book as emerging theories or best practices. As a result, it seemed necessary to make a full revision to the original book. At the same time, I also believed most of the core concepts and theories in the first edition would be still very much relevant and useful for effective supply chain management. Against this backdrop, I decided to write a revision, which could integrate the new ideas and cases with the existing ones, rather than to replace the existing with the new. This philosophy resulted in the second edition, which includes seven in-depth chapters in addition to the original chapters. Complementing the first edition in great detail, these in-depth chapters elaborate on innovative approaches and ideas as well as sustainable competitive capabilities for supply chain management from the learning perspective. I hope that as an integrated and independent volume, the book now can play an essential role in enabling the students to learn and experience effective supply chain management.

Preface to the First Edition

Serendipity (奇遇发现) – the faculty of making fortunate discoveries by accident. This word symbolizes the very capability which I believe management education should enable future managers to develop, i.e., creativity. To be consistent with this perspective, I'd like to make a slight change to the wording. It is not "accident," but "a prepared mind and soul in disguise" that presents invaluable discoveries.

Serendipity should be a quintessential capability of the CEO, the ultimate decision-maker of the firm, because there is no such thing as "the best strategy" or "the core competence" that can sustain *forever*. Serendipity is embodied in the decision-maker's fundamental capacity, such as learning and flexibility. Only the CEO with this capacity can design a self-adapting or self-organizing decision process that makes it possible for the firm to forge the best *dynamic* strategy for the *given* relevant decision time horizon. As such, serendipity is embodied in creativity.

不惑 – the ability not to vacillate. This is another virtue I always value and endeavor to follow. In the Analects of Confucius, the teacher said he had reached a state of perfect calmness at the age of 40. Thus, it presages the age free from vacillation. I admire the concept of 不惑 since it should be another essential capacity of the CEO: I compare 不惑 to "commitment" in decision-making. In addition, the true meaning of 不惑 is deeply involved with the high integrity of the CEO, *lofty ethical and moral standards* the decision-maker must feel obliged to abide by whenever a decision is made.

分析 – deep or thorough investigation into events/facts for objective and systematic understanding of the world surrounding those events/facts. To make a right decision, the CEO must investigate the problem so as to understand it thoroughly and objectively. It is the act of analysis, which I call "calculus," part of the vital qualification of the decision-maker.

Now we have the fundamental underpinning of high-performing decision-making, consisting of 3 Cs: Calculus (分析), Creativity (创意性), Commitment (专念). First, as the ultimate decision-maker, the CEO has to analyze the issues of managerial decision-making. Once a complete calculus is done, the CEO must be able to devise strategic plans based on the analysis, creative enough to provide the firm with superior competitive advantage, which is capable of self-organizing and self-adapting in the constantly changing managerial environment. Then, the CEO should choose a set of strategic action plans for implementation among the plausible, yet possibly numerous alternatives. A significant implementation has to be supported by the decision-maker's uncompromising commitment. Without the full and unwavering commitment from the CEO, even the strategy deemed best from the calculus' point of view might be susceptible to a complete fiasco. A well-balanced commitment doesn't overlook its ultimate link with another cycle of deep analysis, i.e., calculus. Thus, the dynamics comprised of calculus, creativity, and commitment can go on continuously.

This book discusses the dynamic interplay among calculus, creativity, and commitment that constitutes the foundation of this unique perspective. It consists of seven chapters.

Chapter 1. **Supply Chain Management: Creating Value for the Customers**. In this chapter, we learn what a supply chain is, what supply chain management is all about, and why it is important to grasp the fundamentals of supply chain management in creating real value for the customers.

Chapter 2. **Effective Decision-Making for a High-Performing Supply Chain**. We discuss key issues related to the decision-making for effective supply chain management: how to define each of the key elements and to understand its dynamics, how the CEO (i.e., the key decision-maker) can manage these elements effectively, and how they interact with each other to influence the performance of the supply chain. In this context, we also elaborate on fundamental characteristics of supply chain coordination.

Chapter 3. **Dynamic learning for SCM**. In this chapter, we delineate the learning and its dynamics in supply chain management (SCM). We elaborate more on the learning propensity model briefly touched upon in the first chapter, and more thoroughly examine how the learning processes influence the performance of a supply chain system.

Chapter 4. **Strategic management of a supply chain**. We discuss some of the strategic principles of supply chain management. We first contemplate the strategic connection between supply chain management and product life cycle. Then, we focus on postponement. Another important issue in effective supply chain management is how to deal with the so-called "last miles problem." In addition, we briefly mention such issues as quick response or accurate response systems and adaptive channels. As the last subject in this chapter, we discuss how technology affects supply chain management.

Chapter 5. **Coordinating innovation in SCM**. Coordination is the key dimension of infrastructure in supply chain management. In this chapter, we use the comprehensive definition of innovation, i.e., any improvement in technology, engineering, design, and operations. Therefore, we focus on the improvement efforts funneled jointly by the supply chain partners. First, we discuss how to coordinate an innovation in the supply chain. Then, we consider some of the most conspicuous issues in SCM, such as the bullwhip effect, supply chain partner's perceptions, bargaining power balances, and appropriate decision structures for effective supply chain management.

Chapter 6. **Global SCM**. Global SCM (G-SCM) is about managing business activities in the supply chain, which is configured and coordinated on a global scale. In this chapter, we present a dynamic framework for G-SCM, which contains most of the key G-SCM issues/subjects, in a systematic way so that individual study outcomes accumulate, rather than disperse, building on the previous ones.

Chapter 7. **SCM for sustainable competitive capability**. Effective supply chain management needs a capable decision-maker, whose fundamental characteristics we discuss in detail. In order to compete and triumph over world-class companies in the global market, the firm should attain the integrated quality, which requires both labor and management to actively participate in the quality improvement process. The firm should take into account these issues when designing an order-winning strategy for supply chain management.

By thoroughly studying all the chapters, readers will be able to develop a highly effective and well-balanced perspective to understand and solve managerial problems in supply chain management. Since the primary objective of this book is to enable the decision-maker to build up such a perspective, especially in the context of Asian markets, more technical issues and subjects like detailed forecasting methods (e.g., time series analysis, exponential smoothing, regression analysis, and so forth), specific inventory control models (e.g., EOQ model, Q-system, P-system, and the like), and simulation and other quantitative techniques are not discussed in detail. While these issues are equally important, there are other books in the market that are well written to deal with these methodologies. Therefore, readers will benefit from complementing this book with others more focused on such methodological features.

This book is positioned uniquely as a strong reference for MBA students as well as present and future CEOs. It can provide them with both theoretical and empirical knowledge for effective supply chain management. As such, I would like to embark on a continuous process to improve this book so that it can always be useful and relevant for the decision-makers, who have to elucidate dynamic and complex managerial problems in a constantly changing world. Some of the possible ways include exploring interactions between SCM and finance/marketing, investigating emerging "empirical evidences" as well as theories and their impact on the supply chain performance, and the like.

Acknowledgments

When I visited the website of Cambridge University Press, two sentences caught my attention (www.cambridge.org/kr/academic/authors/), i.e., "Publish with Cambridge University Press and you will join a community of award-winning authors including over 60 Nobel Prize Laureates. You will join a distinguished group of authors ranging from the iconic John Milton, Isaac Newton and Albert Einstein to the more contemporary including Daron Acemoglu, Margaret Atwood and Stephen Hawking."

Although I knew that I'm not comparable to those great geniuses in human history, I felt deeply motivated to publish my book through Cambridge University Press. It took over a year before I signed a contract with Cambridge University Press to publish my book *Supply Chain Management: A Learning Perspective*. Throughout the discussion process, Mr. Joe Ng at the publishing company has been a trusted driving force that has enabled me to refine my ideas so that the book could eventually meet all the standards set by Cambridge University Press. I appreciate Joe's unwavering support and encouragement for my endeavor throughout this lengthy and rewarding development process. I would also like to thank Lorenza Toffolon and her team at Cambridge University Press for their wonderful work in completing the book beautifully. Finally, I appreciate my PhD students, Jeong Eun Sim and Sung Hak Kim, for their meticulous help during the final editing process.

I hope this book can make a meaningful contribution to enabling both managers and students as decision-makers to achieve their goals linked with supply chain management.

Abbreviations and Acronyms

ABS	acrylonitrile-butadiene-styrene
ADSL	asymmetric digital subscriber line
BEP	break-even point
BEV	battery electric vehicle
BSC	balanced scorecards
CAD	computer-aided design
CAGR	compound annual growth rate
CAM	computer-aided manufacturing
CE	consumer electronics
CEO	chief executive officer
CFT	cross-functional team
CI	contingent inventory
CIM	computer integrated manufacturing
CIPS	Chartered Institute of Purchasing and Supply
CO_2	carbon dioxide
COGS	cost of goods sold
CPF	central processing facility
CPFR	collaborative planning, forecasting, and replenishment
CRT	cathode ray tube
DC	distribution center
DM	decision-maker
DMP	decision-making process
DOS	days of supply
DRAM	dynamic random-access memory
EDI	Electronic Data Interchange
EHF	empty-headed fellow
EOL	end of life
EOQ	economic order quantity
ERP	enterprise resource planning
EV	electric vehicle
FDA	Food and Drug Administration
FDI	foreign direct investment
FFI	French Fragrances, Inc.
FMS	flexible manufacturing system
FPD	flat panel display
FPSO	floating production, storage, and offloading system
FTE	full-time equivalent
GDP	gross domestic product

G-SCM	global supply chain management
HEV	hybrid electric vehicle
HRM	human resource management
HVAC	heating, ventilation, air conditioning
IC	integrated circuits
ICEV	internal combustion engine vehicle
IEA	International Energy Agency
IICT	internet-based or internet-driven information and communication technology
IoT	Internet of Things
ISDN	integrated services digital network
IT	information technology
JFC	Japan Food Corporation
JIT	just-in-time
JV	joint venture
KDB	Korea Development Bank
KISVALUE	Korea Information Service Value
KOLS	Kikkoman Order Less System
KOLS-CRP	Kikkoman Order Less System Continuous Replenishment Program
KOLS-DEPO	Kikkoman Order Less System Inventory
KOLS-WP	Kikkoman Order Less System Weekly Plan
KOSDAQ	Korea Securities Dealers Automated Quotation
KOSPI	Korea Composite Stock Price Index
KPI	key performance indicator
KSIC	Korea Standard Industry Code
LAB	leader, activist, and believer
LCD	liquid crystal display
LCL	lower control limit
LGC	LG Chemical
LGD	LG Display
LGE	LG Electronics
LGYX	LG Yong Xing
LNG	liquefied natural gas
LNGC	liquefied natural gas carrier
LPM	learning propensity model
LV	Louis Vuitton
M&A	merger and acquisition
M&S	Marks & Spencer
MC	mass customization
MPS	modular production system
MQL	minimum quantity lubrication
MRP	material requirements planning

MRP II	manufacturing resource planning
n.d.	no date
NFC	near field communication
NGO	non-governmental organization
NOV	National Oilwell Varco
NOx	nitrogen oxide
NPD	new product development
NPI	new product introduction/innovation
NPV	net present value
OCP	one company plan
OM	operations management
OR	operations research
OSOE	Ocean Shipbuilding Offshore Engineering
PACE	Partnership for a Cleaner Environment
PC	personal computer
PHEV	plug-in hybrid electric vehicle
PLC	product life cycle
PVC	polyvinyl chloride
QR	quick response
R&D	research and development
RBPP	risk-based production planning
RDD	requested customer dock date
Rel. Freq.	relative frequency
RFID	radio-frequency identification
ROE	return on equity
SBL	styrene butadiene latex
SBU	strategic business unit
SC	supply chain
SCC	supply chain coordination
SCM	supply chain management
SKU	stock-keeping unit
SLA	service level agreement
SOA	sales on assets
SPC	statistical process control
TFT	thin film transistor
TFT-LCD	thin-film-transistor liquid crystal display
TLP	tension leg platform
TPS	Toyota Production System
TQM	total quality management
TR	transistors
UCL	upper control limit
VLC	value life cycle

VLCC	very large crude-oil carrier
VMI	vendor-managed inventory
VMR	vendor-managed replenishment
VOC	volatile organic compound
WIP	work in process
WTI	West Texas Intermediate
WWF	World Wildlife Fund

Part I

Basic Principles in Operations and Supply Chain Management

CHAPTER 1

Value Chain and Value Creation

What is value? **Value** is the defining concept that drives the whole subject of supply chain management (SCM). Let's start with defining and discussing the meaning of value and value creation, since these are the key concepts which underlie our study on supply chain management in this book – *Supply Chain Management: A Learning Perspective*. When we believe a product or service has value for us, it means we are satisfied or happy with the product or service. That is, the product or service gives us great utility, which we as consumers cherish and are willing to pay for. Since each of us can be quite different in terms of feeling satisfied or happy, however, value is subjective and difficult to measure accurately without taking into account unique circumstances each of us is facing. Therefore, ultimately value should be defined and espoused by each customer or consumer who is using or consuming the product or service.

Key Learning Points

- A firm exists to earn profit. In turn, the firm maximizes its profit by creating value for the market.
- The more the customer is involved, the more the company is service-oriented. If this rule is applied, every company has both manufacturing and service attributes to a certain extent.
- Value can be defined from the customer's perspective: it is a function of utility and cost.
- Supply chain management provides an integrating perspective to create the value by analyzing and managing resources, processes, and capabilities across the companies that share the same value chain (i.e., supply chain) together.
- From a supply chain management perspective, value is also a function of responsiveness and efficiency.
- Value life cycle (VLC) is a framework that integrates new product development process and supply chain management, i.e., dealing with the entire process from developing a new product to managing the supply chain throughout the product life cycle (PLC).
- Out-of-the box strategy enables the company to overcome critical trade-offs. But, it requires energetic coordination from all of the participants sharing the same supply chain, i.e., suppliers, manufacturers, distributors, and even the customers.

學 WISDOM BOX 1.1
Wisdom and Insights

Strawberry and Its Value

As human beings, we all consume products and/or services all the time. This morning you woke up and ate your breakfast, e.g., eggs, milk, bread, fresh fruits, and the like. After breakfast, you drove your car to work or school. At your office, you used your computer, perhaps equipped with a 27-inch LCD monitor. During your break, you drank a cup of coffee and played with your iPhone, and so on and so forth. You probably take it for granted that you can enjoy all of these products/services. But if you look at how each of these products/services can be made and eventually delivered to you a little more closely, you will realize that each one of these is nothing short of a miracle.

For example, which fruit do you like? Consider fresh strawberries. In order for the strawberries to reach your breakfast table, some farmers planted strawberry seeds several months ago and nurtured their growth. Once the ripe strawberries were harvested, they were picked and transported to a factory. At the factory, they were washed and packed in smaller boxes. Then the strawberry boxes were again picked up and delivered to retail stores. As an end-consumer, you went to your retail store and looked for fresh strawberries. At last, you bought a box of strawberries and returned home. As we can see from this simple example, there are numerous functions, activities, transactions, and people involved in planting, cultivating, delivering, selling, and consuming strawberries. Moreover, all of these functions, activities, transactions, and people are connected as an integral chain, through which physical products like strawberries themselves and virtual elements such as information and communication flow back and forth constantly. By grouping related functions or activities, we have a supply chain, comprised of four primary functions, such as: (1) supplier, (2) manufacturer, (3) distributor, and finally (4) consumer. A supply chain is essentially a value chain.

For the society or economy as a whole, the goal is to maximize value, i.e., to create satisfactory value without spending too much. In order to create the maximum value for the strawberry supply chain, every participant in the chain must carry out its function efficiently. But, it is just half the condition for value creation. On the one hand, each supply chain member must carry out its role or function effectively. On the other hand, all of the members must coordinate with each other effectively in order to ensure value maximization. For example, in the strawberry supply chain, even if the farmers do their own work superbly, the true value may not be realized unless the transportation function fulfills to deliver the strawberries to the stores on time while still retaining their freshness. We have to face the same issues for almost all the products and services we take for granted in our everyday life, e.g., cars, hamburgers, haircuts, surgeries, movies, banks, restaurants, you name it!

In this book, we want to understand fundamental principles of value creation for the consumers or the market. We try to answer questions like how the product or service is made, how the value-creating activities or functions are coordinated, who

Box continues

should play what leadership roles in realizing all of these, and so on. As our book title hints, we approach all of these issues from a learning perspective, which is dynamic in nature and emphasizes long-term capability building rather than short-term symptomatic problem solving.

Questions
1. What is your favorite product or service? Draw a picture of the processes or functions through which the product or service is delivered to you.
2. What do you think are the most challenging things throughout the processes or functions?

1.1   Value and Value Creation

A firm exists to earn profit. How the firm uses its profit is an important issue, but ethical or moral issues are also involved. As such, in this book we do not discuss how the firm should use its profit. Rather, we focus on how the firm can maximize its profit. The firm maximizes its profit by creating value for the market. In general, there are two ways to create value, i.e., making and selling either products or services to the market. These days, however, it is difficult to make a clear distinction between products and services. In fact, most of the time, it seems futile to make such a distinction. Is McDonald's in the manufacturing sector or service sector? On the one hand, it produces "physical products," e.g., hamburgers, and one may consider it as a manufacturing company. On the other hand, however, customers are very extensively involved in the transaction, and thus one can regard the firm as a service company. As this example implies, whether the firm makes physical outputs or not may not be a good criterion to distinguish between a manufacturing and a service company. Rather, how much involved the customer is in the transaction process can be a relevant criterion. The more the customer is involved, the more the company is service-oriented. If this rule is applied, every company has both manufacturing and service attributes at the same time. Therefore, it is no longer meaningful to categorize a company completely as a manufacturing or a service company. One can only say that a company is more service-oriented or manufacturing-oriented. Then, in the same industry, say, in the automobile industry, it is possible that Company A is more service-oriented than Company B, or vice versa.

1.1.1   Three Fundamental Building Blocks in Creating Value: Resources, Processes, and Capabilities

How can a firm make products or services? First, the firm needs **resources** to make products or services. There are many different forms of resources, e.g., raw materials, facilities, machinery, equipment, land, energy, and human beings. For instance, a global steel company POSCO needs raw materials such as iron ore, limestone, and coking coal, facilities like sinter plant and blast furnace, a huge amount of electricity, and a highly skilled workforce. To make a good car, BMW needs raw materials such as steel, plastics, aluminums, and the like, assembly plants, welding machines, painting plants, and a highly skilled workforce. McDonald's needs many different types of resources to produce hamburgers. A bank also must have a wide range of resources such as a huge computing facility, lots of supplies, and well-educated employees. However, having enough resources does not mean the firm can make products or services. The firm must transform the resources into products and services. POSCO has to process the raw materials, using the plants, machinery, and equipment, to produce quality steel products. BMW must process the raw materials through its assembly line by the workers to produce the cars. The same must apply to McDonald's and a bank as well. The **process** comprises a series of tasks or activities that must be performed to transform the resources into final products or services. Now suppose there are two companies, Company A and Company B. Assume that the two companies have exactly the same resources and utilize the same processes: although these cannot be exactly the same in the real world, we assume that they are sufficiently similar. Given that the two companies have the same resources and processes, can we expect the products or services produced by the two firms to be exactly the same as well? One probably feels uneasy saying "yes" to the question. Why? Somehow, we know there is something more than the two elements, i.e., resources and processes, in producing products or services. For instance, the managers at Company A might have more experience in the industry and have better knowledge about the market and technology directly related with the products or services. Then, even if the two companies utilize the same resources and processes, we know we can expect "better" products or services from Company A than from Company B. We define these largely intangible factors such as experience, knowledge, and technology as the firm's **capability**. Now we have identified three fundamental building blocks in creating value, i.e., resources, processes, and capabilities (Figure 1.1).

1.1.2   What Is Operations Management?

Operations management (OM) is about how a firm manages these three fundamental building blocks effectively to optimize value creation. Here we define "traditional" operations management as operations management focused on a single company's boundary. That is, traditional operations management approaches value creation from a single company's perspective. As such, traditional operations management is more consistent with a "vertically integrated" business model, where a single company owns, i.e., controls, most of its value chain functions. For instance, suppose a carmaker that owns most of its raw material suppliers as well as dealers. Then, the carmaker's operations management is about managing its own resources, processes, and capabilities within its own boundary. That is, it is traditional operations management. In the past, it usually made sense to focus on how to manage the three building blocks within a single company's boundary, i.e., from a single company's perspective. However, more recently

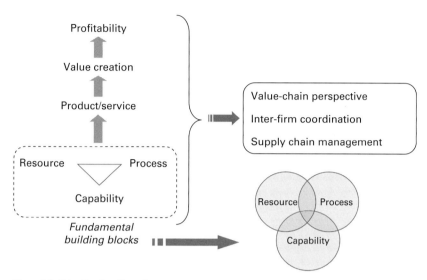

Figure 1.1 Value Creating Hierarchy

it is not reasonable to adopt such an approach. Let us think about Apple. Can one explain the company's value creation by focusing on the company's own resources, processes, and capabilities within the company's boundary only? If one tries to do that, one will fail to understand the true forces driving the company's success, not just as a design company, but also as a profit-making business entity. For instance, one cannot truly understand the value creation without considering the company's manufacturing processes. But Apple usually does not manufacture its products such as iPhone and iPad. Instead, the company works with outsourcing partners in other countries like China. In order to fully understand the company's value creation, therefore, one should look into not only Apple's own resources, processes, and capabilities, but also those of its value chain partners, e.g., outsourcing companies' resources, processes, and capabilities, at the same time. Now one has to shift the perspective from a single company's to that of the entire value chain. The traditional operations management is no longer able to answer critical questions under this new business environment, which calls for an integrating perspective that takes into account various stakeholders and factors throughout the value chain the company shares with its partner companies. We put forth that supply chain management or value chain management in a broader sense enables us to tackle such operations management issues more effectively. That is, supply chain management provides an integrating perspective to approach the value creation issues by taking into account the resources, processes, and capabilities across the value chain companies that share the value chain together. As such, inter-firm coordination becomes one of the most important issues in supply chain management.

There is one caveat regarding the three fundamental building blocks. They are not completely independent or separable concepts. For instance, some people would say that some of the resources are also capabilities, especially if such resources are human beings, where tacit knowledge is embedded. Similarly, some would say that certain processes are indeed part of the capability the firm possesses. It can be a reasonable and often logical contention. We do not intend to refute such arguments. We suggest the three building blocks, not because they can be completely distinguished from each other, but because they are conceptually identifiable and distinct enough to help us analyze the value creation more systematically. As the overlapping circles in Figure 1.1 imply, these three building blocks are sufficiently independent and identifiable to the extent that they help us understand the firm's value-creating process, despite that they are overlapping each other to a certain level. This argument or justification is necessary because in the ensuing chapters, we will define key concepts or constructs to enable us to analyze operations management issues systematically, albeit sometimes these concepts may not be completely independent or separable. That is, we put the "logical, reasonable, and heuristic value" ahead of the "mathematically rigorous or theoretically elegant one."

1.1.3   Value Function

Before discussing the three fundamental building blocks in detail, we want to take a step back and define "value" more formally. How is value determined? Who should judge the value of the products and services made by the company? We put forth that the firm creates value to earn profit from the customers. This means that the value must be defined by the customers or the market. Of course, there might be a case where the company can dictate the meaning of value. However, that was probably in the past, when the supply was far less than the demand, so that whatever the firm made was demanded by the customers. That kind of market condition is no longer prevalent nowadays. It is now a rule, not an exception, that customers have more bargaining power vis-à-vis companies. Then, what are the primary criteria customers use when they evaluate the value of the products or services? First, the customer feels value when the products or services offer utility that meets or satisfies her needs or requirements. For instance, it is likely that the customer is willing to pay more if the products or services are delivered to her at the right time, at the right price, and/or at the right amount. All of these "right attributes" enhance the customer's satisfaction with the products or services. Given the same level of utility, the less the cost or the price the customer has to pay, the more value the customer perceives to get from the products or services. Now we can define the value from the customer's perspective: the value is a function of utility and cost. More specifically, the value is the customer's utility over the cost (Equation 1.1). There are two primary ways to increase the value, i.e., either increasing the utility while maintaining the cost or decreasing the cost while maintaining the utility.

$$\text{Value} = \frac{\text{Utility}}{\text{Cost}} \cong \text{Responsiveness} \times \text{Efficiency} \qquad (1.1)$$

Note that cost and price are interchangeable.

1.1.4   Value as a Function of Responsiveness and Efficiency

Another way to view utility is the firm's **responsiveness** to the customer's needs or requirements. We already postulated that the customer feels value when she obtains the products or services at the right time, at the right price, and/or at the right amount, i.e., she perceives that the firm demonstrates responsiveness to her requirements. Similarly, cost is a factor determined by **efficiency**. The more efficient the firm, the lower the cost the firm incurs to produce the products or services. Since cost is the inverse to efficiency, we have another expression of the value, i.e., the value is a function of responsiveness and efficiency.

1.2   Supply Chain System and Focal Company

In this book, we use a schematic representation of supply chain. It is a much simplified version of the real world. That is, the schematic model consists of four participants only, i.e., supplier (**S**), manufacturer (**M**), distributor (**D**), and customer (**C**) as in Figure 1.2. But, in the real world, many more players get involved in an individual supply chain: even for a single function like supply, there are many suppliers participating in the supply chain coordination, sometimes forming a multi-tier system. Although some functions like R&D and human resource management (HRM) are not explicitly included in the supply chain despite being in the value chain, they are indeed an essential part of the supply chain and we discuss them as such throughout this book. We know that terminologies like supplier and manufacturer have a strong flavor of manufacturing, but we must emphasize that the theories and practices we learn in this book are equally applicable to both service and manufacturing industries. We use manufacturing terminologies because of historical legacy, i.e., the concept of supply chain management was first developed in the manufacturing sectors. Note the corresponding terms like service supporter, service creator, and service contact/provider to use for the service sectors (Figure 1.2).

In Figure 1.2, we combine the three functions of supplier, manufacturer, and distributor and call them a **supply chain system**: it underlines the fact that these three functions or participants must work together to create value and therefore they share the

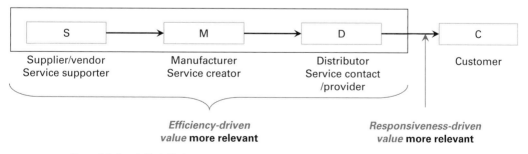

Figure 1.2 Supply Chain System

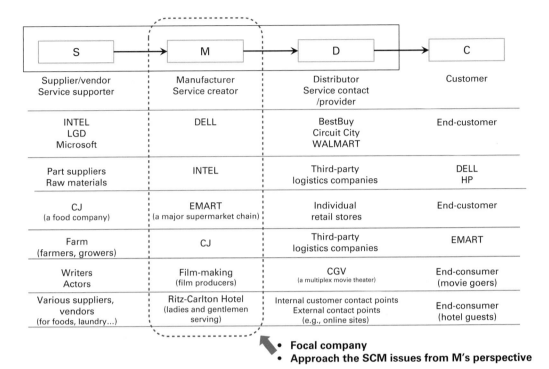

Figure 1.3 Focal Company

same fate. Another point we want to highlight is concerned with the two different types of value, i.e., efficiency-driven and responsiveness-driven. Although the whole supply chain should try to maximize these two values simultaneously, it is sometimes necessary to make a distinction between them. That is, **efficiency-driven value** is more relevant to "within" the supply chain system, whereas **responsiveness-driven value** is more relevant to the interaction "between" the customer and the supply chain system: as in Figure 1.2, the firm's ability to satisfy the changing requirements of the customer is responsiveness, which is conspicuously highlighted at the juncture between the supply chain system and the customer. We elaborate on these issues further, when we discuss supply chain coordination in the next chapters.

Finally, we ask, *From whose perspective do we have to view and analyze the issues of supply chain management?* As alluded to earlier, regardless of whether it is in a service or manufacturing industry, every company has its own supply chain or value chain to manage. Moreover, a company's position in the supply chain may vary as the perspective changes. For instance, if we consider a supply chain, where Dell is the manufacturer,[1] then Intel is in the position of supplier. On the other hand, Intel is also a manufacturing company. As such, if we consider another supply chain, where Intel is

---

[1] As we will explain further, the manufacturer in Figure 1.3 doesn't have to be an actual "manufacturing" company. We use the term "manufacturer (M)" for the company that transforms the input into the output, a physical product or service.

the manufacturer, then Dell becomes a customer and there are numerous suppliers and vendors that work with Intel. In fact, if we are interested in Dell's value creation, we have to design a supply chain from Dell's perspective, i.e., where Dell is sitting in the manufacturer position. In the same vein, if we want to study Intel's value creation, we need to draw a supply chain from Intel's perspective, i.e., where Intel is the manufacturer. In this book, we always try to approach supply chain management from the manufacturer's (i.e., transformation's) perspective, and that's why we call the manufacturer (i.e., the company in the "M" position) the **focal company** (Figure 1.3): note that the manufacturer is not necessarily a manufacturing company; it can be a service creator, if we consider a service industry; we just use the term "manufacturer" for the company in the position of transformation, i.e., manufacturing or service creating. In sum, if we are interested in a particular company's value creation, we need to position that company in the manufacturing function (i.e., M's position) and call it the focal company.

1.3 Value Life Cycle

Traditional operations management has largely focused on those operations issues throughout the **product life cycle** (PLC), i.e., from new product introduction to the growth, maturity, and declining stage. Although researched primarily by those in marketing, new product development has generally remained interdisciplinary. More recently researchers in operations management have started studying new product development as an important part of operations management. Nevertheless, there seems to exist a sizable gap between new product development and operations management. Against this backdrop, we suggest a concept of **value life cycle** (VLC) as an integrated amalgamation of the two historically separated areas, i.e., new product development process and product life cycle.

Figure 1.4 presents the graphical definition of value life cycle. The left side of the figure shows the new product development (NPD) cycle, which moves from concept development to pilot production just before the product life cycle starts. It also indicates that (i) two different types of knowledge are needed during the main NPD process, i.e., NPD process knowledge and product-specific knowledge. By combining multidisciplinary principles, a cross-functional team (CFT) approach can be applied to provide the product-specific knowledge, (ii) during the early stage of the NPD cycle, there are many alternative concepts or designs for the new product, but the number of alternatives is continuously reduced until one final design remains to be ready for the market. During the NPD cycle, the firm may adopt an innovative approach, where lead users are involved in the NPD process: a lead user is a consumer, who tries to design and/or develop her own product or service that meets her own innate needs, when no existing product or service in the market can satisfy those needs sufficiently. During the NPD process, the firm also has to plan a supply chain that can support its operations, i.e., producing the new product or service, throughout the associated PLC. If it fails to prepare the supply chain for the new product's PLC, especially during the growth stage, the firm might not be able to reap the profit as much as it could, when the market demands the product in large quantities.

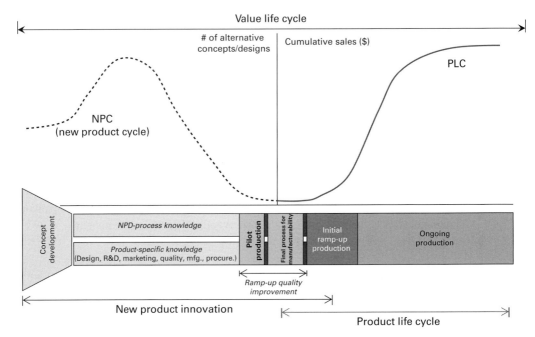

Figure 1.4 Value Life Cycle

Where the NPD cycle closes, the PLC starts. However, the transition should not be so disruptive. In fact, the two cycles overlap each other with a final or transitional process for **manufacturability**, which makes sure that the new product conceived and designed during the NPD process can be effectually manufactured in the current production system equipped with all of its structural as well as infrastructural factors, e.g., machines, equipment, workforces, coordination mechanisms and norms, and the like. As typified in the literature, the PLC moves from introduction, growth, and maturity to the declining stage. At the beginning of the PLC, i.e., during the introduction phase, there are only a small number of consumers, most of them being early adopters, who are willing to take the risk of buying the new, untested product at an early stage. From the growth stage on, the firm in general focuses on the mass market, i.e., general consumers, and expands/manages its supply chain appropriately to accommodate the increasing demand.

From the discussion above, it becomes inevitable to consider the NPD process and PLC as two sides of a coin. That is, the two subjects are and must be closely integrated: in order to optimally manage its supply chain throughout the PLC, the firm must fathom and sometimes guide the NPD process; similarly, in order to ensure successful NPD, the firm must take into account both strengths and weaknesses of its future as well as the existing supply chain. Underlining the significance of amalgamating NPD and PLC, we define "value life cycle," which integrates the NPD process and SCM, i.e., dealing with subjects from developing a new product to managing the supply chain throughout the PLC. In this book, we take up an overarching perspective of the value life cycle.

1.4   Out-of-the-Box Strategy

A manager has to face trade-offs constantly. For example, there is a **trade-off** relationship between managerial capabilities (e.g., controllability and flexibility; see Chapter 2) and also between dimensions of process strategy (e.g., volume and customization; see Chapter 8). Such a trade-off defines a feasible region, where competitive differentiation is rarely successful, i.e., no firm can enjoy sustainable competitive advantage over others continuously. In fact, it is in that feasible region that a vast majority of general or common (i.e., indistinguishable or undifferentiated) companies are in cut-throat rivalry against each other to gain a minimal profit barely sufficient for day-to-day survival. By definition, if a company is in the feasible region, it cannot enjoy any premium profit compared with others. A truly competent company is outside the feasible region. What makes a company stay outside the feasible region?

For example, consider the furniture industry. There are two factors that determine a firm's competitive advantage in the industry, i.e., design and price. It is common sense that if the design of the furniture is highly sophisticated, its price is high, and vice versa. That is, there exists a trade-off relationship between design and price, which defines a feasible region as in Figure 1.5. In effect, any company that can satisfy the **order-qualifying** attributes[2] is able to do business in the feasible region. Being in the feasible region in turn implies that the company cannot enjoy any premium profitability above the normal level, i.e., it earns a minimum profit that warrants day-to-day survival only.

A competitive company that offers differentiated value to the customer can position itself outside of the feasible region. For instance, if a company can build furniture in a highly aesthetical design and at a price affordable by the customer, it positions itself beyond the crowded feasible region, e.g., in the "high-design – low price" cell

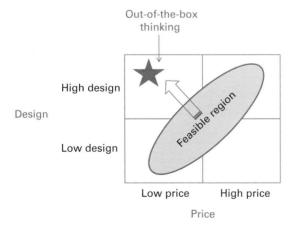

Figure 1.5 Out-of-the-Box Strategy in the Furniture Industry

---

[2] See Chapter 3, where we discuss quality and quality-related attributes.

(see Figure 1.5). Such a move is called "out-of-the-box" thinking or strategy. How can a firm pursue the **out-of-the-box strategy**? In general, it is not possible for one single company to accomplish the strategy alone. As we can learn from the highly capable furniture company IKEA, it requires active coordination from all of the participants sharing the same value chain, i.e., suppliers, manufacturers, distributors, and even the customers.

The collective capability built and shared by the entire value chain partners is the **supply chain capability**. In order for the company to position itself far beyond the foggy feasible region by pursuing the out-of-the box strategy, it must be able to motivate its value chain partners to coordinate with each other, i.e., cultivate the supply chain capability. There are numerous exemplary companies that have helped themselves achieve the out-of-the-box strategy through enhancing their supply chain capability, e.g., BMW, IKEA, Apple, Samsung Electronics, and Daewoo Shipbuilding, to name just a few. In fact, the focus of our study in this book is on advancing the firm's supply chain capability to be truly strong and competitive.

So far in this chapter, we have defined and introduced some of the key constructs, which will comprise the backbone of our study of supply chain management for value life cycle. Our goal is to understand "supply chain management for value life cycle" from two perspectives in action, i.e., value creation and dynamic learning. We will elaborate on these perspectives in the ensuing chapters.

Discussion Questions

1. Can you define value? What are the key determinants of value?
2. Explain the three fundamental building blocks for value creation.
3. What is the primary difference between more traditional operations management and supply chain management?
4. What is the focal company? Why is it important in studying supply chain management?
5. What is the relationship between new product development and supply chain management?
6. Explain the concept of "out-of-the-box thinking or strategy."
7. Suggest an example you know or experience, where the "out-of-the-box strategy" is actually implemented.

案例 CASE STUDY 1.1
Luxury Business Meets Supply Chain Management

In this case study, we would like to learn how a global luxury company has designed its supply chain strategy to meet the challenges in the global luxury market. We interviewed a top manager in charge of supply chain management at Louis Vuitton (www.louisvuitton.com), a prestigious brand in the luxury industry.

What does quality imply to Louis Vuitton (LV)? To us, good quality means durability, details, sophistication, craftsmanship, tradition, and also getting the best materials. We should use the best materials to manufacture products, which are sophisticated at the most detailed level.

What are the overall characteristics of LV's supply chain? Our supply chain is vertically integrated in the downstream, i.e., from manufacturing to distribution. We do about 60 percent of our manufacturing in-house, and own the entire 446 stores worldwide. Although we outsource about 40 percent of our manufacturing to subcontractors, LV is usually the only customer to them and, as such, LV controls almost 100 percent of its manufacturing.

What are the major strengths of LV's integrated supply chain? First, with the integrated supply chain, we know ourselves completely. For each day, we have complete access to all kinds of information such as market demand, inventory amount and its location, which help us forecast most accurately.

Second, it allows us to protect our proprietary knowhow. Let me give you an example. A few years ago, we tried to launch a new product, a fashion shoe line. We wanted to make sure we can make shoes with absolutely high quality and searched for perfect talents for that purpose. In the end, we were able to identify the most ideal craftsmanship available in a small village in Italy. Two options were available to us. One was to find a local manufacturer we could work with as our outsourcing partner and the other to build our own shoe manufacturing plant in the Italian town. We opted to pursue the second alternative and built our own plant in the Italian town, continuing our integrated supply chain strategy. By keeping our supply chain integrated in this way, we can protect our proprietary knowledge and knowhow, and focus on mastering our expertise.

Finally, our integrated supply chain makes it possible for us to have a complete control of price. In the luxury goods industry like the one where LV is, it is very important to manage the price optimally. For instance, if we cannot control our retail stores, some of the stores might be tempted to lower the prices when they have unnecessary inventory in their warehouse. But, offering a discount is fatal in this kind of industry. It will undermine your brand completely. We have to protect our brand. Brand image is everything in the luxury industry. Unless LV controls all of its retail stores, we cannot guarantee a complete price control throughout the world. With the integrated supply chain, we control all of our retail stores all around the world, whether it's in Japan, Hong Kong, the United States, or Germany, and thus make sure that there'll be no discount or no erosion of our prestigious brand image. Another benefit of integrated price control is to

Source: Reprinted by permission: Kim, B. (2013) "Quality Goals and Supply Chain Strategy in the Fashion Industry." *Qualitative Market Research: An International Journal*, 16(2), 214–242. DOI: 10.1108/13522751311317602. © 2013 Emerald Publishing.

enable us to present absolutely consistent brand image throughout the world. Although there might be some small differences due to fluctuating currency exchange rates, LV tries to make sure that every LV product is priced consistently across the world. For example, you won't buy a LV bag at a significantly cheaper price in Hong Kong than in Japan. More importantly, wherever you buy a LV product in Japan, the price will be the same across all of the retail stores in Japan. Consistent pricing and no-discount policy are the two most important tools to prevent any brand value erosion from occurring.

What are the more specific and perhaps immediate goals or objectives of LV's supply chain strategy? First, one of the most important KPIs (key performance indicators) is the product's availability rate, i.e., to maximize the availability rate. We want to make sure that when a customer enters one of our stores, she will find the right product always. This is very important in our industry. When the customer cannot find what she wants in the store, sometimes she may go to other luxury brands or may decide not to buy the product at all, at least for a while.

Second, our goal is to minimize the inventory. It's not just about reducing the inventory cost. More importantly, we have to avoid our products becoming obsolescent. Displaying obsolescent products in the store can tarnish our brand value, sending out wrong signals to our customers. Moreover, keeping unnecessary inventory implies your inability to forecast the demand, which we don't want to accept.

Finally, our supply chain strategy is designed to protect the environment. It wasn't driven by calculating costs, but by proactively selecting our strategy, i.e., it was the result of our strategic intent. Although we don't try to gain immediate profit from our environmental initiatives, we expect our customers and the market in general to value our environmental effort in the future and that might help increase our sales. But, again we have a very long-term perspective in this matter. Three most important initiatives we've started so far are using sea freight more extensively, reducing industrial packaging, and building and utilizing a truly green warehouse. We're currently shipping almost 60 percent of our products via sea and compared with 2004, we've reduced about 40 to 50 percent of carbon dioxide emissions through sea transporting and green warehousing.

Our commitment to protecting environment has not been always favorably accepted inside LV. When we suggested sea freight instead of air shipment, some people pointed out that it would take about four to six weeks to ship products to foreign markets like Japan and Hong Kong, and thus we won't be able to meet the customers' demand in a timely manner. The point was very valid. But, we were able to overcome such an issue with our capability to forecast the demand very accurately. For instance, suppose that the demand for a product for the next five months is forecast to be 100. Based on the forecast information, you ship 20 units via air and the remaining 80 via sea, rather than shipping all of the 100 units via air. Then, you can satisfy the immediate demand for the first month and the demand for the next four months can be satisfied by the products shipped via sea. By using the sea freight along with the air transportation, we can reduce the CO_2 emissions by almost 75 percent. That is a significant improvement! When we actually implemented this strategy, there turned out to be another benefit we neither expected nor intended, i.e., cost saving. The cost of sea freight was just a fraction of the air freight!

As a result, our strategic choice to emphasize the environment was a success. However, it couldn't be made possible without our centralized supply chain. That is, it was possible because we had complete knowledge about our inventory for every SKU (stock-keeping unit) at every store on every day. So we see there is a really close relationship between the goals we have and the supply chain design we've developed over time.

Was there any particular moment or motivation that made LV develop its supply chain strategy in a unique way? Yes, it is very important to understand the context, from which all of our supply chain initiatives sprang. Even just twenty years ago, LV was a manufacturer of leather goods in a stable environment with few uncertainties. The whole thing was dramatically changed in early 1990s, when LV decided to enter new markets such as ready-to-wear fashion products, shoes, and other fashion and accessory items. In fact, LV even set up a goal that 45 percent of its entire product lines should be new products every year. Naturally, the company's business model had to be changed completely. In order to achieve its aggressive sales goals, LV had to find out lots of new customers in many different countries. In fact, LV added almost sixty-two new countries to its customer list. Another phenomenon beyond the control of LV was that the global market became more and more converged. For instance, financial breakdowns in the US were felt not only within the US, but also throughout the world simultaneously. As such, the worldwide market uncertainty is fluctuating more severely. All of these external as well as internal difficulties are combined to make it ever more difficult to forecast the market demand accurately and reliably. LV was in a very delicate situation. On the one hand, it had to deal with the vastly expanded target market, and, on the other hand, the uncertainty became much more complex to make sound planning almost impossible.

In the face of this dire situation, LV decided to make three big decisions. The first one was to centralize our supply chain. Before this change, each store was allowed to place its own orders once a month. Since each store operated independently, it had motivation to inflate its order, believing that the larger the inventory it had, the more likely its sales would increase. Probably the store managers themselves were not very confident about their own ability to predict the demand even for a month. Before centralizing our supply chain, we usually experienced a 30 percent shortage of our products at the store level. Such a massive inefficiency could have been multiplied if we hadn't taken any drastic measures. In this context, we centralized the ordering decision and asked each store simply to sell the products without worrying about inventory, forecasting, and financial performance. Soon we realized that the forecasting at the aggregate level was relatively easy. Each week after we forecast the aggregate demands for all of our regional markets, our SCM teams negotiate with plants regarding which of the products and how many units of them to manufacture. We use either sea or air freight to ship the products to our regional warehouses, from which deliveries to individual stores are made mostly via trucks, trains, or sometimes airplanes.

Another big shift was made toward a very reactive and flexible supply chain. As mentioned already, in the past each store placed an order every month, and thus the delivery to the store was scheduled monthly. As the market uncertainty intensified, however, monthly replenishment was not at all enough. We had to increase the delivery frequency by reducing the lead time considerably. As a result, we were able to reduce the inventory size significantly. There was one psychological barrier to implementing this high-frequency auto replenishment strategy. Store managers falsely believed they needed a large inventory to achieve a high level of product availability for the customers. We had to show that in reality, their belief was groundless. Using some simulation techniques, we proved that a large inventory is usually associated with wrong inventory and makes it difficult for the store to find the right product for the customer, often leading to serious obsolescence as well. Once it was well understood that it should be detrimental to have excessive inventory, we were able to redesign our supply chain to be reactive and flexible. Based on more stable aggregate demand forecast, we make the products and ship them from our central warehouse in France to regional warehouses in other countries. The replenishment at the store level is done very often from a regional warehouse to individual stores using trucks or sometimes airplanes. Now each store receives a small-sized delivery about six times every week. This simple system increased our product availability enormously. In theory, for instance, a LV store in Tokyo sold all of its products including those in stock this afternoon, and then we can replenish the store with a complete set of LV products it needs to open for business tomorrow morning. After implementing the reactive and flexible supply chain, our performance has improved substantially, e.g., the shortage rate is reduced from almost 30 to 5 percent, the overall inventory level from six to three months of sales, and the obsolescence rate is less than 3 percent.

The final decision was about protecting the environment. As already discussed, it was a strategic decision, not resulting purely from a cost-and-benefit analysis. We were committed to embracing social responsibility. Two of the most immediate and visible initiatives we took were using sea freight more often and minimizing the industrial packaging materials. By doing so, we significantly reduced the carbon dioxide emissions and thus our products' carbon footprints. Another more fundamental project was to build our central warehouse in a remote area, which is truly a green warehouse and ISO certified. We used mostly natural materials to build the warehouse and a geothermal heating system is currently used. Although the energy savings and the significant reduction of carbon dioxide emissions are very critical benefits, we also believe that the warehouse provides a very safe and healthy working environment for our employees and therefore helps us enhance the employee productivity.

What are the most serious challenges faced by LV right now? First of all, the greatest potential risk is based on our belief that nothing will stay stable or predictable, and consequently everything will be difficult to forecast. Ironically this is exactly the same belief we had in the early 1990s when we had to make major changes in our strategy. As the market becomes more globalized, we expect, such an uncertainty will extremely intensify. It implies it will be much harder for us to guarantee our product availability at our stores.

Another challenge is concerned with raw materials. So far LV has been successful in forward integrating the supply chain, i.e., we have been in full control over manufacturing and distribution. However, in this luxury industry, it is essential to use the highest quality raw materials like genuine leather and fabrics. Although we haven't faced any serious problems in dealing with our raw material suppliers, we anticipate a future possibility that the raw materials will be in short supply. We don't intend to achieve a complete backward integration of our supply chain, but have to make sure that the coordination with our raw material suppliers should be at the level between our own departments inside LV. In order to do so, we always emphasize close partnership with our raw material suppliers. That is, our relationship with our suppliers is not based on economics only, but on mutual trust and respectable collaboration. It inevitably involves working together to develop new products and improve operations efficiencies. In addition, we'd like to provide visibility to our suppliers by sharing key information and data with them. With more information and data on the actual sales and demand patterns of LV products, the suppliers understand LV's business better and become more willing to share their own information and data, often related with innovative new ideas about advanced raw materials. This is a virtuous cycle, where both LV and the suppliers are getting more and more from the collaborative relationship.

The third issue is concerned with the conflict between the customer's perspective and the factory's perspective. On the one hand, the customer's perspective emphasizes flexibility. On the other hand, the factory's perspective values efficiency. After going through many trial-and-error experiences, we realized that it is essential to strike a balance between flexibility and efficiency, rather than to choose one at the cost of the other. For instance, we believe we can reduce the conflict through implementing a lean production system. For a more fundamental solution, however, we have focused on training and education. We ran forecasting games like the beer game with our warehouse workers. The key lesson was to understand how important it is to have a coordinated supply chain. Another more comprehensive training program was designed to enhance communication skills for effective supply chain coordination. This program put together managers and employees from all functions including marketing and country managers, and highlighted the essential role played by effective communications in improving the supply chain performance. It was a very successful training program.

In fact, we believe we should go beyond simply enhancing supply chain efficiency only. We endeavor integrating all of our critical functions within LV from new concept development to actual delivery of our products to the customer. So far, marketing function has played a major role. It works closely with design function, which is solely dedicated to creative activities. After closely communicating with the design, the marketing decides the launch date for new products. Then, the marketing communicates with the supply chain function to arrange the production and distribution. Of course, when it decides the launch date, the marketing function pays close attention to the feedback from the SCM department. Likewise, the design function accepts feedback regarding the customer voices from the marketing function when it creates new concepts for new products. Also, the SCM department gets inputs from regional SC managers as well as individual stores across the world. It has a SCM team in each regional market and works with all the other functions including the finance department. But such coordination can be improved more, not necessarily jeopardizing our creativity. The key is to find people who can communicate effectively. We believe there are three fundamental building blocks underlying the success of LV, i.e., effective communication, superb teamwork, and excellent information systems for forecasting and replenishment.

Questions
1. How does the company define quality? Is it consistent with the value perceived by the customers?
2. What are the key characteristics of the company's supply chain strategy? How successful has the company's supply chain strategy been? Why?
3. How has the company's supply chain strategy enabled the company to deliver the value to its customers?
4. What are the key challenges faced by the company now?
5. How should the company design (improve or revamp) its supply chain strategy in order to continue its growth and profitability in the global market?

案例 CASE STUDY 1.2
Administrative Quality at an Automobile Company

A Korean carmaker has been notorious for its militant labor–management relationship. For instance, the company usually has to get approval from all of the "multi-layered" ranks of the labor union even for slight changes in production, which can be obviously decided by the management's own discretion in most of the carmakers in the world. This somewhat absurd decision process is the product of a brutal and militant conflict between the company and its labor union over the last several decades. In effect, the company has given in to labor's escalating demands.

There are several explanations about why this has happened. Some say that the traditional corporate and political culture, especially that of the big *chaebol* in Korea, is to blame. A lack of transparency in the relationship between the government and business offered labor an excuse to take a militant stance toward the company, believing that they deserved better treatment and respect from both the company and the government.

Others point to the governance structure of the company. In general, a *chaebol* is said to have a so-called owner, although the actual share owned by the "owner" is only 2 to 3 percent: the magic is a complex web of "cross investments" between subsidiary or affiliate companies belonging to the *chaebol*. Under this kind of non-transparent governance structure, managers don't find any strong incentive to make a decision for the long-term performance of the company, at least in the area of negotiation with the labor union. Instead, they probably find it more than enough to deal with the most imminent issues on an ad-hoc basis and don't care about the risks caused by their decision-making behaviors. One of the most serious risks involves those issues untreated or intentionally ignored by managers today. Although such issues could have been easily resolved should they have received appropriate attention now, they would become enormous burdens that will not be easily removed tomorrow. This pattern of decision-making behavior induces managers to give in to labor's demands, even if they know such demands are unreasonable and harmful to the company's long-term competitiveness, as long as they are assured that such negative impacts don't become visible during their own tenure in the current management position. It has been working well so far primarily due to the fact that the company's sales, in particular its export sales, have been increasing quite fast over the period so that the company can afford a certain level of concession-making to labor.

There might be other, better and more accurate, explanations. But the key issue here is not about finding out the true cause of the absurd decision-making mechanism. It is about answering a question like, *Despite the deteriorating relationship between the company and its labor, how has this company emerged as one of the global top 10 carmakers, boasting world-class quality?* It was really a mystery to outsiders, especially to those who teach and do research on management. We had to grapple to find an answer to this seemingly paradoxical phenomenon.

Source: Developed and written by B. Kim. ©

Finally, a manager of the company offered an answer: "administrative quality" as the quality that is improved through R&D and design activities at the research lab by the engineers and managers without involving the workers' participation during the laboratory phases.

For example, suppose that in order to improve quality, a task must be performed at a particular angle, say 35°, from the worker's right-hand side. However, the labor union objects to performing that task because they believe doing so might cause inconvenience or some hazard to the workers. Due to the contract between the company and the labor, the management cannot force workers to adopt the instruction. Facing the difficulty in reality, the managers decide to change the car design so that the current work method can achieve the intended quality improvement, rather than giving up the opportunity to improve the quality. Perhaps the engineers change the design of the car or production process so that it becomes unnecessary for the worker to perform the task at the 35° angle. Hence, the engineers and managers make it unnecessary for the workers to change their work methods, instead changing the design of the car or production process itself. In Korea, there is a proverb, "If your goal is to go to Seoul, it doesn't matter which way you choose as long as you can get there." This implies that achieving the goal is more important than how to do it! The engineers and managers of the carmaker seem to have certainly believed in the proverb. But the saying is perhaps several hundred years old, when the concept of "effectiveness" was either unimportant or unknown.

We admire the company's achievement for the last several decades: it started as a mere subcontractor for an American carmaker and has become one of the largest automobile companies in the world in a relatively short period of time. It surely is a great company! In this case study, we just want to understand how it has become one of the top players in the car industry and whether it will become one of the truly world-class carmakers eventually. We believe the company can become one of the top global carmakers in terms of both size and quality. But, it will be tough for the company to become a global leader (i.e., one of the very best) unless it develops a new work tenet supported by the integrating forces of both management and labor in a simultaneous and harmonious state.

As Figure 1.6 typifies, we foresee there exists a clear limitation on how far the administrative quality can go when only the engineers and managers are involved in the quality improvement process. It will be possible for the carmaker to become a good company, e.g., a superior "order qualifier," with administrative efforts. However, it will be unfeasible to be one of the true world-class automobile companies if it focuses on the administrative side only. There is a big hurdle between the "order qualifier" quality and the "order winner" quality[3] (Figure 1.7). The carmaker will be able to overcome the hurdle only when it masters the "integrated quality," which has to be designed and implemented by the cooperative participation of both management and labor simultaneously. We want the managers to ask themselves, *How is Toyota perfecting its quality, via the so-called administrative quality alone? Is Toyota's quality philosophy consistent with our administrative quality or the integrated quality?*

---

[3] See Chapter 3 for detailed discussion on quality, order qualifier, and order winner.

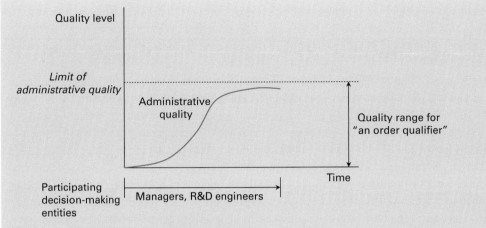

Figure 1.6 Administrative Quality Improvement

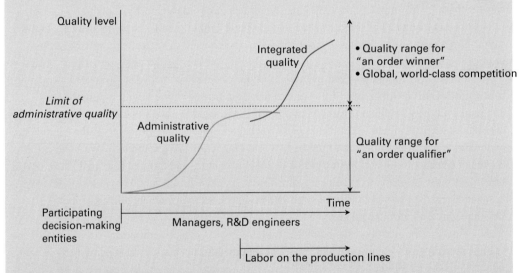

Figure 1.7 Integrated Quality Improvement

Questions

1. Define the concept of administrative quality. How is it different from the usual concept of quality?
2. Is the administrative quality sustainable? Can it be utilized in any operations context? Suggest a real-world example based on your own experience, if you can.
3. What should this company do to improve its quality continuously? Can the company achieve the ultimate level of quality (e.g., the best in the industry), continuing its practice so far?

CHAPTER 2

Learning and Learning Perspective

Learning is perhaps one of the most widely used, but also the most misunderstood, words. In this chapter, we first define learning in a more concrete way and elaborate on the meaning of learning perspective. Learning is one of the fundamental concepts in management. But, it is also an elusive one – it is difficult to clearly define the concept. In this book, we approach the issues of supply chain management from a learning perspective. As such, we have already used the term several times, assuming that there would be no confusion, although the concept has not been formally defined. But now we can no longer delay defining the concept, since we need a finer understanding in order to deal with issues specifically related to the learning processes in SCM. In this chapter, we delve into learning and its dynamics in operations management, in particular, SCM. We define and elaborate more on the **learning propensity model** (LPM). We also examine how the learning process influences the performance of a supply chain system.

Key Learning Points

- Learning in operations is a process through which the company identifies, analyzes, and internalizes complex cause-and-effect relationships among key factors in management.
- Learning capability is the company's ability to enhance its performance through applying its understanding of those cause-and-effect relationships to solving real-world managerial problems.
- Three representative operations or managerial capabilities are controllability (i.e., efficiency), flexibility, and integrating capability.
- There is a trade-off relationship between efficiency and flexibility.
- It is the integrating capability that enables the company to mitigate the trade-off.
- Chain of capability postulates that three capabilities, basic – process – system-level capability, are dynamically linked with each other.
- The principle of "chain of capability" helps the manager understand and reconcile the contrasting relationship between incremental and radical changes in the organization.

Confucian Wisdom – Three Ways to Learn

It is known that **Confucius** taught three ways for a man to learn wisdom. The first was through reflection, the noblest way. The second was through imitation, the easiest way. Finally, one could get wisdom through his own experience, the bitterest way! In modern business terminology, reflection compares to analysis (e.g., experimentation, simulation, and the like), imitation to benchmarking, and experience to "learning by doing." As such, the Confucian teaching some 2,500 years ago is still relevant and even looks stronger now than ever. There might be two explanations. First, Confucius was such a great teacher with a complete foresight, which enabled him to see how the world would work 2,500 years later. Although it can be possible, we would not believe that a human being (after all, Confucius was a human being!) could be perfect. The other explanation is that humankind has evolved very slowly, so slowly that 2,500 years were not enough to make a big change to the way human beings think and behave. In a sense, it is good for us to evolve slowly, because slow evolution gives us more time to learn not only from our own experience, but also through observing the experiences of others. That is, learning occurs robustly and continuously. Drawing an analogy with the Confucian teaching, we suggest we can learn in three different ways – analyzing, benchmarking, and experiencing. What is the fundamental commonality underlying these three methodologies? That is the causal relationship, i.e., cause-and-effect analysis. For instance, we analyze (e.g., experiment, simulate), benchmark, and experience to understand the cause-and-effect relationship between variables, e.g., key factors in managerial decision-making. Unless the manager understands the complex causal relationship among managerial variables and/or factors, she cannot make a decision that can solve real-world managerial problems.

In fact, the cause-and-effect analysis is the fundamental base for a systemic perspective, which is the underlying principle of managerial learning. As such, it is the quintessential perspective for our book!

Questions

1. Do you agree with Confucius regarding the three ways to learn wisdom?
2. Which way do you think is the most effective? Explain why in detail.

2.1 A Learning Organization's Perspective

Learning is an essential part of any **creative activity**. It is also a word many people use for a variety of different purposes and/or in a variety of different contexts. In this book, we define learning in operations as a process through which the manufacturing system (i.e., a company) identifies, analyzes, and internalizes complex **cause-and-effect relationships** among key factors in operations. Thus, learning capability is the manufacturing system's ability to enhance its performance in operations through applying its understanding of those cause-and-effect relationships to solving problems in operations (e.g., manufacturing or service management).

In Figure 2.1 we present an example. Suppose that a company wants to know why its operations performance is poor (Figure 2.1a). Soon it finds out that the market demand for its product is low (Figure 2.1b). The company wonders why its sales are not strong. After some analysis, it finds out that the quality of its product is poor (Figure 2.1c). Now the company has identified at least a simple cause-and-effect relationship that leads to its poor performance. But, certainly it is not enough! The company devotes more effort to understanding why its quality level is unsatisfactory. It figures that there are two primary factors that affect its poor quality (Figure 2.1d): first, its employees simply do not have enough knowledge and experience to control its manufacturing process (inadequate employee education); and second, its machinery and equipment are not in their best condition (dilapidated). The lack of employee education also results in low morale, which in turn affects the quality negatively. Finally, the company wants to fully understand the causes underlying such a miserable environment. Through more in-depth and field-based analysis, it finally sees a closed loop of the cause-and-effect relationship. Dismal market demand along with poor performance causes the company's profit to decline. With little profit, the company can't afford to invest in employee education and equipment. Figure 2.1e shows the closed loop of the entire cause-and-effect relationship.

The above example demonstrates a learning process. Understanding complex cause-and-effect relationships is a starting point. Learning itself is rarely enough for a company. It must be able to utilize its learning to rectify managerial problems. Regarding the example in Figure 2.1, the company should try to find out a link, where it can break the vicious cycle by changing the courses of some of the dynamic forces underlying this relationship. For example, the company might borrow some external resources to educate its employees and/or replace its dilapidated equipment with new technology in order to break the self-destroying cycle. Solving actual managerial problems by applying what the company has learned constitutes an essential part of the company's **learning capability**.

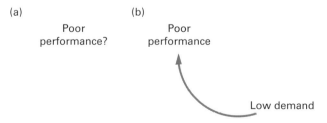

Figure 2.1 Example of Cause-and-Effect Analysis for Learning

(c)

(d)

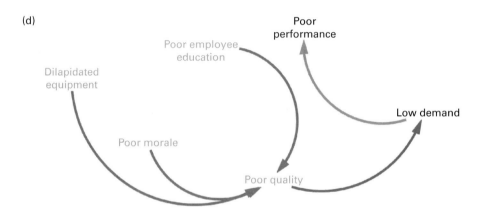

(e)

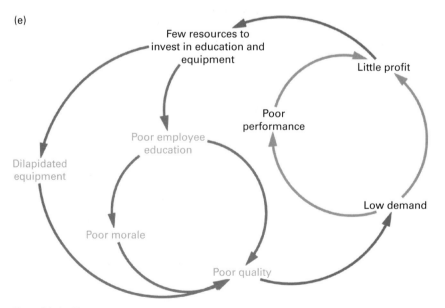

Figure 2.1 (cont.)

2.1.1   Single-Loop versus Double-Loop Learning

There are different types of learning processes. For instance, a learning process can be short-term oriented – focused on mitigating temporary irregularity and/or malfunction in the system. Another learning process tackles more fundamental or **root causes** that underlie a wide range of problem symptoms. Figure 2.2 shows a short-term, **single-loop learning**, where the organization tries to fix the symptoms without tackling more fundamental causes of the problem.

Figure 2.3 depicts the **double-loop learning** that is directly attacking the root causes of the problem. For instance, take a case of maintaining room temperature. A person wants to keep her room at 25°C. She has installed a thermometer system, which turns on the heating system when the temperature drops below 25°C, and turns off when the temperature rises above 25°C. Measuring the room temperature and adjusting the heating system compare to the single-loop learning, which deals with the superficial symptoms, not the underlying causes. After a while, she realizes it is tedious to adjust the heating system too often, and starts wondering why the room temperature rarely stays stable, fluctuating up and down around 25°C. She launches a serious examination of the room, and finds that a window at the far corner is broken. She has learned the underlying or root cause of the unstable room temperature. She replaces the broken window with a brand-new one – she has finally rectified the fundamental cause. With the new window installed, she no longer has to worry about frequently readjusting the heating system. Identifying and rectifying the root causes of the problem consist in the double-loop learning.

Should a company direct its effort to single-loop learning only at the expense of double-loop learning, or vice versa? A truly capable company ought to integrate the two types of learning in a balanced way – it should be able to concentrate on either type, alternately depending on the problem context. There are times when it had better rely on long-term fundamental problem-solving, and others when it had better find quick solutions to cope with short-term problems or irregularities in fast-changing market

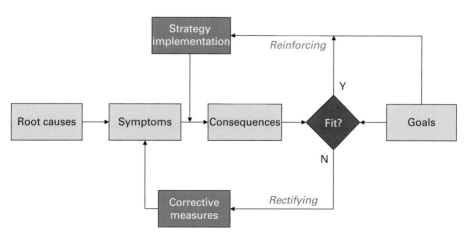

Figure 2.2 Single-Loop Learning

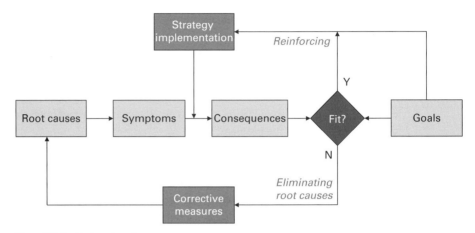

Figure 2.3 Double-Loop Learning

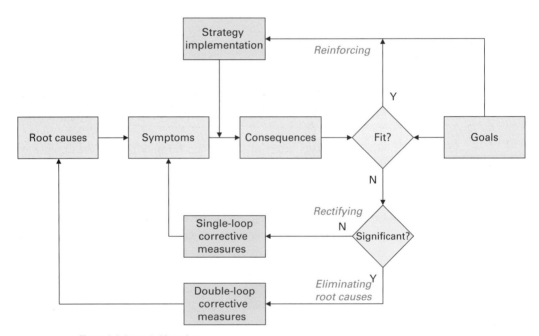

Figure 2.4 Integrated Learning

conditions. The point is that a capable company should retain flexibility to comfortably engage in any type of learning the context deems. Figure 2.4 conceptually portrays the company's integrated capability for such a situation.

2.1.2   Learning Propensity Model

How to integrate two different types of learning is a difficult, yet important, issue. Before delving into that issue, however, it seems in order for us to ask whether the two types of

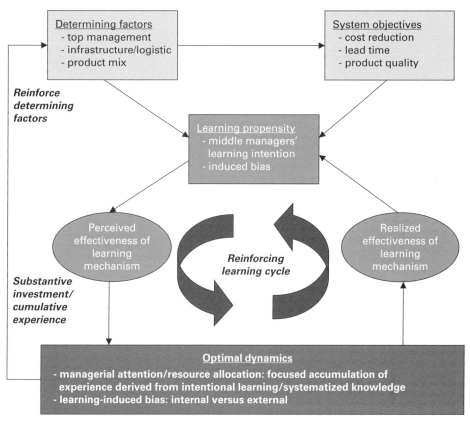

Figure 2.5 Learning Propensity Model (LPM)

learning are actually in action in the real business world and whether balancing them effectively can make a critical difference to a company's performance. Figure 2.5 sheds light on these questions.

In the mid-1990s, we conducted a comparative study on two shipbuilding companies in Korea. The original purpose of the study was to look into the firms' shipbuilding processes and find out key driving forces behind their operational efficiency. While conducting the research, however, we were able to make an intriguing observation: despite the fact that the two companies shared much in common in terms of their historical, geographical, and structural characteristics, their strategies to solve operational problems were very different. Thus, our research focus shifted from identifying factors for operational efficiency to explaining such a counterintuitive discrepancy between the two firms' learning strategies.

Company D tried to solve operations problems on site, using its own knowledge and experience embedded in its own employees, and leveraging its internal resources. It was the field workers who were actively participating in the **problem-solving process**. In effect, Company D's approaches to solving operations problems were **on-shop** or internal methods. On the contrary, Company S adopted a completely different approach.

Its primary problem-solving was dependent on **off-shop** approaches. For instance, when there was a serious problem in the shipbuilding process, say its welding operations, the company brought the problem to its R&D laboratory distant from the production process. Unlike Company D, the engineers and researchers in the R&D lab were the primary forces behind the problem-solving process to analyze the problem, identify plausible causes, and suggest solutions. In addition to its formal R&D resources, Company S sometimes outsourced some of its problem-solving activities to external research institutes such as consulting firms, universities, and other R&D institutions. Company S's approaches to operations problem-solving could be defined as off-shop or external methods.

Although their approaches to solving operations problems were very different, the two companies had started their shipbuilding operations under similar circumstances: both were part of large business groups in Korea, their shipyards were on the same island close to the southern end of the Korean peninsula, they initially hired managers and engineers who had comparable educational as well as professional backgrounds, and so on. Despite these initial similarities, the two companies have developed completely different capabilities of problem-solving and learning.

In Figure 2.5 we try to explain why. Although their structural conditions were similar, Company D and Company S had top management teams with very different wills and philosophies. The top management of Company D valued a close relationship with yard workers because they learned a lesson from a severely violent and militant labor dispute shortly after it took over the shipyard from its previous owner. Since then, Company D emphasized a basic principle of resolving issues and problems jointly between field workers and managers. Another critical factor was concerned with the physical structure of the company's production system. Its dry dock and crane were huge, much bigger than those at other shipbuilding companies in Korea, or even in the world. This gigantic physical structure imposed a set of constraints on the company's internal infrastructure and logistical system. For instance, because the huge size of the dry dock implied enormous overhead costs, the company had to keep high utilization of its physical structure. This motivated the company to concentrate all of its infrastructure-related arrangements, e.g., communication systems and logistical arrangements (on-shop trans-porting systems) on and around the dry dock. The dry dock became a natural place where most of the shipbuilding activities, including problem-solving, were conducted. These physical characteristics also impacted on the firm's decision concerning its product mix. In order to fully utilize its gigantic dry dock, Company D had to focus on building huge vessels such as VLCCs (Very Large Crude-oil Carriers) in large quantities. Hence, the employees accumulated knowledge and experience specific to a limited range of vessels, and therefore utilizing the field workers' expertise was indeed the most efficient way to solve operations problems.

These three factors – top management, infrastructure, and logistical system – and product mix constituted **determining factors**: they were not separate factors, but in fact they interacted with each other through a close cause-and-effect relationship. Managers, especially the middle managers, at Company D formulated their objectives in accor-dance with these determining factors. For instance, since the company's physical structure dictated focusing on the large vessel types, the managers set up a system-level objective of minimizing the production cost: a primary competitive advantage in the VLCC market was derived from low cost more than any other factor.

By taking into account the determining factors, along with the resulting system-level objective, the managers started forming a particular direction for learning – **learning propensity** leaned toward internal or on-shop learning methods. Initially, the managers' belief in such methods was based only on "perceptions," which presumed that somehow they needed to accommodate directions designated by the top management. Following their initial "perceived effectiveness" of such approaches, the managers planned, allocated more resources and managerial attention to, implemented, and tried to perfect those on-shop learning methods on the production field. Although the initial belief was based on rather murky "perception," as the managers "intentionally" fueled their efforts to the selected methods, these methods indeed started generating actual results in the shipyard. The managers' initial "perceived effectiveness" of their chosen learning methods transformed into "realized effectiveness," which in turn reassured the managers about the validity of their choice of such methods. Buoyed by the realized effectiveness, the managers formulated a similar strategy to allocate resources including their own attention in favor of on-shop learning methods over the other off-shop approaches. The managers' initial learning propensity toward on-shop learning methods was strengthened and reinforced by verifiable positive results from the successive implementation of such approaches. Now this "virtuous" cycle repeated itself.

We were able to observe similar dynamics in Company S. This company belonged to a business group, the core business of which was in hi-tech industries such as consumer electronics and semiconductors. Therefore, the top management of Company S's parent company was inclined to more scientific and formal methods when solving problems and developing new products. This inclination was imbued into the group's shipbuilding business as well. Company S's physical shipbuilding structure consisted of smaller docks, which were sometimes distant from each other. In order to accommodate this structural condition, Company S designed its infrastructure and logistical system accordingly and had to focus on building smaller ships compared to those built by its rival. In order to make a profit by building smaller vessels, the company needed to concentrate on high-end products such as container ships and more sophisticated small vessels. Thus, the product line was broader than Company D's. In addition, primary competitive advantages in the small and sophisticated vessel markets were derived more from short lead time and/or high quality than other factors. Thus, Company S's managers developed their own system-level objectives that clearly emphasized lead-time reduction and high vessel quality.

Given such determining factors and system-level goals, what kind of learning propensity should the managers at Company S have developed? Because the product line was broad, it was difficult for the managers to accumulate enough experience to solve production problems associated with a particular vessel type. Moreover, the physical structure was small so that there was not enough room in and around the docks for them to test on-shop problem-solving approaches. Fortunately, Company S was affiliated with a parent corporate, which was good at conducting sophisticated engineering and R&D

projects and helped its shipbuilding unit to borrow such sophisticated off-line or **off-shop learning** techniques. Given all of these conditions, it seemed natural for the company's managers to form a learning propensity consistent with off-shop learning approaches supported by formal engineering and R&D functions, both inside and outside the company itself. Again, the managers' initial belief in off-shop learning was in large part based on their perceived effectiveness of those methods, which in turn was formed after taking into account their determining factors and system-level objectives.

In order to show that their initial perception was indeed legitimate, the managers planned and allocated resources including their own managerial attention, implemented, and monitored the off-shop learning methods. Like in Company D's case, as the managers accumulated their intentional experience to successfully solve problems through off-shop ways, their initial perceived effectiveness was transformed into "realized effectiveness," which reinforced the entire learning process through the off-shop methods selected by the managers in the first place.

The two shipbuilding companies were both among the most successful shipbuilders in the world. But, as discussed above, they adopted very different strategies to learn in their shipyards. How was that possible? We were able to draw a conclusion from this comparative study on the two shipbuilding firms: what is important is not the learning method a company chooses, but how to choose a method consistent with the firm's structural as well as infrastructural conditions and to manage the learning process so as to have a reinforcing virtuous cycle in place. Thus, one can't say that a particular problem-solving method is always better than others, without taking into account firm-specific conditions.

As shown in Figure 2.5, the cycle of "learning propensity → perceived effectiveness → optimal dynamics (resource allocation and implementation) → realized effectiveness → reinforced learning propensity" can be compared to the single-loop learning, which repeats continuously in the short run. We now know that despite the difference in their learning strategies, both Company D and Company S have been successful in operations problem-solving. But, it is possible that the single-loop learning leads the organization in a negative direction – the learning process becomes a vicious cycle rather than a virtuous one. There is no guarantee that the single-loop learning enables the system to improve. What should a company do when it faces such a vicious learning cycle? Once the single-loop learning has repeated for a relatively long period of time, it will be extremely difficult for the company to change the dynamics by simply attempting to curb the negative single-loop learning process only. As in most dynamic systems, the learning propensity model is also affected by such dynamic inertia as chaos, path-dependence, administrative heritage, and so forth. One of the most effective and promising intervention methods is to tackle the determining factors – to modify top management's will, the system's infrastructure or logistical mechanism, and/or other relevant factors of any fundamental belief systems. More ideally, the company might want to check the validity of its determining factors from time to time when implementing its learning strategy. This more serious learning cycle of attempting to redirect or modify determining factors can be compared to the double-loop learning.

Learning is an important factor when managing a supply chain effectively for all of the participating organizations. Understanding how an organization, e.g., a partner company in the supply chain, develops a learning propensity that has ramifications in the long run should be an essential part of any SCM strategy. Going a little further, a competent participant in the supply chain should be able to identify a leverage point, through which it can intervene in the vicious cycle (e.g., a deteriorating or negative learning process) and rectify those problems that are jeopardizing effective coordination in the supply chain.

IN-DEPTH CONCEPT 2.1
On-Shop versus Off-Shop Problem Solving

Let's discuss the two contrasting methods of managerial problem solving, i.e., on-shop versus off-shop. Note that a managerial problem-solving method is a learning routine, which is a set of procedural steps through which a formalized learning process proceeds. There are pros and cons for each of the approaches (Table 2.1).

Table 2.1 Pros and Cons of On-Site versus Off-Site Learning Approaches

	On-Site (On-Shop) Approaches	Off-Site (Off-Shop) Approaches
Pros	– System-specific solutions – Utilizing internal expertise – Avoiding leakage of knowledge	– Avoiding interruption of operations – Utilizing wide range of expertise – Developing generalizable solutions
Cons	– Interrupting the ongoing operations – Solutions with limited applicability	– Difficulty in maintaining fidelity – Excessive lead time

An on-shop approach to learning has the following advantages. First, since the learning occurs in the production system itself, the solutions from the learning activity are system-specific in that the solutions can be implemented straightaway – as soon as the learning routine is completed. This approach also utilizes internal resources, including tacit knowledge and expertise embedded in the firm's own workforce. Therefore, the decision-maker (DM) doesn't have to worry about leaking the knowledge developed from learning to those outside the organization – e.g., to its competitors.

This approach has its fair share of cons as well. The most serious one is concerned with interrupting the current operations. Since the learning has to involve experimenting with the production system, it cannot completely avoid interfering with the current operations, which might not be affected by any significant "deviating causes." For example, an automobile company conducts a learning activity inside its production line. Suppose that the problem is related to fixing the stiffness of the front doors. Using an on-shop approach, the managers experiment with the car doors on the

Box continues

assembly line, interrupting the flow of normal operations. The solution to this problem might be found in the welding equipment at the particular process where the door is welded to the car body. Then, although the solution is pretty much system-specific – fixing the problem tailored to the unique context of the production system – it interrupts the normal flow of operations and thus causes additional costs, which might offset any benefits from utilizing the internal resources. A related issue is that the solutions might lack generalizability. Since the solutions are system-specific, they might not be able to be applied to other production environments: when the company operates multiple plants, learning at one location might not be transferable to other sites.

An off-shop approach has pros, which mirror the cons for an on-shop approach. Since this approach conducts learning outside the production system, e.g., moves the learning activity outside the present operations, it doesn't interrupt the normal operations. This approach utilizes external resources: it uses knowledge as well as expertise external to the production system, sometimes still in the same company (e.g., corporate R&D centers or engineering labs), or outside the company (e.g., consulting companies, universities, external R&D institutes, and so forth). Thus, the company has an option to tap into a much wider range of expertise from simple technical knowledge to profound scientific technology from a variety of external R&D sources. As a result, the solutions rooted on a rather generic pool of knowledge could have more generalizability compared with those developed specifically to the production system in question.

Despite these advantages, the off-shop approach has a serious difficulty in maintaining **fidelity** (e.g., similarity or congruence) between the production environment and the R&D environment. For example, let's look at the automobile company again. Suppose the company outsources its problem-solving to an outside R&D institute. Since the R&D institute resides in a university 100 kilometers from the assembly line and studies multiple projects from different companies, it cannot afford to tailor its learning environment to the automobile company's assembly line. Therefore, the solution might not be able to take into account the unique production environment that might have caused the problem in the first place. The solution would be purely generic: suppose that the solution suggests installing a new welding machine to fix the door stiffness. However, it turns out that the machine cannot operate to its fullest potential under the current production environment of the company. The lack of fidelity between the production environment and the R&D environment can be a serious problem. Similarly, when the lack of fidelity is excessive, communication between the company and the R&D institute can be tardy, incurring an excessive lead time for the problem-solving. The DM must take into account the pros and cons of each of these approaches before selecting the primary learning method.

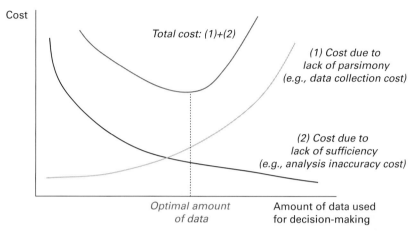

Figure 2.6 Parsimony versus Sufficiency

2.1.3   Parsimony versus Sufficiency

Managing the learning process requires the chief executive officer (CEO) to make decisions incessantly. Thus, an important question arises: *How much information does a CEO need when making a decision?* Note that in this book, the term "CEO" is equivalent to "decision-maker." The answer will be dependent on the particular situation in point. In general, the CEO probably has to consider various factors, which are sometimes contradicting each other – there exists a trade-off relationship between relevant factors. For instance, other things being equal, the more information the better. However, it also costs the CEO to get information – utilizing information requires searching, recording, classifying, retrieving, and analyzing activities, all of which involve cost expenses.

   We suggest two conceptual criteria that a CEO can contemplate when thinking about an optimal amount of information for effective decision-making: sufficiency and parsimony. The **sufficiency** criterion puts forth that the CEO must have enough information so that she won't omit any critical factors when making a managerial decision. Following the sufficiency criterion, one can say the more information the better. But, as mentioned already, processing information incurs costs. The **parsimony** criterion dictates that the CEO must utilize as little information as the decision environment permits. Thus, following this rule, one would say the less the better. In a real-world environment, the CEO should not solely rely on either rule at the expense of the other. Balancing between the two criteria is important. Figure 2.6 depicts such a situation.

2.2   Learning in Operations

What is learning? How can we properly define the concept? A general definition of learning is "the process of gaining knowledge through studying." First, learning is a process that must be dynamic and continuous, not just a one-time single isolated event. Second, it involves accumulating knowledge, which is useful for further learning and/or solving problems. Finally, the knowledge generation/accumulation is done through conscious effort – through studying, not just haphazard experiencing. Of course, this definition is not perfect. At least it provides us with a starting point. In this chapter, we want to define operations learning and to understand how it is related to SCM; e.g., how learning can be used to improve supply chain performance.

We define operations learning as the process of:

- identifying and understanding the complex cause-and-effect relationship between critical factors in operations;
- generating operations knowledge based on that understanding; and
- applying the knowledge to solving problems in operations to enhance the operations performance and to further improve the capability of identifying and understanding the cause-and-effect relationship.

This definition consists of several key components.

Learning is a process. Like the generic definition, we view operations learning as a process; i.e., operations learning should be dynamic and continuous. Since it is a process, operations learning could consist of multiple related sub-processes or components. It is dynamic – past learning influences present learning, which in turn affects future learning. In general, an organization is a system consisting of multiple parts or decision units. Thus, being dynamic also means that learning in one part of the organization affects learning in other parts of that organization, and vice versa. For instance, operations learning in one area affects and also is affected by operations learning in other areas. If we extend this concept to other functional areas in the firm, we would say that operations learning is closely related to learning in marketing, IT, HRM, and the like. Operations learning should also be continuous, implying that the process is moving forward incessantly. It is a process with the aim of expanding the firm's knowledge in operations, and the entire space of potential knowledge the firm has to pursue is boundless in theory, and thus the expansion process can go on forever theoretically. It is dynamic also in that operations learning encompasses continuous feedback and feed-forward between sub-processes consisting in the whole process or system. We will return to this point after discussing other components.

Understanding the complex cause-and-effect relationship. The starting point of a learning process is to identify critical cause-and-effect relationships in operations and to try to fathom the complexity of them. There are perhaps an infinite number of factors that interact with one another to bring about an infinite number of different phenomena or outcomes in operations. To understand such webs of complex cause-and-effect relationships should be the first immediate goal of operations learning.

Why is it important to understand the complex cause-and-effect relationship? This leads us to recall that management is all about decision-making to enhance the firm's performance. However, unless the DM understands how different factors in the firm interact with each other to produce a certain outcome, she cannot figure out how to improve the performance. By viewing "understanding the complex cause-and-effect relationship" as the first step in operations learning, we suggest that the ultimate goal of operations learning should be to maximize the operations performance, and eventually to optimize the firm's performance as a whole.

Generating operations knowledge. To understand the complex cause-and-effect relationship between key factors or dimensions in operations means to know about such a relationship. Hence, while trying to understand the cause-and-effect relationship, the DM accumulates knowledge about how the system behaves – how the firm's numerous factors dynamically interact with one another to determine the system's behavior. As the learning process iterates, the knowledge level becomes higher and the DM becomes more sophisticated in generating more knowledge.

Applying the knowledge to solving operations problems. The potential real value of knowledge about the system's behavior becomes fully realized only when the DM can solve real problems in operations by utilizing that knowledge. Here the problems are comprehensively defined to encompass a wide range of issues and phenomena that prohibit the firm from realizing its performance potential to the fullest extent. Therefore, this step for the DM to apply the knowledge to solving substantive managerial problems is an essential part of the learning process.

Improving performance and capability. Resolving critical managerial problems in operations helps the DM enhance the firm's performance. At the same time, through this iterative process from understanding the cause-and-effect relationship, generating useful knowledge about the system's behavior, to solving substantive managerial problems, the DM enables the firm to improve its own capability of learning – learning how to learn.

Figure 2.7 depicts the learning process: as we mentioned, it constitutes a closed loop comprised of continuous feedback interactions. An important observation is that just like the complex cause-and-effect relationship between crucial factors in operations, the learning process itself consists of successive cause-and-effect relationships. Therefore, understanding the causal relationships between steps of the learning process is key to enhancing the firm's learning capability.

There is a powerful obstacle that makes it difficult for the DM to manage the learning process optimally. This obstacle is the **delay** underlying the cause-and-effect relationship between learning steps. For instance, understanding the complex cause-and-effect relationship between factors in operations does not simultaneously generate a complete knowledge about how the operations system behaves. It takes time for such an understanding to transform into a useful form of knowledge that can be directly utilized for problem-solving. In effect, the delay makes the cause-and-effect relationship between learning steps unclear. When the cause-and-effect relationship is vague, the DM might find it difficult to commit resources to facilitating the interaction between the learning steps. What the delay does in the learning process is in essence to decouple time from space so as to make the whole process inherently complicated. Such a delay interferes

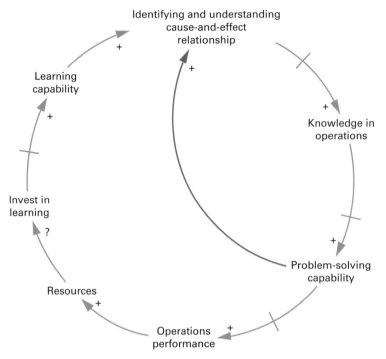

Figure 2.7 Operations Learning

with the learning process at multiple points; e.g., a delay intervenes in the relationship between knowledge-generation and problem-solving capability, between problem-solving capability and performance improvement, and also between investing in learning capability and learning capability improvement.

This multitude of delay in the learning process is the most serious threat to the firm's effective learning. Figure 2.8 shows an example of the dilemma faced by the DM. When the DM has to decide resource allocation, there are alternative ways to invest. Should the learning process not be affected by the delay, the DM finds it straightforward to recoup any investment in improving the learning capability. In reality, however, that is not the case. Now the DM has to decide whether to commit resources to an uncertain (due to the delay) learning process or to fund short-term projects that might help the firm realize a quick profit. The problem is that in general, a quick profit does not provide the firm with lasting competitive advantages for ongoing profitability. In most cases, short-term profit opportunity is associated with non-learning activities. By funneling resources into short-term initiatives, the firm might get quick profits in a relatively short period of time. But, then it is very much likely that such short-term projects help the firm realize quick profits at the expense of its capability of generating a lasting source of profitability. Even if the DM is well aware of the existence of delay, however, the issue can be still elusive since there remains another inhibitor: uncertainty – it is still uncertain whether allocating resources to learning that may become successful causes the delay. Thus, the delay becomes more detrimental since it is also intertwined with uncertainty to a great extent.

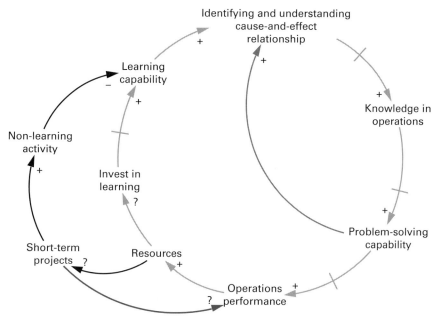

Figure 2.8 Operations Learning and Competing Alternatives

The discussion so far hints at a few characteristics that an effective DM must have, in order to nurture the operations learning for her organization. First, the DM must be able to comprehend dual complexities, one existing between learning steps and the other between crucial factors determining the firm's operations outcomes. Second, she must appreciate the value of learning as founding a lasting ground for sustainable profit generation for the foreseeable future. And based on this appreciation, she must be willing to take into account the delay factor when designing an operations strategy. Encompassing the delay in decision-making often implies a painful patience that the DM has to have, especially when there are other alternatives that might generate much quicker profits. The DM will be in a serious dilemma and the uncertainty would seem much greater than it is in actuality. The DM will be enormously tempted to make a decision for short-term solutions rather than for learning commitment. Unless necessary measures are taken properly, such short-term endeavors will weaken the firm's capability of sustainable growth and profit generation.

2.3 Dynamic Operations and Knowledge Development

As implied above, learning is an essential part of operations management. But, it has not been the case for long: learning in operations has become a crucial concept only in the 1980s. Before then, operations management was viewed as static, assuming that it would be done mechanically. A new perspective that incorporated the learning into an essential part of operations is the dynamic approach to operations management. There are critical

Static OM   *Dynamic Approach*

- Known production technology; no need for internal organizational learning or research; "one optimal way"
- Labor's role: performing procedures; "procedure" = defined set of actions; management = specify procedure and monitor

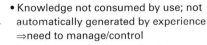

- Knowledge not consumed by use; not automatically generated by experience ⇒need to manage/control
- Learning must be intertwined with production

- Known and stationary environment; product markets, input markets, workers, machines = deterministic + unchanging
- Homogeneous inputs: labor, raw materials . . . standardized and available in complete markets
- Known goal/purpose/objective function: well-defined

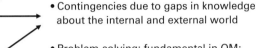

- Contingencies due to gaps in knowledge about the internal and external world

- Problem-solving: fundamental in OM; identify and solve the problems that lead to pinpointing contingencies; implications for control = focus on contingencies and related problems

Figure 2.9 A Static versus Dynamic View of Operations Management
Source: Jaikumar and Bohn (1992)

differences between the static and the dynamic view of operations. Figure 2.9 summarizes them.

Production technology. The first difference between the two perspectives is concerned with production technology and the role of learning in developing the technology. The static view assumes that the production technology is well known, and therefore an operations system does not have to try to improve its production technology because it doesn't provide the firm with any competitive advantage vis-à-vis its competitors. An implicit assumption that there is an optimal way to do operations and it is already known to the players in the market underlies this perspective.

Assuming the existence of one optimal way to conduct an operations activity causes a significant ramification: it implies that it is useless for an operations system (a production system) to try to nurture an internal learning capability inside the organization. Should one subscribe to the assumption, it perfectly makes sense not trying to enhance the learning capability because learning is futile when everybody already knows the optimal way to do a task.

On the contrary, the dynamic approach views the learning capability as a quintessential part of effective operations management. Underlying the dynamic approach, uncertainty takes a crucial role. Unlike the static view, every event in the world is affected by uncertainty, albeit the impact varies significantly, depending on numerous other emotional, as well as physical, factors. Once the uncertainty is accepted, one can no longer say that there exists only one optimal way to do a task and therefore the production technology is already known completely.

The dynamic approach also assumes that the knowledge – production technology – is not automatically generated by experience. It is true to a certain extent that one can acquire knowledge through experience. But, there are serious flaws in that reasoning. First, depending solely on learning through experience severely limits the DM's learning capability. It usually takes too long to learn through experience only. Suppose that a company tries to learn how to globalize its operations successfully. Should the company depend on its own real experience related to its globalization, it might take at least several years and perhaps cost millions of dollars for the company to obtain useful knowledge about the globalization. Learning through experience takes too long and costs too much. Because of the extremely long time lag between the time when the company needs the knowledge and the time when it accumulates enough experience to provide a useful answer, the knowledge might be useless when it eventually becomes available to the company.

Another peril of "learning solely through experience" is that the knowledge might be wrong, which could hamper the DM's ability to make a right decision. If in a bid to gain useful experience the DM observes only the events that are occurring currently, it is usually impossible for her to control lots of factors surrounding those events. Thus, when all of the events end and it becomes time to systemize the experience, all of a sudden the cause-and-effect relationship among those factors looks too confusing for the DM to establish any definitive correlation that should support formalizing that knowledge.

In order to avoid these risks, the dynamic approach advocates the firm's conscious effort to initiate, manage, and maintain the learning process. Moreover, knowledge is something that is not consumed away by use, and therefore investing in learning capability is a very effective resource allocation decision. Because of the dynamic approach, knowledge and learning become strategic fundamentals in operations management, and now the question is how and where to generate such capabilities.

Labor. Presuming that it is unnecessary to nurture production technology, the static view considers labor's role to be passive. According to the static view, the main role played by labor in the production system must be to perform procedures established by the management. A procedure defines methodology and sequence for a set of tasks necessary to produce goods and services. The static view also suggests that the management's role is to specify procedures and monitor whether labor follows the set procedures properly. According to this view, there exists a huge gap between the role of management and the role of labor. Since management prescribes the procedures and labor follows them, there is no need for communication between management and labor.

From the dynamic approach's perspective, this gap is damaging to the learning. This issue is also concerned with who should take an active role in the learning process. Effective learning in operations must be supported by all the members in an organization – from field workers, supervisors, R&D engineers, and middle managers, to top managers. Of course, depending on specific attributes of learning, different weights need be given to the participants in the learning process. The critical point is that collaboration and communication among various groups of DMs in the company are essential in taking on an effective learning process. In addition to emphasizing the importance of operations learning, the dynamic approach puts forth that the learning process must be intertwined with the production process.

Input markets and the environment. Consistent with the assumption about one optimal way to solve a managerial problem, the static view presumes that the inputs are homogeneous and the business environment is stationary. Homogeneous inputs imply that critical inputs to production, such as labor, raw materials, and capital equipment, are standardized and readily available in the market. Therefore, the company should not try to identify inputs tailored to its own production context: it can buy the best inputs from the market, whenever necessary, implying that any internal effort to develop skills or capabilities is of less use. Assuming that the business environment is stationary is consistent with believing that the environment is deterministic and unchanging over time, or changes very slowly at best. The business environment consists of diverse forces and elements such as product market, labor market, input market, capital market, and competitors. Therefore, assuming a stationary environment alleges ignoring the uncertainty in the market. These assumptions about the business environment and input market's characteristics are all consistent with the static view's presumption about technology and labor as mentioned above.

On the contrary, the dynamic approach suggests that the environment, including the input market, is inherently uncertain. Thus, the organization has to constantly try to find out the driving forces behind such changes. In effect, the market situation is systemic in that when one part of the market changes, its impact goes far beyond that portion of the market, affecting the entire market system. The company has to prepare itself for readjusting its strategy so as to take into account the dynamic changes in the market. As such, the learning process must be dynamic and flexible enough to accommodate those changing forces constantly. Otherwise, the company will lose competitiveness.

The dynamic approach, therefore, assumes that the current state of the company's knowledge about how the production system behaves is always incomplete – there always exists a gap between the current knowledge and the theoretical knowledge in the environment. Such theoretical knowledge is governed by physical laws that might not have been revealed yet. For instance, suppose that a field worker wants to drill a 10-mm hole on a printed circuit board, but the actual diameter of that hole turns out to be 9.999 mm. Why does this 0.001-mm gap occur? There probably exists the theoretical best way to drill the hole to its exact specification, but such theoretical knowledge is probably never known to the worker. Instead, the worker has her own idea about how to perfect the drilling; i.e., an incomplete knowledge about drilling. The gap of 0.001 mm reflects the gap between the theoretical complete knowledge and the worker's practical incomplete knowledge – the gap is between the internal and the external world. The dynamic approach calls this gap "contingency." Contingencies due to gaps in operations play an important role in the learning process. These contingencies help the DM initiate the learning process – they constitute a mechanism for triggering the learning. The DM should try to deal with these contingencies by engaging in problem-solving activities, which are the backbone of operations learning.

Organizational goals. Compatible with its perspective on the existence of one optimal solution, the static view considers that the company can define its goal clearly. It is again consistent with the static view's other perspectives as well. Since the company knows what it wants to accomplish and the market environment is very stationary, the management just needs to set up procedures of operations, which are simply supposed to be followed and implemented by the workers.

On the contrary, the dynamic approach strongly questions the validity of the assumption that the organization has clear goals and knows exactly what it wants to accomplish. Although it is true that any organization must have a well-defined mission as part of its long-term strategy, it is not warranted to say that such a mission is infallible in the constantly changing market. When a child is asked about her life goal, she might reply with a seemingly naïve answer. As she grows older, she will probably answer the same question with different replies. Why does her answer change over time? It is because as she grows older, she learns more about her ability as well as the environmental constraints surrounding her. As she learns more about herself and her environment, she modifies her goal so as to reflect the reality or the gap between her ideal and the environmental reality. Changing her life goal constantly should not be viewed as the child's weakness. Rather, such changes enable her to adapt to the world – she becomes stronger and nimbler.

As the child's example shows, an organization has to be prepared for refining and adapting its goals dynamically so as to cope with market changes more effectively. In fact, the dynamic approach suggests that the problem-solving activities must help the DM re-evaluate and adjust the organizational goals. Since the problem-solving focuses on contingencies that are caused by the gap between the incomplete organizational knowledge and the theoretically complete knowledge in the market, the organization can accumulate knowledge by engaging in the problem-solving processes. Through trying to understand the contingencies, the organization will be more capable of grasping the underlying forces of the market and therefore enhancing the likelihood of success in that market by properly adjusting its goals so as to be more compatible with the market forces.

In sum, the dynamic view regards learning as one of the most fundamental activities in operations management. The actual implementation of the learning process starts with identifying and solving managerial problems that are caused by significant contingencies: problem-solving itself will enable the organization to be more capable of pinpointing critical contingencies. This problem-solving process is the key part of the learning process. Its implication is that the DM must focus on contingencies and related problems in operations.

A brief thought on the relationship between learning and SCM. So far, we have discussed the profound differences between two perspectives on operations management: the static versus the dynamic view. If we summarize the differences in one sentence, it is that the dynamic approach views operations learning as the quintessential part of operations management, whereas the static view ignores it. Now one may want to ask, *So what? What is the relationship between operations and SCM?*

Although we will have more chances to elaborate on such a relationship in the subsequent chapters, it is the right time for us to think about it at least briefly. First, we have emphasized "coordination" as the key to successful SCM. Coordination is a joint learning process involving more than one organization participating in SCM. The principles applicable to operations learning are applicable and should be applied to supply chain coordination and collaboration.

Second, the learning process is a dynamic one that explores complex cause-and-effect relationships between basic factors or forces in operations. We view SCM as a dynamic process, too. In order to improve the supply chain performance, the decision-makers in the supply chain system should be able to fathom the complex webs of cause-and-effect relationships between various forces of the supply chain participants.

Finally, we view "learning" as a philosophy the decision-maker should accept. It is the philosophy that guides her in reaching a decision on resource allocation, organizational structure, strategic alliance building, technology or new product development, and so forth. The learning principles we have discussed so far, and will discuss continuously, should play the role of a guiding light for decision-makers: they must craft sustainable supply chain strategies.

2.4   Learning Propensity Model II

In Figure 2.5, we briefly discussed the learning propensity model (LPM) and how it affects the firm's technology development. The original LPM was successfully employed to explain two carmakers' globalization strategy so that we were able to develop LPM II (Figure 2.10).[1] The refined LPM is primarily different from the original LPM in that it has a formal mechanism to evaluate the validity of the current learning (i.e., dynamics of the original learning propensity) and thus to enable the company to decide whether to halt an undesirable dynamic or vicious circle.

Having a screening procedure put in place inside the LPM resolves an important issue. In essence, such a screening mechanism provides the company with flexibility in sustaining its learning process. It is far easier to break a vicious cycle before than after it is solidly formed: economically speaking, pre-emptive intervention costs much less than ex-post fixing. By changing the course of a potentially damaging propensity among its managers, the company increases its chance to learn in the right direction. But, even after implementing the screening method, a fundamental difficulty still remains in early determining of whether a certain learning propensity would be eventually helpful or detrimental to the company.

In fact, the only solution to such a dilemma in the learning process is to **learn how to learn** in a simulated, as well as actual, environment. And the firm has to pursue and refine such a solution incessantly. A constant **learning-and-updating process** might be an answer. Although it is not an easy task, however, it could be a rewarding strategy for the decision-maker.

---

[1] B. Kim and Y. Lee, "Global Capacity Expansion Strategies; Lessons Learned from Two Korean Carmakers" (2001) 34(3) *Long Range Planning* 309–333.

IN-DEPTH CONCEPT 2.2
Learning Propensity Model II

Incorporating the globalization case studies into the original learning propensity model (Figure 2.5), we put forth an extension, the "global LPM or LPM II," which offers a coherent and convincing explanation for the cases (Figure 2.10).

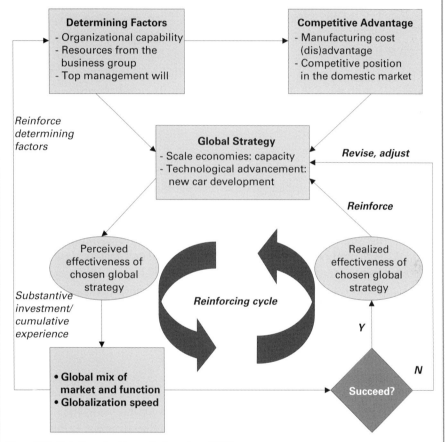

Figure 2.10 Global Learning Propensity Dynamics – LPM II

Determining factors such as organizational capability influence the firm's competitive position in the domestic market. Along with the determining factors, the firm's competitive position shapes its globalization motivation, goal, or objective. This globalization motivation dictates *what global strategy the firm should pursue.* Initially, the firm has a perception that the chosen strategy would work fine in the global market: it is logical because, after all, the chosen strategy fits well with its organizational capability and also its competitive position in the domestic market.

Believing in the effectiveness of the chosen globalization strategy, the firm decides *which market to concentrate on* and *which particular value chain activity (business function) to globalize and how.* Also, the firm probably has to decide *how*

Box continues

> *fast it could afford to expand into the global market.* Commitment to the selected
> strategy would eventually bring about higher performance that reinforces the
> "perception."[2] The critical moment arrives when the firm evaluates its performance
> in global operations following the selected strategy, and asks, *Has it been successful
> or not?*
>
> Should the strategy prove successful, the firm could feel satisfied with its choice of
> the strategy and reinforce it. This process will continue iterating and it will accelerate
> until serious challenges indicate otherwise. *What if the selected strategy fails to
> realize the promised performance improvement in the global market?* When the
> strategy proves unsuccessful, the evaluation sends a negative feedback to the com-
> pany, which will try to rectify the problem by adjusting its globalization strategy.
> With this new strategy, the firm restarts its global expansion dynamics.

Learning and SCM. We would like to clearly state why and how learning is related
to supply chain management. As discussed already, coordination between strategic
supply chain partners is the key to successful implementation of various initiatives
for effective SCM and such coordination cannot be forged without mutual learning
between the partners. Structural constructs in SCM are important, but the infrastructural ones that bond together the structural factors must be the prerequisite to
high-performing SCM. In that sense, building a relationship that facilitates the
coordination between strategic partners is the process of learning, *learning from
each other as well as learning how to solve supply chain problems together more
effectively.*

2.5   SCM and Operations Capability

The company should have strong operations capabilities in order to implement its supply
chain strategy effectively. There are two perspectives that help us understand essential
characteristics of operations capability. We discuss these two perspectives, horizontal
and vertical.

2.5.1   Horizontal Perspective: Controllability, Flexibility, and Integrating Capability

Effective supply chain management requires the firm to have strong operations capabilities. One can group various operations capabilities into three representative capabilities:
controllability (i.e., efficiency), flexibility, and integrating capability.[3] In order to be

---

[2] P. Ghemawat, *Commitment: The Dynamics of Strategy* (New York: Free Press, 1991).
[3] B. Kim and C. Park, "Firms' Integrating Efforts to Mitigate the Tradeoff between Controllability and
Flexibility" (2013) 51(4) *International Journal of Production Research* 1258–1278.

competitive in the market, the firm must retain high levels of these capabilities. When the firm has **controllability** on its operations, it is able to control its processes so that it can attain an enhanced level of efficiency. For instance, a high level of controllability enables the firm to achieve a high conformance quality. Then, how can the company raise its controllability? One important source of controllability is the scale economy – when a company is producing a limited number of products in large quantities, e.g., mass-producing a limited product line, it will become more and more efficient in producing the *same* products. Mass production based on the scale economy can provide the company with a capability of "doing limited things very efficiently."

Whereas controllability requires doing a limited number of functions repeatedly, i.e., rigid repetition of similar operations continuously, **flexibility** enables the firm to be nimbler to deal with uncertainties in the market. Unlike controllability, the essence of flexibility is "responsiveness" to diverse market demands. Without a proper level of flexibility, the firm will find it difficult to make a diverse range of products demanded by customers, who in most cases reside in different parts of the world and have a great deal of diversity. Since one of the most conspicuous uncertainties a company has to deal with in the market is demand uncertainty, we may conclude that the crucial role played by flexibility is to cope with market uncertainty by enhancing the firm's responsiveness to the changing market.

It is important for the firm to have *both* controllability *and* flexibility: to be competitive in the market, the firm needs both efficiency and responsiveness at the same time. The problem is that there exists an inverse relationship between controllability and flexibility. For instance, the more the firm wants to increase its controllability, the less it will be able to enhance its flexibility, and vice versa. The reason why there exists such an inverse relationship is that the critical sources of these two capabilities contradict each other. As mentioned already, the key source of controllability is the scale economy and its effect is enhanced operational efficiency. On the contrary, the primary source of flexibility is the firm's ability to deal with diverse dimensions simultaneously and its effect is superior responsiveness. It is difficult for the firm to deal with diverse operational dimensions when it wants to focus on producing a limited product line repeatedly. Likewise, when the firm is busy coping with diversity, it can't enjoy the scale economy to the fullest extent. Figure 2.11a depicts an example of such an inverse relationship between controllability and flexibility: when the firm enjoys a higher level of controllability, C_1, it can have a relatively low level of flexibility, F_1. Suppose the firm wants to enhance its flexibility, say from F_1 to F_2, then, according to the inverse relationship, its controllability might have to decrease, say from C_1 to C_2. Fundamental questions arise such as, *Should there always be such an inverse relationship between the two capabilities?* and *Is there any way for the firm to overcome such a contradiction?*

We doubt that the underlying characteristics of the inverse relationship between the two could ever change radically. Despite the irreversibility of the relationship, there *is* a possible way for the firm to mitigate the negative impact of the inverse relationship. Figure 2.11b indicates such a possibility. Although the pattern of inverse relationship between controllability and flexibility remains intact, as the curve moves upward, the severity of the relationship lessens. For instance, suppose the relationship is changed

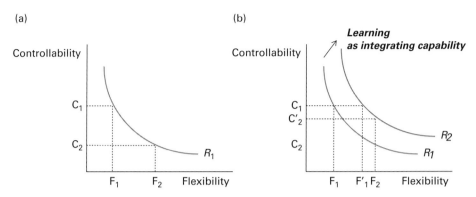

Figure 2.11 Controllability, Flexibility, and Learning Capability

from curve R_1 to curve R_2, which is at a higher position. Now, if the company has its controllability at C_1, its flexibility level is F'_1, which is larger than F_1, its previous flexibility level under the curve R_1. Similarly, if the company has its flexibility at F_2, its controllability level is now C'_2, which is larger than C_2, its previous controllability level. According to Figure 2.11, curve R_2 indicates that the company has more capability than under R_1. More precisely, the company represented by R_2 is more capable of mitigating detrimental impacts resulting from the inverse relationship between controllability and flexibility than that associated with R_1. We define **integrating capability** as the capability that enables the company to shift its capability curve from R_1 to R_2. How to enhance such an integrating capability? The integrating capability should be tightly based on the company's learning ability.

In order for a supply chain to function effectively, it is important for the supply chain partners to actively seek ways to improve their individual operations capabilities. Understanding the potential "inverse" relationship between capabilities is key to developing critical capabilities in a balanced manner. In particular, the role of integrating such needs must be highlighted.

2.5.2   Effects of Integrating Capability on the Trade-Off

Consider the discussion of capabilities, i.e., controllability, flexibility, and integrating capability (Figure 2.11). We postulated that the relationship between controllability and flexibility is inverse in the short term. In fact, we did not talk about the long-term relationship. For instance, one might say, "I think BMW improves both controllability and flexibility simultaneously every year. Then, isn't it true that the relationship between the two capabilities is positive?" Such a question seems reasonable and calls for rethinking about the proposition. In order to reconcile the seemingly contradicting observations, we put forward an example. Let's consider a hypothetical case, where BMW has improved its integrating capability continuously. Figure 2.12 presents the company's capability improvement dynamics for the last five decades. In the figure, there are two observations we note:

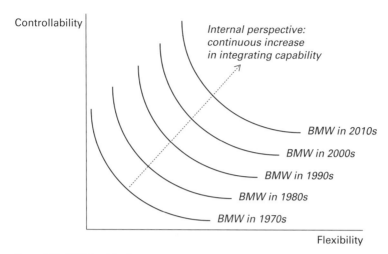

Figure showing axes labeled Controllability (vertical) and Flexibility (horizontal), with "Internal perspective: continuous increase in integrating capability" and curves labeled BMW in 2010s, BMW in 2000s, BMW in 1990s, BMW in 1980s, BMW in 1970s.

Figure 2.12 BMW Capability Curves

- At a particular point of time, there exists an inverse relationship between controllability and flexibility. For instance, in 1970 as well as 2010, BMW was struggling with the trade-off relationship between controllability and flexibility. This is consistent with the proposition we postulated regarding the short-term trade-off between the two capabilities.
- Over time, BMW was improving its integrating capability and thus the company's capability curve was moving upward continuously. This observation indicates that the company continues enhancing its ability to communicate and coordinate with its supply chain partners across the value chain.

With its capability curves as in Figure 2.12, BMW has made specific choices about the combination of flexibility and controllability. That is, the company made a strategic choice regarding its actual operations capabilities in a way consistent with its corporate strategy. Figure 2.13 shows an example series of choices made by the company. For instance, from 1970 to 1980, BMW seemed to decide to increase its controllability and flexibility proportionally as its integrating capability improved; but, from 1980 to 1990, it seems like BMW made a strategic choice that emphasized controllability more than flexibility (the slope linking the two strategic choices is steeper), perhaps due to the change in its target market to call for more controllability, i.e., efficiency.

Is the company's improvement path externally observable? For instance, is it possible for outsiders to observe BMW's capability curve improvement over time? The answer is no in general. It is probably impossible for those outside BMW (i.e., not involved in the detailed planning or management of operations capabilities) to observe the dynamics of the company's capability improvement. What about the strategic choices made by the company? The strategic choices made by BMW are not proprietary to the company only. In fact, such choices are part of public knowledge. For instance, the market can have knowledge about how much flexibility or controllability the company is capable of by

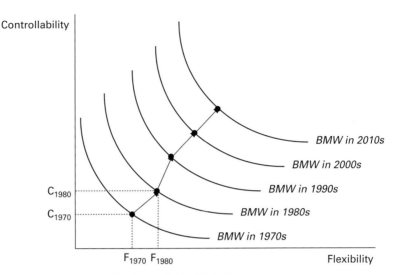

Figure 2.13 BMW Capability Choices

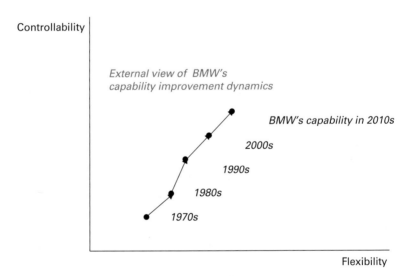

Figure 2.14 External View of BMW Capability Improvement

observing the products and services delivered by the company. As such, the strategic choices of capabilities are visible to outsiders such as customers, competitors, and the general public. Figure 2.14 draws BMW's capability improvement dynamics from the external perspective, i.e., in the way observed by outsiders, deleting other internal portions of the capability curves, which could be observable only to the BMW managers. As we can see in Figure 2.14, it is plausible for an outsider to say that the relationship between controllability and flexibility is positive. Indeed, the long-term relationship between the two capabilities can be positive as long as the company improves its integrating capability continuously. These long-term dynamics are not contradicting our proposition about the short-term trade-off relationship between capabilities. In fact, the framework we put forth to explain the trade-off relationship can be applied to explaining the long-term capability dynamics.

A summary caveat is that although in the long run the company can overcome the trade-off between capabilities as long as it enhances its integrating capability, that doesn't mean that the company can ignore the short-term trade-off completely. In fact, the trade-off stays there all the time and thus the company must try to manage it effectively. Unless the company deals with the short-term trade-off successfully, it might not be able to improve its integrating capability in the first place. What is critical is not whether to manage both short-term and long-term capability dynamics, but how to balance resource allocation to deal with both dynamics optimally.

2.5.3　Vertical Perspective: Chain of Capability – Basic, Control, and System Capability

The three capabilities mentioned above – controllability, flexibility, and integrating capability – constitute the typology focused on fundamental roles played by the capabilities. Another way to look at the firm's operations capability is to analyze the cause-and-effect relationship between key capabilities. We present a new typology, from a more hierarchical perspective. This typology categorizes the operations capabilities into basic, control (process), and system capability.

Figure 2.15 shows another set of capabilities and their linkages; Figure 2.16 graphically describes a general hierarchical relationship among the capabilities. The **basic capability** consists of the most elementary knowledge and skills a company must have – e.g., employees' general understanding of production processes, quality, safety, quantitative skills, economic and engineering concepts, and cultural aspects. The company can raise the basic capability by educating and training its employees regularly under a long-term plan. This basic capability is the backbone of the company's comprehensive capability. However, the basic capability often seems less relevant to the current operations at the company since it deals with a broad range of issues – i.e., employees might view this capability as remote and non-imminent, and focus on more urgent task-specific matters.

Dealing with those task-specific problems requires control or process capability, which is specifically tailored to a limited range of production processes. Consider a steel company's production process in Figure 2.17. In order to effectively operate the "melting" process, the steel company has to utilize a set of skills and know-how, which could be very different from those related to the "casting" process. Each of the other processes requires a specific set of knowledge and skills – i.e., a different capability. Capability specifically coupled with a particular process or processes is defined as **control (or process) capability**. Compared with basic capability, process capability is more focused and clearly attached to a certain process or processes. This also implies that the process capability is "less general" than the basic capability in that the process

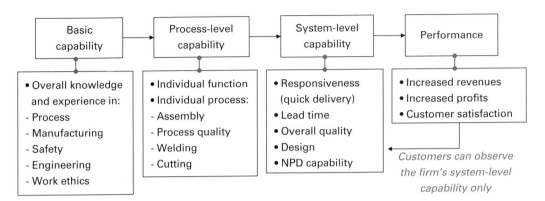

Figure 2.15 Chain of Capability

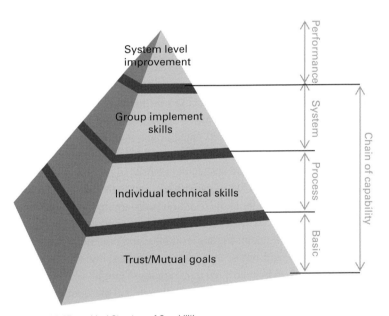

Figure 2.16 Hierarchical Structure of Capabilities

Figure 2.17 Production Process at a Steel Company

capability specifically associated with one particular process may not be useful for other processes.

Let's think about the steel company again. The customers of the steel company are most concerned with the quality and/or delivery speed of the final products –

wire rods, plates, or hot rolled steel. They probably don't care about how much control capability the steel company has for, say, its melting process or casting process. Although the steel company must try to develop a high level of control capability for each of the processes, the customers care only about the attributes of the final products such as high quality, diverse product lines, high delivery speed, and responsive after-sales services. The company's capacity to meet the customers' such demands is defined as **system capability**. The company can expect to have a satisfactory level of system capability only when its control capabilities for the production processes are well developed, which in turn need to be firmly based on the basic capability.

2.5.4 Incremental versus Radical Improvement

An intriguing issue in the innovation literature is whether a firm should innovate incrementally or radically. This issue seems a bit controversial: some people advocate for **radical innovation**, while others emphasize **incremental improvement**. But we need not be binary in taking a position regarding this issue. We can find an integrated framework to reconcile the potential conflict. We suggest that there are both incremental and radical elements in a company's innovation or improvement dynamics. Figure 2.18 shows such reconciliation. Since it takes a long-term, sustained effort to build basic capability, the company might observe only "incremental improvement" in basic capability over time. As discussed previously, control capability is rooted in basic capability. But, the time frame might be different – a small improvement in basic capability might not be instantly translated into the same improvement in control capability. For

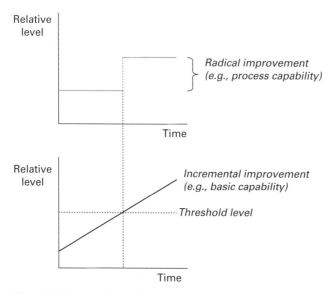

Figure 2.18 Incremental versus Radical Improvement

example, suppose the employees took a class on **statistical process control** (SPC)[4] today. Probably their basic capability level slightly improved. It is, however, doubtful that their slight improvement in basic capability can contribute much to enhancing their control capability for the refining process tomorrow. Suppose further that the employees take the SPC course for the next few weeks and practice the method thoroughly. With their accumulated knowledge and practices of SPC, they will eventually be capable of improving their process capability for the refining process. Hence, an accumulation of incremental improvements in basic capability will help the employees enhance their process capability in a discontinuous, radical manner. Sometimes a certain improvement seems radical from an outsider's perspective. But, in most cases, such a radical improvement/innovation is triggered by an accumulated impact of incremental improvements for a longer period of time. Thus, the more critical issue is not whether a company focuses more on a particular type of improvement, but on how it harmonizes the two different types of improvement in order to optimize its operations performance.

Discussion Questions

1. Can you define a learning organization?
2. Why is it important to take a learning perspective in studying supply chain management?
3. Explain and compare single-loop and double-loop learning.
4. What is the learning propensity model (LPM)?
5. Can you suggest a case to which you can apply the LPM to analyze a managerial problem?
6. What are the major differences between static and dynamic operations management? Why do you think such differences occur?
7. Define controllability, flexibility, and integrating capability, respectively. Why do you think there is a short-term trade-off relationship between capabilities? Is there such a relationship in the long run? Why or why not?
8. Explain the concept of chain of capability. In what ways is it different from the horizontal model consisting of controllability, flexibility, and integrating capability?
9. Define radical and incremental improvements. Which one do you think is more realistic for your (future) business? Explain why.
10. Explain how you can reconcile the two different improvement patterns by using the chain of capability.

---

[4] See Chapter 3 for a detailed discussion on SPC.

CASE STUDY 2.1
Global Knowledge Management at Danone (A) (Abridged)

By Amy C. Edmondson and David Lane[5]

At Danone we don't talk about strategy, we react to the context around us. For me, it's like a Lego box that you buy for your children. They start to play, trying to find a way to build the image on the Lego box. At the end of the day, they give up, throw out the box, and put the pieces away. The next weekend you put all the Lego pieces on the floor and then the strategy starts. They try to imagine something. Not what was on the box, but what they have in their heads. That is strategy at Danone for me: It's Lego.   Franck Riboud, Chairman and Chief Executive Officer, Groupe Danone

At the Paris headquarters of consumer goods company Groupe Danone, Executive Vice-President of Human Resources (HR) Franck Mougin had been implementing a concept called the Networking Attitude to accelerate knowledge sharing across country business units (CBUs) in a company with employees in 120 countries. "At Danone we don't have time to reinvent the wheel," he explained in May 2007. "We want our time to market to be shorter than that of our competitors, who are much bigger than us. If we cannot be big, at least we can be shrewd." In 2006, Danone had revenues of €14 billion, compared with Swiss packaged food giant Nestlé with revenues of €60 billion, and America's Kraft Foods with revenues of €25 billion.

After joining Danone in May 2002, Mougin had hired Benedikt Benenati as organizational development director in April 2003 and gave him responsibility (and a very low budget) for the Networking Attitude initiative. Together they had developed several tools – notably knowledge "marketplaces" and "sharing networks" – to help employees connect with each other and share good practices horizontally, peer-to-peer, rather than relying on hierarchical lines of communication. From 2004 to 2007, Danone employees shared almost 640 good practices with colleagues, making practical information accessible to some 5,000 of Danone's 9,000 managers around the world.

Mougin and Benenati were pleased that 86 percent of general managers surveyed saw the Networking Attitude as highly successful. But now, in July 2007, the two wanted to take the work further. Benenati had recently experimented with variations on the original concept, extending the Networking Attitude events from managers to all employees. Other new events invited Danone managers to share practices with suppliers and customers.

Source: © 2012 by the President and Fellows of Harvard College. Harvard Business School Case 613–003. This case was prepared by Amy C. Edmondson and David Lane, as the basis for class discussion rather than to illustrate either effective or ineffective handling of an administrative situation. Reprinted by permission of Harvard Business School.

---

[5] Professors Amy C. Edmondson (HBS) and Bertrand Moingeon (HEC Paris), Executive Director of the Europe Research Center Vincent Dessain, and Research Assistant Ane Damgaard Jensen prepared the original version of this case, "Global Knowledge Management at Danone (A)," HBS No. 608-107. Professor Amy C. Edmondson and Global Research Group Senior Researcher David Lane prepared this abridged version.

Finally, Benenati was working on "co-building events," where employees from different Danone units networked to create *new* practices and products rather than to share existing ones.

Extending the concept's application posed management challenges. Increased complexity and breadth strained the Networking Attitude's informal spirit, which was to Mougin its essence. Some managers wanted to give the process more structure, by tracking results or rewarding employees for networking. But Mougin feared that the spirit of the Networking Attitude might get lost. He knew he needed to make a decision on how to proceed.

Danone's corporate growth. The company that became Danone was originally established by the Greek doctor Isaac Carasso in Barcelona, Spain, in 1919. Carasso was the first person to perfect an industrial process for making yogurt and named his company after his son Daniel.[6] Daniel Carasso moved to France in the late 1920s where he ran the company after his father's death. After World War II, he merged Danone with French cheesemaker Gervais, creating Gervais Danone, and acquired companies producing pasta, ready meals, and fresh packaged foods. In 1973, Gervais Danone merged with BSN, the leading French manufacturer of beer, mineral waters, and baby food, creating BSN Gervais Danone, the biggest food company in France. CEO Antoine Riboud saw the merger as an opportunity to enter new markets with a decisive shift toward food products and to integrate his social enterprise interests with his work. In a speech in the early 1970s, Riboud insisted that companies including Danone have social goals and be managed "with the heart as well as the head."[7] He then sold off non-food assets and bought Italian and Spanish food companies; a 1986 acquisition brought operating companies in Germany, the Netherlands, Belgium, France, and Italy; the collapse of the Soviet Union opened up Eastern Europe. To reach consumers in emerging markets in Asia, Latin America, and South Africa, BSN Gervais Danone relied on acquisitions and partnerships. In 1994, it became Groupe Danone.

Franck Riboud: In 1996, Franck Riboud took over from his father Antoine as chairman and CEO of Groupe Danone. The youngest of Antoine Riboud's children, Franck Riboud was a sports enthusiast and an engineer by training. He had held various positions within Danone, working his way up to a top position in the beverages division. When he took the helm, some accused the family (which held 1 percent of firm capital) of nepotism: "I had no legitimacy," he recalled.[8]

---

[6] Matthew Gwyther, "The MT Interview: Franck Riboud," *Management Today*, August 1, 2006, via Factiva; "Danone: from Greek Shop in Spain to Empire Rooted in France," Agence France Presse, July 21, 2005, via Factiva; Donna Larcen, "Yogurt Snack Trend Booming – New Varieties Are Keeping Fat-Free Snack Lovers Satisfied," *Charleston Daily Mail*, March 8, 1995, via Factiva; Thomas Fuller, "PepsiCo Says It Won't Try to Buy French Company," *The New York Times*, July 26, 2005, via Factiva; and Dannon Company website, www.dannon.com/about_company.aspx.

[7] Dominique Vidalon, "Danone Founder Antoine Riboud Dies," *Reuters News*, May 5, 2002, accessed via Factiva.

[8] Gwyther, "The MT Interview: Franck Riboud" (n. 7).

Riboud proceeded to restructure the company, which in 1996 had a broad product offering and an operating margin of 8.9 percent. While primarily a French-Spanish group, the French market then accounted for 42 percent of Danone revenues. Riboud consolidated Danone's portfolio from nine to three divisions, selling non-core brands such as sauces, pasta, beer, and cheese and retaining the Danone, Evian, and LU brands to spearhead the company's Fresh Dairy Products, Beverages, and Biscuits product divisions. Said Pierre Deheunynck, Vice-President of People and Organization Development: "[Riboud] did three very smart things. He directed the company's focus towards health and nutrition. He turned a Western European company into an international organization with operations worldwide. And he changed how the organization was managed. He created the expression *jeu de jambe*,[9] which perfectly describes Danone's approach to dealing with many issues in a flexible way."

Danone in the twenty-first century. *Health through food:* Riboud continued to build on his father's vision of dual social and economic goals, seeking to bring health through nutrition to people around the world. He explained:

> When I visit a CBU I am always given a presentation about the buying power of the consumer in category A, B, C, D, or E. For instance, out of 250 million people in an area we can launch a product for the 50 million of them who are in category B. But I started to wonder why we didn't look at category C, so we developed a strategy focused on making our blockbuster brands affordable for those consumers. But what about category D, or the people living on two dollars a day? They are also part of our mission to bring health through food to a maximum of people, because they make up 80% of the population in emerging countries. It's not charity; it's sustainable development. We have to create a new economic model.

In 2004, Danone started a project with that objective in South Africa, where the local subsidiary launched the yogurt Danimal in the city of Soweto. The nutrient-fortified yogurt retailed for 13 US cents and sold through a distribution network of local women known as "Daniladies." In 2006, Danone formed a joint venture in Bangladesh with the microfinance organization Grameen Group and created a yogurt targeting the poor in Bangladesh living on less than $2 per day. Shakti Doi, meaning "power yogurt," would retail for 3 to 4 cents and be launched in fully biodegradable plastic.

A strong position in 2006 and beyond: Under Riboud's leadership, Danone was a thriving international company. Riboud had launched a research center in Paris in 2002, and established a vital business division in the Asia-Pacific in 2004. Danone had acquired more than forty businesses in Asia, Latin America, Eastern and Central Europe, Africa, and the Middle East. In 2007, the company showed an operating margin of 13.4 percent,

---

[9] "Jeu de jambe" means dribbling and is a term used in various team sports such as soccer or basketball for players moving a ball in a series of changes in direction and position to create opportunities to score a goal. According to a company glossary, *Danone words*, "Footwork is a matter of flexibility, pragmatism and daring, the capacity to bounce back and get over past failures. Just as sportsmen continually and rapidly replace their feet, managers have to take the right strategic stance."

with France accounting for 22 percent and Western Europe 54 percent of revenues. Of the 90,000 employees working for Danone worldwide, 47 percent were employed in the Asia-Pacific region, another 23 percent in Western Europe. Danone was the global leader in fresh dairy products and was tied with Swiss packaged food giant Nestlé in beverages. Danone was second only to American food company Kraft Foods in biscuits and cereal products worldwide. Of Danone's €14 billion in 2006 revenues, €8 billion were generated in the dairy division, €2 billion in biscuits, and €4 billion in beverages. Europe still accounted for a majority of Danone revenues, down from 66 percent of sales in 2004; Asia-Pacific contributed 17 percent, and the rest of the world generated the remaining 26 percent in 2006. Danone's four blockbuster products, Activia, Actimel, Vitalinea, and Danonino (all in the dairy division), represented €4 billion, or nearly 30 percent, of group revenues.

In July 2007, Kraft Foods offered to purchase Danone's biscuits division for €5.3 billion; the deal was expected to go through by the end of 2007. A week later, Danone launched a takeover offer to acquire Royal Numico NV, a Dutch baby food company, for €55 per Numico share, or €12.3 billion. To Riboud, these developments were in sync with the company's mission to bring health through food to the majority of people. In January 2008, Danone planned to reorganize into four business lines: Fresh Dairy Products, Water and Beverages, Baby Food, and Clinical Nutrition.

Managing knowledge for competitive advantage. Making product, customer, and operational information available to Danone employees around the world where and when needed was a challenge: Mougin and his colleagues recognized a tension between a more efficient top-down approach and local managers' desire for autonomy. They also confronted questions about the role of information technology in managing knowledge.

Local markets: By the early 2000s, Riboud was committed to maintaining close touch with local markets, despite Danone's presence on five continents. Mougin saw decentralization as essential to firm strategy: "At Danone, a managing director who is in charge of an activity in a country is the decision-maker, with P&L responsibility. Headquarters can merely suggest options to him, but cannot impose conditions. We think that there are more disadvantages than advantages in looking for synergies, and the success of our decentralized management can be seen in our local brands."[10]

Mougin believed that varying products by market and staying close to local consumers allowed Danone to move quickly, a critical skill in competitive markets where it was not the largest player. "We can launch in three months while it takes Nestlé an average of 12–18 months to get a new product to the market," he noted. "Some of our competitors have a lot of good ideas for new products, but we get them to the market earlier because our frontline manager can execute quickly."

Decentralization and integration: Yet, decentralized operations could confuse frontline managers when they lacked clear directions from headquarters, did not know to whom to turn for

---

[10] Adapted from Franck Mougin and Benedikt Benenati, "Story-Telling at Danone: A Latin Approach to Knowledge Management," Les Amis de l'École de Paris, April 1, 2005.

advice, and saw little horizontal communication between Danone's large divisions. Fabien Razac, a marketing director, explained that it was difficult for CBUs to learn from each other:

> At Danone, we don't have a lot of quantified organizational expertise. The expertise that we have is the sum of our individual knowledge. We don't have a library with a bunch of files where you can go if you need to know how to perform a certain task. The key learnings are embedded in individuals around the world, and there is little incentive to formally categorize things into databases. You have to talk to people and network to do your job.
>
> The schizophrenia between bottom-up and top-down is there all the time. You need the top-down to re-prioritize and re-concentrate, and you need the bottom-up to nourish – to listen to the market, the latest ingredients, the latest innovations, to know what works with the competition ... It's because of this confrontation and the local autonomy that we create value.

Prior approaches to knowledge management: Danone had made prior attempts to leverage company talent – people, knowledge, and products – without centralized governance. In the late 1990s, Jacques Vincent, a former vice-president, had initiated the Growth Program to foster growth through sharing brand assets among the CBUs to develop blockbuster brands. Deheunynck elaborated:

> The Growth Program was a short-term focus shift from portfolio management to growth management. We had 2% to 5% quarterly growth, but it was very volatile. Jacques Vincent pushed us to use our CBUs to leverage existing practices rather than to use consultants. We looked for good performers in areas such as renovation, innovation, proximity, affordability, etc. When we put these ingredients into one basket, we would out-perform our competitors. The Growth Program enabled us to maintain consistent growth at around 5%.

In 2003, the Growth Too program accelerated growth further by identifying, analyzing, and formalizing good practices and promoting their adoption by all seventy Danone CBUs. Next, Danone created "Acceleration Units" – international working groups that specialized in one concept or brand – comprising four to forty high-level members from one or more functions (e.g., directors of marketing, R&D, or supply chain). Acceleration Units sought to identify good practices within a specific area (for instance, in marketing, or within the Activia brand) and then to formalize and circulate them, enabling CBUs to improve performance, or roll out new products faster.

Elsewhere, challenges of implementing enterprise resource planning (ERP) software in 2001 to help boost productivity further led Mougin to an epiphany about the potential for networking. As Deheunynck explained:

> We struggled a lot with ERP. We thought it was necessary because the organization was so decentralized. We didn't realize it at the time, but I think that the project was countercultural, simply because we are not process-driven. Being controlled by headquarters has always been a challenge for Danone. Managers cannot be P&L responsible while having any sort of tool or system imposed upon them from above.

Instead of imposing an approach to implementation, Mougin therefore encouraged direct discussion between departments about the software, leveraging the experiences of those who had already tested it. This networking and the informal exchanges of practices that followed opened Mougin's eyes to the value of networking for CBU managers.[11] Emmanuel Faber, Executive Vice-President of Danone Asia-Pacific, explained the insight and the resultant emphasis on frontline managers:

> The head of the logistics depot in Finland should network with those in the Czech Republic, Italy, Argentina, and China who all have the same function. At the end of the day these people know which processes we need to change and what the consequences of changing the processes are. The frontline managers deal with the issues on a daily basis. They may not be the most important people in the hierarchy, but they are the critical-mission people.

Whereas general managers collaborate to "drive top-line growth" – perhaps sharing advertising strategies – frontline managers traditionally lacked such opportunities, Faber noted. Yet, "networking among frontline managers is about optimizing processes to generate the resources that can fuel this top-line growth."

The human connection: Mougin concluded that traditional knowledge management – using technology, uploading files, building databases – was not optimal for Danone. Most employees did not use online portals and felt most comfortable talking to each other. Some managers claimed systems and processes also slowed down the business. Mougin therefore decided to look at behavioral patterns, especially interactions between people, and hired Benenati to help him. He found that "sharing wasn't a natural thing. We had to find a way to encourage people to share." Direct discussions between top managers were efficient, but sharing at lower levels clashed somewhat with traditional managerial culture:

> Managers may be reluctant to let their teams discuss among themselves. If members of their team find solutions, then managers are of no further use. But in a group with 90,000 employees, the solutions to the problems of one team are likely to exist entirely or partly elsewhere. So we had to organize these contacts to increase communication between the levels at the bottom of the pyramid. Our target was the 8,400 first-level managers.[12]

Instead of starting out by creating databases, filling them with content, and finally establishing personal networks, Benenati wanted to reverse the process, starting out by creating a culture of discussion, contact, sharing, and solidarity, helping managers to want to work in networks. "That is why this process was managed by the human resources department rather than by the IT departments," he explained. "I wanted it to be first of all a change in behavior. It's about attitude."

The Networking Attitude. The Networking Attitude was launched in fall 2002. Mougin recalled, "We presented the Networking Attitude to Danone's general managers as our way to circulate good practices and make people in units far from each other share knowledge." Razac illustrated: "The objective of the Networking Attitude is to show people that 50% of their daily work should be copy-paste, at least in marketing." Said Catherine Thibaux,

---

[11] Adapted from Mougin and Benenati, "Story-Telling at Danone" (n. 11).   [12] Ibid.

director in charge of the Danone Way and rating agencies relations, "To me, the Networking Attitude lets the company move faster and perform better. It's a way to work horizontally and to break silos, to absorb and combine talents and knowledge coming both from within and outside the organization."

"Make it yours": To differentiate the Networking Attitude from previous knowledge-sharing attempts, Benenati wanted the Networking Attitude to appear informal. He said, "People had to embrace the Networking Attitude like a game and accept it like it was their own project." Mougin and Benenati designed social tools to stimulate sharing and use of knowledge.

Marketplace: "Marketplaces" were information-sharing events held during other meetings or conferences. Thus, participants were not invited specifically to them and were usually unaware that they would occur during the conference they were attending. Mougin's team normally requested two hours to run a marketplace; it ran between other, already scheduled, conference sessions. Mougin called this the "cuckoo" strategy, as the cuckoo bird borrowed other birds' nests to lay its eggs.

Facilitators arranged and ran marketplaces, acting as intermediaries to organize the exchange of practices. They chose a strategic business topic and contacted five to ten colleagues about three weeks in advance to mobilize them to act as *givers* – offering *good practices*, or solutions to problems. The rest of the participants were to act as *takers*: managers with problems or issues to resolve. Before the marketplace, the facilitators collected givers' good practices and recorded them in *The Little Book of Good Practices*, printed before the event. On each page the book displayed one good practice, summarizing a problem, presenting a solution, its tangible advantages, and practical implementation details. No idea was too small; in fact, if an idea was too large or complicated it would be split up into smaller ideas that were easier to handle. Said Mougin, "The most important thing is to make it simple." A photo of the giver appeared along with her idea, to help takers recognize them easily at the marketplace. "This is our old-fashioned version of the intranet," said Benenati (see Figure 2.19).

Marketplaces were devised around a theme (e.g., a French food market, Star Wars, the Wild West) (see Figure 2.20). Givers and takers wore costumes and played the role of a character, obscuring hierarchical rank to help overcome inhibitions. "It's much easier to ask for help when you are pretending to be someone else," noted Mougin. The event would be filled with colors and music to create a lively atmosphere. "Though designed to look haphazard and informal to make people relax and have fun, it's actually very organized," Benenati said. Preparing for a marketplace took weeks.

While Mougin and Benenati encouraged the use of videos, stories, and symbolic objects, PowerPoint was banned. "We wanted to avoid having people sit in a room looking at a presentation. They do that all day in conferences and we wanted to take them out of that setting," Benenati said. However, Benenati understood that managers had to be convinced of the benefit of asking for help from their peers. He reported, "To make sharing happen, you have to show the nice story. Start with a good ending and explain how you get there afterwards. We use videos to show the exchanges that take place. The story has to be short, like a 30-second elevator pitch."

B1

scorecard reporting based on actual figure

ON DISPLAY TODAY!

simplify

my problem
- closing deadline d+5 does not allow a scorecard based completely on actual and analysed numbers

the solution
- tighten the deadline for sales, manufacturing and subsidiary book closing => closing at d+1; cost split and variance split at d+2.
- automisation for monthly accruals.
- reorganisation of trade terms management.
- own development for the forecast in essbase.
- "closing meeting" floating during d+3 between controlling and financial accounting.

the benefits
- more transparency in ttm => can per customer and product at d+2.
- time for analysis from ar1 at d+3 plus last postings.
- time for analysis of OFCF.
- scorecard reporting based on actual and analysed numbers.
- result reporting at d+4.

praticalities
- no time for delays, substitutes must be clear.
- the rule for cost center reposting should be very tough.
- do as many actions as possible in the old month (e.g. interface run payroll).
- the whole company must be included in this process, that means they must know and understand the necessity of being fast.

more questions? just call me!

Stefan Kost
Danone Germany **DANONE**
+49-8962733240
stefan.kost@danone.com

networking attitude

the little book of *Day+4* good practices

Figure 2.19 A Good Practice
Source: Groupe Danone.

Figure 2.20 A Marketplace
Source: Groupe Danone.

The Little Books compiled the stories told. One book featured thirty-three summaries of transferred good practices in diverse functions. One story entitled "If time is not on your side" described how the marketing team at Danone Brazil had helped the marketing team at Danone France. The story involved Marie-Laure in France, who faced Nestlé's launch of a new fat-free dessert in her segment, and a colleague in Brazil, Cecilia, who had a new, somewhat similar dessert product in her portfolio, *Corpus Delicious*. Marie-Laure took Cecilia's concept, renamed it *Taillefine*, changed the packaging, and launched the new brand in France in less than three months. Not only was time saved, but a €20 million business was created and sales were superior to those of the competitor. Added Benenati, "We used the successful launch of Taillefine in France to show that networking could bring together two countries as far apart as Brazil and France. For the first time we had someone from the French unit saying thanks to someone from outside of France."

While takers could review the good practices in the book to prepare for the marketplace, givers would prepare their stands. To symbolize the value of the knowledge transferred, takers could "pay" givers whose ideas they most valued with one of seven (non-monetary) "checks" from an "interest check book." The number of checks acquired by a giver was a sign of the relevance of a good practice, which would be noted by the facilitator to follow the idea exchanges in his or her community.

Juliette Penot managed HR for the nine factories and three warehouses of LU France, Danone's French biscuit subsidiary, and helped organize its first marketplace on safety issues in 2005, with a mix of workers, plant managers, and union representatives in attendance, including Riboud, Vincent, and Mougin. Penot and her colleagues established a network of twelve members working on plant safety, who met quarterly for one or two days to share good practices, and connected between meetings as well. At one point, one member notified the network of an incident with potentially grave consequences. Said Penot, "In three days, all members of the network had replied to his e-mail with their own suggestions on how to improve this procedure in the future. Everyone had checked their equipment to avoid an accident waiting to happen."

In September 2006, Penot held a second marketplace to demonstrate continuing commitment to these practices. These interactions on workplace safety reduced the number of lost-time incidents at LU France from 116 in 2004 to seventy-six in 2005 (a 35 percent reduction), and from seventy-six in 2005 to forty-one by the end of August 2006 (another 25 percent reduction).

By the time of the case, Danone had undertaken nineteen marketplace sessions in fifteen countries. "They have all been quite successful," Benenati noted. "Only one marketplace didn't work out, and that was due to the sponsor of the marketplace refusing to include costumes. Without the costumes and the role-playing, it doesn't seem to work." He believed that success required emotions. "You have to feel humility, love, and joy, all in a loosened-up environment with a lot of music. People don't like to stand up in a room and ask a question that everyone can hear," he explained.

Message-in-a-bottle: The message-in-a-bottle session brought takers with problems to a smaller audience of potential givers. Said Mougin, "It's like an Alcoholics Anonymous meeting: problems and helpers and many do's and don'ts." Benenati added, "These givers are more than willing to help because they in turn will become takers. It's a bottom-up approach with more spontaneous connecting." Sessions took place without observers so that people did not feel inhibited to ask for help or raise issues. At the time of the case, about 115 message-in-a-bottle sessions had been organized involving more than 3,000 people. When time was too short to run a full marketplace or message-in-a-bottle session, Benenati ran T-shirt sessions, in which participants wrote suggestions on the front of their T-shirts and problems on the back and then mingled in an energizing learning session.

Follow-up: After a marketplace or message-in-a-bottle session, the facilitators – with Benenati – organized follow-up measures to help participants take the acquired knowledge and the new network to the next steps of the journey. Benenati maintained, "We don't want to teach people how to network. We want to give them the motivation to do it by showing them what can come out of it." Several tools had been put in place to ensure that this could happen.

Who's Who: The Who's Who was an internal directory on the Danone intranet that had a box entitled "Networking Attitude." All employees had a profile and the option to check a box with some key topics saying *I'm happy to share.* Explained Benenati, "The idea is that if you have a problem, you can with a few search words find someone who can help you in the area where you need help." While some employees used the directory daily, others did not find it helpful. "It was supposed to be a tool to get to know people and help people find colleagues that possessed specific knowledge," Thibaux said. "If you punch in a keyword, for instance 'diversity,' then you will see all the people that have put that as a competence. But it doesn't work at all. I think very few people use it. At Danone you can't just say that from now on everybody will be doing this. That's just impossible."

Communities: Communities (*networks*) ensured that people continued to exchange good practices even without marketplaces. Danone had identified fifty-nine networks, each with a leader and ten to fifteen members. Members met regularly, once every six to eighteen months. Between meetings, members fed the network with information and questions to keep it alive. In some communities, participation in meetings was mandatory. Over time, however, the need for top-down pressure to participate diminished as interest grew at the local level.

Assessing the Networking Activities. Mougin and Benenati believed they had reached the Networking Attitude's initial objectives: people across Danone had strengthened personal networks and shared practices with colleagues (see Figure 2.21). Tangible results proved that people from different divisions benefitted from each other's experiences. Thibaux agreed: "Benenati has clearly done an extraordinary job and I think that today, even though we can go even further, we have progressed a lot compared to when he arrived. Benenati's strong advantage is his personality, which is the reason this has worked at Danone. All the things that happen at the marketplaces are not always to my taste, but I have to admit that it works – it contributes, people participate. They let go, and there are fewer barriers [to sharing]."

CEO Riboud was supportive of this informal approach to knowledge management also: "At Danone we promote good practices through networking. We do not do this through technology, because IT systems are not enough to a network [sic]. You need the relation and exchange between people. At Danone, we foster games between people during which they can exchange ideas. I see this as our competitive advantage."

Explaining why one or two marketplaces fell short of the others' success, Benenati reflected, "For Anglo-Saxons, the Networking Attitude was nothing new . . . They were a bit 'so what?' about our sessions. For Latin companies, however, networking is not normal practice, and for Asian companies it was even less so, which is probably why it has been a significant success in Asia."

Marketplaces had become popular in Mexico, where Martin Renaud, the general manager for the mineral water Bonafont, had organized a marketplace involving distribution centers and employees below management level. He noted, "People are so proud to present their ideas to someone else – ideas that they developed themselves. It empowers people, because the ideas come from their own ranks instead of from the head office." After the marketplace, Renaud and his team selected the ten most popular practices and asked all the Mexican distribution centers to implement them.

A finance marketplace in Budapest, Hungary, had as its objective to help people to close their accounts at D+4, the target of the company. Marie-Catherine Boinay, Director of Reporting Consolidation, testified, "Many people were not closing at D+4, but at the Budapest marketplace we showed them how to do it. The objective has definitely been reached, because all of our units close at D+4 now and it has had a lot of benefits in terms of organization."

Benenati wanted to assess the Networking Attitude's impact. Since no formalized tracking existed, he followed up on a 2004 marketplace in Morocco by sending e-mails to the 300 participants who indicated an interest in a good practice through the check system. Yet, one colleague argued against follow-up: "We shouldn't police and track the impact of this. We shouldn't act as bean counters."

As the number of marketplaces grew, some saw the impact as limited. Beverages Supply Chain Director Kim Cartledge observed, "Many great ideas are implemented as a result of networking, but not as many or as fast as we'd like. We should help the takers implement the ideas they take home." Others wanted even more networking, but believed that the framework was lacking. In his capacity as R&D Director for Consumer Science at Danone Research, Alain Montembault lived this every day. He highlighted, "IT is an absolute key success factor for this company. But in Danone it is seen as a cost. We need IT and we need more facilities to support our research, to share folders, to store research, and to maintain the long-lasting management of our data." Yet, other managers believed that more stimulation was needed. Thibaux worried that managers simply had too much work to do to make networking a top priority – especially when it was not rewarded:

Function	Issue	Solution from Colleague	Result	Transfer
Marketing	In Finland they don't eat biscuits for breakfast, so the LU breakfast biscuit was difficult to implement.	With an adapted communication campaign, the French breakfast concept was repositioned into a biscuit for little hungers in the mid-morning.	The biscuit became the best launch in Finland in five years, more than 18 months of product development was saved and a €1.5 million business was created.	From LU France to LU Nordic
Sales	Wanting to increase sales of beverages in German petrol stations where 57 percent of people didn't buy water or dairy drinks.	By installing lane chillers in petrol stations, consumers were challenged to change habits.	Increase of sales by 47 percent in water and 100 percent in dairy drinks in three countries. Turnover increase by 35 percent in twenty first German Total stations.	From Danone Group to Danone Germany
HR	Finding a Danone-adapted sales training program with high quality material at a low price.	Seven different colleagues shared their experiences and material with training programs in their businesses.	A tailor-made training program based on existing experiences and saving more than €100,000 on external consultants.	From Danone France to Danone Canada
R&D	Making a 0 percent fat mousse is a difficult process and would take a lot of time and money.	Borrow the development technology from a colleague that already had a market-leading product.	Six months of development processes were saved and a $20,000 test avoided.	From Danone Canada to Danone Brazil
THEMIS	A new manager had to get up to speed on a software program that the team had used for months.	A colleague gave tricks, tips, and advice based on his own team's experience with the new software.	The colleague rescued the manager and the manager rescued the team from lagging behind.	From Danone Germany to Danone Belgium
Quality	Eliminating the risk of complaints over Plexiglas in biscuit packages.	Replace Plexiglas boxes using screws with boxes without screws – a safer solution.	No more Plexiglas in biscuit packages and no more complaints from consumers.	From LU France to LU France
Operations	Cost reduction in purchasing and supply chain.	Two colleagues with different ideas collaborated on implementing a global cost reduction project in all warehouses.	More than €1 million saved.	From Danone France to Danone France
Finance	Commercial overspend due to lack of visibility.	Visit to colleague in Germany to see implementation of monitoring tool.	Improved workflow, £1.5 million of overspend avoided, and 3 months saved in developing own intranet-based tool.	From Danone Germany to Danone UK

Figure 2.21 Selection of Exchanged Practices – Nice Stories

"To me, people's workload is a major obstacle to the Networking Attitude. It happens that people tell me, '*well, if it's not in my objectives then I'm not going to help you.*' It's rare, because it's not the Danone style, but it happens." Meanwhile, some saw differences across groups, believing that the dairy division was more likely to network than the beverages division, for example, due to the cultural history in that group.

Extending the Networking Attitude. Mougin and Benenati believed that the Networking Attitude could be furthered to deeper, wider, or richer sharing. Some attempts had already been made.

Deeper: More employees: Mougin believed that all Danone employees could benefit from the Networking Attitude to share good practices. Mougin had tested this belief with a marketplace for administrative assistants that worked well, with some assistants claiming that it was the first time anyone had asked their opinion. "This is about empowerment and appraisal," said Benenati.

While almost everyone saw the benefits of going deeper, some barriers remained. Cartledge noted that "much of the richness of the Networking Attitude comes from crossing countries, but when you get to a certain level, there are language barriers." "I would focus more on the quality of the networking rather than going deeper," added a manager. "You need proven successes, and then it will extend." Deheunynck believed that Danone's emphasis on marketing and sales left manufacturing, supply chain, and purchasing with less senior management attention. "Quite a few general managers don't visit their factories on a regular basis, which can be an issue when more than 50% of our employees worldwide are in manufacturing." Firm performance, he argued, did not depend on just 10,000 senior managers, but on all 90,000 employees. However, he continued, "some still believe that the contribution of non-managers to total performance does not merit including them in networking activities and that we will not gain what we spend to make it happen. What we do know from our own surveys is that performance is always better when there is clear alignment between senior management and employees."

Wider: Outside the company: To use the sharing tools to build external bridges to partners, suppliers, and customers, Danone had tested a marketplace in Spain, Poland, and France, with preselected suppliers. In these events, renamed The Innovation Challenge, suppliers competed to devise the best solution for Danone on a strategic business issue that Danone had communicated to them in advance. The supplier with the best solution won a contract with the company. Danone also invited consumers to discuss products in development. Furthermore, Danone, which had no direct contact with consumers, could share practices with retailers such as Walmart or Carrefour. "When there is a shortage of our products on the shelf, Danone is penalized by the retailer for its loss of sales," explained Deheunynck. Danone was starting to collaborate with mass retailers to find ways to ensure on-shelf availability. "It's direct profit at no cost," Deheunynck noted. "But we cannot run the show by ourselves. To reach this common goal we need our customers, and they don't have the Danone DNA. It's also more dangerous for us, because if we help our customers to progress, our competitors will benefit as well."

Richer: For innovation: Mougin and Benenati considered going a step further than sharing knowledge – to create new knowledge by inviting employees from various divisions to network with the aim of coming up with new processes or products. So far, Danone had conducted seven so-called co-building sessions. One was focused on shifting from water to beverages. During one week, the members of the executive committee of the beverages division discussed the strategy with the general managers of all the CBUs. On the third day, another group was brought in and in total 160 people fine-tuned Danone's beverages strategy. Said Deheunynck: "It made people aligned in one week. That's what we call getting richer. If we just keep sharing practices we are not going to survive, because the good practices of today are not going to be the good practices of tomorrow." Cécile Diversy, HR director at Danone Waters France, saw potential: "Nestlé has 10 times as many resources as we do, but we still manage to create new solutions and processes . . . because of the human aspect."

In 2004, the Innovation Task Force had been established with about eighty Danone employees and some external experts to promote innovation. Essensis, a yogurt that nourished the skin from the inside, was an outcome of this team effort and launched in 2007. The idea of launching a product in the cosmetofood[13] category was then tested in Belgium, Spain, France, and at headquarters. Razac elaborated, "Essensis is an example of a very centralized project. It was born out of two or three local ideas. We brought together those working on the project in the various countries and integrated them in a corporate project group." The cross-functional team managed to get the product to the market in seven months. "For the people involved, this work was done on top of their normal job," Razac explained. That meant that "you have to motivate them even more, because it means working for the central business, for an idea that could benefit their own business as well. You need to convince a local general manager [to support it] because people have other things to do than to work on a product that might be launched in five years."

The Future. Mougin and Benenati had much to discuss. Networking involved so many stakeholders that satisfying everyone would be difficult. Should they extend the concept to be deeper, wider, or richer? Should they impose more structure, evaluation, or rewards on the Networking Attitude to make it more viable for the long term? Or should it remain as it was? Benenati wondered whether formal reward systems would be at odds with the spontaneous nature of networking and its aims. Mougin preferred developing new ideas to structuring and evaluating systems anyway, believing, "That's the Danone way of doing things." It was clear to him that some divisions were more advanced than others when it came to networking and innovation, but he wished he had more systematic quantitative measures of the Networking Attitude and its impact on Danone.

Questions

1. What is your assessment of the company's knowledge management?
2. What are the most important knowledge management challenges faced by the company? What does the company need to do well to succeed?
3. What is your assessment of the Networking Attitude initiative?
4. What should the company do next? Which of the three options (go wider, go deeper, go richer) do you recommend? Why?
5. How does the CEO's approach to leading Danone affect your recommendation?
6. Can you suggest some of the concepts or theories in this chapter, which you can employ to analyze the case? Show how you apply them to the case analysis.

---

[13] "Cosmetofood" is food that has health or beauty objectives and can be considered somewhat medical.

CHAPTER 3

Fundamentals of Operations and Supply Chain Management

In this chapter, we show what a supply chain is, what supply chain management (SCM) is all about, and why it is important to grasp the fundamentals of SCM in creating real value for the customers. We try to understand these issues from a learning perspective, i.e., a dynamic and systemic viewpoint. First, we draw a supply chain and define key decision dimensions and considerations associated with it. By doing so, we can better appreciate the dynamic interrelationship between key factors in SCM, and develop our own capability of designing a well-balanced SCM strategy. Since we view the SCM issues from the learning perspective, it is necessary for us to refer to qualitative concepts like **organizational capability, learning dynamics** (e.g., single-loop versus double-loop learning), and how these capability factors interact with each other to develop an effective SCM strategy. Note that we already defined "operations management" in Chapter 1: "Operations management is about how to manage the three fundamental building blocks (i.e., resources, processes, and capabilities) effectively to optimize value creation. Traditional operations management has focused on a **single company's boundary**. That is, traditional operations management approaches the value creation from a single company's perspective." Although most of the theories and principles in operations management are also valid for supply chain management, SCM is fundamentally different from traditional operations management in that it approaches the operations issues from the **value chain perspective**, i.e., coordination among supply chain or value chain partners sharing the same supply chain or value chain should be at the center of any SCM.

Key Learning Points

- Supply chain management is about how to manage the supply chain in an optimum way to create the maximum value for the customers.
- Over time, the boundary of supply chain management has expanded to encompass the entire value chain and now it seems very natural to use the two terms, supply chain and value chain, interchangeably.
- The structural dimension of supply chain management consists of such structural or physical elements as configuration, connection, inventory, and logistics.
- The infrastructural dimension of supply chain management is coordination or collaboration among supply chain partners.

- In order to be competitive in the market, the firm should achieve fit between its operations strategy and corporate strategy.
- Total quality management (TQM) is a managerial philosophy, which endeavors to improve and innovate every aspect of the organization and its value creating continuously by empowering the employees and taking the customer-oriented perspective, i.e., becoming a true learning organization.

學 WISDOM BOX 3.1
Wisdom and Insights

Supply Chain Management for an Automobile Company

Have you ever wondered how your car has reached you? Suppose you have just bought a new Hyundai (www.hyundai.com) Sonata. The design of Sonata was probably done several months or even years ago at one of Hyundai's design centers in Korea. Once the design was approved by the head of the product division in charge of the model, the head of production department planned the production by scheduling detailed production batches, ordering materials from appropriate suppliers on the company's list of cooperating suppliers, and allocating production orders to individual production units at three assembly plants scattered around Korea.

One such supplier was POSCO (www.posco.com), which was one of the largest and most efficient steel companies in the world. As soon as POSCO received the order from Hyundai, it developed its own production plan: the company itself dealt with hundreds of different suppliers and vendors. POSCO would soon deliver steel parts to Hyundai, which could be used for fabricating the chassis and doors of Sonata. Another supplier was Hyundai MOBIS (http://en.mobis.co.kr/): it was supplying Hyundai Motor with various car modules, which constituted key components of a Sonata. Hyundai MOBIS also dealt with many different suppliers. In addition to POSCO and MOBIS, Hyundai was receiving key parts as well as materials from hundreds and thousands of different suppliers around the world. As alluded to already, these suppliers were also dealing with their own suppliers, sometimes as many as several thousand.

Once Hyundai Motor received all the necessary parts and materials from its numerous suppliers, it could start assembling cars, including the Sonata (Figure 3.1). Hyundai Motor had three main plants scattered across Korea: each was specialized in producing particular car models, although the plant network retained a certain level of flexibility so that the plants could produce cars not in their specialization, if necessary. It usually takes several hours to complete assembling a Sonata. But, it would take a little more time and effort from now until the Sonata finally reaches its owner. It first needs to be shipped to one of Hyundai's warehouses, and stay there until a dealer picks it up. The potential owner, a customer, probably contacted the

Box continues

dealer and decided to buy a Sonata. Finally, the dealer would deliver the Sonata with options and colors of the customer's choice to the owner, and the deal would be closed. As this simple case shows, a product (or service) should go through lengthy and complex processes before it eventually reaches its final customer. Numerous managerial issues are involved in such processes. *What do you think these issues are?*

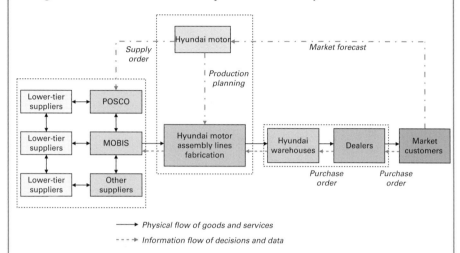

Figure 3.1 How a Sonata is Made through Lengthy and Complex Processes

Questions
1. Which industry are you most interested in? Draw a supply chain (like Figure 3.1) for the industry of your choice.
2. What kinds of physical flows and information flows do you think are critical to the supply chain of the industry?

3.1   A Supply Chain and Key Dimensions of SCM

A supply chain is an **interrelationship**, through which information, physical goods, and services flow back and forth, consisting of business entities that undertake value-creating activities involved in supplying necessary materials, transforming various supplies into valuable goods and services, and distributing the final outputs to the customer markets. SCM is the study of how to manage the supply chain in an optimum way to create the maximum value for the customers.

Figure 3.2 is an example supply chain for **BMW**. As the manufacturer assembling car components, BMW is at the center of the supply chain. In the upstream of the supply chain, there are many **first-tier suppliers**, who provide such key supplies as tires, car seats, and electronic parts to BMW directly. There are numerous second-tier suppliers, who do business with the first-tier suppliers. In theory, there are an unlimited number of tiers of suppliers in the supply chain, each of which performs a critical role in enabling

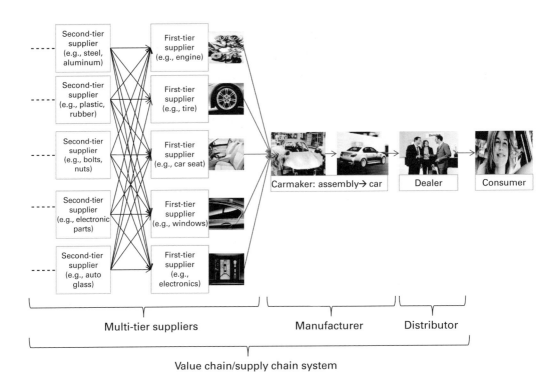

Figure 3.2 An Example of a Supply Chain

the entire supply chain to function properly. What about the downstream of the supply chain? Once BMW cars are completed, the company delivers them to the warehouses, e.g., dealer shops, where the end-consumers buy and pick up the cars they like. In order to create value, BMW must make cars using all the parts and suppliers from its upstream and sell them to the consumers through its downstream. That is, the company should coordinate all of the functions in its supply chain so as to create value.

3.1.1   Supply Chain or Value Chain?

As in Figure 3.2, sometimes we use **value chain** and supply chain interchangeably. Although they are almost considered as synonyms these days, they were developed separately. It was Michael Porter[1] who popularized the concept of value chain (Figure 3.3). Porter defined a value chain as a systematic collection of functions or activities a firm must perform to create value. There are two different types of functions: primary and secondary activities. **Primary activities** consist of such functions as **inbound logistics** (to bring resources or inputs into the firm), operations (to transform inputs into outputs, i.e., finished goods), **outbound logistics** (to move the outputs to the market), marketing and sales (to promote the outputs, i.e., finished goods or services,

---

[1] Porter, M. E., *The Competitive Advantage: Creating and Sustaining Superior Performance* (New York: The Free Press, 1985).

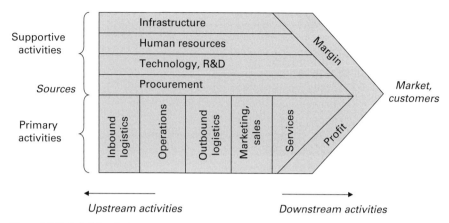

Figure 3.3 Porter's Value Chain

to the customers), and services (to provide maintenance or aftersales services throughout the product life cycle). In fact, the primary activities constitute a vertical chain: the firm needs to perform these activities in a more or less sequential manner. These are called "primary," since the firm *must* perform *all* of these activities to create value in the market or they are the *major activities critical* to the firm's creating value. In addition to the primary activities, there are more supplementary ones, which the firm needs to execute in order to perform the primary activities more effectively. They are the supportive activities, such as the firm's infrastructure (e.g., IT, communication systems), HRM, R&D (e.g., new product development), and company-wide procurement (to procure materials or supplies to help all the other functions to perform appropriately).

Downstream or upstream activity is a relative concept. That is, a function closer to the source (i.e., the beginning of the value chain or the very beginning of the inbound logistics) is an upstream activity for a function closer to the market (i.e., the end-customers or -consumers): considering two primary activities, the one on the left is an upstream function for the other on the right, or the one on the right is a downstream function for the other on the left.

When the concept of value chain was first introduced, people thought it was the primary activities that were related to the concept of supply chain, i.e., a supply chain was part of the value chain. Over time, however, it becomes clear that effective supply chain management should involve *not only* the primary activities, *but also* most of the **supportive activities** in the value chain. As a result, the boundary of supply chain management has expanded to encompass the entire value chain and now it seems very natural to use the two terms, supply chain and value chain, interchangeably. Throughout this book, we regard the two concepts almost as synonyms, unless doing so causes any misunderstanding.

3.1.2 Structural and Infrastructural Dimensions in SCM

There are many issues involved in managing a supply chain. In this book, we deal with key issues grouped into two: structural and infrastructural dimensions. These issues are

Key issues
- Structural dimensions
    - ✓ Configuration – geographic/physical placement
    - ✓ Connection – matching between SC functions
    - ✓ Inventory – uncertainty management
    - ✓ Logistics – shipping/transportation options
- Infrastructural dimensions
    - ✓ Coordination, collaboration
        - ➤ Information sharing
        - ➤ Innovation – product development
        - ➤ Improvement – quality, process
- Supply chain performance
    - ✓ Customer satisfaction
    - ✓ Financial performance
    - ✓ Value creation

Figure 3.4 A Simplified Supply Chain and Key SCM Issues

closely linked with each other: in order for a company to have an effective supply chain, it must be able to consider these issues simultaneously and in an integrated way. In addition, we need **key performance measures**, a set of criteria with which we can evaluate and compare supply chains to suggest more generalizable principles of SCM. Key performance measures should be based on the customers in the market, where the real, substantive value must be created.

Figure 3.4 shows a simplified supply chain, highlighting only the essential processes, i.e., supply → operations (manufacturing and service) → distribution → market (customers). In order to optimize the supply chain performance, managers must take into account various decision factors related to supply chain management.

First, there is a **structural dimension**, which consists of configuration, connection, inventory, and logistics. **Configuration** is about geographic and/or physical placement of supply chain processes, e.g., suppliers, facilities such as plants and warehouses, and distribution centers. *Which process (or function) should be located where?* is a critical decision problem which will determine the effectiveness of the supply chain in the long run. When a company decides on this "configuration" issue, it has to take into account many important factors such as current production cost structure, as well as its long-term trend at different locations, taxes, tariffs, duties, duty drawbacks, existence of skilled labor forces, and other location-specific costs.

Once the configuration of the supply chain is decided, the company, or the decision-maker in the supply chain, must decide how to link or connect scattered functions (i.e., processes) in the supply chain. In effect, the issue of **connection** is concerned with how to match different supply chain processes or partners and also which product or service the firm should flow through the supply chain, i.e., the choice of product or service. For instance, for each product or service, the company has to decide which supplier should supply which plant, which plant produces which products and ships them to which distribution center, and which distribution center should serve which customer market. While matching different supply chain functions/processes, the company has to think about the role and location of inventory existing between consecutive processes. How to connect or match supply chain functions is a decision problem of medium- to long-term impact.

Inventory plays several critical roles in supply chain management. Its most common purpose is to buffer against uncertainty. For instance, there exists inventory between supplier and manufacturer. From the supplier's perspective, it is desirable to supply goods to its customer (the manufacturer) consistently, even when the manufacturer is not ready to accept them: when the manufacturer can't process the goods from its supplier as soon as they are finished at the supplier's site, the goods will be stored at the inventory between the supplier and the manufacturer. Likewise, the inventory plays a similar role for the manufacturer. Suppose that the manufacturer is processing at a higher speed than its supplier's during a particular period of time. Should there be no inventory stored between the supplier and the manufacturer, the manufacturer would have to stop processing when its supplier can't supply as fast as the manufacturer requires. If the manufacturer processes faster than its supplier all the time, this supply chain system is unstable – it can't work normally in the long run. On the other hand, if this kind of imbalance between the processing speeds should be temporary, then the inventory can mitigate possible disruption at the manufacturing function because of the irregularity at the supplier site. Each of the players in the supply chain can utilize inventory to cope with the uncertainty it has to face.

At a more comprehensive level, inventory plays a role as an indicator about the overall effectiveness of the supply chain system. More specifically, having more inventory than needed implies that the company is not performing as well as it should. In general, the inventory occurs or increases when the supply is larger than the demand. Hence, a company accumulates inventory when it produces more than the market wants. Why does the company produce more than it should? There are many reasons, such as a lack of accurate forecasting and/or market information, retarded product innovation, an inability to factor its long delivery time into planning, and so forth. Regardless of the specific reason causing such a mismatch between supply and demand, the very existence of unnecessary inventory indicates a potential illness at the company.

In addition to these important roles, inventory plays a role as a key performance measure in supply chain management. Sometimes an important objective of SCM is to optimize the inventory level across the supply chain system. By reducing the inventory, the supply chain system as a whole should be able to *not only* solve some of the critical operational problems mentioned above, *but also* save costs associated with carrying and managing the inventory.

The last element of the structural dimension is **logistics**, which is involved with the issue of how to transport goods from one process to another in the supply chain. In general, a fast logistical option (e.g., air shipment) is more expensive than a slow logistical option (e.g., surface or sea transportation). If the unit value of a product as inventory (e.g., raw material, part, semi-finished, or finished) is high and thus its

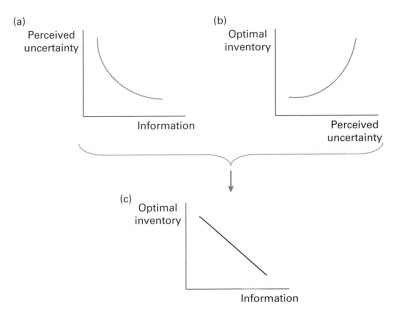

Figure 3.5 Information, Uncertainty, and Inventory

inventory holding cost is also high, other things being equal, it would be more economical to use a fast (or expensive) logistical option to ship the product from one process to
another while keeping a low level of inventory. Thus, one can see that there is a close
relationship between the logistics and the inventory decision.

For effective SCM, there is also an **infrastructural dimension**; i.e., **coordination** or
collaboration among supply chain partners. As some of the examples above indicate, in
order for the supply chain as a whole to function effectively it is critical for the partner
companies in the supply chain to cooperate with each other. On what specific areas and/
or functions need the supply chain partners cooperate? One such area is **information-
sharing**. As pointed out earlier, there exists inventory between supplier and manufacturer: the role of this inventory is to buffer against uncertainty at each side of the
partners. Uncertainty is inversely related to information (or knowledge). The more
information the firm has, the less uncertainty it has to cope with. As the level of
uncertainty perceived by the company lessens, it can afford to reduce the amount of
inventory. Figure 3.5 shows an example relationship among the information, uncertainty, and inventory level.

To retain competitive advantage in the long run, companies must be able to develop
new products. However, it becomes increasingly difficult for a single company to invest
in developing a new product from the beginning to the end: due to increasingly
complicated technical requirements involved in new product development, the R&D
activity has fast become an area where a single company (or only a few companies) can't
take care of the full extent of necessary investment. In a supply chain, therefore, partner
companies could find it essential for them to collaborate to develop and introduce new

products together. Coordinating innovation (e.g., new product development) in the supply chain is a critical area of the infrastructural dimension.

Another area where supply chain partners cooperate with each other is **quality** and **efficiency improvement** in current operations. For instance, the supplier might cooperate with its customer, the manufacturer, in improving the quality of the current product, or enhancing the manufacturer's operational efficiency. In order to improve quality and enhance efficiency of current operations, it is essential for the supplier and the manufacturer to collaborate on analyzing the production processes in addition to the supply chain conditions.

So far we have considered key dimensions related to effective supply chain management. It is assumed that should the decision-maker take into account these dimensions when designing a supply chain strategy, she will manage the supply chain more effectively. But, how should one define "*being effective*"? If we want to say that something is more effective than another, there should be a criterion on which we can base our decision. Then, what are such criteria in SCM? Note that the most right-hand-side of a supply chain is "market or customers." This implies that the whole supply chain pursues meeting the demand (e.g., desire or requirement) of the customers. How to satisfy our customers should be the number one criterion, with which one decides the **effectiveness of supply chain management**. There are more specific measures that enable the decision-maker to "operationalize" the rather abstract concept of customer satisfaction. One such measure is the "**line-item fill rate**" or "**service rate**," which measures how much (in percentage terms) of the customers' demand is met when it has first arrived at the company. Here, again, inventory is a key element. There are other measures as well, but sometimes they are more or less concerned with the company's internal performance. For instance, some financial measures can be utilized to evaluate the supply chain's effectiveness. In addition, the company can do an extensive market survey to find out whether its products or services satisfy *not only* the explicit market demand (i.e., the customers' desire or requirements), *but also* the innate and/or implicit desire the customers have but do not necessarily know explicitly.

3.2   Basic Motivation and Typologies of SCM

Why is SCM regarded as vital in staying competitive in the market? Several factors contribute to the new way of thinking. From a more traditional economic perspective, there are two extreme modes of transaction: **spot market transaction** versus **vertical integration** (Figure 3.6). The spot market transaction assumes no specific, regular, and/or long-term relationship between transaction entities, whereas the vertical integration is based on a tight ownership between those entities. For instance, buying and selling crude oil involves spot market transactions. When a buyer wants to buy crude oil, she simply visits a spot market such as Brent Spot either physically or via the internet. The buyer does not have to worry about building up a long-lasting relationship with crude oil sellers. From the sellers' perspective, they don't have to worry about servicing the buyer in the long run. The price and quantity of a transaction would be determined by pure

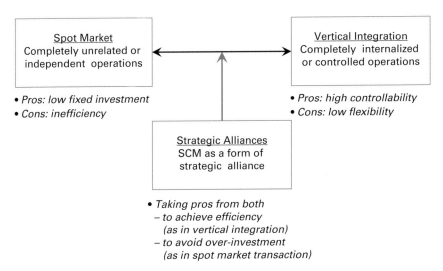

Figure 3.6 Spot Market Transaction versus Vertical Integration

economic, in general, short-term, forces of supply and demand. Thus, the spot market transaction requires neither buyers nor sellers to invest in capital equipment specific to their transaction.

On the contrary, vertical integration requires internalizing the transaction entities completely – buyers and sellers would be part of the same economic entity. For instance, a construction company might own construction equipment such as fork cranes and heavy trucks, that is, internalizing or owning such equipment by itself. In the crude oil example, one might own the crude oil as well, so that she does not have to worry about from where to buy the crude oil whenever she needs it.

What are the pros and cons of each of the two extreme options of economic transaction? First, since the spot market transaction doesn't require any long-term resource commitment, buyers and sellers of the spot market transaction don't have to pay overhead costs. It is true that burdens due to overhead costs are not usually noticeable when the business is booming – when the company grows rapidly. But, when the company stops growing, the overhead costs become quite visible: now the company does not earn enough to cover its fixed overhead costs. Therefore, the spot market transaction enables the company to retain a certain level of flexibility to deal with uncertain fluctuation of business conditions. Despite its flexibility, the spot market transaction might cause inefficiency to the transaction. Since the companies do not have any long-term arrangement, they have to look for new transaction partners whenever they need to buy or sell goods and services. Again, consider the crude oil case. In the spot market transaction context, a company has to find out the best deal whenever it wants to buy crude oil. This process would involve constant negotiation, haggling, and controlling, which significantly reduce the transaction efficiency. In sum, the primary benefits of the spot market transaction include retaining flexibility and avoiding downside risks when the business is in recession, while its most serious problem is "transaction and operational inefficiency": the spot market transaction could reduce the transaction and operational efficiency due to the increase in search and controlling costs.

Vertical integration has its own pros and cons, which are exactly opposite to those associated with the spot market transaction. Hence, the pros of vertical integration include enhanced efficiency due to increased controllability over the supply-side functions. Similarly, the cons of vertical integration are mainly the inflexibility as well as the increased downside risks when the business is in turmoil.

One can raise a question, then: *Is it possible to arrange a transaction mode that can mitigate the cons and enhance the pros of both spot market transaction and vertical integration?* Strategic alliances have emerged as such arrangements to offer companies transaction options without huge fixed investment (i.e., free of ownership obligation), yet at the same time with predictability of transactions via a long-term collaborative relationship. SCM, in a certain sense, is a form of strategic alliance.

3.2.1   Intra-Firm SCM versus Inter-Firm SCM

Having said that supply chain management is a **strategic arrangement** between economic entities to take advantage of both spot market transaction and vertical integration simultaneously, i.e., retaining efficiency and at the same time avoiding **downside risks**, it is reasonable that coordination between those partners in the supply chain should be viewed as critical. Such coordination need be highlighted not only between different organizations or companies, but also between different functions or departments at a single company. We want to distinguish **inter-firm coordination** from **intra-firm coordination**, although the two have much in common with regard to the fundamentals of SCM. One example of intra-firm SCM is coordination between the production department and the marketing department at the same company. Inside a company, we can identify an intra-firm supply chain consisting of supply, operations, and distribution (marketing) functions, which have a great deal in common with those in an inter-firm supply chain. We already emphasized that in order to create value in a (inter-firm) supply chain, supply chain partners must cooperate with each other. Likewise, in order for a company to enhance its value, various supply chain functions inside the company must perform in a coordinated, systematic manner. Thus, a firm should be able to manage two different types of supply chain at the same time, one for intra-firm functions and the other for inter-firm functions. Only when the firm manages the two supply chains effectively, will it be able to optimize its value creation (Figure 3.7).

3.2.2   Production Process versus Supply Chain Process

Another typology-related issue is concerned with a distinction between production processes and a supply chain. Figure 3.8 shows the production processes of a steel company, from raw material procurement (coal and iron ore) to differentiating final products (wire rod, plate, and hot rolled steel). It is difficult to make a clear distinction between a company's production processes and its intra-firm supply chain. Regarding its production processes, the company could use a couple of alternative strategies. First, the

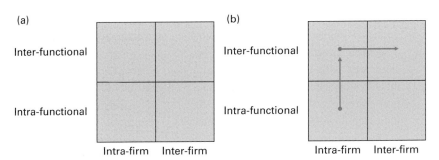

Figure 3.7 Typology of Coordination

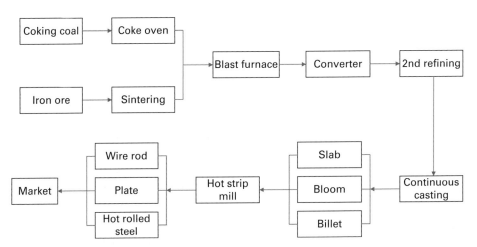

Figure 3.8 Production Process in a Steel Company

company might want to **outsource** some of its processes to contract manufacturers. Then issues related to the internal production processes become SCM issues. Another complication could occur when the company wants to globalize its operations. For instance, suppose the company wants to enter China's steel market (Figure 3.9). Then, it has to decide which production processes it must bring into China, e.g., *Should it bring a furnace into China, thus moving "upstream functions" into the foreign country or just rolling functions only?* It becomes very complicated to make a clear distinction between the company's internal production process chain and its supply chain. Sometimes it is not necessary to make such a distinction, and at other times it is clear to do so. For the purpose of this book, we believe it will be clear when we need to make such a distinction so that we do not have to worry about any serious confusion regarding this issue. In addition, we also think that looking into the issue itself would enable us to make a clever decision whenever we are involved in a confusing situation, thus to avoid reaching a false conclusion.

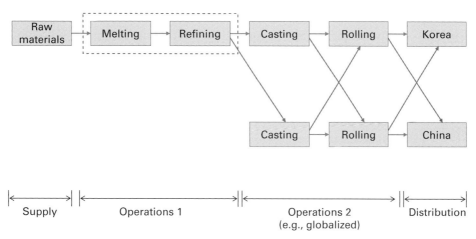

Figure 3.9 Globalizing a Supply Chain

3.2.3   Decision-Making – from Whose Perspective to See the Issue

As discussed above, in order to properly understand and analyze a supply chain, we need to make logical definitions of key components and aspects of a supply chain, e.g., whether to look at intra-firm or inter-firm issues, and internal production processes or a supply chain as we have defined. In addition, it is important to have a consistent perspective when analyzing the SCM issues. In this book, we focus on the decision-making issues from the perspective of a manufacturing company, which has to transact with its suppliers and distributors, and also take into account the end-customers in the market. Considering that every company has to do business with both downstream and upstream partners, the assumption is not such a stringent one; in fact, having a manufacturing company's perspective will enable us to focus on basic SCM issues more clearly and systematically. It is useful to refer to the discussion of the focal company in Chapter 1.

3.3   Fundamentals of Operations Management

In Chapter 1, we suggested a definition of operations management, which is the bedrock of supply chain management. In fact, we even suggested the only difference between supply chain management and operations management is concerned with the perspective, i.e., from whose perspective to look into the issues in operations: supply chain management calls for an integrating perspective, which embodies coordination between functions within a company, between companies sharing the same value chain, and even between companies and various stakeholders surrounding them. Although in this book we are mainly focused on supply chain management, therefore, we want to discuss some of the fundamental theories or concepts in operations management, which can be a solid base of supply chain management throughout the book. In particular, we delve into such key concepts as **process analysis**, **fit** between operations strategy and corporate strategy, quality and quality failure costs, and process control.

3.3.1   Process Analysis and Strategy

To produce a product or service, a firm must perform certain activities or functions. Usually a **process** is a series of such activities or functions, connected by flows of materials and/or information. Sometimes a process means *one* particular activity or function, since each activity or function may also consist of smaller activities or functions. As such, it depends on the particular context in point whether a process implies a specific activity or a set of activities. In order to avoid possible confusion, we make a distinction that a production system consists of individual processes, whereas each process is an activity or a function, which is comprehensive enough to be an independent task. Consider an example of car making. In order to build a car, a carmaker must perform "individual processes, i.e., activities," like cutting, fabricating, and assembling either in sequence or in parallel, depending on unique features of the firm's assembly plant.

A firm can maximize its performance by managing its **production system** effectively. There are several measures of performance, such as **productivity** and **utilization**: productivity is the ratio of outputs to inputs in production, a measure of production efficiency, whereas utilization measures the degree to which equipment, space, or labor is actually being used, compared to capacity. We informally define capacity as a measure of how many customers the system (i.e., the firm or its plant) can serve or how many units it can produce in a certain period of time under a normal (i.e., in a regular or steady state) condition. Since capacity can constrain outputs as well as inputs, it also affects productivity. As such, it is important to estimate capacity properly, in order to enhance the firm's performance.

Process analysis enables the firm to determine its capacity. The first step toward achieving the goal is process analysis. A manager can find ways to improve productivity as well as utilization by analyzing the process. For further explanation, we consider a simplified production system for bread making. Figure 3.10 shows a set of processes to make bread: for the sake of simplification, we assume three processes are necessary, i.e., to mix, proof, and bake. To express the production system, we use a sort of conventional notation for inventory, process, and flow of material or information as in Figure 3.10.

For process analysis, we use time as a unit: in fact, time is an appropriate unit in most cases. **Run time** measures how long it takes to process one unit at a particular process. In Figure 3.11, we assume that it takes 40 minutes to process one unit at the mix process, 60 minutes at the proof process, and 50 minutes at the bake process. Under this condition, what is the monthly capacity of the production system, assuming it operates 8 hours a day, 20 days per month? To answer this question, we first need to calculate the cycle time of the system. **Cycle time** is the time interval between two units being successively completed. Suppose that you are standing at the end of the system, say just after the bake process, and measure the time when a unit is completed and just coming out of the bake process. What is the average interval between successive units' completion times?

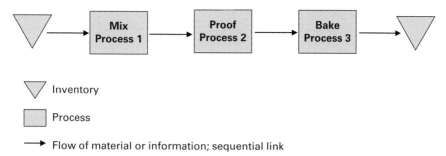

Figure 3.10 Bread-Making Processes

Figure 3.11 Process Run Time

To show how to estimate the cycle time, we utilize graphs in Figure 3.12. Suppose that the company starts making bread at time 0, i.e., the first unit enters the production system at $t = 0$ (Figure 3.12a). Since it takes 40 minutes to complete one unit at the mix process, unit #1 is finished at $t = 40$ minutes and moved to the next process immediately: that is, unit #1 starts the proof process at $t = 40$ minutes (Figure 3.12b). Again, since it takes 60 minutes to finish the proof process and 50 minutes to complete the bake process, unit #1 finishes all of the processes at $t = 2 : 30$, 2 hours and 30 minutes (Figure 3.12c). When can the firm start the second unit? Although there might be many factors that affect when to start unit #2, for the sake of simplicity, we assume that the firm starts a new unit as soon as the first process becomes available. Therefore, unit #2 enters the production system at $t = 40$ minutes, when the first unit is finished at the first process.

Figure 3.13a shows that unit #2 starts the first process at $t = 40$ minutes. Since it takes 40 minutes to finish the mix process, unit #2 completes the process at $t = 80$ minutes. But, unit #2 cannot proceed to the next process, the proof process, when it is done at the first process. Why? Since the proof process is still occupied by unit #1 at $t = 80$, it has to wait for 20 minutes before moving to the second process at $t = 1 : 40$, i.e., 1 hour and 40 minutes (Figure 3.13b). By the time unit #2 is completed at the proof process ($t = 2 : 40$), however, the bake process becomes available and thus unit #2 moves to the last process without any delay. Eventually, unit #2 completes all of the processes at $t = 3 : 30$, 3 hours and 30 minutes (Figure 3.13c).

With careful attention to whether the next process is still occupied by the previous unit, we can estimate that unit #3 completes the entire processes at $t = 4 : 30$, i.e., in 4 hours and 30 minutes (Figure 3.14).

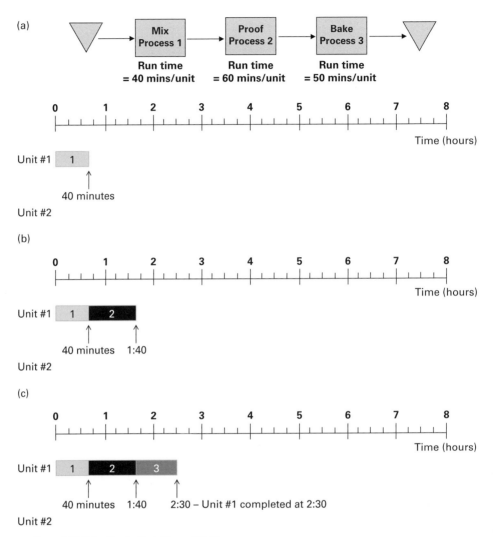

Figure 3.12 Estimating the Cycle Time – Unit #1

From Figure 3.13d, we see the time interval between unit #1's completion and unit #2's completion is 60 minutes. In addition, the time interval between unit #2 and unit #3 is also 60 minutes (Figure 3.14). If we continue this exercise for ensuing units, i.e., unit #5, unit #6, and so on, we will see that the time interval between successive completions of the units is always 60 minutes. That is, the cycle time of this production system is 60 minutes: of course, it is valid under the current assumptions made for this particular example.

It is intriguing to see that the run time of the proof process is 60 minutes as well. Is it simply coincidence that the cycle time is equal to the run time of the proof process? Actually, it is not a simple coincidence. Among the three processes, the proof process is the **bottleneck process** since it requires the longest run time in the sequential production

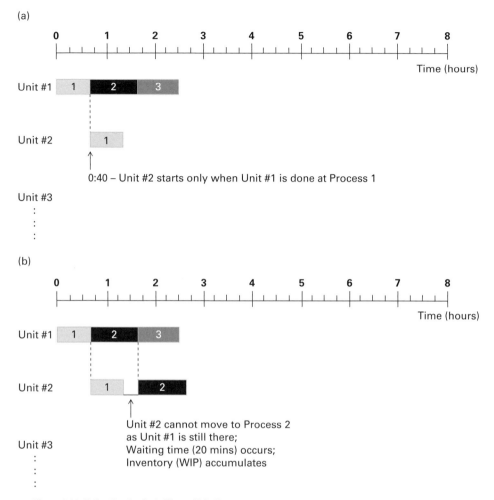

Figure 3.13 Estimating the Cycle Time – Unit #2

system, i.e., it is the least efficient among the three. In fact, the cycle time is in general determined by the bottleneck process in the system.

Now, what is the monthly **capacity** of the system described above, assuming 8 hours a day and 20 days per month? Since it takes 60 minutes to complete a unit, the monthly capacity is:

$$\frac{Total\ available\ time}{Cycle\ time} = \frac{20\ days\ \times\ 8\ hours\ \times\ 60\ minutes}{60\ minutes} = 160\ units/month.$$

There are a few assumptions for the calculation:

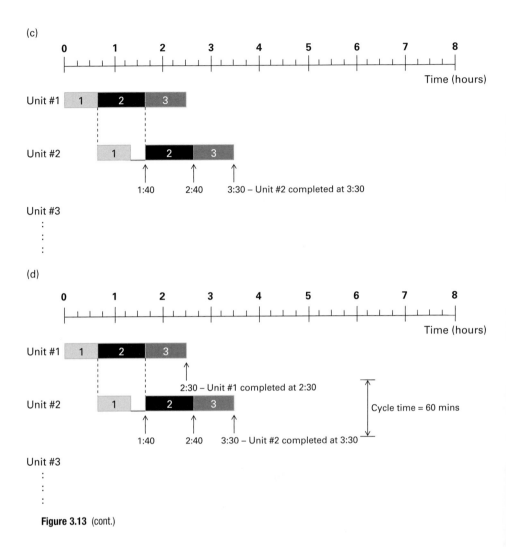

Figure 3.13 (cont.)

- The production system operates continuously in the long run. That is, a steady state is assumed. It means that we can ignore irregular or abnormal states, e.g., part of the initial state during which unit #1 is being processed.
- A WIP (**work in process**) unit can be worked on again after a pause and become completed. For instance, a unit can be half processed at the end of the day, and the next day the system can pick up the unit and work on it to be completed.

Another measure similar to the cycle time is the **throughput** or **manufacturing lead time**. It measures how long the unit stays inside the production system, i.e., the interval between when the unit enters and when it exits the system. For instance, the throughput time of unit #1 is 2.5 hours because it enters the system at $t = 0$ and exits at $t = 2 : 30$ (Figure 3.15). Similarly, the throughput time of unit #2 is 2 hours 50 minutes and that of unit #3 is 3 hours 10 minutes. Unlike the cycle time, the throughput time is different

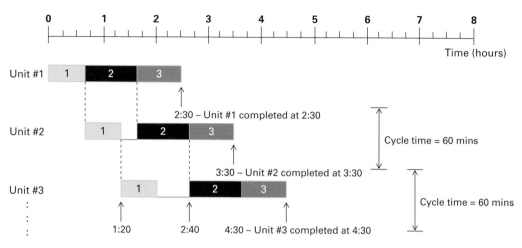

Figure 3.14 Estimating the Cycle Time – Unit #3

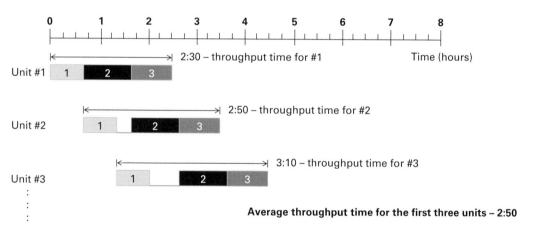

Figure 3.15 Estimating the Throughput Time

across the units. In fact, the throughput time can vary depending on the production policy: for instance, if the system adopts a policy to enter a new unit at every 30 minutes (rather than the current policy to start a new unit whenever the first process becomes available), then the throughput time will be completely different. Since the throughput times vary across the units, we need to take an average: in Figure 3.15, the average throughput time for the first three units is 2 hours 50 minutes. While the cycle time is needed to calculate the capacity, the throughput time helps the manager determine whether the system operates productively or efficiently, i.e., whether the system is doing value-added activities or being idle.

There is another approach to estimate the cycle time and the throughput time: Figure 3.16 shows the process-centered approach, which focuses on the individual processes, not the units, resulting in the same cycle and throughput times.

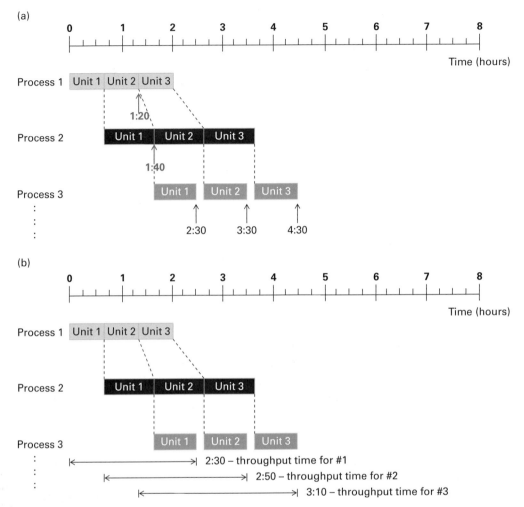

Figure 3.16 Process-Centered Approach

So far we have assumed that the production system processes one unit at a time. But, let's consider a different context. Suppose that the bakery company makes a few different types of bread in batches or lots. A **batch** is all the loaves of bread baked at the same time: more generally, it is a collection of things or units to be processed together. Why does the company bake the bread in batches? Suppose the bakery makes two kinds of bread, e.g., wheat and corn breads, using the same oven, which can bake a maximum of 10 units of bread at a time. Since the ingredients for the wheat bread are different from those for the corn bread, the bakery doesn't want to bake two types of bread at the same time, since doing so reduces the efficiency of the production system. For instance, using the same oven, the bakery makes 10 units (loaves) of wheat bread, then 10 units of corn bread, so on.

It takes time to switch from one batch to another. The time needed between two consecutive batches is the set-up time, which is the time necessary for preparation to move from one batch to the next. Why does the production system need the set-up time between batches? Consider the bakery example again. The company needs a preparation time between the batch of wheat bread and that of corn bread, since the ingredients are different. That is, after baking one batch of wheat bread, before starting to bake the corn bread, the bakery probably has to clean the oven and prepare the ingredients suited to the corn bread. Thus, it needs a set-up time. Even if the bakery makes batches of the same bread, it needs a set-up time between batches. Suppose that the bakery has to make fifteen loaves of wheat bread. Since the oven can bake a maximum of ten loaves at a time, it has to first bake one batch, i.e., ten loaves, of wheat bread. After processing the first batch, it is probably necessary to clean the oven anyway and to prepare more ingredients for the next batch.

Is there any special meaning of the batch size, e.g., a small versus large batch size? The units in the same batch are mostly identical in product characteristics, e.g., size, color, taste, or even functionality. As such, other things being equal, the company utilizes a large batch size when it plans to serve the mass market, i.e., a large number of customers, whose demands or requirements are similar and undifferentiated among themselves. On the contrary, a specialty or niche market usually consists of a small number of customers. Therefore, the company had better use a smaller batch size when it aims to serve such a market.

Let's return to the bakery example. Figure 3.17 shows the case where the set-up time occurs: in addition to the run times, the set-up times are specified in the figure. For example, the bake process requires a set-up time of 700 minutes per batch with the run time of 50 minutes per unit (i.e., a loaf), which is the same as before. What does the number mean? Figure 3.18 shows how to calculate the total time required to process one batch (of ten loaves) at the bake process.

Table 3.1 presents calculations for three different cases, i.e., the batch size of 8, 15, and 100 units. For instance, consider the batch size of 8 for explanation. Using the same logic in Figure 3.18, we calculate the "batch run-time" at each process: the batch run-time is the total time needed to process one batch, including the set-up time and the sum

Table 3.1 Monthly Capacity

Batch Size	Mix	Proof	Bake	Capacity*
8	40×8+800=1,120	60×8+500=980	50×8+700=1,100	(20×8×60)/1,120=8.57 batch=69 units
15	40×15 +800=1,400	60×15 +500=1,400	50×15 +700=1,450	(20×8×60)/1,450=6.62 batch=99 units
100	40×100 +800=4,800	60×100 +500=6,500	50×100 +700=5,700	(20×8×60)/6,500=1.48 batch=148 units

Note: * monthly capacity, assuming 8 hours/day, 20 days/month.

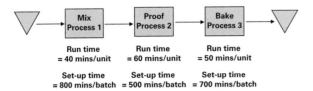

Figure 3.17 Bread-Making Process with Set-Up Times

Batch run time = Total time needed to process one batch at the bake process

= set-up time + total run times = 700 minutes + 10 units × 50 minutes/unit

= 1,200 minutes

Assumptions

● The batch size is 10, i.e., the oven bakes 10 loaves of bread as one batch.

● After completing one batch, it takes 700 minutes to prepare (set up) for the next batch.

● Inside the bake process, it takes 50 minutes to bake one unit (loaf) of bread individually.

Figure 3.18 Total Time to Process One Batch at Bake Process

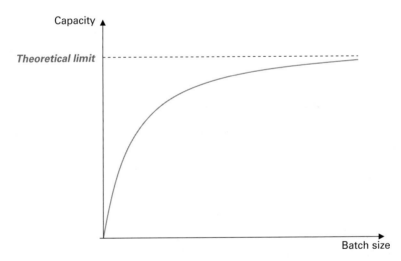

Figure 3.19 Theoretical Limit to Capacity Increase

of the individual units' run-times. For the ensuing discussion, we assume that the production system processes only one type of batch continuously. Table 3.1 shows that it takes 1,120 minutes to process one batch of 8 units at the mix process, 980 minutes at the proof process, and 1,100 minutes at the bake process. As in Figure 3.11, we need to identify the bottleneck process to determine the cycle time of the production system. Assuming the production system is processing only the batch of 8 units, we determine that the bottleneck process, i.e., the least efficient process, is the mix process, since it takes the longest time to process one batch. Provided that the bakery operates 8 hours a day, 20 days a month, continuously, the monthly capacity of the production system is 8.57 batches or 69 units (8.57 batches × 8 units/batch). Similarly, the monthly capacity is 99 units (loaves) if the production system processes only the batch of 15 units, and 148 units if it processes only the batch of 100 units.

One very important observation here is that the bottleneck is changing as the batch size varies. That is, when the batch size is 8 units, the bottleneck is the mix process, whereas the bottleneck is the bake process if the batch size is 15 units and the proof process if the batch size is 100 units. This phenomenon is the **bottleneck shifting**. We see that the bottleneck process is not an absolute fixed concept. In fact, it is a relative concept, which can be changed as the structural condition such as the batch size changes.

Is there any relationship between the batch size and the capacity? Table 3.1 hints at a positive relationship between the two, i.e., as the batch size increases, so does the capacity. Figure 3.19 sketches a general pattern of such relationship, demonstrating a positive curvilinear one that increases at a decreasing rate. Can the capacity increase indefinitely? In fact, the capacity cannot increase forever, i.e., there is a theoretical limit on the capacity. Consider the examples in Table 3.1. What happens to the "unit set-up time (i.e., the set-up time divided by the batch size)" as the batch size increases? Yes, the unit set-up time decreases as the batch size increases. How long can this phenomenon continue? Theoretically, the batch size can become infinite, i.e., approach ∞, then the unit set-up time becomes zero. That is, that the batch size is ∞ is equivalent to there being no set-up time. For the bakery example, the theoretical limit on the capacity is 160. Can you explain why?

3.3.2   Fit between Operations and Corporate Strategy

Now let's think about whether the choice of batch size has any strategic implications. We already talked about the phenomenon of bottleneck shifting, i.e., as the batch size changes, the bottleneck process shifts as well. What determines the batch size? We previously alluded that the batch size is related to the **target market**. That is, if the company targets a **mass market**, then it must use a large batch, which makes the product in large quantities, not differentiated. On the other hand, if the company plans to serve a **niche market**, which is in general small and requires a highly differentiated product or service, then it needs to use a small batch. Figure 3.20 shows the relationship between the firm's target market and its batch size. A small batch size is compatible with a high-end, premium market and the **make-to-order** process strategy: under the make-to-order strategy, the firm starts making the product only when the customer places an order for it. On the contrary, a large batch size is more desirable for a low-end, mass market, where the demand is not finely differentiated and the make-to-stock process strategy is more relevant: under the **make-to-stock** strategy, the company makes and stocks the product without a concrete order from the market, and the customer buys and picks up the product from the stock or inventory. Then, who decides the firm's target market? In fact,

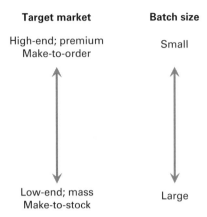

Figure 3.20 Target Market and Batch Size

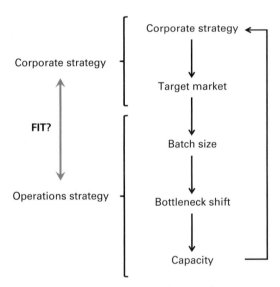

Figure 3.21 Fit between Corporate and Operations Strategy

it is the top management that determines which market to serve. Therefore, the target market is in the realm of corporate strategy.

Corporate strategy defines the firm's vision, mission, long-term strategic direction, and boundary, i.e., the business as well as the market the firm intends to be in. Under the corporate strategy, there are functional strategies at the firm, e.g., marketing, finance, human resource, and operations strategy. Each functional strategy has to be designed to support the corporate strategy by utilizing the functional resources. **Operations strategy** defines the firm's operations regarding how to utilize the three fundamental building blocks, i.e., process, resource, and capability, effectively so as to optimize the firm's value creation by making products or providing services. Figure 3.21 shows the relationship between corporate strategy and operations strategy. As discussed already, corporate strategy determines the firm's target market. The target market affects the batch size, which in turn decides the bottleneck process. Since the bottleneck process determines the capacity of the production system, it effectively implies that corporate strategy at the top of the company has a continuous chain effect on capacity. Finally, capacity will have an impact upon corporate strategy in the long run, by constraining the firm's ability to serve the market.

The link from batch size, bottleneck, to capacity is part of operations strategy. As such, we establish the need for a fit between corporate strategy and operations strategy. Consider a simple example that helps us see the importance of the strategic fit (Figures 3.22 and 3.23).

- Consider a company, which is currently pursuing a corporate strategy to focus on a mass market. In order to support the corporate strategy, the firm is implementing the operations strategy, which uses a relatively large batch size of S_0 and achieves a current capacity of EC_0.
- The company suddenly revises its corporate strategy by changing its target market from a mass to premium market. Without paying attention to the potential variations in operations due to such a change in corporate strategy, the company plans the corporate strategy for the new target market, assuming it can still enjoy the capacity at EC_0.
- The problem is that due to the sudden change in corporate strategy, the company should adjust its effective capacity. Because of the change in the target market, there should be an appropriate change in the batch size, e.g., from S_0 to S_N. Then, the new effective capacity becomes EC_N, no longer EC_0.
- Although the company assumes the capacity to be EC_0 (i.e., the assumed capacity $AC_N = EC_0$) when it changes its target market, the effective capacity the company can achieve for the new strategy is just EC_N, not EC_0.

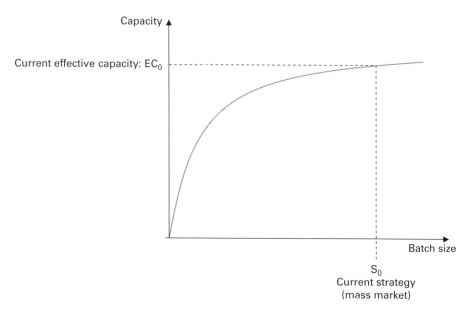

Figure 3.22 Current Operations Strategy

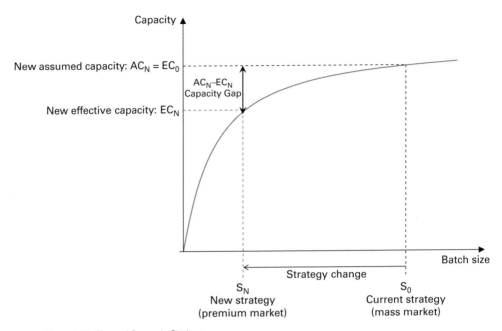

Figure 3.23 Changed Corporate Strategy

- Thus, there exists a capacity gap, EC_0-EC_N, when the company changes its corporate strategy without taking into account the systemic change in the capacity. The capacity gap can be so large that the new corporate strategy to focus on the premium market can fall apart, i.e., it can be a fiasco. For example, suppose that the company accepts an order to deliver an amount of EC_0 by a certain due date, believing that the level of capacity remains the same despite the strategy change. Since the change in the target market reduces the effective capacity to EC_N significantly below the current level EC_0, however, it turns out that the company cannot honor its delivery promise when the due date arrives. Any manager knows that failure to keep the delivery promise has a disastrous consequence for the business.

Although the above example is somewhat simple for the sake of clarity, it is a very powerful demonstration about the potential problem when the company fails to achieve the fit between corporate strategy and operations strategy. There are many real-world cases that corroborate the managerial implications derived from the simple example.

3.4   Quality and Value

Value creation is the foremost goal of the firm. In Chapter 1, we defined value as a function of utility and cost. **Quality** is one of the most important factors that determine the utility. That is, the higher the quality, the larger the utility experienced by the

- Conformance – meeting specification
- Performance – functionality
- Reliability – reliable performance
- Durability – long product life
- Features – supplementary functions
- Serviceability – maintenance, repair
- Aesthetics – feel, look, touch, subjective
- Perceived quality – brand, image, status

Figure 3.24 Garvin's Eight Dimensions of Quality

customer. But, quality is not a one-dimensional concept. In fact, it is a highly complex, multi-layered one. Garvin[2] put forth eight dimensions of quality as shown in Figure 3.24.

We can group these multiple attributes of quality into two: order-qualifying and order-winning attributes. **Order-qualifying attributes** are basic attributes a product should have in order for it to be in the market in the first place. That is, they constitute the very basic requirements of the product. Consider the passenger car market. What are the basic requirements of a car? First of all, in order for the car to be in the market, it must meet engineering specifications, perform basic functionality reliably as expected by the customer, and last for a certain period of time at the least. Unless the car satisfies these basic requirements, it cannot expect the customer to consider it as a candidate car to purchase. Suppose the car meets the order-qualifying attributes and thus is eligible to be in the market, say the show-window at the dealership. Is this the end of the story? No, to be in the market doesn't mean that the customer buys the car eventually. There are probably many alternative cars that meet the basic requirements in the market. When the customer shops around the market, she has to choose one among the many alternative cars. What factors should the customer take into account for her final decision to buy a particular car? Since the order-qualifying attributes were already taken into account, they are no longer relevant when the customer tries to choose one among the many "order-qualifying" cars. It is the **order-winning attributes** of quality that help the customer to make her final choice. For instance, the customer probably wants to consider which car has more extra features that make the driving experience a pleasure, which carmaker offers better services of maintenance and repair, which car looks or feels more beautiful, which carmaker or car heightens her social status because of its luxurious brand image, and so forth.

Figure 3.25 presents an example grouping of order-qualifying and order-winning attributes of quality dimensions, where the four dimensions such as features, service-ability, aesthetics, and perceived quality are grouped as order-winning attributes, and the others as order-qualifying. In fact, it depends on the unique situation or condition of the market in point which attributes are order-qualifying or order-winning. For a less developed economy, in order to be in the market, it might be enough for a product to

---

[2] D. Garvin, *Managing Quality* (New York: The Free Press, 1988).

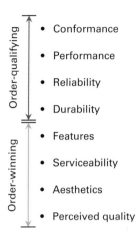

Figure 3.25 Order-Winning versus Order-Qualifying

meet the very basic quality attributes like conformance and performance, whereas in a more developed or advanced market, even features and serviceability might be considered as basic requirements and grouped as order-qualifying attributes.

"Quality is free" dynamics. Considering it costs a lot to take an action for quality improvement, it is practical to ask whether it is always necessary to make an effort to improve quality.

The cost side: In order to enhance quality, the firm has to take quality improvement activities funded by its resources, which are in turn based on its profits. That is, the more the profits, the more the resources available for quality improvement. Similarly, the more the firm's quality improvement activities, the more the quality improvement. On the other hand, it costs for the firm to embark on quality improvement activities. The dynamics described above can be depicted in Figure 3.26. There is a negative closed-loop from profits → resources → quality improvement activity → costs → profits. It is negative since as the firm makes more effort to improve quality, the profit actually decreases; the decreased profit reduces the resources available for quality improvement; in effect, this **closed-loop** is a kind of balancing loop, where no direction for continuous improvement exists.

The "expected" profit side: Observing the negative loop, one can ask, *Is it better to make an effort to improve quality at all?* In fact, the dynamics in Figure 3.26 are incomplete. What is the goal of quality improvement in the first place? The firm expects the improved quality to increase the sales by meeting the customer requirements better. That is, there is a positive closed-loop from quality improvement activity → quality → customer perception → sales → profits → resources → quality improvement activity as in Figure 3.27. This loop is positive since as the firm improves its quality, its profit

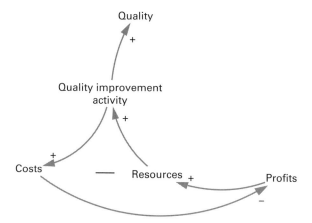

Figure 3.26 Quality Improvement Dynamics 1

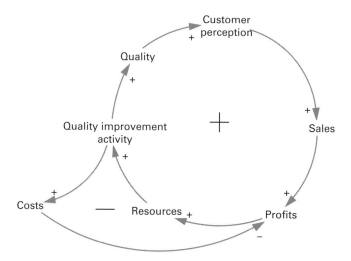

Figure 3.27 Quality Improvement Dynamics 2

increases more and enables the firm to enhance quality even further. That is, a **self-reinforcing**, virtuous cycle is setting in.

The "unexpected" profit side: Although the positive loop in Figure 3.27 makes a reasonably strong case for investing in quality improvement, it doesn't seem to be an overwhelming support for devoting all of the firm's energies to quality improvement. Let's think about what actually happens when the firm tries to improve its quality. As the dynamics in Figures 3.26 and 3.27 show, the firm should take quality improvement activities such as quality circles and six sigma projects. Consider the managers at the firm are engaged in a six sigma project. The project is likely initiated with a specific goal, e.g., to fix a broken machine, to change a work procedure, to modify a production

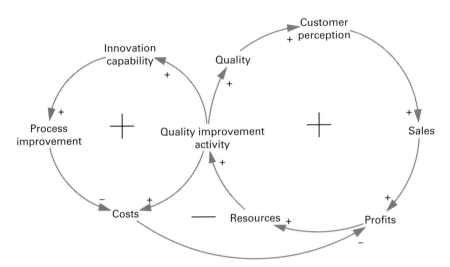

Figure 3.28 Quality Improvement Dynamics 3

scheduling, and the like. In order to tackle the specific quality problem at hand, the members of the six sigma project work very hard together: they probably observe the problem thoroughly, analyze the causes of the problem, discuss technical or engineering details, and brainstorm intensely to find solutions. In doing so, they not only deepen their understanding about the problem itself, but also increase their knowledge about overall process improvement, which can enable the firm to optimize its operations and eventually reduce the production cost throughout the manufacturing system. This is the "unexpected" profit side of the quality improvement dynamics: another positive closed-loop consists of quality improvement activity → innovation capability → process improvement → costs → profits → resources → quality improvement activity (Figure 3.28).

Now the two profit sides seem to dominate the cost side (Figure 3.28). Our discussion on the quality improvement dynamics so far makes a very strong argument for the firm's conscious effort to devote resources to quality improvement. In fact, it powerfully advocates **Philip Crosby**'s[3] postulation of "quality is free," which implies that the cost spent on quality improvement will be more than fully compensated through sales increase and process improvement.

We want to point out one potential caveat. "Quality is free" is a conceptual maxim. Can the firm implement it without any real-world obstacles? Suppose that by presenting the dynamics in Figure 3.28, we want to persuade the CEO to follow the maxim and invest a huge amount of money in quality improvement right away. Will the CEO be satisfied with our reasoning and take an action without any concern or hesitation? We posed the question to several CEOs. When asked, at first most of them said they agreed with the proposition that the costs to improve quality would be fully compensated by sales increase and process innovation. But, when asked again, they paused for a little

---

[3] P. B. Crosby, *Quality Is Free: The Art of Making Quality Certain* (New York: McGraw-Hill, 1980).

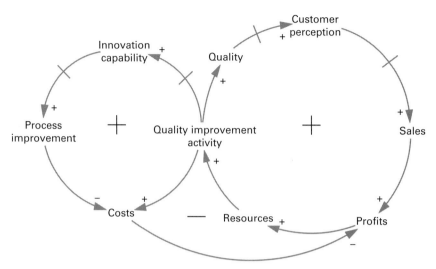

Figure 3.29 Quality Improvement Dynamics 4

longer and became more serious or less enthusiastic. Then, some of them started expressing their concerns. Yes, they indeed could see that the sales would increase and also the process improvement would occur if they should make an effort to improve quality. Yet, what they were concerned about was the timing. Even if they accepted that the improved quality would eventually make the customer perception more favorable for the firm's product, they acknowledged that it was not clear how long it would take for such a change to be realized. Similarly, it was not clear how long it would take for a more favorite customer perception to translate into increased sales. That is, there would be a time lag or **delay** between an action and its consequences. In Figure 3.29, the time delay between a cause and its effect is denoted on the arrow as +. There is a similar time delay between quality improvement activity and innovation capability and also between innovation capability and process improvement. In effect, the firm can expect the benefits of quality improvement to be materialized in the long run, not instantaneously. On the contrary, the costs spent on quality improvement are instantaneous, i.e., reflected in the current income statement. In general, the CEO is evaluated annually. If she spends money on improving quality, such costs are included in the current performance evaluation as a negative factor. But, the benefits of improved quality will be reaped in the future, possibly long after the CEO leaves the company. Under this condition, can the CEO make a decision to invest in quality improvement without any reservation? Practically, it is quite a challenge for the CEO to ignore such an obstacle. This is an example of **time discrepancy** in managerial decision-making: the time discrepancy caused by the time delay between cause-and-effect relationships is one of the most serious factors that make it difficult for the CEO to make a decision with a long-term, strategic perspective. Another is **space discrepancy**, which is a discrepancy between cause-and-effect relationships due to the existence of some physical, e.g., geological, differences. For instance, it might happen that when the manager makes a decision at the marketing department, serious consequences of the decision emerge in the production department, not the marketing department; or, when the firm takes an action in area A, but the effects of the action appear in area B, not A – these are possible examples of space discrepancy.

Both time and space discrepancies are detrimental to effective decision-making by the CEO: they make it difficult for the decision-maker to see the problem from a long-term perspective; as such, the CEO is forced to be myopic when making a decision. Relying on the short-term at the expense of long-term, strategic decision-making jeopardizes timely and effective decision-making. Therefore, for sustaining competitive advantages, the firm must design a performance evaluation system that encourages the CEO to look beyond the short-term constraints and make a decision with a longer-term, strategic perspective. One such system is to establish a compensation scheme that recognizes significant contributions made by former CEOs or top managers: for instance, suppose in 2012 the CEO makes a decision to invest in an R&D project that is expected to complete a new product in five years; the CEO retires in 2013; as the CEO anticipates, the R&D project completes the new product, which becomes a hit in 2017 and generates an enormous profit for the company. If the company is just mediocre, it probably has no formal mechanism to compensate the former CEO: under a situation like this, an average CEO would not be motivated to take an action that will bear fruit long after she is gone from the company. But, if the company has a forward-looking system that recognizes the contribution made by the former CEO, it can compensate the former CEO for her insightful decision to embark on the R&D project even if she is no longer employed by the company: if this is the case, the CEO is willing to take risks to make the company stronger in the future, despite the short-term obstacles getting in the way. Of course, when designing such a forward-looking system for measuring a long-term performance, the company must also take into account the opposite cases, in order to curb such negative behaviors as taking unreasonably extreme risks and moral hazards. As always, it is indispensable to have a system based on balanced perspectives.

Finally, we underline that in the face of complicated dynamics affected by time and space discrepancies as in Figure 3.29, the company should make an effort to identify "leverage points": a **leverage point** is a decision factor or point so that if the company makes an effective decision at this point, it can realize the best outcome by spending the least amount of resources; that is, a leverage point is the most economical, i.e., effective, decision point. For instance, in Figure 3.29, the "quality improvement activity" is the most substantial leverage point for the company, of course as long as it recognizes the time delays in the dynamics and understands their implications.

Total quality management (TQM).   Quality is so important for a firm's competitive advantage that nowadays the entire organization, and not just part of the company like the quality or production department, is engaged in quality improvement initiatives. That is, quality management has become an issue of the whole, i.e., "total," company. Hence there is the concept of "total quality management (TQM)." To understand the origin of TQM, we need to recognize two streams of development (Figure 3.30).

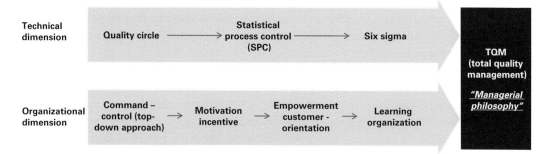

Figure 3.30 Technical and Organizational Dimensions of TQM

The technical dimension: First, there is a stream of technical dimension. In the 1960s and 1970s, companies realized the importance of quality and embarked on formal quality improvement activities such as quality circles. But, these activities were not scientifically sophisticated, although they were effective enough to enhance quality during the time. A more sophisticated, statistical approach began to be extensively utilized not only in manufacturing, but also in non-manufacturing sectors. Although it was originally conceptualized in the 1920s, the statistical process control (SPC) became an important quality improvement tool in the 1980s and 1990s, when it was stylized to differentiate common causes from assignable causes as sources of variations; in fact, statistical variations were central to the SPC approach. Since the 1990s, companies made an effort to go beyond simple quality improvement to **continuous process improvement** or innovation. Although the concept of "**six sigma**" was first developed by Motorola in 1986, soon it outgrew its original meaning tied to an extremely high statistical accuracy and began implying incessant organizational dedication to process innovation.

The organizational dimension: There has been a mirroring development in the organizational side. From the early 1900s to the 1950s, a typical organization theory was based on classical theories such as Weber's theory of bureaucracy and Taylor's scientific management, advocating a command-and-control, i.e., top-down, management approach. Since the original **Hawthorne** study in 1924, researchers in organizational behavior started paying attention to softer aspects of organizational behavior such as motivation and non-monetary incentives, which became very powerful factors to explain organizational behaviors in the 1970s and 1980s. As the technological innovation, e.g., the internet, was accelerating from the early 1990s, consumers became better equipped with high-tech tools that helped them to be more sophisticated in making a purchase decision. Accordingly, companies found it essential to be responsive to the market and consumers and realized they could enhance such a capability by empowering their employees, i.e., delegating more decision-making powers to the managers and employees. The culminating point of the development in organizational behavior was the learning organization, where the members of the organization, e.g., managers and employees alike, were continuously learning and solving managerial problems, innovating the management system and process, creating and accumulating new knowledge through problem solving and innovation, and transferring and sharing such knowledge among the members. The learning organization is a self-adapting, self-organizing entity.

TQM is rooted on the two dimensions, the six sigma principle as the technical dimension on the one hand and the learning organization as the organizational dimension on the other. In effect, TQM is a managerial philosophy, which endeavors to improve and innovate every aspect of the organization and its value-creating continuously by empowering the employees and taking the customer-oriented perspective, i.e., becoming a true learning organization.

3.4.1   Quality Failure and Cost

Defects are made when quality fails. Thus, quality failure incurs costs. There are two different types of **quality failure** – internal and external. When the defect is discovered during the production process, i.e., before it is sold and delivered to the customer, it is the internal quality failure. On the contrary, when the defect is discovered by the customer during the product's life cycle, it is the external quality failure. Each quality failure costs. Between the two quality failure costs, the external quality failure costs overwhelm the internal quality failure costs (Figure 3.31).

Quality costs.   There are three categories of quality-related costs, i.e., costs associated with the firm's internal efforts for quality improvement, **internal quality failure** costs, and **external quality failure** costs (Figure 3.32).

Internal efforts for quality improvement: The firm should make an effort to improve quality and process. Such an effort incurs costs including those involved with prevention, appraisal, and other improvement activities.

Internal quality failure costs: If the defect is discovered inside the firm, i.e., the firm's production system, it means internal quality failure, which incurs costs such as rework, repair, and scrap or disposal costs.

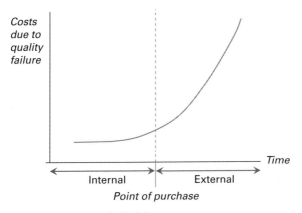

Figure 3.31 Cost Due to Quality Failure

- Internal efforts for quality improvement
    - Goal: to eliminate both internal and external quality failures
    - Costs
        - Prevention cost
        - Appraisal cost
        - Process and quality improvement activity cost
- Internal quality failure
    - Costs
        - Rework, repair, scrap costs
- External quality failure
    - Costs
        - Short-term
            - Return, repair, rework costs
            - Customer compensation
        - Long-term
            - Customer perception ↓→ Reputation ↓→ Customer loyalty ↓→ Future sales ↓
            - Rework ↑→ Disruption ↑→ Process variability ↑→ Quality deterioration ↑

Figure 3.32 Quality-Related Costs

External quality failure costs: If the defect is discovered by the customer, it is external quality failure. External quality failure incurs two different types of costs – short-term and long-term. Short-term external quality failure costs are similar to the internal quality failure costs, i.e., return, repair, and rework costs, along with the cost of compensation paid to the customer to pacify her complaint. Long-term external quality failure costs are more damaging than short-term ones in that they have a huge negative impact on the firm's competitive advantage. For one thing, the external quality failure causes a chain effect as follows: external quality failure → decreased customer perception → reputation down → customer loyalty down → future sales down. Another serious ripple effect is: external quality failure → unscheduled rework increased → increased disruption in the production system → increased production variability → quality deterioration. These two chains of events have grave consequences for the firm's long-term competitive standing and capability. That's why the external quality failure costs are much larger and more rapidly accelerating than the internal ones.

Value and quality proposition – a VLC perspective. In Chapter 1, we defined the value life cycle (VLC), which encompasses both the firm's new product development process and the product life cycle. That is, VLC covers the entire life of the product from its conception to its demise. We want to compare the customer's value proposition with the firm's quality proposition throughout the product's VLC.

Customer's value proposition: What factors does the customer take into account when making a decision to purchase a product or service? In order to understand the true value for the customer, we have to look at the entire product life cycle, rather than focusing on

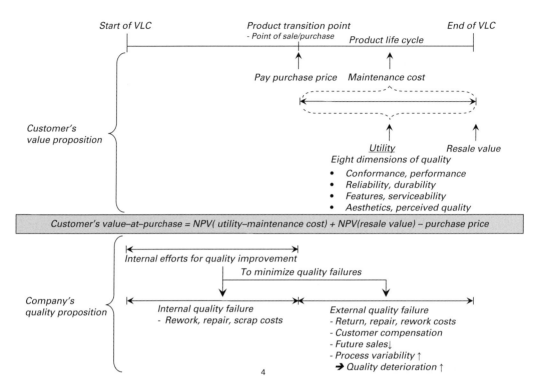

Figure 3.33 Value and Quality Proposition

the point of purchase only. There are four factors the customer takes into account, explicitly or implicitly, when making the decision, i.e., the purchase price, total costs for maintenance throughout the PLC, total utility the customer experiences throughout the PLC, and the resale value (Figure 3.33). Even if she doesn't calculate the total value of the product systematically or explicitly, the customer is applying the following reasoning:

$$\text{Value at purchase} = \text{NPV (utility)} + \text{NPV (resale value)} - \\ \text{NPV (maintenance cost)} - \text{purchase price}$$

where NPV is net present value.

That is, the customer's **value at purchase** is the NPV of utility and resale value minus the NPV of purchase price and maintenance costs. The most important managerial implication is that the customer doesn't base her decision on the point of purchase only; on the contrary, she looks at the value she experiences throughout the entire product life cycle. Therefore, the firm has to design and manufacture a product or service, which can maximize the value felt by the customer throughout the product life cycle, and be not just obsessed with the product transition point, i.e., the point of sale or purchase.

Company's quality proposition: Facing the customer value proposition, the firm has to design its own competitive strategy throughout the value life cycle. It must embark on quality and process improvement inside the production system, i.e., before the product transition point. The goal should be to minimize both internal and external quality failures at the same time. It must work hard to enhance all of the multiple dimensions of quality from the very moment of product conception, i.e., throughout the whole VLC, including new product development and product life cycle. In addition, as in the "quality is free" dynamics, the firm must plan to integrate its quality improvement activities with process and capability improvement for the sustainable competitive strategy. While engaging in the activities, the firm must deal with various types of costs optimally. All of these are going to enable the firm to realize TQM in the entire organization.

3.4.2 Quality and Process Control

We defined value as a function of utility and cost. Since we also defined quality as a multi-dimensional concept closely related with the customer's utility, quality is the essential element of utility. When quality fails, however, a defect is produced. From an analytical perspective (Figure 3.34), a quality problem occurs due to **deviation**, i.e., the difference between the goal and the actual outcome. Deviation in turn is caused by **process variability**. Finally, there are two different types of causes that make the process deviate from its target, i.e., **common causes** and **assignable causes**.

Process outcome distribution. Suppose there is a process that makes a mini cereal box. The target weight of the cereal box is 200 g. That is, the process is designed to package 200 g of cereal in each cereal box. If the process is in perfect condition, in theory it should produce cereal boxes, each of which weighs exactly 200 g. But, in reality, there is no such thing as the "perfect" condition. Even if everything is realistically perfect, the process cannot produce things exactly as designed. That is, the process makes the cereal boxes with a certain level of deviation. Assume that the process outcomes (e.g., the "actual" weights of the cereal boxes) follow a normal distribution as in Figure 3.35, where the mean or target value is 200 g.

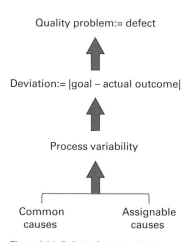

Quality problem:= defect

Deviation:= |goal – actual outcome|

Process variability

Common causes   Assignable causes

Figure 3.34 Defining Quality and Defect

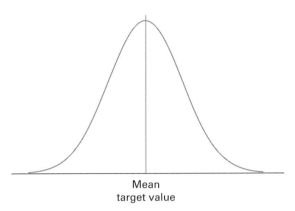

Mean
target value

Figure 3.35 Process Outcome Distribution

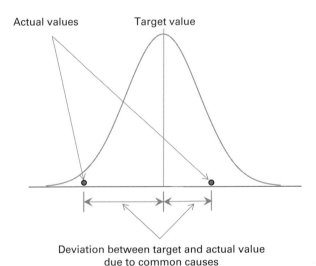

Actual values   Target value

Deviation between target and actual value
due to common causes

Figure 3.36 Deviation Due to Common Causes

Common versus assignable causes.

Even if the condition is normal or very close to perfect, the process makes cereal boxes weighing not exactly 200 g. For example, the process can make a cereal box weighing 175 g or 210 g even if it is **in-control**, i.e., not **out-of-control**.

Why? Under this situation, we state such deviation is due to a common cause, which is random in its own nature. That is, it is common causes that make the process outcome deviate from the goal or target value even when the process is in-control (Figure 3.36). On the contrary, assignable causes are systematic reasons that force such deviation. Assignable causes are systematic, implying that it is possible for the firm to identify fundamental sources of the quality problem and fix them as long as it has enough skill and knowledge: in contrast, the firm cannot find out the fundamental forces underlying the common causes given the current level of its knowledge; this logic helps us infer that as the

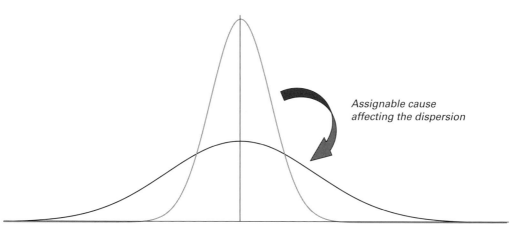

Figure 3.37 Process Affected by Assignable Causes 1

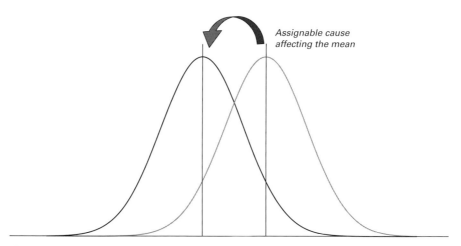

Figure 3.38 Process Affected by Assignable Causes 2

firm accumulates more knowledge about the process, some of the causes previously thought to be random may become assignable causes so that the firm can identify the underlying reasons of the causes and fix them. Analytically speaking, assignable causes can affect and change the dispersion of the process, i.e., the standard deviation of the process outcome distribution (Figure 3.37), or the mean value (Figure 3.38). Either way, the process becomes less reliable, producing more defects. We think of some examples of assignable causes such as broken machines and damaged morale among the employees.

Statistical process control (SPC). As in Figure 3.34, **process variability** is the foremost reason underlying the quality problem. That's why the methodology of SPC (statistical process control) plays an important role in quality improvement. Here we sketch the skeleton of SPC. Consider the process that makes the cereal boxes. Knowing that even when it is under normal conditions, the process can produce defects, the firm decides that a cereal box is acceptable as long as its weight is smaller than 230g, but larger than 170g: the

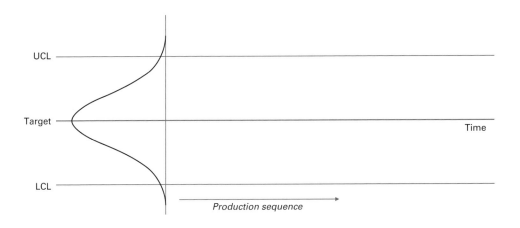

Target = 200g; UCL = 230g; LCL = 170g

Figure 3.39 Basic Concept of Statistical Process Control

maximum value is "**upper control limit** (UCL)," whereas the minimum is "**lower control limit** (LCL)"; the range between UCL and LCL is the **tolerance range**.

An example SPC chart is shown in Figure 3.39: it is easy to see the logic by rotating the normal distribution 90° to the left. How can the firm utilize the SPC chart? The most important role played by the SPC approach is to enable the firm to determine whether the process is affected by assignable causes: if the assignable causes are indeed present in the process, the firm must stop its current operations, search for the fundamental reasons, and fix them. It is conceptually easy to divide the causes into two categories, i.e., common versus assignable. But, in reality, it is not at all straightforward to make such a distinction. Hence, the SPC principle comes in handy.

Figure 3.40 shows an example of how to use the SPC chart. As it produces each unit, the firm plots the outcome of the unit on the chart: since it is concerned with meeting the "weight" specification given by the customer, the firm plots the weight of each unit, following the production sequence. Let's return to the example in Figure 3.40. The first 9 units are within the tolerance range, i.e., between the upper (230g) and lower (170g) control limits. But, the ninth and tenth units are outside the tolerance range, i.e., larger than the upper control limit. Observing these units outside the tolerance limit, the firm determines that the process is affected by assignable causes. A logical next step the firm can take is to stop the production process and search for the fundamental causes. Once it identifies the assignable causes, the firm tries to fix them before restarting the production process.

Although the scenario described above is conceptually straightforward, it might not be that crystal clear in the real world. Can the firm definitely determine whether the process is being impacted by assignable causes based on simple observation of the SPC chart? We already mentioned it is possible for the process to make a defect even when it is in control. That is, it is inherently difficult for the firm to make a completely foolproof decision by observing the SPC chart, because of the process's innate variability.

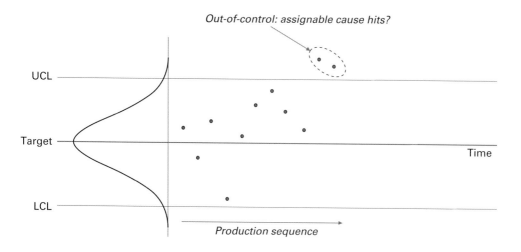

Target = 200g; UCL = 230g; LCL = 170g

Figure 3.40 Detecting Assignable Causes

Discussion Questions

1. What is value chain? What is supply chain? What are the similarities and differences between the two?
2. What is the structural dimension of supply chain management?
3. What is the infrastructural dimension of supply chain management?
4. What is the relationship between the two dimensions of supply chain management?
5. What is the general relationship between a firm's information and inventory level?
6. What are the differences between a spot market transaction and vertical integration?
7. How is supply chain management different from the more traditional operations management?
8. Why is it important for the firm to achieve a fit between operations strategy and corporate strategy?
9. Explain the statement that "quality is a multi-dimensional concept."
10. What are the quality failures and the resulting costs?
11. Define the order-qualifying and order-winning attributes of quality.
12. Explain the concept of "quality is free." What are some discrepancies the manager should understand?
13. Define TQM (total quality management) from a historical perspective.
14. What are the common causes and assignable causes?
15. Explain how to detect an assignable cause, using the SPC principle.

Elizabeth Arden: Executing Global Supply Chain Re-Engineering

By David Wood and Norman Gao[4]

Pierre Pirard, Senior Vice-President of Global Supply Chain at Elizabeth Arden in New York City, was troubled with the challenges that lay before him. It was mid-2008 and, less than a year after joining Elizabeth Arden, he had already made a significant impact in forecasting, inventory control, and service performance. However, Pirard knew that the company would need much more. He was hired to make sweeping changes to how the company managed the supply chain and his next move would require a radical consolidation of suppliers, make dramatic changes to inventory management, have a far-reaching impact on product development, and require major lead-time reductions. Given such a disruptive move, could current suppliers be able to meet his expectations? Could Elizabeth Arden's current employees keep up with the pace of change expected? And were significant results to shareholders really achievable? Pirard was determined to execute the re-engineering in a manner that would best address all these concerns.

Cosmetics industry. "Cosmetics" are products used to enhance the appearance or odour of the human body. They are generally mixtures of chemical compounds, some derived from natural sources, many synthetic.[5] The practice of caring, cleansing, and decoration of the skin has been in existence for over a millennium. For instance, castor oil was used several thousand years ago in ancient Egypt as a protective balm. Galen of Pergamon (AD 129–199), a prominent Roman physician, surgeon, and philosopher, developed one of the first precursors of modern skin creams from a mixture of beeswax, olive oil, and rosewater (Aqua Rosae).

Elizabeth Arden, Helena Rubinstein, and Max Factor developed the modern cosmetics market in the United States during the 1910s. These firms were joined by Revlon just before World War II and Estée Lauder shortly after.[6] In 2007, the worldwide cosmetics and perfume industry generated an estimated annual turnover of $170 billion.[7] Europe was the leading market, representing

[4] Norman Gao wrote this case under the supervision of Professor David Wood solely to provide material for class discussion. The authors do not intend to illustrate either effective or ineffective handling of a managerial situation. The authors may have disguised certain names and other identifying information to protect confidentiality.

[5] *Ullmann's Encyclopedia of Industrial Chemistry* (Weinheim: Wiley-VCH, 2012).

[6] Company websites, www.revlon.ca/Revlon-Home/Revlon-Corporate/Corporate.aspx and www.esteelauder.com/cms/about/index.tmpl, accessed July 15, 2013.

[7] www.clickpress.com/releases/Detailed/82987005cp.shtml, Eurostaf, May 2007.

approximately $86 billion.[8] In comparison, the US cosmetics revenue for 2007 was $51.52 billion.[9] Market volume information by product category for 2005 in the United States, Japan, and Europe is available in Figure 3.41.

Market for Cosmetic Products (2005)			
Product	Market Volume (€B)		
	US	Japan	Europe
Skin and face	5.6	6.8	8.7
Body care	3.8	1	4.7
Hair treatment agents	5.5	4.2	6.2
Perfume	2.4	0.2	3.2
Decorative cosmetics	3.2	3.1	3.3
Other	2.6	1.4	4.1
Total	**23.1**	**16.7**	**30.2**

Source: *Ullmann's Encyclopedia of Industrial Chemistry*, vol. 33, section 15, Table 2.

Figure 3.41 Market for Cosmetic Products in the United States, Japan, and Europe (2005)

The manufacture of cosmetics is currently dominated by a small number of multinational corporations that were founded in the early twentieth century, but the distribution and sale of cosmetics is spread among a wide range of different businesses. As of 2004, the top 100 cosmetics manufacturing firms worldwide had a combined market share of $124.5 billion, of which the five largest – L'Oréal Group ($17.7 billion), Procter & Gamble Company ($16.5 billion), Unilever ($9.3 billion), Shiseido Company Limited ($5.9 billion), and Estée Lauder Companies, Inc. ($5.8 billion)[10] – accounted for 44 percent or $55.2 billion. There were many worldwide distribution channels for cosmetics manufacturers to choose from, including department stores, mass merchandisers, drug stores, TV shopping networks, internet retailers, distributors, supermarkets, and salons.

Due to a large portion of the cosmetics industry power being concentrated among a few large companies who all possess significant resources, competition among leading cosmetics manufacturers is fierce. A deep understanding of the drivers of consumer demand (fashion trends, demographics, and consumer spending) is needed to build successful brand portfolios, engage positively with consumers, and manage available inventory. To capture revenue and market share, cosmetics manufacturers must not only have a clear focus on offering products that are valuable in the eyes of the consumer, but also strategically decide between numerous channels to deliver their products to these consumers in an effective manner.

---

[8] 2007 average Euro to US$ = 1.37, www.oanda.com/currency/average, accessed June 20, 2013. All monetary amounts are in US dollars unless stated otherwise.

[9] Inflation adjusted. "Cosmetic Industry," Statista Dossier, 2012; "Cosmetic & Beauty Products Manufacturing in the US," 2011, *IBISWorld*, p. 31.

[10] "The Beauty – Top 100," *WWD Beauty Report International*, available at www.scribd.com/doc/3027409/Top-100-Cosmetic-Manufacturers, accessed July 8, 2013.

Since consumer perception heavily impacts revenue generation, it is common to see dominant cosmetics players enter into licensing agreements or conduct acquisitions in order to obtain brands or to gain access to preferred distribution channels. The structure of these agreements and acquisitions can have a direct effect on materials management. For example, in terms of obtaining brands, Elizabeth Arden acquired Liz Claiborne's fragrance portfolio in 2008, structured as a long-term licensing deal whereby Elizabeth Arden acquired inventory and hard assets and would pay a royalty stream to Liz Claiborne. In terms of obtaining distribution, a US fragrance manufacturer, Inter Parfums Inc., signed a four-year licensing agreement with the clothing company Gap for international distribution of personal care products through Gap and Banana Republic stores in the United States and abroad, as well as in select specialty and department stores internationally.[11] A ranking of the top 10 personal care brands and their respective brand value is available in Figure 3.42.

Top 10 Personal Care Brands (2008)				
Rank	Brand	Parent Company	Brand Value* ($B)	Brand Momentum**
1	Gillette	Procter & Gamble	18	7.5
2	L'Oréal	L'Oréal	12.3	6.5
3	Colgate	Colgate-Palmolive	7.7	5
4	Avon	Avon Products Inc.	6.6	5.5
5	Garnier	L'Oréal	4.2	5
6	Nivea	Beiersdorf	3.2	4.5
7	Lancôme	L'Oréal	3.1	6.5
8	OralB	Procter & Gamble	2.6	5.5
9	Crest	Procter & Gamble	2.3	5.5
10	Olay	Procter & Gamble	2.3	6

Notes:
* Brand value is the sum of all earnings that a brand is expected to generate.
** Brand momentum is an index of a brand's short-term (one-year) growth rate compared to the average short-term growth rate of all brands in the ranking.
Source: Millward Brown Optimor (including data from Brandz, Datamonitor, Bloomberg), *International Cosmetics News*, June 1, 2008.

Figure 3.42 Top 10 Personal Care Brands (2008) in Broad Category of "Cosmetics"

Unlike cosmetics manufacturers, suppliers in the cosmetic industry are very fragmented. Cosmetics supplies must comply with the standards of the Food and Drug Administration (FDA), which defines and regulates the extremely broad category of cosmetics in the United States. Even when considering only the cosmetic chemicals market, hundreds of suppliers provide the broad array of organic and inorganic chemicals that are the essential ingredients of cosmetics and toiletries.[12] To be competitive, suppliers focus on the ability to produce exciting and innovative products, to deliver on time, and to integrate with their clients' supply chain preferences. Also as a result of the abundance of competitors, successful suppliers often seek to

[11] *International Cosmetics News* (ICN), June 1, 2008, p. 8.
[12] See www.ihs.com/products/chemical/planning/scup/cosmetic.aspx, accessed June 20, 2013.

secure long-term relationships and contracts. For instance, Swiss flavour and fragrance manufacturer Givaudan has signed a creative partnership deal with US consumer goods group Colgate-Palmolive that will establish a dedicated team to work directly with Colgate's internal perfumery resources on fragrance development across all categories. Givaudan is hoping the partnership will help it secure a spot on Colgate's list of preferred suppliers.[13] However, large cosmetics manufacturers may not necessarily favour long-term contracts due to the cost savings associated with lower prices when many suppliers compete for business.

Given the fierce rivalry in cosmetics manufacturing as well as the abundance of both channels and suppliers, operational success in the international cosmetics industry is increasingly dependent upon the ability to handle complexity in addition to effective brand management. Not only must companies align their operations in a way that allows them to benefit from multiple upstream and downstream choices in the cosmetics value chain, they must be able to do so in a way that capitalizes on the fast-moving trends of the international cosmetics market. For instance, sales of prestige beauty products, primarily sold in department stores, dropped 3 percent following a fifteen-year low in US consumer confidence at the end of 2007.[14] However, despite weaker than normal global market conditions, Brazil's cosmetics and toiletries industry is the second fastest growing market worldwide, with a growth of nearly 14 percent in 2007.[15]

Elizabeth Arden Inc. Elizabeth Arden established the modern concept of the US beauty industry a century ago. Born Florence Nightingale Graham, she traveled from rural Canada to New York City, where she opened her company, initially named the "Red Door" salon, on Fifth Avenue in 1910. Her fundamental belief was that beauty should not be a veneer of make-up, but an intelligent cooperation between science and nature in order to develop a woman's finest natural assets. She lived by her mantra, "To be beautiful is the birthright of every woman."[16] She was largely responsible for establishing make-up as proper and appropriate, even necessary, for a ladylike image, when before it had often been associated with lower classes and such professions as prostitution. She targeted middle-aged and plain women for whom beauty products promised a youthful, beautiful image.[17]

Elizabeth Arden's company grew from a small start-up to an international corporate success. It was acquired in the 1970s for $38 million by the pharmaceutical company Eli Lilly & Co. It changed hands twice more before 1990, when Unilever PLC purchased it. Unilever then sold it in 2001 to French Fragrances, Inc. (FFI), a perfume marketer that dealt in prestige as well as mass-market products. FFI paid approximately $190 million in cash for Elizabeth Arden, plus an exchange of stock that gave Unilever an approximately 18 percent stake in the publicly owned company. Shortly after the acquisition, FFI changed its name to Elizabeth Arden, Inc.[18]

Since its inception, Elizabeth Arden had become one of the world's leading makers of prestige perfumes and cosmetics, goods that were sold in over ninety countries worldwide, with major markets in the United States and Europe. Examples of brands included Elizabeth Taylor's White

---

[13] *International Cosmetics News* (ICN), June 1, 2008.

[14] See www.marketoracle.co.uk/Article3859.html, accessed June 20, 2013.

[15] See www.klinegroup.com/news/speeches/cosmeceuticals-27jun08.pdf, accessed September 14, 2013.

[15] See www.klinegroup.com/news/speeches/cosmeceuticals-27jun08.pdf, accessed September 14, 2013.

[16] See corporate.elizabetharden.com/about-elizabeth-arden/, accessed June 20, 2013.

[17] See womenshistory.about.com/od/fashion20th/p/elizabeth_arden.htm, accessed June 20, 2013.

[18] See www.fundinguniverse.com/company-histories/elizabeth-arden-inc-history/, accessed June 20, 2013.

Diamonds, White Shoulders, Red Door, 5th Avenue, Visible Difference, and Millenium. However, sales were in decline by the turn of the century – annual sales were estimated at $890 million, well below the company's peak in the early 1990s – and under new ownership, things were about to change.

Situation in 2007. Under the direction of Chairman and Chief Executive Officer (CEO) Scott Beattie, fiscal 2007 was a milestone for Elizabeth Arden as it surpassed $1 billion in net sales. Total net sales increased by 18.1 percent to a record $1.127 billion, and reported earnings per diluted share grew 18.2 percent to $1.30 from $1.10.[19] Main contributions to this net sales were from North American fragrances (23 percent), international businesses (12 percent), and branded skin care and color cosmetics (16 percent). Select financial information can be found in Figure 3.43.

This achievement was driven by the successful integration of two strategic acquisitions in the year, continued successful innovation on product offerings, and further expansion and development of international markets. The company aimed to continue this progress and to grow from approximately $1.2 to $2 billion in the next three years. However, a top-line focus was not in itself sufficient; the company must drive operational results and increase value for its shareholders. As CEO Beattie stated in the 2007 annual report:

> Our business strategy is to grow our brand portfolio by investing behind our core brands and to acquire control of and develop additional prestige brands through brand development, acquisitions and new licensing and distribution agreements . . . We are also focused on improving our cash flow and operating margins, particularly through improving our extended supply chain and logistics functions, managing the advertising spend behind our new fragrance launches and leveraging our global overhead structure more efficiently.

Elizabeth Arden offered more than 400 prestige fragrance, skin care, and cosmetic brands to retailers in the United States,[20] including department stores such as Macy's, Dillard's Saks, JCPenney, Belk, and Nordstroms; mass retailers such as Walmart, Target, Sears, Kohl's, Walgreens, Rite-Aid, and CVS; and international retailers such as Sephora, Marionnaud, Hudson's Bay, Shoppers Drug Mart, Myer, and Douglas, as well as several travel outlets. It also sold online via e-commerce. In 2007, the ten largest customers accounted for more than 39 percent of net sales; the only customer that accounted for more than 10 percent of net sales was Walmart (Sam's Club).[21] See Figure 3.44 for categories of customers and their respective contribution to 2007 net sales. As was customary in the industry, Elizabeth Arden generally did not have long-term or exclusive contracts with retail customers, but relied instead on purchase orders.

The cosmetics industry competed primarily on brand strength, merchandise selection, reliable order fulfilment, and delivery. Elizabeth Arden therefore focused on product recognition, quality, performance, price, and providing value-added services to certain retailers (e.g., category management services).

---

[19] Elizabeth Arden Annual Report 2007.

[20] Of Elizabeth Arden's distribution, 100 prestige brands were owned or licensed and 300 additional prestige fragrance brands were manufactured by other beauty companies.

[21] Walmart (including Sam's Club) represented approximately 15 percent of consolidated net sales and approximately 25 percent of the North American fragrance segment net sales.

	Year Ended June 30		
	2007	2006	2005
Selected Statement of Income Data			
Net sales*	$1,127,476	$954,550	$920,538
Gross profit	$461,319	$404,072	$411,364
Income (loss) from operations	$74,006	$68,257	$78,533
Debt extinguishment charges	$–	$758	$–
Net income (loss)	$37,334	$32,794	$37,604
Accretion and dividend on preferred stock	$–	$–	$–
Accelerated accretion on converted preferred stock	$–	$–	$–
Net income (loss) attributable to common shareholders	$37,334	$32,794	$37,604
Selected Per Share Data			
Earnings (loss) per common share			
Basic	$1.35	$1.15	$1.35
Diluted	$1.30	$1.10	$1.25
Weighted average number of common shares			
Basic	27,607	28,628	27,792
Diluted	28,826	29,818	30,025
Other Data			
EBITDA**	$98,524	$89,608	$100,038
Net cash from operating activities	$58,816	$65,276	$35,549
Net cash from investing activities	$110,518	$24,335	$17,508
Net cash provided by (used in) financing activities	$53,120	$(37,584)	$(15,785)
	Year Ended June 30		
	2007	**2006**	**2005**
Selected Balance Sheet Data			
Cash	$30,287	$28,466	$25,316
Inventories	$380,232	$569,270	$273,343
Working capital	$298,165	$280,942	$275,628
Total assets	$939,175	$759,903	$719,897
Short-term debt	$97,640	$40,000	$47,700
Long-term debt, including current portion	$225,655	$225,951	$233,802
Convertible, redeemable preferred stock	$–	$–	$–
Shareholders' equity	$320,927	$277,847	$259,200

Notes:
* Comparison of US and international net sales = 63:37 (2007), 60:40 (2006), 62:38 (2005).
** EBITDA: earnings before interest, taxes, depreciation, and amortization. *Source:* Company files.

Figure 3.43 Select Financial Data (in $ Thousands)

The challenge of translating growth into profit. In 2007, the supply chain was performing suboptimally when compared with both industry benchmarks and internal aspirations.[22] For instance, logistics costs (i.e., distribution, outbound freight), as well as supply chain overhead (i.e., demand and materials planning labour, purchasing labour), had been increasing as a percentage of

[22] Company files.

Region	SBU*	Total FY06 Sales ('000)	No. of Customers in SBU	No. of Customers Making up Top 80% of SBU Sales	Percent of Total SBU
North America	**Mass**	$483,647	361	17	5%
	Prestige	$182,065	82	23	28%
	Department Store Fragrance Group	$59,593	127	4	3%
International	**All Other**	$317,073	2,016	177	9%
TOTAL		**$1,042,378**	**2,586**	**242 [sic]**	**9%**

Note:
* SBU: strategic business unit.
Source: Company files.

Figure 3.44 Elizabeth Arden Customer Breakdown by Sales Volume (2007)

net sales. The existing supply chain processes and infrastructure were determined to be manually intensive and inefficient and created an unnecessary amount of low-value-added work. However, even though these processes were necessary for the business at that moment, focus would have to be on a fundamental shift in the operating model for the future. It was clear that this change wasn't just a supply chain initiative, but rather a transformation of Elizabeth Arden, involving more pieces of the company.

Since being hired a little less than a year earlier, Pirard had already completed improvements on production planning and sales forecasting. Forecasting and demand planning at Elizabeth Arden had been tedious and focused on the short term without extensive use of market intelligence and strategic account management. The company had been using a forecasting practice that enabled each division along a product delivery chain to add its own contingencies to forecasted numbers. This led to overestimation of necessary product as contingencies accumulated, with only 33 percent of the top 100 stock-keeping units (SKUs) in FY2006 forecasting "well" (within plus or minus 25 percent error), resulting in a total accuracy of only 70.5 percent. To improve the inventory accuracy and order fulfillment rate, Pirard utilized a single, more accurate forecast and sold off slow and obsolete products to make room for faster moving SKUs.

Although progress was being made, Pirard knew that the internal process improvements conducted to date would not be sufficient for Elizabeth Arden to meet the expectation of CEO Beattie and the board. He believed that a complete re-engineering initiative would be necessary, centering on a "turnkey strategy." In this new approach, Elizabeth Arden would seek to consolidate suppliers and the suppliers that remained would be given additional responsibility for undertaking the entire manufacturing process from materials procurement to product completion. Ideally, this would enable Elizabeth Arden to simplify procurement efforts. However, Pirard was concerned about the enormity of this change and wondered how to best approach the transformation.

Manufacturing, supply chain, and logistics. *Materials management:* Elizabeth Arden used independent suppliers to obtain substantially all raw materials, components, and packaging products and contract fillers to manufacture finished products relating to owned and licensed brands. As was customary in its industry, Elizabeth Arden also generally did not have long-term or exclusive agreements with contract manufacturers.[23] Purchases were made through purchase orders, and Elizabeth Arden believed it maintained a good relationship with numerous manufacturers of brands and, although costly, could replace manufacturers should some become unavailable.

Since individual purchase orders were made to many independent suppliers, Elizabeth Arden had to assume the responsibility of orchestrating a large portion of the product completion process. For instance, for a bottle of perfume, Elizabeth Arden bought the fragrance, pump, box, glass, cellophane wrap, and label separately from six independent suppliers and then had all these purchased materials shipped to a third-party manufacturer. After the third-party manufacturing was completed, Elizabeth Arden then arranged for the finished product to be shipped to either distribution centers around the world or directly to a customer. In an effort to minimize logistics complexity and reduce delivery time, "drop shipping" (sending the product directly from source to customer) was used wherever possible. Although Elizabeth Arden hoped to be more flexible and have lower risk with a diversified independent supplier base, Pirard was concerned that the orchestration efforts detracted from the company's strategic strengths.

In 2007, material and indirect purchases of $350 million[24] were converted into more than 9,000 items of finished goods SKUs. At a quick glance, 12 percent of SKUs sold in 2006 made up 80 percent of total sales (see Figure 3.45). A high level of complexity and customization in addition to the numerous SKUs put a burden on the fulfillment group, especially given that 12.2 million customized units represented only 17 percent of total 2007 unit volume. In addition, Pirard was concerned that even though direct spend from purchasing was increasingly concentrated with the Top 10 suppliers[25] (see Figure 3.46), it was not translating into volume benefits. In FY2007, the top 10 suppliers were estimated to represent 40 percent of all items purchased.

1–10	11–20	21–30	31–40
CURIOUS	PROVOCATIVE	HALSTON Z14	IN CONTROL
WHITE DIAMONDS	TOMMY GIRL	DESIGN LADIES	RED DOOR REVEALED
FANTASY	DRAKKAR NOIR	TRUE STAR	OTHER CHEEK
RED DOOR	FIFTH AVENUE AFTER 5	BLOCKBUSTER	ARDEN CORP/ COFFRET
SIGNATURE	TOMMY BOY	OTHER EYE	ETERNITY LADIES
CERAMIDE SKINCARE	EIGHT HOUR	MILLENIUM	OTHER MAKE-UP
FOUNDATION	SUNFLOWERS	ARDENBEAUTY	POLO SPORT MEN
5TH AVENUE	PAUL SEBASTIAN	COFFRET WOMEN	A/ANAIS
GREEN TEA	LIPSTICK	WHITE SHOULDERS	ETERNITY MENS
PREVAGE	PASSION WOMEN	PROVOCATIVE INTERLUDE	OSCAR LADIES

Source: Company files.

Figure 3.45 Elizabeth Arden Top 40 Selling Brands in FY2006

[23] Exception: Cosmetic Essence Inc. (third-party) manufacturing agreement ending January 31, 2010.
[24] As of January 2008.
[25] Top 10 suppliers, by volume order: Jackel, Matic Plast, IFF, Pochet, Givaudan, Arkay Packaging, Heinz, Rexam, Quest, and Interasia.

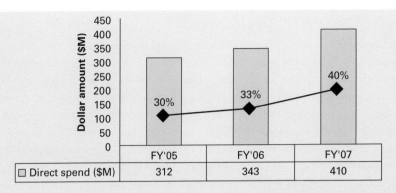

FY2007 amount was a forecast based on the quarterly spend pattern of FY2006, materials and indirect purchases actually amounted to $350 million as of January 2008. Source: Company files.

Figure 3.46 Percentage of Total Direct Spend in the Top 10 Suppliers (April 2007)

The high level of customization, slow-moving SKUs, and long lead times all led to extremely large inventory levels. Inventory days of supply (DOS) were 225 days, well above the industry standard (approximately $340 million inventory investment). Finished goods alone accounted for 120 DOS. Inventory carrying costs were estimated to be 4.2 percent of net sales and 7.2 percent of cost of goods sold (COGS). Furthermore, almost 30 percent of unit volume forecast changes occurred within the supply lead time period, which drove logistic costs well above average. In 2007, Elizabeth Arden spent $3.2 million on airfreight costs and 0.3 percent of sales on materials planning. Despite the high level of inventory and an increase in the expediting of finished goods, the current fill rate was only 85 percent, 10 percent below the industry.

Although Pirard had already done some work to improve the fill rate by focusing on selling off some slow-moving SKUs to make room for faster-moving products, he was still very concerned with the very poor fill rate. He wondered how the re-engineering effort could not only further alleviate fill rate concerns, but also help address the multitude of other materials management problems. How much impact could this re-engineering have on delivering bottom-line operational results?

Organizational design and full-time equivalents (FTE). As of September 4, 2007, Elizabeth Arden had approximately 2,250 full-time employees and approximately 600 part-time employees in the United States and seventeen foreign countries. Within the scope of the supply chain re-engineering, there were 217 full-time equivalents (FTEs) across eighteen locations and six process areas (see Figure 3.47).

Pirard was worried about the very manual and labour-intensive purchasing process – buyers spent most of their time on purchase order generation and expediting for both the individual components and finished goods, leaving limited time for strategic sourcing and value analysis. There was also no centralized management to perform strategic purchasing, resulting in a high direct material spend and an inability to consolidate spend across brands/commodities and utilize volume leverage to negotiate better pricing with suppliers. Pirard was concerned that this purchasing issue might only get worse as changes to the organization unfolded.

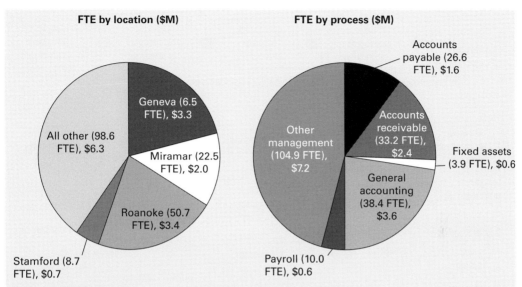

FTE = Total dedicated staff + documented part-time staff contributions: 217 in-scope FTEs.
Source: Company files.

Figure 3.47 Full-Time Equivalents (FTEs) Breakdown by Location and Process

Elizabeth Arden's organizational design was functionally organized with employees interacting through hand-offs. For example, departments included demand planning, generic supply planning, confined supply planning, and raw material planning (see Figure 3.48). In anticipation of the supply chain re-engineering effort, examples of transactional processes performed by employees can be found in Figure 3.49. It had already been determined that a more "customer-oriented" approach to the organizational design might align more with a turnkey approach (e.g., in the Skin & Color Department). Pirard wondered if employees could handle the ambitious rapid re-engineering effort and, if so, what the best way of managing the workforce to deliver the expected results would be.

Moving forward. Beattie had hired Pirard because he knew he could make the necessary changes. The supply chain needed work, and there were many areas of proposed improvement that included, but were not limited to: enhancing the effectiveness of demand management; developing a more collaborative, turn-key approach with key suppliers; simplifying material flows and collaborations with key accounts; utilizing strategic sourcing; and developing more cross-functional ability. However, many questions still remained unanswered with regard to Pirard's task of carrying out the re-engineering and turning Elizabeth Arden's tremendously successful growth into operating results. Pirard wondered which execution initiatives should be prioritized. Would the execution of the re-engineering vary by product type (e.g., glass sourcing versus fragrance sourcing)? Also, would the organizational design change and, if so, how much would it change and what would the end result look like? Would the savings be direct savings, indirect savings, or both?

Pirard knew that the supply chain re-engineering effort would be critical to the future success of Elizabeth Arden – more importantly, he knew that how he chose to execute the changes to the various components to the supply chain would directly affect the level of impact that the effort

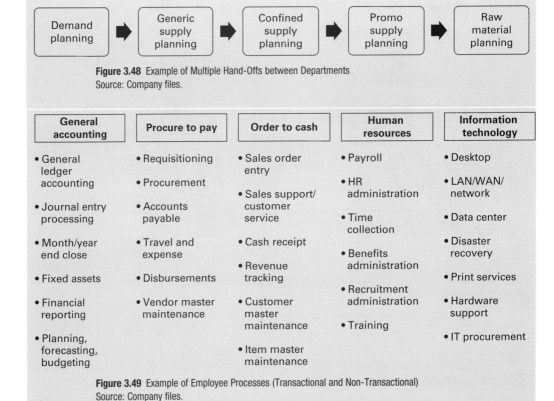

Figure 3.48 Example of Multiple Hand-Offs between Departments
Source: Company files.

General accounting	Procure to pay	Order to cash	Human resources	Information technology
• General ledger accounting	• Requisitioning	• Sales order entry	• Payroll	• Desktop
	• Procurement	• Sales support/ customer service	• HR administration	• LAN/WAN/ network
• Journal entry processing	• Accounts payable		• Time collection	• Data center
• Month/year end close	• Travel and expense	• Cash receipt	• Benefits administration	• Disaster recovery
• Fixed assets	• Disbursements	• Revenue tracking	• Recruitment administration	• Print services
• Financial reporting	• Vendor master maintenance	• Customer master maintenance	• Training	• Hardware support
• Planning, forecasting, budgeting		• Item master maintenance		• IT procurement

Figure 3.49 Example of Employee Processes (Transactional and Non-Transactional)
Source: Company files.

would have. He wanted to remain "results oriented" and therefore be able to tie the supply chain strategy to quantifiable outcomes. He turned his attention to three main questions in the turnkey strategy: how to effectively manage the consolidation of suppliers; how to execute the optimal organizational structure for this change; and, lastly, how to maximize the monetary impact of the re-engineering for Elizabeth Arden and its shareholders. How much money would be saved; where would the savings come from; and when would they be realized?

Questions

1. Analyze the differences between the current supply chain and the proposed turnkey strategy. What will the change mean for suppliers and their roles? What will it mean for current employees and their roles?
2. Calculate the total financial impact for the re-engineering effort. What does this mean for Elizabeth Arden and its shareholders?
3. Assuming the role of Pierre Pirard, what would you do and why?
4. Which concepts have you learned in this chapter that you can apply to analyzing the case? Explain in detail.
5. How can the company's supply chain strategy help the company implement its corporate strategy successfully?

Part II

Structural Dimension of Supply Chain Management

CHAPTER 4

Supply Chain Configuration and Connection

In Chapter 3, we defined supply chain management and its key dimensions. In this chapter, we discuss the first two elements of the structural dimension, i.e., configuration and connection. **Configuration** is about *what*, *where*, and *how much*, whereas **connection** is about *how to relate diverse supply chain activities* scattered across the supply chain. Throughout the book, we regard the **chief executive officer** (**CEO**) as the key **decision-maker** (**DM**) in an organization. As such, we use the two terms, CEO and DM, interchangeably. The key decision-maker at a company is expected to make decisions that enable the company to perform exceptionally in managing the supply chain. Configuration and connection are part of such critical decisions.

Key Learning Points

- Decision hierarchy shows how corporate strategy is implemented through business strategy and its associated planning steps. In turn, every element or step in the decision hierarchy is affected by various forms of uncertainty.
- The goal of supply chain management is to improve the performance of the supply chain, i.e., to maximize both efficiency-driven and responsiveness-driven values at the same time.
- Customer feels satisfied when she believes that she is receiving a distinctive "value" from the product and service provided by the company.
- The first decision element in the structural dimension of supply chain designing is configuration, which calls for several key questions to answer, e.g., what (product or service), where (location), and how much (capacity).
- Once configuration of the supply chain is decided, the decision-maker should define an informational relationship among the supply chain functions, i.e., how to connect or link the supply chain activities, which are physically or geographically scattered according to the configuration decision, in order to achieve the goal most effectively.

學 WISDOM BOX 4.1
Wisdom and Insights

Designing a Supply Chain
ReignCom (now known as iriver; www.iriver.com) was a rapidly growing Korean company that sold MP3 players. In 2003, it enjoyed a 52 percent market share in Korea and almost 25 percent worldwide. In order to make and sell an MP3 player, there were several steps involved, such as developing a new product concept, designing, fabricating, and distributing (Figure 4.1). First, ReignCom developed a concept for its new MP3 player model, but didn't do the entire **designing**. Instead, it outsourced the "**outer design**" to an industrial design company, **INNO Design** in Silicon Valley, California.

Once the external design was done and returned to ReignCom, the company started the "**inner design**" that drew the circuits of electronic parts inside the case body of the MP3 player. Hence, the inner design should be made congruent with the outer design, not the other way around!

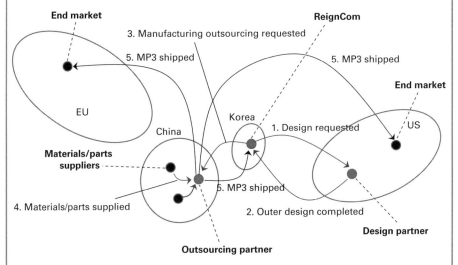

Figure 4.1 Designing a Supply Chain at ReignCom

With the outer and inner design completed, ReignCom made a **prototype** of the MP3 player and sent it along with detailed design blueprints to AV Chaseway in China, which was a manufacturing **outsourcing** partner for ReignCom. Most of ReignCom's MP3 players were fabricated in the plant at AV Chaseway. ReignCom viewed its relationship with AV Chaseway as strategic – the **outsourcing contract** was not just based on a short-term transaction, rather it was strongly based on mutual trust and supported by ReignCom's extensive investment in AV Chaseway's operations. AV Chaseway, in turn, had its own suppliers, who provided the company with raw materials and key parts essential for manufacturing the MP3 players.

Box continues

Completed MP3 players were shipped to customer markets around the world. In fact, the United States was the largest market for ReignCom's MP3 players. Such players were very popular also in Korea and China. Some of the company's products sold in the European Union market as well. Who shipped these MP3 players to the markets around the globe? Integrated logistics companies like **UPS** and **FedEx** were doing the job. ReignCom decided which logistics company to employ by taking into account such factors as transportation costs, inventory levels in each market, timing of sales seasons in the markets, production schedules at AV Chaseway, competitors' moves, and so forth.

Questions
1. How did ReignCom create value?
2. How could its supply chain strategy be characterized?
3. Why did the company develop the particular configuration for its supply chain? What were the reasons for the company to develop the particular sequence of transactions/activities described in Figure 4.1?
4. What were the advantages and disadvantages of the supply chain strategy implemented by ReignCom?

4.1   Decision Horizon

Before considering key decision elements, the decision-maker should understand the **decision horizon**, i.e., **decision time frame**, associated with each decision. At the very top of the company, the CEO has to decide the firm's overall strategic direction (**corporate strategy**), which generally involves very long-term planning. Once the company has developed a well-designed long-term strategy, it can decide on business strategy; e.g., each business division should have its own long-term strategy that must be consistent with and supportive of the corporate strategy.

For a **business strategy**, we focus on the operations division. The decision-maker in the operations division should design the overall operations systems to effectively perform value-creating activities. Among other things, she must decide what kind of **product** the system should produce and what kind of **process** the system must employ to produce the product; i.e., the product and process planning. Once the decision on product and process is made, the decision-maker needs to start **capacity planning** – the physical capacity of the production system, its location, operating rules, and the like. The decisions so far are relatively long term and thus strategic, involving substantial resource commitment.

Given these strategic conditions, the decision-maker can start an **aggregate planning**, which translates "strategic goals and visions" into working sub-plans, through which the actual tasks are conducted within an intermediate, say annual or quarterly, decision time horizon. This is the backbone of overall operations activities. Based on the aggregate planning, the decision-maker can develop a **master production scheduling** followed by a **material requirements planning** (MRP) and finally by a detailed order scheduling for manufacturing, or an intermediate and short-term workforce planning for service

Figure 4.2 Decision Hierarchy

operations. Stages from the aggregate planning to MRP or the intermediate workforce planning form the medium-range decision time horizon, whereas the detailed order or workforce scheduling is a short-term planning process. Figure 4.2 depicts the **hierarchical relationship** among these strategic planning processes.

Key factors to consider and types of uncertainty. At each stage of the decision hierarchy, there are several key factors the decision-maker must consider (Figure 4.3). For the corporate strategy, the CEO (i.e., the decision-maker) must conduct a strategic competitive analysis by taking into account macroeconomic and industry level trends, which have a significant and long-term impact on the market as a whole. In developing a business strategy for operations, the decision-maker has to pay keen attention to significant changes in the markets and customers, which include dynamics of technological innovation and various dimensions in managing the supply chain. After properly understanding the **market dynamics**, the DM must decide on target products and processes to make the products, and also the physical structures such as capacity of the processes, by taking into account the long-term demand trends that determine the firm's product mix strategy. From this long-term demand pattern, the DM needs to develop the aggregate planning that translates the annual and/or quarterly demand into

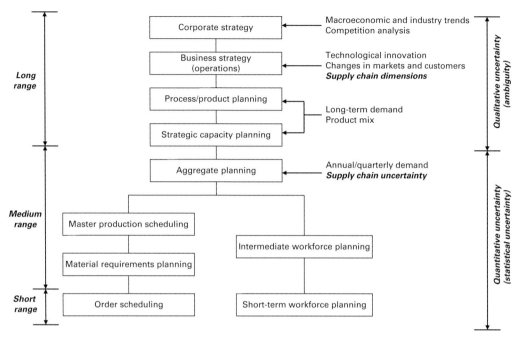

Figure 4.3 Decision Hierarchy and Decision Time Horizon

feasible work plans, each of which can be implemented realistically under the current system's conditions affected by the various uncertainties in the supply chain.

In fact, uncertainty involves every stage of the decision hierarchy. Since strategic and long-term decisions are vulnerable to macroeconomic and industry-level changes, which are in many cases well beyond a single firm's control, high-level decisions must deal with "ill-structured" uncertainties, which we define as "qualitative uncertainties." **Ambiguity** underlies these ill-structured uncertainties. These uncertainties affect not only the highest planning stage – corporate strategy – but also most of the long-range decision-making, including business strategy, product/process planning, and strategic capacity planning.

For the medium- and short-range planning, the DM has in general more data and information than can be readily applicable. Therefore, the decision-making process becomes more systematic in the sense that more analytical and systematic formal methods are available. This should not imply that this decision-making is immune to uncertainty. There remains uncertainty, but of different types. For the relatively shorter decision horizons, the uncertainties are in general well-structured in that the DM can formalize her assumptions about the uncertainty, such as its probabilistic distribution. We define these uncertainties as "quantitative, i.e., quantifiable uncertainties" or "statistical uncertainties." One of the most striking differences between ambiguity and statistical uncertainty is that the DM can reasonably reconstruct the formal and probabilistic shape (distribution) of the statistical uncertainty, whereas she has no clue about the reliable probability distribution for the ambiguity (Figure 4.4). Thus, the DM needs

(a) Ambiguity – *which distribution?*

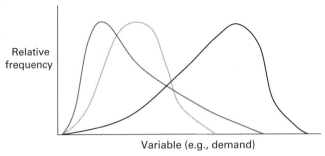

Relative frequency

Variable (e.g., demand)

(b) Statistical uncertainty – *how much probability given the distribution?*

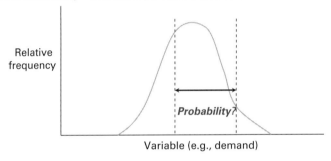

Relative frequency

Probability?

Variable (e.g., demand)

Figure 4.4 Ambiguity and Statistical Uncertainty

qualitative and sometimes judgmental methods to make a decision, when faced with ambiguity.

4.2   Decision-Making Factors in the Supply Chain

The goal of SCM is to improve the performance of the supply chain, more specifically, *to maximize both efficiency-driven and responsiveness-driven values concurrently.* Then, *how can the DM design her supply chain strategy to accomplish this goal?* In this section, we consider critical performance measures for the supply chain and discuss key decision variables the DM must take into account when developing her supply chain strategy.

4.2.1   Performance Measures for Effective SCM

The first and most important performance measurement of SCM is customer satisfaction. Figure 4.5 presents the simplest form of a supply chain consisting of supply function → manufacturing (transformation) → distribution function → end-customer market. The chain encompassing supplier, manufacturer, and distributor constitutes the **supply chain system**, which must function harmoniously under the most ideal condition of complete coordination. The primary point of Figure 4.5 is that substantive values must

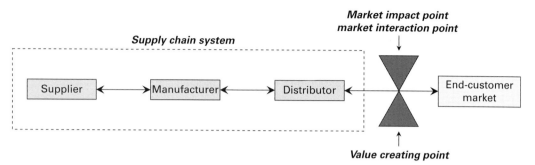

Figure 4.5 A Simplified Model of a Supply Chain System

be created at the market interaction (or impact) point at which the supply chain system faces or interacts with the end-customer market, in order to have a sustainable supply chain partnership. Recall Figure 1.3, which showed that the primary value created at the market interaction point is "*responsiveness-driven.*"

Of course, any improvement between the supply chain system's partners can be regarded as "value creation." Suppose that the manufacturing company is able to negotiate a lower supply cost from its supplier: note that it is an example of efficiency-driven value as in Figure 1.3. This lower supply cost will improve the manufacturer's profitability. But, this relationship can't be sustainable unless the supplier gets additional value from lowering the supply cost. One way for the manufacturer to help its supplier to realize more value is to support, say, subsidize, the supplier's quality improvement efforts. It is a give-and-take relationship. Then, in the long run, the sum of the manufacturer's profit and the supplier's profit would remain the same, unless their coordination generates more sales in the end market – the end-customers become more willing to pay for the same products and/or to buy more of the products. In this respect, we suggest that the real value for the supply chain system as a whole must be created at the market. Therefore, the most important criterion of performance improvement is the end-customer satisfaction.

In turn, the concept of **customer satisfaction** itself is a very comprehensive one. How can a firm tell that its customers are satisfied? Customers will feel satisfied when they believe that they receive a distinctive "value" from the products and services provided by the company. The value (v) is defined as $v = \dfrac{\text{Utility}}{\text{Price}}$. The utility is a function of diverse factors such as a core product's *functionality, quality,* and *services*. More intuitively, we put forth that "utility" comes from "happiness" the customer feels from consuming the product or service made by the firm. That is, the happier the customer, the larger the utility.

The core product's **functionality** can be measured by the extent the product performs as expected by the customer (product performance). Suppose the customer bought a car. Then, the functionality of the product is related with transporting the customer from one place to another. The difficulty in defining functionality lies in that customers often require more than just basic functionality. For instance, a customer wants to have safe transportation, whereas another customer might want to have a comfortable ride.

As a result, the core product's functionality is something that initially and primarily motivated the customer to buy the product. But, the utility is something the customer enjoys during the entire life of the product, not just at the time of purchase. Therefore, the functionality is in many cases a necessary condition, not a sufficient condition for customer satisfaction. In addition to the core product's functionality, **quality** is also important in determining the utility the customer enjoys by using the product (or service). It is a composite concept, which is dependent on the context as well as the customer's unique preference system. The concept of quality seems widely understood, yet is still very elusive. Garvin[1] suggests eight dimensions of quality:

- performance
- features
- reliability
- conformance
- durability
- serviceability
- aesthetics
- perceived quality

As mentioned above, the first dimension, the performance that refers to primary operating characteristics of the product, constitutes the essence of the core functionality. In view of this relationship between quality and functionality, we put forth that the quality dimensions except for the performance are peripheral or supportive functionalities, which enhance the utility of the product as perceived by the customer since they fulfill complementary desires the customer wants to have from utilizing the product in addition to the essential, yet very basic, performance – the core functionality. In this book, we see quality consisting of seven dimensions among the eight originally summarized by Garvin.[2]

The core functionality and the quality dimensions are specifically linked with the product's characteristics. On the contrary, the product's **services** constitute the logistical, informational, and organizational supports for the core product in order to help the customer to start utilizing the product faster, more reliably, and more efficiently. For example, the company could improve its customer interaction when it gets customer orders, delivers the product, tracks the product's usage, and responds to the customer's changing needs in relation to her continuous utilization of the product until the end of the product's life cycle. These are involved in customer **order fulfillment** processes, **after-service** implementations, product **recycling**, and the like. These services will surely help the customer to be satisfied with the product; hence, more utility will be generated from the customer's viewpoint.

The **price** represents several things. One is concerned with the company's operating capability. If the company operates more efficiently, it has more room to reduce the price. Sometimes companies try to undersell their products even when their operations are not very efficient. In this book, we will discuss important issues connected with how to

---

[1] Garvin, D. A., *Managing Quality: The Strategic and Competitive Edge* (New York: The Free Press, 1988).
[2] Ibid.

improve the company's operations capability. For the purpose of understanding the value function, it suffices to say that the price is determined by both market forces and the company's internal operations capability.

Therefore, given the same price, the more utility the customer enjoys from consuming the goods and services produced by the firm, the more value the customer perceives. Similarly, given the comparable utility, the lower the price, the more value the customer perceives from the goods and services offered by the company.

Now the next question is how the firm can enhance customer satisfaction so that the customers will either demand more or pay more. In order to enhance the end-customer's satisfaction, the DM has to design the supply chain in an optimal way. There are key decision variables, which will determine the performance of the supply chain. We group such variables into two dimensions, *structural* and *infrastructural*.

4.2.2 Structural Dimension

The first dimension of supply chain design is the structural one, which mainly involves physical and/or tangible factors. There are four elements in the **structural dimension**:

- configuration
- connection
- inventory
- logistics

These four elements are closely interrelated with each other, although their relevant time horizons are different (Figure 4.6). We consider two different decision time horizons: *strategic* and *operational*. The **strategic decision** requires heavy resource commitment in the long run – the strategic decision time horizon is critical to the organization in the long term. The strategic decision time horizon implies at least a one-year or longer time span. On the contrary, the **operational decision** is focused on relatively short-term issues, which require fast decision-making, although the resource commitment might not be as significant as that for a strategic decision. In general, the operational decision deals with a time horizon of less than a year.

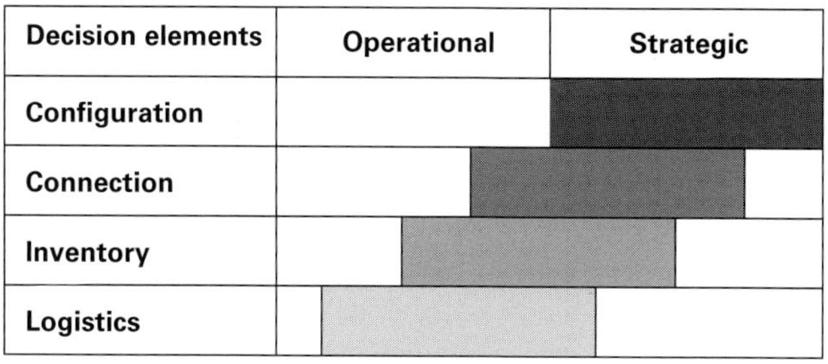

Decision elements	Operational	Strategic
Configuration		
Connection		
Inventory		
Logistics		

Figure 4.6 Structural Elements and Decision Time Horizon

Table 4.1 Characteristics of Configuration and Connection

Element	Key Questions to Answer	Key Factors to Consider
Configuration	• What – which product/service • Where – location, placement • How much – capacity; can increase/ change gradually • Other issues √ Ownership – vertical integration *versus* spot market transaction √ Concentration (integration, economies of scale) *versus* dispersion (differentiation, localization, responsiveness to the local market)	• Investment in physical facility, equipment • Production costs and limitations • Current and long-term possibility to have qualified workforce • Taxes, tariffs, duties and duty drawbacks, tax incentives • Local contents, trading policies • Proximity to markets, input materials • Qualitative factors, including psychological, emotional, political, strategic aspects
Connection	• How to connect/link supply chain activities, which are scattered/ located according to the configuration decision • For example, which supplier supplies which plant, which plant ships product to which distribution center, which distribution center covers which end market	• Strategic fit/compatibility between activities/functions/partners to be linked • Transportation cost, geographic proximity • Uncertainty, i.e., reliability of each activity/function • Time (speed to meet the market's needs), cost, quality • Qualitative factors, including psychological, emotional, political, strategic aspects

Configuration.   This is the first element of the structural dimension in designing a supply chain. As in Table 4.1, a configuration decision calls for several key questions to answer, i.e., *what, where,* and *how much.* The first question is concerned with *"what,"* i.e., *which product or service to produce* through the supply chain. For instance, if the company plans to make automobiles in its supply chain, it should ask a question like: *Which specific models should we make?* It is obvious that the answer to the question *"what"* could change over time as the market conditions vary. In other words, the specific car model to produce can change from one to another as the various conditions vary over time. It implies any configuration decision should be dynamic in nature. Only when the *"what"* part is answered, the company can ask *"where to locate the supply chain functions."* It is basically about the geographic or physical placement of supply chain functions. *Where should we locate our suppliers, plants, distribution centers, and customer markets?* After answering "what" and "where," the company should ask,

How large should each function be? It is essentially an issue of capacity, i.e., *how much capacity to have for each supply chain function.* How much capacity should our supplier have? How much capacity should our manufacturing plant have? How much capacity should our warehouse have? How large should each customer market be? These are the questions to be answered for the question of *how much*.

Regarding configuration, the company should take into account two additional issues. The first one is concerned with the ownership or mode of transaction, i.e., vertical integration versus spot market transaction (Figure 3.6). The other is about the level of concentration. That is *concentrated versus dispersed* configuration. When the company believes it can benefit from a close integration of its supply chain functions and/or capitalize on the economies of scale among its functions/facilities, it would design a concentrated configuration. On the contrary, if the company expects each local market to have unique characteristics and value responsiveness from the company, i.e., a great deal of differentiation or localization is a competitive advantage in each market segment, the company would prefer a dispersed, i.e., decentralized, configuration.

We recapitulate the issues involved with configuration as follows. In essence, configuration is about how to locate the functions of a supply chain across regions, e.g., across the global markets. It is about geographic placement of supply chain functions such as suppliers, inventory warehouses, plants, distribution centers or warehouses, retailers, dealers, and finally target markets (Figure 4.7).

Consider the Hyundai Motor case. Hyundai maintained most of its manufacturing capacity in Korea until very recently. But, the company started globalizing its operations by building plants in foreign countries. Currently, Hyundai has assembling plants in China and also in Alabama in the United States. The company now has its own global manufacturing network consisting of plants in Korea, China, and the United States. Its configuration of manufacturing plants, a function in the supply chain, is the pattern (that is, geographic placement) of its plants throughout different regions in the world.

Once the company has built its new facilities in a particular geographic region, it becomes difficult to physically change its location or make a decision to close it down without paying excessive costs. It is true for any critical functions in the supply chain: suppliers, warehouses, distribution centers, and so on. In addition, the configuration decision requires a huge resource commitment from the company: think about how much it costs for Hyundai to build a plant that could churn out 500,000-plus cars per year. It is obvious that the configuration decision is of a strategic and long-term nature.

In order to make a decision on configuration, the DM has to take into account many factors, as follows:

- How much it costs to invest in physical facilities and equipment, e.g., construction costs.
- How much it costs to establish a business relationship with a partner company for a supply chain function.
- How much it costs to produce the product/service at the physical location or place in point.
- What are the production/functional limitations for a particular configuration?

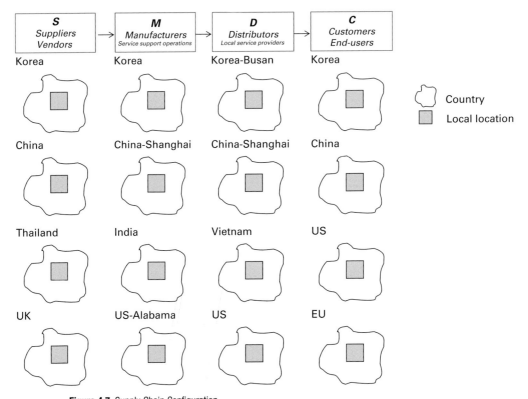

Figure 4.7 Supply Chain Configuration

- Whether the company can have access to qualified workforce, i.e., labor supply, now and in the long run.
- What are the various forms of taxes, such as customs, tariffs, duties and duty drawbacks, and tax incentives, now and in the long run?
- Whether and how the host country government enforces the "local contents" rule.
- What kinds of trading policies the host country government has.
- Whether the company can have an effective access to markets and/or input materials under the configuration it currently considers.
- What impact the qualitative factors, such as psychological, emotional, political, and strategic aspects, have. Note that sometimes these qualitative factors override some of the more objective and quantitative ones. For example, even when a particular location is not appropriate due to an expected high production cost, the company might decide to build a manufacturing plant there since it wants to build a trust-based relationship with the local community, which is a large customer base for the company's other products. Whenever it is possible to quantify these qualitative factors, the company should do so to make the decision as accurately as possible.

When the company tries to answer these questions, it must take into account *not only* the current, *but also* the future trends of each factor. That is, the

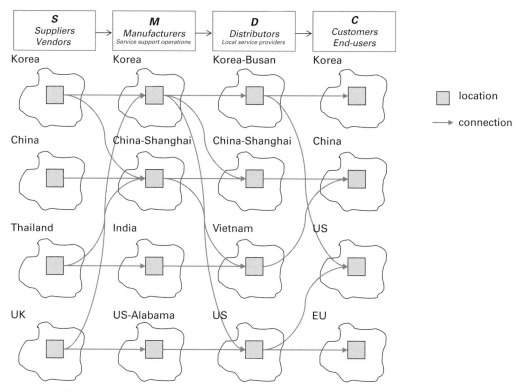

Figure 4.8 Supply Chain Connection

configuration decision should be dynamic, i.e., it should change as the environment evolves over time. After estimating and factoring in all of these issues, the company can decide the most effective configuration and should be ready to dynamically refine it as the market as well as the technological environment changes over time.

Connection. Once the geographic placement of supply chain functions is decided, the DM has to establish an informational relationship between functions (Figure 4.8). That is, she should decide *how to connect/link supply chain activities, which are scattered/located according to the configuration decision.* For instance, which supplier function uses which inventory warehouse, which supplier or inventory warehouse supplies which plant, which plant produces which products and to which distribution center the plant ships the products, and finally which distribution center delivers products to which customer market. There are key factors to take into account when making a decision on the connection, i.e., establishing the connection between adjacent functions:

- **Strategic fit** – it is essential to ensure compatibility between activities, functions, and/or partners to be linked.

- **Logistical factors** – the DM should take into account various transportation options and their associated costs, which are primarily affected by geographic proximity.
- **Uncertainty** – the DM should factor in uncertainty and/or reliability at each supply chain function or activity, e.g., whether the supplier is capable of supplying the materials reliably, whether the manufacturing plant is able to produce the amount demanded by the market on a reliable basis, and so forth.
- **Others** – there are other important factors such as quality and timing or speed, i.e., how fast to meet the market's needs, which is related to the firm's responsiveness as well as flexibility.
- **Qualitative factors** – similar to the configuration decision-making, the company should take into account psychological, emotional, political, and strategic aspects when making a connection decision.

As a factor to consider when determining the connection, flexibility has a strategic implication. Thus, we elaborate on manufacturing process flexibility, which is the firm's capability of coping with uncertainty in the supply chain by adjusting the product mix produced by each plant in this chain. We apply this concept to the element of "connection." Let's focus on the connection between plants and distribution centers, which deal with a single product. The complete "connection flexibility" means each of the plants is linked with every one of the distribution centers in the supply chain (Figure 4.9). Although the complete connection flexibility is supposed to provide the company with the largest benefit from utilizing the flexibility, it can be expensive to achieve this level of completeness. In this regard, the partial connection flexibility would be a more feasible (probably better) option to the company. Figure 4.10 illustrates an example of partial connection flexibility, where each plant is linked with only two distribution centers rather than every distribution center. Our discussion about connection flexibility so far is very abstract in that there are many more factors to consider in the real world. Our goal is to understand the principles of connection flexibility, and knowledge about the fundamental theory will be useful in designing a complicated supply chain connection in the real world. Since the primary motivation for a company to retain flexibility is to cope with uncertainty in the market, the DM must take into account the future, as well as the present, changes in uncertainty in the market when designing the supply chain connection.

Plains   DCs

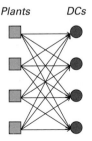

Figure 4.9 Complete Connection Flexibility

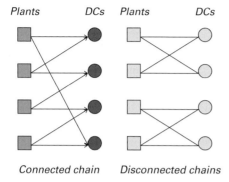

Figure 4.10 Partial Connection Flexibility

It is also necessary to consider the cost implication of a certain design of connection, i.e., a manufacturing network. For instance, connecting plant A and distribution center 1 might be costlier than connecting plant A and distribution center 2, but the A-1 link is affected by less uncertainty than the A-2 link. Then, the question is how to quantify the uncertainty in the same unit of cost so that the DM can compare the two alternatives unambiguously. This is another example of trade-off decision-making.

Like the configuration decision, the firm's decision on connection should be dynamic. That is, the firm must be ready to revise and refine its connection as the competitive, technological, and/or market environment changes over time. The reason is that these changes will surely affect the cost-benefit balance of the factors which the firm should factor in when determining its connection. Although it is mostly strategic, however, the firm's decision on connection is less strategic than the configuration decision, i.e., the decision horizon for connection is shorter than that for configuration. For instance, consider the case of Hyundai Motor. Building an assembly plant in Alabama is a very long-term decision, which the company cannot revoke or change in a short period of time. On the contrary, albeit not so easy, it is not impossible to change the connection temporarily. Suppose that there is a link between a Chinese supplier and its Korean assembly plant. The connection can be changed, for instance, if the Chinese supplier's plant is hit by a natural disaster such as an earthquake and thus it cannot supply to the Korean plant temporarily. Then, Hyundai should come up with an alternative connection, e.g., to link another supplier in Hong Kong with the Korean assembly plant while the Chinese supplier cannot function normally.

In effect, the company should take into account all of the factors discussed above and consider the trade-off relationship among them, based on the configuration decision. Only then can it make an optimal decision on its connection as a key element of the structural dimension for designing the supply chain so as to maximize both values, *efficiency-driven* and *responsiveness-driven*, simultaneously.

IN-DEPTH CONCEPT 4.1
An Example of Analytical Modeling for Configuration and Connection

We present a simple quantitative modeling for configuration and connection. Consider the example at a steel company. The company is to decide its configuration in Korea and China, e.g., how much capacity of each supply chain function it should have in Korea and China. More specifically, we assume a decision problem described in Figure 4.11, where the company's supply chain is divided into supply (raw materials), furnace (melting and refining), casting and rolling, and the final consumer market. Suppose that the company has decided to retain the upstream manufacturing function, i.e., furnace, in Korea and needs to make a configuration decision, e.g., how much capacity of casting and rolling to have in China. The company's decision is affected by various factors such as the size of the end market in China as well as Korea, production costs, inventory holding costs, and transportation costs in the two countries. Note that the transportation cost is also an important factor in the connection decision. In order to simplify the problem, we do not consider the inventory holding costs for this particular example.

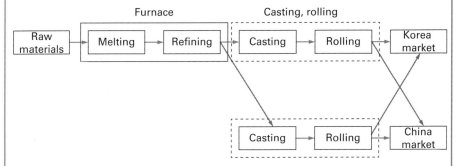

Figure 4.11 Simple Configuration and Connection Decisions at a Steel Company

In order to answer the configuration questions, we define decision variables in Figure 4.12. Note that for the downstream manufacturing and the end market, "1" represents Korea and "2" China.

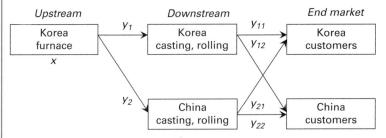

Figure 4.12 Decision Variables for the Configuration/Connection Example

Note that it is an advanced modeling based on mathematical programming. Although we believe its managerial or conceptual implications can help you understand supply chain configuration and connection much better, we suggest you may skip this part unless you feel familiar with the subject. Please note that in our analysis chapter, we will explain a little bit more about the mathematical programming.

x : Total capacity of the upstream manufacturing in Korea

y_i : Total capacity of the downstream manufacturing in country i

y_{ij} : Shipment of final product from country i to j

Using these notations, we develop an analytical model in Figure 4.13, which consists of two parts, an objective function and constraints.

Maximize $\quad b_1(y_{11} + y_{21}) + b_2(y_{12} + y_{22}) - \{c(y_1 + y_2) + ty_2 + c_1(y_{11} + y_{12}) +$
$\qquad\qquad c_2(y_{21} + y_{22}) + t_{12}y_{12} + t_{21}y_{21}\}$

Subject to $\quad y_1 + y_2 \leq S$
$\qquad\qquad y_{11} + y_{12} \leq y_1$
$\qquad\qquad y_{21} + y_{22} \leq y_2$
$\qquad\qquad y_{11} + y_{21} \geq D_1$
$\qquad\qquad y_{12} + y_{22} \geq D_2$
$\qquad\qquad y_i, y_{ij} \geq 0,\ i, j = 1, 2$

Parameters:

S : furnace capacity, i.e., $x = S$

b_i : unit revenue in market $i = 1$ (Korea) and 2 (China)

t : unit transportation cost from Korea to China (casting)

t_{ij} : unit transportation cost from i to j (market)

c : unit (upstream) production cost in Korea

c_i : unit production cost in market $i = 1$ (Korea) and 2 (China)

D_i : market demand in market $i = 1$ (Korea) and 2 (China)

Figure 4.13 Analytical Model to Solve the Example

First, consider the objective function, which consists of the following terms:

- Total sales revenue $b_1(y_{11} + y_{21}) + b_2(y_{12} + y_{22})$: $b_1(y_{11} + y_{21})$ is the sales revenue the company earns in Korea, by selling its product produced in Korea (y_{11}) and also in China (y_{21}); similarly, $b_2(y_{12} + y_{22})$ is the sales revenue the company earns in China, by selling its product produced in Korea (y_{12}) and also in China (y_{22}).
- Total upstream (furnace) production cost in Korea, cx: x is the total production capacity for furnace in Korea and c is the unit production cost.
- Total transportation cost from upstream production in Korea to downstream production in China $ty_2 = t(y_{21} + y_{22})$: y_2 is the shipment amount of the refined steel from the furnace in Korea to casting and rolling in China; t is the unit transportation cost involved in the shipment; note $y_2 = (y_{21} + y_{22})$ and no transportation cost from Korea to Korea assumed.
- Total production and transportation cost for the downstream production in Korea $c_1y_{11} + (c_1 + t_{12})y_{12}$: $c_1y_{11} + c_1y_{12}$ is the total production cost for the downstream production in Korea; $t_{12}y_{12}$ is the total transportation cost of the finished product from Korea to China.

Box continues

- Total production and transportation cost for the downstream production in China, $(c_2 + t_{21})y_{21} + c_2 y_{22}$: a similar explanation can be given as for the same cost in Korea above.
- The objective function is to maximize the firm's total profit after taking into account all of the revenues and costs, given the parameters (e.g., unit costs) and the constraints to be defined below.

Now consider the constraints.

- Total upstream capacity to meet the total downstream capacity, $y_1 + y_2 \leq S$, $y_{11} + y_{12} \leq y_1$, $y_{21} + y_{22} \leq y_2$: assuming no outsourcing for the downstream production, we impose a constraint that the upstream capacity is larger than or equal to the total downstream capacity.
- Total downstream capacity to meet the end market demand $y_{11} + y_{21} \geq D_1$: $y_{11} + y_{21}$ is the total shipment of the finished product from the downstream production in both Korea and China to the end-consumer market in Korea; D_1 is the total end-consumer demand in Korea; we offer the same explanation for $y_{12} + y_{22} \geq D_2$ for the end-consumer market in China.
- Non-negative production and shipment, x, $y_{ij} \geq 0$: it is necessary to assume that there cannot be negative production or negative shipment.

We have defined the objective function and constraints for the configuration and connection problem. Once we estimate the associated parameter values (for revenues, various costs, and demand amounts), we can solve the analytical model in Figure 4.13 to determine the decision variables x and y_{ij}, which answer the configuration and connection questions, i.e., how much capacity to have where (in Korea or China), which plant (in Korea or China) to ship the product to which market (Korea or China), and the like.

Dynamic Nature of Configuration and Connection Decision

Note that the example problem above is a very simple case, which we use only to illustrate the basic principles of decision-making for configuration and connection. For instance, it is a static model, which assumes that the firm already knows the parameter values and these values remain steady. But, in the real-world business setting, such an assumption is rarely valid. In order to utilize the decision model effectively, therefore, the firm must continue to reassess the parameter values as well as the model structure (i.e., the functional forms of the objective and constraints) itself, reformulate them appropriately, and solve the problem again to update the configuration/connection decision, as the market and competitive forces plus the firm's own internal conditions change over time. That is, as the external and internal environments change over time, the firm must dynamically revise and refine its configuration and connection continuously.

4.3   An Illustrative Case

In this section, we present an illustrative case, with which we show how a company actually makes a decision on configuration and connection in its global supply chain. While reading the case, please think about how to answer the following questions:

- What are the characteristics of the company's configuration and connection? Draw a simple figure, which shows only an overall (i.e., not detailed) structure of the company's configuration and connection.
- What are the important factors the company took into account when designing its configuration and connection?
- How can you characterize the company's capacity expansion in China from 1996 to 2006? Why did the company expand its capacity as it did?
- What will be the important changes in the industry? How do you think such changes will impact the company's configuration and connection?

案例 CASE STUDY 4.1
Global Configuration and Connection of LG Chemical

LG Yong Xing ("LGYX") was established in October 1996, devoted to producing and selling ABS (acrylonitrile-butadiene-styrene) in the Chinese market. From its foundation, LGYX had targeted Chinese manufacturers who served the domestic (i.e., Chinese) market and made just one type of low grade ABS. In the decade since its inception, LGYX had increased its capacity tenfold from 50,000 to almost 500,000 tons a year. By the end of 2006, LGYX was the largest company in the Chinese ABS market, boasting a 27 percent market share and sales of US$709 million annually. China's consumption of ABS accounted for 54 percent of the world's usage, and it was estimated that the demand for ABS in China would increase by 200,000 tons every year in the foreseeable future. However, the market for ABS was not just expanding, it was also changing. With exports by Chinese manufacturers growing, demand was shifting to higher grades of ABS. Moreover, LGYX was facing competitive pressure from both local producers and producers in the Middle East.

The global chemical industry. Chemical companies manufactured their products through chemical processes such as chemical reactions and refining. Chemical reactions using diverse catalysts required special equipment that was corrosion resistant at extremely high temperatures and pressures. Multiple production processes, such as distillation, precipitation, crystallization, absorption, filtration, sublimation, and drying, were used. The products were packaged in bottles, boxes, drums, and cylinders and transported to customers through pipelines or via tankers such as rail cars, trucks, and ships.

The chemical industry could be characterized by its cyclicality in terms of capacity in the global market and its profitability. It was also capital intensive, as chemical companies had to invest in special equipment for chemical reactions. In order to make sure that the chemical products met quality standards throughout the chemical processes, a chemical company had to be able to perform quality inspections with precise controllability. This required the company to do advanced research in both chemical and manufacturing engineering. It was usual for a company's R&D laboratory to have pilot plants whose manufacturing environments resembled those of the actual plants. Although these facilities could be located far from the actual plants, it was preferable that they be nearby.

Among many different types of products, LGYX focused primarily on ABS. ABS was a common thermoplastic used to make light, rigid, molded products such as piping, golf club heads, automotive body parts, wheel covers, enclosures, protective head gear, and toys, including LEGO bricks. Even though ABS plastics were used largely for mechanical purposes, they also had good electrical properties that were fairly constant over a wide range of frequencies. The key mechanical properties of ABS were resistance and toughness. A variety of modifications could be made to improve impact resistance, toughness, and heat resistance. As such, while the cost of producing ABS was roughly twice that of producing polystyrene, ABS was considered superior.

LG Chemical's globalization via localization in China. LG Chemical (LGC) was the leading chemical company in Korea in terms of both size and performance and was the mother company of LG Group. In 1995, the company entered the Chinese market by establishing LG Dagu for PVC manufacturing as a joint venture with Dagu Chemical Investment in Tianjin. In October 1996, LGC boosted its presence in China by setting up LGYX, a joint venture for ABS production with Yongxing Chemical Investment, an investment company of Ningbo, Zhejiang Province. By the end of the 1990s, LGYX was the largest ABS manufacturer in mainland China. By successfully running both PVC (polyvinyl chloride) and ABS plants in China, LGC's global strategy was put on the right track. In 2004, it established LGYX Latex in Ningbo and began the construction of an ABS plant in Guangzhou. LGC pursued its globalization strategy in terms of several key dimensions such as globalization motivation, location, capacity, and product mix.

Motivation to enter China: China was the world's largest consumer of plastics and, due to a lack of domestic plastic producers, was heavily dependent on foreign imports. Many feared that the Chinese government would heighten trade barriers by enhancing tariffs and enforcing anti-dumping regulations in a bid to protect its domestic companies and increase domestic production of industrial chemicals. With this scenario in mind, LGC decided to enter the Chinese market. LGC viewed the issue from a broader strategic perspective – that of setting up its manufacturing network on a global scale. It was believed that the supply shortage of plastics in China could continue for a long time, e.g., the total annual demand for ABS in China being 3.1 million tons in 2005 and China having to import more than 60 percent of this.

Location decision: Once the company had decided to build a plant in China, LGC had to select the plant's location. There were many factors the company had to take into account. ABS was used for manufacturing consumer products such as refrigerators, washing machines and TVs, IT and office automation products like computer monitors, copiers and fax machines, and various parts for automobiles and toys. It was essential for an ABS manufacturer to stay near the manufacturers who were their major customers. In addition, it was critical for a chemical plant to have easy access to raw materials such as benzene, and to have logistical infrastructure, such as a nearby port with some chemical processing facility.

Evaluating various locations that could meet these requirements, LGC chose Ningbo, a port city in the northeast of Zhejiang Province. At the time the decision was made, a raw material processing plant had been planned for construction near the city, and the company believed that this plant would make LGYX cost-competitive by supplying raw materials through pipelines. In addition to these objective criteria, LGC's managers were attracted to the city's surrounding countryside, which was reminiscent of rural Korea.

Capacity expansion strategy: Initially, LGYX had difficulty positioning itself in China. In 1997, the Korean economy was afflicted severely by the Asian financial meltdown and was barely rescued by funds from the International Monetary Fund. Due to the financial squeeze felt by its parent, LGC, LGYX was unable to transfer money to China for constructing the plant on time. That was the most critical moment for LGYX, recalled by Hanseob Kim, the former head of LGYX. The company managed to survive the crisis only with the emergency financial support of the LG Group, the *chaebol* to which LGC belonged and which had made a strategic decision to support the company in need.

In the decade since signing the joint venture in 1996, LGYX gradually increased its production capacity. The company initially built a plant with a annual capacity of 50,000 tons and expanded to 150,000 tons per year in 2000. In 2002, the capacity was increased to 300,000 tons per year and, by July 2006, the capacity had been expanded to 450,000 tons per year. The company's total investment in capacity increase amounted to US$290 million, including US$76 million for the last expansion. As a separate endeavor, in 2004 LGYX formed LGYX Latex, a joint venture between LGC and Ningbo Yongxing Chemical Investment. LGYX invested US$30 million for the construction of a new plant with an annual production capacity of 70,000 tons of SBL, a raw material key to paper coating. Due to the rapid increase in paper production, demand for SBL in China had increased sharply, and the market was estimated to grow by 10 percent each year. By establishing a new cutting-edge plant, LGYX planned to capitalize on this expanding market.

A top manager at LGC summarized the reason for this gradual approach in capacity increase, saying:

> When we first entered China, nobody had much knowledge about the market. What we all knew was just the potential, which we believed the Chinese market would soon have. But, the potential was a pretty obscure thing. So we decided to have a rather small presence at first. Then, we wanted to see and feel the market, where and how fast the market will move. As we accumulated more understanding as well as knowledge about China and its market, we became more confident and felt comfortable with adding more capacity. Of course, what we learned was not just about the market demand patterns. We became more familiar with the legal systems and the Chinese people as well. Back in 1996, we didn't have much information about the legal system in China and didn't know how to interact with the officials in Chinese governments. That was the primary reason why we started as a joint venture rather than a wholly owned subsidiary. In addition, in the early days, we were not good at managing and communicating with the Chinese employees, and that inability caused lots of difficulties.
>
> In order to overcome these obstacles, we tried hard to establish a family-like bond with our Chinese workers, and were actively engaged in helping the community as well as building good business relationship with the Chinese officials. Our incessant efforts paid off! Gradually, we became more knowledgeable about the market and its people. With this enhanced confidence, we

were rapidly assimilated with the community and our company image improved more and more. As a result, the Chinese began recognizing LGYX almost like a truly Chinese company and we were able to recruit more talented Chinese employees.

Product mix strategy: There were many different grades of ABS. Thus, whenever a capacity decision was made, the company had to contemplate whether to make a single grade of ABS or several grades. Although one could make different grades in the same factory, several reactors were required, each used exclusively for a certain grade. From the beginning, LGYX concentrated on producing a single low-grade ABS. Generic ABS was low grade, while there were many special ABS grades that were high-end products.

"When we had to decide the product mix, we took into account the market demand for ABS in China. We also had to factor in our corporate strategy," explained the manager. In 1994, the demand ratio between generic ABS and special ABS had been almost nine to one, gradually decreasing to about seven to three by 2007. In this context, LGYX decided to position itself as a local company that employed only Chinese and sold low-grade ABS to Chinese manufacturers whose products were meant for the domestic market only. Thus, LGYX didn't sell its product to LG Electronics (LGE) in China because LGE's primary goal was to export the products it made in China to countries in North America and Europe. Once it chose its product type, LGYX worked hard to enhance its brand value. The company's efforts paid off: by 2007, its generic ABS could command an almost 50 percent premium, compared with the same grade of ABS produced by its Chinese competitors. Analysts believed that the gradual increase in demand for special grades of ABS would continue after 2008, when Beijing was to host the summer Olympic Games.

This particular product mix strategy was also based on LGC's global manufacturing strategy. LG Chemical's Yeosu plant in Korea had a capacity of 500,000 tons per year. The Yeosu plant dealt in over 260 different high-end ABS products. LGC wanted LGYX to concentrate on producing a single generic-grade ABS so that the Chinese subsidiary could enjoy economies of scale in a short period of time. Moreover, the Chinese demand was big enough to require the entire capacity at LGYX, a trend that was believed to continue at least up until the Beijing Olympics. LGC also calculated that, when the demand pattern in China eventually changed, the company would have enough time to adapt. Therefore, until that happened, it was deemed better for LGYX to focus on generic ABS and enhance its brand recognition by concentrating on a clearly defined product. If the company could enjoy a premium brand value, LGYX believed that it would command a competitive advantage. In order to better prepare for the future, LGYX started gradually investing in manufacturing for higher grades, e.g., buying compounding machines for coloring of special ABS. The company was paying particular attention to demand patterns in southern China, which covered Guangxi, Guangdong, and Hainan provinces – in the past, the demand patterns in this region had led the overall changes in the industry.

Sources of synergy. In order to avoid potential cannibalization between the Yeosu plant and LGYX, it was critical to coordinate operations in the two countries. LGC's organization was structured to support such coordination. As the manager explained:

> The coordination between Yeosu and LGYX was possible because I was in charge of managing both plants. If each plant was under a different senior manager, such coordination would be very challenging. I also made a clear distinction between the two plants' products, even if they were

the same grade products. LGC's Yeosu plant could make 500,000 tons per year. Out of these, 50% was used for low-margin generic grade, whereas the other half for high-margin special grade. In fact, the 250,000 tons of low-margin generic-grade ABS were exported to China, and there was possibility that the Yeosu's products competed against those made by LGYX. Again, since I could control the two operations, I enforced that the generic ABS made in Yeosu could only be sold to the exporters in China that would sell their final products outside China. That was, Yeosu plant could not sell its generic grade ABS to local Chinese companies, which sold their products domestically only. These were the customers of LGYX. In this way, I could make sure that the two companies didn't compete against each other. There was another more economic consideration as well. Due to tariff drawbacks, there was difference in price between domestic selling and exporting. We would have an option to exploit this difference to our advantage.

In addition to avoiding cannibalization, there were other benefits to the concentrated management. The manager continued:

I believed we had an extra advantage since I controlled the operations together. It's "integrated marketing." For example, there was a local Chinese company that was selling in the domestic market by using the generic grade ABS supplied by LGYX. Over time, the company had grown and eventually become capable of exporting to foreign markets. Then, the company required a high-end special grade ABS as well as low-end generic grade. At this critical transition time, LGYX referred its customer to the Yeosu plant, since it could not sell its products to exporters due to our synergistic policy. The customer had been doing business with LGYX and highly valued the LG brand. Therefore, when it was referred to LGC in Yeosu by LGYX, the customer instantly felt familiar with the new supplier, simply because the LG brand was there too. This transition could occur very rapidly so that other competitors could not find any time to contact the customer.

Chinese competitors. Although LGYX was far ahead of its Chinese competitors in terms of product quality, the company knew that the Chinese would definitely catch up with LGYX. However, the company didn't feel keenly threatened. The manager explained why:

Even if the Chinese improve their quality level so that it becomes almost same as ours, we will continue to be more competitive since we can make the same product at 5% lower cost. It is huge cost advantage. How can we do this? There are many reasons. For instance, first mover advantage, higher brand value, so forth. Another important reason is that we have been able to enjoy economies of scale due to concentrating on making a single grade ABS even as we increased our capacity continuously. In addition, I believe we have superior learning capability, which enables us to have a highly efficient production process.

In the production process adopted by most ABS manufacturers, three monomers (i.e., acrylonitrile, butadiene, and styrene) were converted into powders through a reactor for polymerization. ABS was produced after drying, mixing, and re-extruding these powders, a process called the "dry process." However, LGYX adopted a process called the "wet process," which moved the wet powders directly from the first reactor to the second, bypassing the expensive drying process in order to reduce cost. To use the wet process, however, the company needed a special extruder.

LGYX and its key supplier of equipment and machinery developed the special extruder together, and the supplier provided the extruder only to LGYX. Therefore, the wet process was proprietary to LGYX, enabling the company to enjoy another competitive advantage in cost vis-à-vis its competitors.

Most of LGC's process innovation was done in Korea, where the company had an R&D center in Daeduk, about 150 kilometers south of Seoul, and a small R&D branch in Yeosu. Daeduk was a major R&D hub in Korea, where many companies as well as research institutes funded by the Korean government had R&D facilities. LGC employed about sixty-five scientists and engineers in Deaduk and Yeosu. Once an innovation project was done, it would be transferred to and promptly implemented at LGYX, which didn't have its own R&D function. When such a technology transfer was conducted, LGC charged LGYX a license fee. Although the Chinese government owned 25 percent of the shares of LGYX and LGC owned 75 percent, the company believed that there was little risk of technology leaking to competitors during the transfer process.

Localization: One big family. LGYX had always believed that the most important asset of the company was its employees. As such, ever since its establishment in the mid-1990s, the company had sought to harmonize its workforce. In particular, it emphasized family spirit among its local Chinese employees. This family orientation was not just for the employees, but also for the customers, as most of the customers of the company were also Chinese. "Our customers and LG are one big family! (LG大家庭)" was the company slogan, which could be seen everywhere. The manager said confidently, "Our customers trust and depend on us and we also trust and depend on our customers. Thus, it is an unchanging truth that our customers and LG are a big family!"

The "one big family" concept originated toward the end of the 1990s, when many chemical manufacturers, both local and foreign, emerged in the Chinese market and drove up competition. LGYX contemplated possible measures to deal with the difficult times. Finally, the company decided that the best solution would be to embark on building trust from its customers by declaring that it would honor every promise it made to its customers at any cost.

Changes in the global ABS market. In the early 2000s, there had been many changes in the ABS market, mainly due to heightened competition in the global market. As the raw materials used to produce ABS were becoming more expensive, cost competitiveness was becoming more critical in the ABS industry.

Potential substitutes for ABS: Industry experts believed that there was a high positive correlation between the price of ABS and the cost of styrene monomer, a key ingredient of ABS. This could have serious implications for the industry. At 2007 price levels, ABS enjoyed advantages of higher performance and functionality vis-à-vis similar products such as polypropylene or polystyrene. However, if ABS became more expensive, polypropylene or polystyrene might replace ABS, at least in some segments of the market.

Advantages in the Middle East: Companies in the Middle East had a competitive advantage in the area of feedstock. ABS consisted of three primary raw materials: acrylonitrile monomer (20 percent), butadiene monomer (20 percent), and styrene monomer (60 percent). In general, the styrene monomer was made by mixing seven parts benzene with three parts ethylene and naphtha-cracking them. But in the Middle East, styrene monomer was made of ethane gas, which was abundant in the region. As a result, companies in the Middle East could produce styrene monomer at a per-ton cost about US$100 lower than the average. Even with a US$50 per-ton transportation cost, Middle Eastern competitors would still have a huge cost advantage. Moreover, 1 kilogram of ABS required about 2 kilograms of oil for raw materials and energy, bringing the oil-producing Middle Eastern countries more potential advantage for ABS manufacturing. Although there were few companies in the Middle East actively pursuing ABS, the situation could change suddenly if they decided to capitalize on the potential cost advantage they had in the industry. The manager said:

> Of course, the Middle East is a threat to LGC, which is producing styrene monomer itself. But, from LGYX's perspective, it might not be a bad thing after all. LGYX imports styrene monomer and can enjoy the low cost offered by the Middle East. Thus, what I am most concerned about is not the styrene monomer, but the possibility that the companies in the Middle East opt to enter the Chinese ABS market themselves. In the end, who has the strongest competitive advantage in this market will be decided not only by who has the most efficient manufacturing process, but also by who buys the cheapest feedstock (i.e., raw materials).

Competitors in East Asia: By the early 2000s, one could characterize China's chemical industry in two ways. First, its market size was huge. For instance, the synthetic resin industry in China was expected to become the world's largest market, demanding almost 40 million tons per year by 2010. However, the country's self-sufficiency rate was terribly low, requiring that more than 50 percent of the demand be satisfied by imports. Due to geographical proximity and some cultural affinity, companies from Korea, Japan, and Taiwan accounted for most of such imports, making up almost 60 percent in 2003.

However, proportions of import from Japanese and Korean companies had been declining continuously, while that of the Taiwanese companies had steadily increased. For instance, Korea's share in the import of synthetic resin to China was over 30 percent in 1998, but it had reduced to about 22 percent by 2003, while the Japanese share during the same period changed from about 18 to 12 percent. The Taiwanese share, on the other hand, had increased from less than 20 to almost 25 percent during the same period. The trend looked more drastic in the synthetic fiber industry. In the case of primary synthetic fiber materials such as ethylene glycol, acrylonitrile, and purified terephthalic acid, Taiwanese companies increased their share from less than 5 percent in 1998 to almost 20 percent in 2003, whereas Korean companies reduced their share from almost 30 to about 20 percent and Japanese companies from over 30 to less than 15 percent during the same period.

There were several possible explanations for the growing presence of Taiwanese chemical companies in China. Up until early 2000, the country's chemical industry had not been fully realized, as it had been monopolized by a state-run enterprise, CPC Corporation. Only in the early 2000s did some of the big Taiwanese companies in the private sector recognize the strategic importance of the chemical industry, possibly observing the rapid encroachment of Korean and Japanese companies on the Chinese chemical market. Companies like Formosa Group and Chi Mei Corporation significantly increased their capacity for producing chemical products in Taiwan and also started investing heavily in building new capacity in China, a trend that was most conspicuous in the ABS market. As these companies were adding more capacity, they were also becoming more competitive by capitalizing on more economies of scale. Another advantage enjoyed by Taiwanese companies was the linguistic and cultural affinity between Chinese and Taiwanese. This affinity was believed to enable Taiwanese companies to do business in China more efficiently than their Korean and Japanese counterparts. Although Taiwanese companies could not match the Koreans in terms of productivity and quality, the situation could be reversed rather quickly if the Taiwanese would continue to increase their market share in China by building up such advantages as manufacturing capacity.

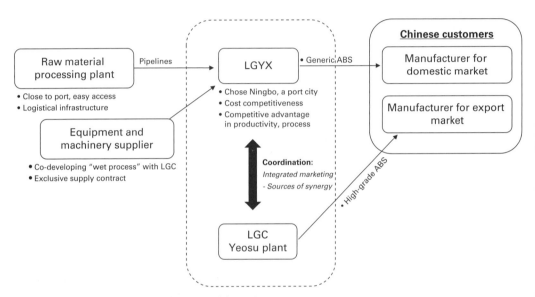

Figure 4.14 LGYX's Configuration and Connection

Now let's recall and answer the questions we raised just before presenting the illustrative case:

- characteristics of the company's configuration and connection
- important factors to consider
- company's capacity expansion pattern
- important changes in the future

4.3.1   Characteristics of the Company's Configuration and Connection

We can draw the company's configuration and connection in Figure 4.14. As part of its global configuration, LGC formed a manufacturing network with its operations in China (LGYX) and Korea (Yeosu plant). But, in terms of its connection, LGC differentiated its global operations, i.e., LGYX specialized in manufacturing and supplying generic ABS for the Chinese manufacturers, which served the Chinese domestic market only, whereas LGC's Yeosu plant produced and exported high-grade ABS to the Chinese customers, who were manufacturing and exporting their final products to foreign markets. In addition, LGYX was connected with two types of suppliers, one for raw materials and the other for equipment and machinery. In deciding the geographic location of its raw material processing plant, the company took into account whether it had easy access to a port as well as a sound logistical infrastructure. When choosing its equipment and machinery supplier, LGC paid attention to whether the supplier could cultivate partnership to develop the wet process together with LGC and also be willing to accept an exclusive supply contract.

4.3.2   Important Factors to Consider

When it decided to build its plant in Ningbo, the company took into account many of the factors listed in Table 4.1. The first factor was its proximity to the market, i.e., LGC wanted to stay near its customers. It was also crucial for the location to have easy access to raw materials and functional logistical infrastructure. In addition, LGC was also considering a subjective criterion, i.e., the area felt very much like a Korean rural area. A primary factor to consider for the connection was to maximize the synergy effect between its operations in China and in Korea so as to minimize the possibility of inter-firm competition or cannibalization.

4.3.3   Company's Capacity Expansion Pattern

Table 4.2 summarizes the company's history of capacity expansion at LGYX. In addition, Figure 4.15 shows the timeline of the company's capacity expansion along with its decisions. As the two indicate, LGC increased its capacity at LGYX gradually from 50,000 tons/year in 1998 to 450,000 tons/year in 2006. Let's look at the decisions the company made during the time period. Before it had decided to enter the Chinese market, LGC had determined its motivation to globalize into China, e.g., to pre-empt the market before competition became fiercer. The company decided to form a joint venture as its entry mode in 1996. This was due to the fact that the company didn't have enough knowledge and experience to enable it to pioneer the Chinese market independently. Once it entered the Chinese market, LGC tried to grow there by

Table 4.2 History of Capacity Increase

Oct. 1996	Established as a joint venture with LGC and Yongxing Chemical Investment
Jul. 1998	Capacity started from 50,000 tons/year
Oct. 2000	Expanded to 150,000 tons/year
Dec. 2002	Expanded to 300,000 tons/year
Jun. 2004	Start of construction of Yongxing latex plant (SBL 70,000 ton/year)
Sep. 2004	Cumulative ABS sales of 1 million tons
Jul. 2006	Expanded to 450,000 tons/year of ABS

Source: LG Chemical document.

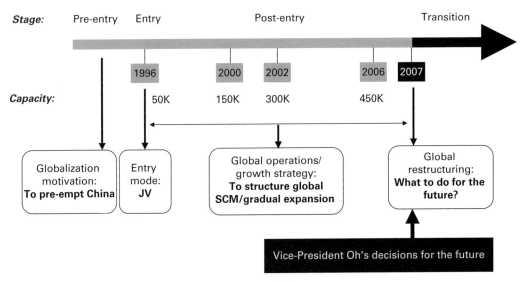

Figure 4.15 LGYX's Configuration – Capacity Expansion Strategy

increasing its capacity and assimilating itself to the local market as much as possible. The capacity expansion continued during the period. As of 2007, the company was facing a difficult future and had to make decisions regarding its supply chain configuration and connection.

Why did LGC increase its capacity gradually? As mentioned above, LGC didn't have enough knowledge and experience about China and its market, despite firmly believing that the Chinese market had a strategic importance and that it had to enter the market. As such, the company needed a partner, who had sufficient knowledge, experience, and relationship in the Chinese market so as to complement those of LGC. That's why LGC decided to use the joint venture as its choice of entry mode in 1996. Once the company had presence in the Chinese market, LGC was able to accumulate knowledge and experience about the local market by interacting with various stakeholders, including suppliers, vendors, distributors, customers, government officials, community members, and non-government activists. As its knowledge and experience about the local market increased, the company became more confident in its ability to build and manage its capacity and grow in the local market. This iterative and dynamic cycle, "small-scale presence in the market → direct interaction with stakeholders in the market → knowledge and experience accumulation → enhanced capability → capacity or scale increase → more intensive and relevant knowledge and experience → further growth," is an example of market-based learning. Figure 4.16 shows the dynamic cause-and-effect relationship of market-based learning. Although the company develops its capability through an indirect accumulation of knowledge and experience, it should facilitate the capability-building process by engaging in the direct learning process. Market-based learning doesn't have to start with a large scale. It is more effective to start with a small scale, say a relatively small-to-moderate presence in the market. Once it has entered the

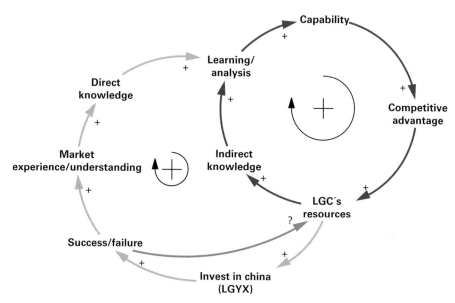

Figure 4.16 LGC's Market-Based Learning – Fast-Cycle Learning

market on a small scale, the firm has numerous ways to interact with all the stakeholders as well as key players in the market and can accumulate knowledge and experience in a much more direct and relevant manner. As its knowledge and experience about the market grow, the company has more capability to manage a larger presence, i.e., capacity or scale. With the enlarged capacity or scale, the company has more opportunities to gather massive knowledge and information, which are probably more relevant and precise and thus further strengthen the company's ability to manage the scale. If the company carries out this process effectively, it enters a virtuous cycle, which can be self-adapting and self-organizing and enables the company to improve continuously.

4.3.4   Important Changes in the Future

The case points out that some big changes were underway in the ABS industry, describing: "In the early 2000s, there had been lots of changes in the ABS market, mainly due to heightened competition in the global market. As the raw materials used to produce ABS were becoming more expensive, cost competitiveness was becoming more critical in the ABS industry." Some of the strong potential competitors seemed to be from the Middle East with abundance of oil as an advantage and also Taiwan with cultural affinity and geographic proximity as competitive advantages. In the face of the potentially huge changes in the market's competitive landscape, sooner or later LGC should reassess its competitive positioning in both China and Korea, and make strategic changes in its global configuration and connection. For instance, should the company increase its capacity? If it should, for which product, generic or special ABS? Where should it add the capacity – in China or Korea? Should the company make any changes to its connection so as to cope with the pressure on cost reduction? For example, should it find a new supplier in another country, which can provide the raw materials at a lower price reliably in the long run? In order to establish such a connection with the new supplier, what should the company do? Should the company design a more attractive contract to support the supplier's effort to increase its technological capability or offer an exclusive contract so that the supplier can focus on the quality without worrying about the renewal of a contract every year?

These are examples of questions LGC should ask and answer in order to redesign its configuration and connection optimally. They also highlight the dynamic nature of the firm's decisions on its supply chain configuration and connection.

Discussion Questions

1. What is decision hierarchy? How is it relevant to supply chain management?
2. What is the difference between ambiguity and statistical uncertainty? How is it relevant to supply chain management?
3. How should we define performance measures for effective supply chain management?
4. What are the quality dimensions put forth by Garvin? How can these dimensions be related with the performance measures for effective supply chain management?
5. Define the structural dimension for designing a supply chain.
6. Define configuration as an element of the structural dimension. What are the key factors the company should take into account when determining its configuration?
7. Define connection as an element of the structural dimension. What are the key factors the company should take into account when determining its connection?
8. Is there any difference between configuration and connection in terms of decision time horizon?
9. Characterize the relationship between configuration and connection.
10. What is market-based learning? Under what circumstances can it be an effective strategy for a company to globalize?

案例 CASE STUDY 4.2
Locating a Business to Enhance the Customer Experience: Enterprise Rent-a-Car

One of the most important decisions a business has to make is where to locate. The location of the business can have a significant effect on how it performs. Businesses will aim to operate from locations that provide the maximum competitive advantage. These decisions need to be reviewed regularly.

By selecting the best location, a business could get more customers, improve its efficiency, and generate greater profits. For example, choosing an out-of-town shopping park instead of a high street may allow a retail business to have greater shop space, better overheads, and attract more customers because parking is easier.

Multinational businesses need to make many decisions about the location of their operations. At an international level, they might need to choose which countries or territories to operate within to maximize opportunities. Within each country, they would need to locate the head office. At a more local level, they may need to choose whether to locate within or around major cities.

Enterprise Rent-A-Car is an internationally recognized brand, operating within the United States, Canada, the United Kingdom, Ireland, and Germany. It is the United Kingdom's largest car rental company. As the company has developed, it has sought to retain the personal feel of a smaller business.

The company encourages its branch managers to take responsibility for local operations. This approach helps to create a dynamic service driven by the individual branches. This means that each branch is free to focus on the needs of its local customers, while delivering Enterprise's values and high standards of customer service.

Competitive market place. Car rental is an extremely competitive market. There are many car rental companies operating in the United Kingdom. Enterprise aims to outperform its competitors through a focus on customer service. Service is a core element of Enterprise's ethos and, as such, employees seek to provide the highest standards of customer care. This is the driving force and key differentiator of the business.

As part of this strategy, Enterprise attempts to locate its branches as close as possible to its customers. It has an extensive branch network. Within the United Kingdom, the company operates from 350 locations. Most people (over 75 percent of the country's population) live within five miles of an Enterprise branch.

This case study focuses on how Enterprise Rent-A-Car decides where to locate its new or relocated branches.

Factors affecting the location of a business. There are several reasons why an organization might decide to open new branches or relocate its existing operations. It might want to expand the business, so it will open branches in cities where the organization did not previously have a presence.

A business might also want to restructure or modernize its operations. It might do this by bringing together some existing departments into new purpose-built premises. It might decide to

Source: Reprinted with permission from Business Case Studies LLP.

shut its less profitable operations and open branches in locations that offer more business potential.

A business will have to consider many factors when determining where to locate a new branch or operation. Usually, it will have to balance several factors in making a decision. Sometimes one factor may sway the decision:

- It may choose a site with the cheapest land or buildings.
- It might decide on a location that is convenient for key employees. A business needs to be able to recruit staff with the right skills base.
- It might choose a site that has easy access to raw materials. For example, many frozen food factories are located near fishing ports to reduce transport time taken and to keep fish fresh.

The key factor could be the transport and service infrastructure. Many businesses require easy access to good road and railway links and modern telecommunication services. These ensure that they can meet service or delivery deadlines.

Enterprise Rent-A-Car is a service business. Its customers include:

- businesses, who may require regular car rentals for their staff or visitors; and
- individual customers, who may want to hire a car when they are on holiday or if their own vehicle has been involved in an accident.

Enterprise makes it as easy as possible for customers to use its services. For example, business customers may need a car delivered to their doorstep. Alternatively, retail customers can use Enterprise's unique pick-up service, where the customer will be collected from their location and taken back to the branch to collect the car.

Customers can also pick up cars direct from branches, so all Enterprise sites need to have good transportation links and easy access. They also need to be close to their customers. This helps to ensure Enterprise can keep its promise to customers on the speed and efficiency of its service.

Types of locations: Enterprise has branches in two types of locations:

- First, there are "home/city" branches. These are located in areas close to long-term business partners, as well as to a large market for personal customers. These branches meet the demand for car rental from businesses and individuals wanting a car for accident cover or for leisure purposes and represent 95 percent of all Enterprise's locations.
- Second, there are branches at airport locations. These provide a service for people flying into or out of a region.

By locating branches in busy areas and near to its customers, Enterprise can also increase awareness of its services by using its premises to project a strong visual brand. The signs and fittings at each branch premises display the Enterprise corporate logo and reflect the company's colors and branding.

Enterprise also needs to be open to changing customer demand. For example, a major new housing development may generate a new source of customers in an area. The growth of residential housing could also encourage new businesses, such as shops and offices, to open nearby to provide services and goods to this new market. Enterprise needs to be in a position to adapt its locations to meet any changes in its market efficiently.

Return on investment. When an organization makes an investment, it is taking a business risk. When a company spends money on opening or moving to a new location, it will hope to see a return on this investment through increased profits. For example, by opening a new branch close to a buoyant or developing market, the business would hope to increase its sales. This in turn should lead to higher profits.

Setting up a new Enterprise branch generates costs. These relate to:

- set-up costs, such as for obtaining planning permission, decorating and fitting out the buildings, and installing fire alarms and security;
- fixed costs, including rent and other overheads such as heating and lighting; and
- variable costs, which will depend on the volume of business. These include staff salaries – as the business grows, a company will hire more staff – and, for Enterprise, the cost of owning and maintaining vehicles.

There are several ways in which Enterprise assesses whether a new branch or relocation will generate sufficient return on the required investment. The starting point for any method of investment appraisal is to forecast how much additional revenue the new operation will generate.

However, this also needs to be considered against how much that business may take away from other Enterprise locations nearby. This revenue forecast can then be used to obtain a profit forecast.

Projected revenues and profits: Projected revenues and profits can be linked back to costs in several ways:

- **Payback** measures the length of time it will take to generate sufficient profit to cover the costs of the initial investment. When assessing different project options, companies sometimes choose the project that has the shortest payback period.
- **Return on capital employed** expresses the amount of profit generated in a given period (usually a year) as a percentage of the costs of the project. Investors would usually only back projects where this percentage is greater than prevailing bank interest rates. It would make little sense to back a business project if investors could get a greater return by simply keeping their money in a bank account.
- **Break-even analysis** is a way of assessing how long it will take (or how many customers are required) for a new business venture to generate a profit. This analysis relates sales revenue to total costs. The break-even point is achieved when the revenue equals the costs incurred to date.

A large multinational company like Enterprise may sometimes take a location because it offers a strategic advantage. For example, it may stop a competitor obtaining the location or may be situated in a developing area where the longer-term projections are very good.

Identifying a new location. Before selecting a new location for a branch, Enterprise undertakes a detailed analysis. Initially, local managers identify the potential of possible new locations. This is done through a detailed process of forecasting based on existing information, such as how many customers currently use each branch. This process enables the business to spot where existing branches are at maximum capacity and where there might be opportunities for new branches to win business from competitors.

At this early stage, managers look at the population in the catchment area of the proposed new branch. They assess how many cars have been rented by customers in this catchment area from surrounding branches. They aim to understand the amount of business in the area, as well as what level of business is currently being missed because Enterprise does not have a presence in that local market.

Enterprise sets a boundary for a new location aiming to be within a 6-minute drive time for its customers. It also needs to be close to referral sources, such as vehicle repair centers, mechanics, and dealerships. These are some of the places where Enterprise may acquire new customers, such as people who urgently need a rental car because their own car has broken down or been involved in an accident.

Once it has been decided to establish a branch in a particular location, Enterprise managers consider the suitability of potential sites. Enterprise needs its branch sites to have good access and parking space. They should be easy to get to at all times. If the area around the site experiences frequent traffic jams, this might inconvenience customers and create negative perceptions of Enterprise's service.

Enterprise managers undertake an initial property analysis to see if a site is worth further investigation. They use a comprehensive checklist to evaluate each location. This includes looking at other planning applications being made in the area, estimating the cost of setting up the branch, and considering the impacts promotional signs will have at and around the site.

Enterprise sets high standards: Enterprise sets high standards so that every new branch will provide a better service for customers. For example, the new Enterprise Rent-A-Car branch at Heathrow airport has a convenient and accessible position between the airport junctions on both the M4 and M25 motorways. This means customers coming from different directions can find it easily. It also has prominent signage to make it easier for customers to see where they should leave rental vehicles that are being returned.

The new branch also has operational advantages for Enterprise. It is a bigger site and allows more efficient operations. Its location means that shuttle times to the airport terminals have reduced. It now takes 10 minutes less to transfer customers from the Enterprise offices to the terminal buildings.

The new branch also offers Wi-Fi and has a rest area for customers. The improved facilities not only mean customers generally feel more comfortable, but also that business people can keep using e-mail and the internet while waiting.

Qualitative influences. There are also other factors that influence Enterprise in its choice of location for a new site. It is important that safety requirements are met, for example, making sure the road conditions are suitable. Ideally, there should be the space to expand operations in the future, so managers assess if the local facilities and infrastructure will allow this.

Managers also take into account environmental considerations. Enterprise aims to make new branches as environmentally friendly as possible:

- Long-life bulbs are used within Enterprise signage. These last five times longer than standard bulbs. This reduces environmental waste and cuts the labor hours spent replacing bulbs.
- Photocells are used to switch on outside lights and signs only when they are needed. This reduces electricity consumption.
- Regulators are placed on car wash and jet wash machines to reduce the amount of shampoo used.
- Printing is kept to a minimum and documents are only printed on recycled paper.

- A "last person out" switch turns off all non-essential electrical devices at the end of the day.
- Special window blinds reduce heat gain, which reduces energy costs.
- Offices use efficient lighting that generates less heat, so that cooling systems are not required.
- Furniture is recycled by donating replaced items to charities.

As there are 7,700 Enterprise Rent-A-Car branches worldwide, even small environmental improvements at branch level produce a big difference globally.

Conclusion. Setting up new branch locations gives Enterprise the opportunity to expand the business and improve on the quality of its customer service. The key factor that often differentiates a service business from its competitors is the quality of the care and attention given to customers.

When looking for new sites, Enterprise aims to locate the business as close to customers as possible. This means that it can respond more quickly to their requirements. It also makes it more easy and convenient for customers to access the services of Enterprise.

In evaluating potential new locations, Enterprise also aims to address environmental concerns. During refurbishments and the setting up of new branches, Enterprise puts in place measures to reduce the carbon footprint of the business. This not only improves the customer experience, but also helps Enterprise to reduce its costs and grow as a business.

Questions
1. How do you characterize the competitive situation of the car rental business?
2. What are the key factors that might affect the location of a business?
3. What analysis does Enterprise undertake before selecting a new location for a branch? What are the factors that influence the company in its choice of location for a new site?
4. How does the company's location affect its competitive position in the market?

CHAPTER 5

Strategic Roles of Inventory

If we want to know the state of our health, we go to a hospital and have a medical check-up. The hospital conducts many tests to examine our body. Among those numerous tests for the medical check-up, which one do you think is the most important, if you have to choose only one? The most likely answer is a blood test. To see whether our body is healthy, we need to test our blood: the blood test result reveals many things about our body. In fact, our blood performs several vital functions that are extremely essential to our body and eventually our life itself. One of them is to transport oxygen to every part of our body, including the most quintessential, our brain: we cannot be alive without oxygen, i.e., without blood. **Inventory** is to a company as blood is to a body! That is, inventory is much like blood. Should we want to check the condition of a company's health, we first need to look at the inventory the company has. Both too much and too little imply something wrong at the company. In this chapter, we delve into inventory not only as a key element of the structural dimension, but also as a strategic lever for the company.

Key Learning Points

- The primary role of inventory is to buffer against uncertainty.
- There are conflicting forces, i.e., some forces for large inventory and others for small inventory. Therefore, it is possible to find out an optimal inventory level. In fact, a company is supposed to identify such an optimal point.
- EOQ (economic order quantity) and newsvendor problem are examples of analytical models to help the company determine an optimal inventory level by trading off the conflicting forces.
- Inventory has additional key implications for such concepts as flexibility, flow strategy, and supply chain forecasting.
- A company has to face two different types of uncertainty, aggregate level and product-mix level. It is often that the product-mix level uncertainty poses a greater threat to the company.
- When there are little information and few historical data for a new product, the company should use a qualitative forecasting method. The Delphi method is a very strong methodology to enable the company to forecast for a new or innovative product.
- In addition to buffering against uncertainty, inventory has two more roles, which are strategically important for the company. Excessive inventory dampens the company's innovation speed and also deters its learning capability.

學 WISDOM BOX 5.1
Wisdom and Insights

Innovation versus Inventory

In 2009, we interviewed a recently retired CEO at a global consumer electronics company. He talked about his thirty-plus years of tenure at the company with a gratifying smile on his face. As the interview was approaching the conclusion, he became a little emotional and started telling a story about how his company began the journey to be a global company, which was obviously one of his most beloved and proudest experiences as its CEO. In 1998, at the peak of Korea's economic crisis triggered by the Asian financial meltdown, he took the helm of the company as CEO. What he did first as CEO was to take a tour of the company's retail stores in Europe. When he visited the company store in London, he was so shocked. Despite the company churning out new and more innovative products in Seoul, the retail store displayed old models with the new ones dusted and stacked at the store's warehouse. Customers seemed uninterested in the old products and thus the inventory of old models increased further. As no shelf space became available, the store manager could not pull out the new products from the warehouse and display them on the front shelf. Since all products on the shelf were oldies, no customers had interest in the products. Inventory accumulated. New and more innovative products sat on the floor of the dusty warehouse. The vicious cycle continued. The CEO knew the old inventory was killing any sales at the store. But he couldn't do anything either, since he also knew the store manager's motivational system, i.e., the manager hated "writing off the inventory," since doing so could seriously harm his performance evaluation. The CEO visited stores in different cities and found that the problem was not unique to the London store. In fact, the problem was spread throughout the company's global retail network and was destroying sales everywhere.

For the next several days, the CEO was up all night worrying about the impasse and trying to contemplate a solution. Then, one night, after excruciating efforts, he came up with an answer. Next morning, he hurriedly summoned all his senior managers and announced: "Today, every store manager must write off the bad inventory, i.e., products that were on the shelf for more than 2 months, and I will not hold you responsible for the loss due to the write-off." That was a really pivotal moment. The entire "dead" inventory throughout the company's global supply chain was exposed and eliminated at once. The CEO recalled: "As soon as the non-performing inventory disappeared from our stores, the new and more innovative products started flowing through the pipeline and our global sales increased slowly at first then much more rapidly soon. I still believe that was the turning point, from which my company started growing in the global market and becoming one of the best companies in the world." At the end of the interview, he offered his final words **"Bad inventory** kills **innovation!"**

Box continues

Questions

1. Do you agree with the CEO's assertion? Explain why or why not.
2. Is it possible for you to identify and suggest certain circumstances where the CEO's statement is valid or invalid?

5.1 What Is Inventory?

We stated "inventory to a company is as blood to a body." To assess the statement, we need to define inventory more clearly. What is **inventory**? Why should the firm need inventory? Let's consider a **production system** consisting of three processes as in Figure 5.1. The system is well-balanced in that each process performs at the same **production rate**, 100 units per minute. If there is no **uncertainty** in the production system, i.e., each process performs exactly as it is designed, then the firm doesn't need any inventory between processes. But unfortunately that is not always the case in the real world. Uncertainty is everywhere and it is impossible for the firm to avoid uncertainty completely.

For example, suppose that uncertainty hits Process 2 and as a result it can now process 80 units per minute only, not 100. Then, what happens to other processes? Let's further assume that the other two processes, Process 1 and Process 3, are not affected by the uncertainty and therefore both of them perform as they are designed, i.e., 100 units per minute. Even if Process 1 and Process 3 are not hit by the uncertainty and can perform at the full production rate, they are not able to perform as they like, of course, unless they have inventory between themselves and Process 2 (Figure 5.2). First, without inventory between Process 1 and Process 2, Process 1 cannot make 100 units per minute since Process 2 can only take 80, not 100. Likewise, without inventory between Process 2 and Process 3, Process 3 cannot process 100 units per minute since it can receive only 80 units from Process 2 every minute. Process 1 is **blocked** by Process 2. Process 3 is **starved** by Process 2. In fact, without inventory between processes, they are tightly **coupled** with each other.

Is it possible to decouple the processes, i.e., to make the processes more independent of each other? Inventory plays such a role, i.e., **decoupling** the processes (Figure 5.3). If there is inventory between Process 1 and Process 2, Process 1 can perform as it likes without being concerned about the situation at Process 2: it can

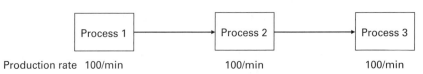

Production rate   100/min   100/min   100/min

Figure 5.1 Process under Normal Condition

Random variation hits Process 2

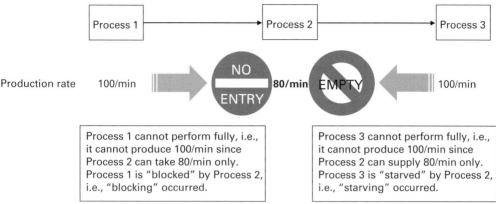

Figure 5.2 Process Coupling – Blocking and Starving

Random variation hits Process 2
with inventory between processes

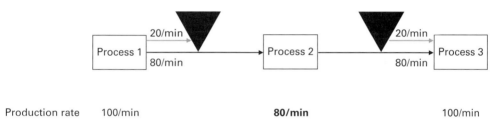

Figure 5.3 Process Decoupling

still make 100 units per minute, 80 units received by Process 2 and 20 stored in inventory. Similarly, inventory between Process 2 and Process 3 makes Process 3 independent of the problem faced by Process 2, i.e., Process 3 can make 100 units per minute, 80 coming from Process 2 and 20 from the inventory. By keeping inventory, the firm can effectively decouple the processes so that each process can perform as it is designed without being too much constrained by its neighboring processes. In fact, it is the primary reason why the firm wants to keep the inventory. There are advantages and also disadvantages to keeping an inventory between processes. We will elaborate more on the pros and cons of inventory. When making a decision on the **size of inventory**, the firm must take into account both advantages and disadvantages of keeping a certain amount of inventory. There are several methodologies the firm can use to determine the **order size**, which ultimately affects the firm's inventory size. Before introducing two such methodologies, we define different types of inventory and discuss how they are determined.

We discuss two approaches to categorize or define inventory. First, we define inventory depending on where it occurs in the supply chain. When the firm has inventory in its upstream supply chain before processing it inside its own production system, it is **raw material inventory**. When the inventory occurs inside the firm's production system, i.e., in the middle of a production process, it is **work-in-process inventory**. Once the product is completed and stored at a storage space ready for shipping to the customer, it is **finished goods inventory**. These three types of inventories are the **supply chain inventories** (Figure 5.4).

The other approach is to define inventory depending on the context under which it occurs. Using this method, we discuss three types of inventory, i.e., base inventory, safety inventory, and transit inventory.

Base inventory is an average inventory between consecutive order-receiving times, which define an ordering or inventory cycle (Figure 5.5). This is the inventory that the company keeps due to the time interval between order receipts. For example, assume that the demand occurs constantly, e.g., 100 units demanded and sold each day. If the company orders and receives 1,000 units, then it takes 10 days for one cycle to complete. That is, at the beginning of each cycle, the company starts with 1,000 units, and at the end of the cycle, none will remain. Then, the average inventory for the company to keep during the cycle is $\dfrac{\text{beginning inventory} + \text{ending inventory}}{2} = \dfrac{1000 + 0}{2} = 500,$

which is the base inventory or base stock. In effect, the base inventory is largely determined by the **order quantity**, i.e., the larger the order quantity, the larger the base stock.

Before the inventory level becomes too low, the company has to place another order. Assume the company continuously monitors the inventory and determines the level at

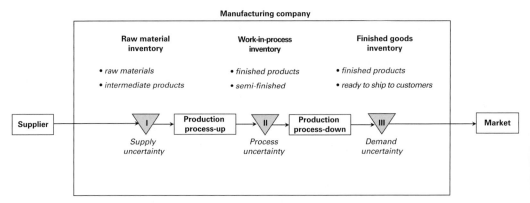

Figure 5.4 A Firm's Supply Chain Inventories

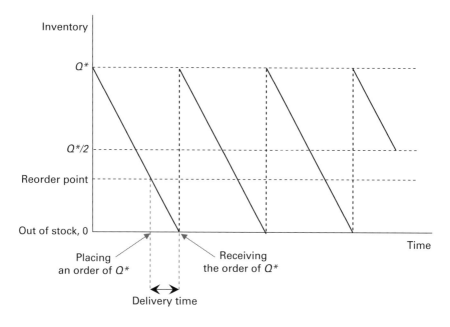

Q* : order amount

Q*/2 : average inventory, base inventory

Figure 5.5 Base Inventory – Assuming Deterministic Demand

which it should place the next order. Such an inventory level at which the company places another order is the reorder point (Figure 5.5). In general, the **reorder point** is affected by the **delivery lead time**, i.e., how long it takes for the supplier to deliver the order to the company after the company places an order. If the demand is constant at 100 units per day and the delivery lead time is four days, then the company should place an order when there are 400 units left, i.e., when the inventory level is at 400. When determining the reorder point, the optimum order quantity is not relevant, since it is determined by factors other than the delivery lead time: note that we will elaborate further on this later.

Figure 5.5 describes a deterministic case, where the demand rate is constant and the delivery time is deterministic, i.e., fixed. But, in reality, the company has to face uncertainty all the time. In particular, the demand rate is not, in general, constant. Figure 5.6 depicts a more realistic situation. In Figure 5.6, the demand is uncertain, causing the inventory level to decrease unevenly. Despite the uncertain demand, let's assume that the company still has the policy to place another order at the reorder point. Further suppose that like the demand, the supplier's delivery time is also uncertain, i.e., the delivery lead time varies. Then, the company might experience **stock-out** due to the uncertain demand rate during the uncertain lead time. The company should be prepared to cope with the stock-out during the lead time. One strategy for the company to achieve this goal is to keep an extra inventory, whose specific role is to make sure the

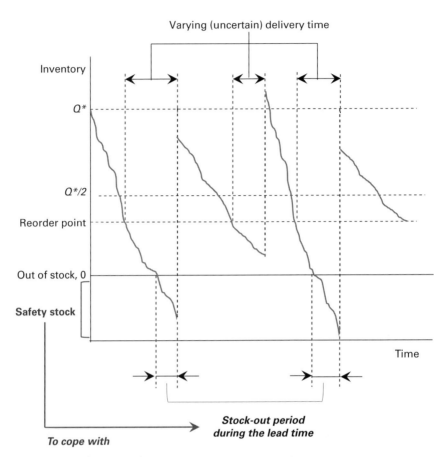

Figure 5.6 Safety Stock – Assuming Uncertain Demand

stock-out doesn't occur during the uncertain lead time. It is the **safety stock** or **safety inventory**.

Finally, there is a **transit inventory**, which is in transit from the supplier to the company as the customer. For example, suppose that the company orders 1,000 units today, but the supplier will deliver the order in 5 days, which is the delivery lead time. In general, the ownership of the goods or materials in transit belongs to the company, but the company doesn't physically possess them. Although it can be temporary, the transit inventory comprised those goods and materials in transit, which sometimes cause difficult accounting and/or financial problems for the company.

Optimal inventory. *Why does the firm want to have a large inventory? Why does the firm want to have a small inventory?* The firm decides an optimum amount of inventory by taking into account both costs and benefits associated with keeping inventory (Table 5.1). Let's first consider the factors that encourage the firm to have more inventory. If the company fails to meet the customer's demand due to its

Table 5.1 Forces Driving Small versus Large Inventory

Forces for Large Inventory	Forces for Small Inventory

- To increase customer service, minimizing lost sales
- To continue production as planned
- To save fixed costs associated with ordering
- To cope with possible price hikes for raw materials
	- To save inventory management costs such as
	  • financial costs such as warehouse costs, interests, taxes, insurances
	  • opportunity costs due to having an excessive inventory
	  • obsolescence, deterioration, shrinkage, theft
	  • excessive management, supervising
	
	- To challenge operations inertia by coupling the processes
	- To facilitate learning and innovation

stock-out, then the company's **service level** (i.e., to meet the customer's requirement when it first comes in) deteriorates. One of the easiest ways to increase the customer service level is to keep plenty of inventory. Note that in order to implement this strategy, the firm has to keep more and more inventory as the customer's demand uncertainty becomes larger. To stay efficient or productive, the firm should be able to continue its production as planned without much **disruption**. There are forces that cause a serious disruption to the production process. If the necessary raw materials arrive at the warehouse irregularly in an unpredictable way, the firm cannot avoid a disruption. Similarly, if the uncertainty affects the firm's internal production process, a disruption occurs. Often, the firm can prevent or overcome these disruptions by keeping plenty of inventory. If the fixed costs associated with placing an order are excessive, the firm can reduce the total **ordering cost** by ordering a large quantity for each order, which eventually implies a large base inventory. Sometimes the firm views inventory management as a tool to cope with financial issues. For instance, it is not unusual that in anticipation of price hikes for raw materials in the future, the firm purchases raw materials which are far larger than the normal order size without such expectation.

There are other factors that discourage the firm from having a large inventory. As already mentioned, keeping inventory costs the firm in many ways. There are many financial costs involved with inventory management. For instance, there are financial costs such as warehouse costs, interest costs, taxes, and insurances, in addition to **opportunity costs** due to having an excessive inventory (e.g., lost opportunity to invest the money in other more profitable projects). There are other costs due to **obsolescence, deterioration, shrinkage**, and theft of the inventory, and also excessive management and supervision.

Which costs are more serious and dominating depends on the industry, market, and/or the company's unique characteristics and conditions. The firm must take into account all of its unique factors, forces both encouraging and discouraging to keep inventory, by conducting an appropriate **cost-and-benefit analysis**.

Now it is time for us to discuss methodologies that help the company determine an optimal order size, which as we have discussed can affect the inventory level. The first one is the method to determine an economic order quantity, i.e., the **EOQ (economic order quantity)** model. In-Depth Concept 5.1 explains the model in great detail. In essence, EOQ determines an optimal order size by trading off the costs associated with making an order. The other is the **newsvendor model**. In-Depth Concept 5.2 thoroughly explains the logic of the model. Unlike EOQ, the newsvendor model considers opportunity costs, i.e., what if the last unit can be sold or cannot be sold? It essentially deals with a probabilistic problem, whereas the EOQ assumes a deterministic context, e.g., a constant demand without any uncertainty. Although we believe these two methodologies, EOQ and newsvendor, shed an important light on understanding the fundamental trade-off issues in determining the optimal order size, they are also limited in that their assumptions are sometimes too simplistic and/or unrealistic. As such, the two in-depth concepts are only for those who are interested in learning analytical tools in operations management, i.e., these are optional readings.

IN-DEPTH CONCEPT 5.1
Economic Order Quantity (EOQ)

There is a classic model to help the manager decide an optimal level of inventory. It is **economic order quantity (EOQ)**, which trades off costs of ordering and keeping inventory.

Notation
D: annual demand for the product
Q: order quantity, i.e., the amount of product the company orders each time
n: number of orders per year, i.e., $n = D/Q$
c: unit ordering cost, i.e., the cost the company pays whenever it places an order
h: unit inventory holding cost per annum, i.e., the cost the company pays for each unit of product it keeps as inventory for a year; and
Q/2: average inventory the company keeps, assuming a constant demand for the product, throughout the year.

Note that this is an advanced modeling. Although we believe its managerial or conceptual implications can help you understand inventory much better, we suggest you may skip this part unless you feel familiar with the analysis method.

An EOQ model takes into account two types of cost, total **ordering cost** and total **inventory-holding cost**. That is, total inventory management cost per year *(TC)* = total ordering cost + total inventory holding cost per year:

$$TC = c\frac{D}{Q} + h\frac{Q}{2}.$$

In order to determine an **optimal ordering quantity**, Q^*, we differentiate TC with regard to Q and equal the result to zero:

$$\frac{dTC}{dQ} = -\frac{cD}{Q^2} + \frac{h}{2} = 0.$$

Therefore, the optimal order quantity is $Q^* = \sqrt{\dfrac{2cD}{h}}$.

Example: A fashion company needs 10,000 tons of dyes for the next 12 months. Whenever the company places an order, it costs $5,000. The company estimates that it costs $300 to keep 1 ton of dyes as inventory for one year.

(1) What is the optimal order size for the company?
(2) If the ordering cost is reduced to $500, what is the optimal order size?
(3) If the inventory holding is increased to $600, what is the optimal order size?

Solution

(1) $\quad Q^* = \sqrt{\dfrac{2cD}{h}} = \sqrt{\dfrac{2 \times 5000 \times 10000}{300}} \cong 577.35 \approx 578.$

That is, each time the company places an order, the order size should be 578 tons.

(2) $\quad Q^* = \sqrt{\dfrac{2cD}{h}} = \sqrt{\dfrac{2 \times 500 \times 10000}{300}} \cong 182.57 \approx 183.$

That is, each time the company places an order, the order size should be 183 tons.

(3) $\quad Q^* = \sqrt{\dfrac{2cD}{h}} = \sqrt{\dfrac{2 \times 5000 \times 10000}{600}} \cong 408.25 \approx 409.$

That is, each time the company places an order, the order size should be 409 tons.

Box continues

There are several assumptions for the EOQ model:

(a)   There is no demand uncertainty, i.e., the demand is deterministic and the company knows the exact amount of the demand.
(b)   The demand occurs regularly, i.e., the demand rate is constant.
(c)   The costs remain the same for the relevant decision horizon, e.g., for a year.

These assumptions are sometimes too simple and unrealistic. That's why the EOQ model is not utilized in the real-world context as extensively as one might expect. Nevertheless, it can help the manager understand the key trade-off relationship between important factors, which affect the economics of keeping inventory. If used wisely, it can be a simple, yet effective tool to offer a great insight for inventory management.

Figure 5.7 graphically shows the logic to determine the optimal order size. As the order size increases, the total ordering cost per year decreases, while the total inventory holding cost per year increases linearly due to the assumption of a constant demand rate. The company's goal is to minimize the total cost, not just either the ordering or holding cost alone. The total cost, which is the sum of the two costs, is a convex function. Therefore, the smallest total cost identifies the optimal order size for the company.

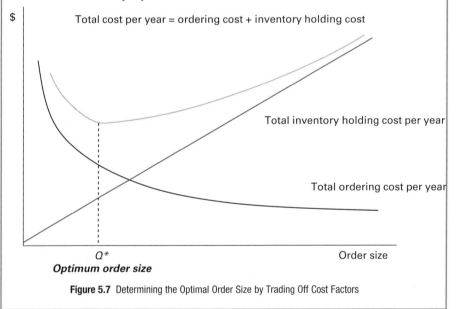

Figure 5.7 Determining the Optimal Order Size by Trading Off Cost Factors

IN-DEPTH CONCEPT 5.2
Newsvendor Problem – Trading Off Inventory Management Costs

There is another important analytical tool that helps to determine an optimal order quantity. Suppose that there is a newspaper boy or girl, i.e., newsvendor, who every day has to decide how many units of newspaper to order for tomorrow's sales. It is a difficult decision problem since the demand is uncertain, i.e., she has to deal with a **demand uncertainty** each day. She pays c for one copy of a newspaper, which she sells to the customer at p. She can return the **leftover**, i.e., unsold, newspapers to the newspaper company, but at a discount s, which is smaller than c. How many copies of the newspaper should she order now for tomorrow's sales?

First, we define the variables and parameters as follows:

D: demand variable;
Q: order quantity (decision variable);
p: sales price per unit;
c: purchase cost per unit;
s: salvage value per unit;
π: total expected net profit;

$C_u = p - c$: understocking cost, the cost due to having one unit less than demanded;
$C_o = c - s$: overstocking cost, the cost due to having one unit more than demanded;
Prob$(D \leq Q)$: probability that the demand is less than or equal to the order quantity;

$$\textbf{Prob}(D \leq Q) \equiv F(Q)$$

Now, the newsvendor's decision problem is to determine the order quantity which generates the largest net profit. Since there is demand uncertainty, it should be an expected net profit.

What is the net profit if the newsvendor orders more than the demand? That is, "net profit if $D \leq Q$" $= Dp - Qc + (Q - D)s$, i.e., sales revenue (Dp) minus total purchase cost (Qc) plus total salvage value for the leftover units $((Q - D)s)$.

Then, what is the net profit if the demand is larger than the order? Similarly, "net profit if $D > Q$" $= Qp - Qc = Q(p - c)$, i.e., sales revenue (Qp) minus total purchase cost (Qc). Note that if the demand is larger than the order quantity, the maximum the firm can sell is the order quantity, not the demand, and there is no leftover.

Therefore, the expected net profit (π) is the average net profit of the two cases, i.e.,

$$\pi = F(Q)\{Dp - Qc + (Q - D)s\} + \left(1 - F(Q)\right)Q(p - c)$$
$$= F(Q)\{Dp - Qc + (Q - D)s - Q(p - c)\} + Q(p - c)$$

Box continues

$$= F(Q)D(p-s) - F(Q)Q(p-s) + Q(p-c)$$
$$= F(Q)D(p-s) + Q\{(p-c) - F(Q)(p-s)\}$$

If $(p-c) - F(Q)(p-s) > 0$, then it is always better to order one more unit, i.e., by ordering one more, the firm can increase its profit. On the contrary, if $(p-c) - F(Q)(p-s) < 0$, then it is always better to order one less, i.e., by reducing the order by one unit, the firm can increase its profit. But, either case cannot be an optimal solution: only when $(p-c) - F(Q)(p-s) = 0$, do we reach an equilibrium, i.e., an optimum order quantity. That is, the optimum order quantity, Q^*, is achieved when $F(Q) = \dfrac{p-c}{p-s}$: the firm should increase its order quantity up to the point when the "probability that the demand is less than or equal to the order quantity $(\text{Prob}(D \le Q) \equiv F(Q))$" becomes $\dfrac{p-c}{p-s}$, which is called the **critical ratio**.

To better understand the managerial implication of the critical ratio, we define two additional costs – understocking and overstocking. An **understocking cost** occurs if the firm orders an amount smaller than the demand by one unit. That is, if the firm cannot sell the last unit demanded by the customer, then it loses the profit, $p-c$, which it could have earned should it have ordered one more unit. Therefore, the unit understocking cost is $C_u = p - c$. Similarly, if the firm orders an amount larger than the demand by one unit, an overstocking cost occurs, which equals the purchasing cost minus salvage value, $C_o = c - s$: if the firm cannot sell the last unit, it loses the unit purchasing cost (c), but earns the salvage value (s) by salvaging the leftover unit at a discount.

Now we can rearrange the critical ratio as follows:

$$F(Q) = \frac{p-c}{p-s} = \frac{p-c}{p-c+c-s} = \frac{C_u}{C_o + C_u},$$

i.e., the critical ratio is the understocking cost over the sum of overstocking and understocking costs. Here, again, we see that the optimal order quantity is determined by trading off the inventory management costs.

Example: Suppose the newsvendor faces the market with the parameters as follows:

- D: demand follows a probability distribution in Table 5.2;
- p: sales price per unit is $7;
- c: purchase cost per unit is $3;
- s: salvage value per unit is $1.

Box continues

Table 5.2 Demand Distribution (*D* is the random variable of demand)

Actual Demand (d)	Probability, Prob(D=d)	Cumulative Probability, Prob (D≤d)
1	0.010	0.010
2	0.050	0.060
3	0.060	0.120
4	0.070	0.190
5	0.085	0.275
6	0.090	0.365
7	0.095	0.460
8	0.098	0.558
9	**0.100**	**0.658**
10	**0.090**	**0.748**
11	0.070	0.818
12	0.065	0.883
13	0.055	0.938
14	0.050	0.988
15	0.012	1.000

How can she estimate the probabilities in Table 5.2? One possible way is to use the **historical data**. For instance, she can obtain the demand data for the last 1,000 days. Of these 1,000 days, the demand for the newspaper was just one copy for 10 days, five copies for 85 days, nine copies for 100 days, and so on. In order to use the empirical frequency for estimating probability, we need an assumption that the events, i.e., how many copies were demanded for each day of the last 1,000 days, were independent of each other: e.g., the demand on the 515th day was independent of the demand on any other day of the other 999 days, i.e., it was not affected by the demand on any other day. In addition, we need another assumption that the demand pattern in the past will repeat in the foreseeable future, i.e., the past demand distribution will be valid in the future as well. Although in a real-world setting it is not always easy or possible to make these two assumptions completely, for a practical sense, it is reasonable to use the historical frequency for estimating the future probability.

Suppose that she is confident that the past demand information will be valid in the future. Now she has to decide how many copies of the newspaper to order for tomorrow's sales. Using the profit equations developed here, we calculate the expected profit as the order quantity changes, assuming that the demand follows the probability distribution in Table 5.2. See Table 5.3 for calculating the expected profit when she orders nine copies of the newspaper, i.e., she can expect to earn $23.77 if she orders nine copies tonight. Table 5.4 and Figure 5.8 show the relationship between the order and the expected profit: both indicate that the newsvendor's optimal decision is to order ten copies and then she expects to earn $23.82 tomorrow.

Box continues

Table 5.3 Total Expected Profit When the Newsvendor Ordered Nine Units

Price	7	
Cost	3	
Salvage	1	
Order	9	
Demand	Probability	Profit
1	0.010	−12
2	0.050	−6
3	0.060	0
4	0.070	6
5	0.085	12
6	0.090	18
7	0.095	24
8	0.098	30
9	0.100	36
10	0.090	36
11	0.070	36
12	0.065	36
13	0.055	36
14	0.050	36
15	0.012	36
Total expected profit		**23.77**

Table 5.4 Total Expected Profits

Order	Total Expected Profit
1	4.00
2	7.94
3	11.58
4	14.86
5	17.72
6	20.07
7	21.88
8	23.12
9	23.77
10	23.82
11	23.34
12	22.43
13	21.13
14	19.50
15	17.57

Box continues

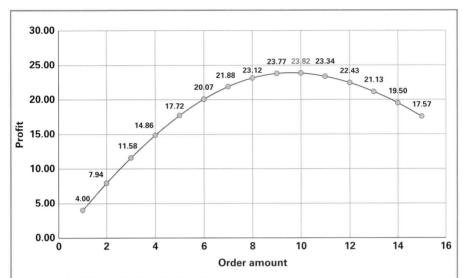

Figure 5.8 Total Expected Profits as the Order Size Changes

So far we have used Microsoft Excel to obtain an optimal order size. Could we have attained the same answer using the critical ratio? Recall that the critical ratio is $\text{Prob}(D \leq Q) = F(Q) = \dfrac{p - c}{p - s}$. Thus, the critical ratio of this example is $F(Q) = \dfrac{7 - 3}{7 - 1} = \dfrac{4}{6} = 0.67$. According to Table 5.2, the critical ratio is between 0.658 ($\text{Prob}(D \leq 9)$, i.e., the probability that the demand is less than or equal to 9, and 0.748 ($\text{Prob}(D \leq 10)$). If the demand quantity can be expressed as a real number, i.e., a continuous variable, we might be able to identify the order quantity matching the critical ratio exactly. When the demand is a discrete variable, e.g., an integer as in our example, however, we have to use an approximation. That is, since the critical ratio is between $\text{Prob}(D \leq 9)$ and $\text{Prob}(D \leq 10)$, we know that the optimum solution is to order either nine or ten. A rather practical guide in this case is to choose the larger one, i.e., the ordering of ten for this example. That is, the optimum solution is the order quantity whose **cumulative probability** is the one that is greater than the critical ratio for the first time.

Question: Suppose the newsvendor faces the market with the parameters as follows:

- D: demand follows a probability distribution in Table 5.2;
- p: sales price per unit is $7;
- c: purchase cost per unit is $4;
- s: salvage value per unit is $1.

How many copies should she order tonight in order to maximize the expected profit tomorrow? First, calculate the optimal order size using Microsoft Excel. Then, calculate the optimal order size using the critical ratio. Is the answer different from that in the example above? Explain why.

5.2   Fundamental Roles of Inventory

Now we look into inventory from a more strategic perspective. Although our discussion so far has been rather focused on basic characteristics of inventory and slightly analytical, it helps us better comprehend the strategic issues involved with inventory and its effective management. As such, the ensuing discussion is more in-depth and at times refers to the concepts previously touched upon when necessary to make them clearer and more relevant.

Inventory's role. The most important role played by inventory is to cope with uncertainty. We have already discussed the relationship between inventory and uncertainty in Chapter 3. Other things being equal, the more uncertain the market demand, the more inventory the company has to retain at the same service rate. Large inventory means excessive inventory holding costs. In general, the inventory holding cost is the single most important element in a company's income statement – it is usually the largest expense a company has to make: note that, in this chapter, we define the inventory holding cost as a very comprehensive concept, which includes all tangible and intangible as well as opportunity costs involved with managing the inventory. One estimate says that the inventory holding cost is about 20 to 40 percent of the inventory's value. This implies that if the company can't sell its product for two to three years, it would have been better not to make the product in the first place.

For effective SCM, it is critical for the company to make the right decisions regarding the inventory: where to locate the inventory in the supply chain, how much inventory to hold, and so on. To answer these questions, the decision-maker needs to understand the specific characteristics and roles taken by the inventory at different points in the supply chain.

(1) Supply chain inventory. The characteristics of inventories held at various points in a supply chain are different, depending on where the inventory is retained (Figure 5.9). We have already defined various inventories in the supply chain as "**supply chain inventory**." The inventory between the supply function and operations takes the form of raw materials and intermediate products, and copes with **supply uncertainty** in the upstream and **process uncertainty** in the downstream. There is inventory inside the production system, which is the **work-in-process inventory** dealing with process uncertainty within the production system. The inventory between operations and the distribution function takes the form of finished or semi-finished products, and copes with process uncertainty in the upstream and **logistical uncertainty** in the downstream. Finally, the inventory between distribution function and the market, which usually consists of finished goods, deals with logistical uncertainty in the upstream and **demand uncertainty** in the downstream.

The supply uncertainty is related to various risks on the part of suppliers. For instance, the most prevalent supply uncertainty is the **delivery uncertainty** from the supplier to the manufacturer – it is uncertain how long, exactly, it will take for the supplier to deliver supplies such as parts and raw materials to the manufacturing

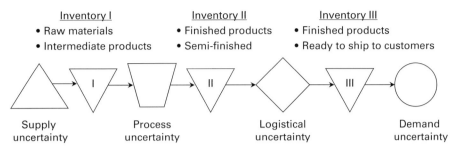

Figure 5.9 Types of Inventory

company. Others include the supplier's own process uncertainty and the possibility of finding defects in the supplies. The process uncertainty is observed internally at the operations function, e.g., the manufacturing system. The production process is vulnerable to numerous causes of uncertainty. Machine or equipment breakdown causes the process to slow down or even completely halt. Human behavioral irregularity among workers could also cause process uncertainty – a labor strike could force the production process to a standstill. There are other random or systematic factors that might affect the process, leading to process uncertainty. In essence, the process uncertainty makes it difficult for the company to plan and schedule the production in a predictable way. In order to mitigate the negative impact due to the process uncertainty, it is necessary to keep inventory before and after the operations process. The logistical uncertainty is concerned with the delivery uncertainty in the **outbound logistics**. For instance, when the **distribution center** does not function properly, the manufacturing company can't distribute its finished products in a timely manner. Similarly, if third-party logistics companies such as UPS and FedEx do not perform as expected, the manufacturing company has to face logistical uncertainty. In order to avoid this kind of uncertainty, there needs to be inventory held between the operations process and the distribution function. Finally, there is demand uncertainty in the market: it is very difficult to forecast exactly the volume of the demand for the finished goods by the customers. Sometimes the product line or product mix demanded by the customers is mismatched with that anticipated by the company, and this discrepancy causes a significant inefficiency in the supply chain. Another serious problem is that the features of the product demanded by the customers are different from those the company forecasted and designed. In sum, we can think of three categories of demand uncertainty: **volume**, **product mix**, and **product features**. In order to respond to the market's fast-changing demand characteristics – the demand uncertainty – the company finds it necessary to keep inventory between the market and the distribution function in the supply chain.

(2) Inventory value and flexibility. There are two important issues in managing inventory: how much inventory to keep and where. There are quantitative tools available to determine an optimal level of inventory. For example, we already discussed that the EOQ model enables the company to decide the optimal order quantity by taking into account such factors as total demand of the product, inventory holding cost, and ordering cost. Once the optimal order quantity is decided, it is easy to estimate the average inventory. However, this model's most serious limitation is its assumption about deterministic demand. Since there exists uncertainty in numerous forms in the market, managers need to use more sophisticated models to control the inventory, which help the managers estimate the safety, as well as average inventory level, and also the ordering frequency and quantity.

In this section, we focus more on where to keep the inventory. Consider a supply chain for French fries at fast food restaurants. At the very upstream of the supply chain, there are farms that grow potatoes. Once the farmers harvest the potatoes, they sell them to a processor that washes, rough slices, and packages the potatoes in large quantities. The processor supplies the frozen potatoes to a wholesaler, who cuts them to various shapes for different uses and packages them in smaller bags. The wholesaler sells small-size bags of different shapes to the retailers. Each fast-food restaurant buys frozen French fries from an appropriate retailer and fries them. Finally, individual customers buy tasty French fries from the restaurant. As the potatoes travel through the supply chain, their physical attributes have changed, e.g., raw potatoes (unprocessed potatoes) ➔ rough processed frozen potatoes ➔ frozen French fries ➔ cooked French fries. As the potatoes move from an upstream activity to a downstream one, the unit value has increased because of **value-added activities** performed on them. For instance, 1 kilogram of raw potatoes costs much less than 1 kilogram of ready-to-eat French fries. Therefore, other things being equal, keeping 1 kilogram of raw potatoes as inventory costs less in terms of inventory holding cost than retaining 1 kilogram of fully cooked French fries as inventory.

Now consider the same supply chain and think about flexibility. One can use the raw potatoes in many different ways. For example, rather than making French fries, one can make potato chips with the raw potatoes, cook them as a side dish to a main entrée, or even transform them into cooking ingredients. But, once the potatoes are cut into rough shapes and frozen, their potential use becomes limited; perhaps, now they can be used for either chips or French fries only. Finally, once the frozen potato slices are fried at the restaurant, they can no longer offer any alternative use. The point is that as the potatoes move from an upstream to a downstream activity, their flexibility to be useful for multiple purposes diminishes fast.

Figure 5.10 shows the overall patterns of inventory unit values and their flexibility as they move through the supply chain. Now we can answer the question about where to retain the inventory more confidently. Other things being comparable or unchanged, it is better to move inventory to an upstream position in the supply chain as much as possible. It is true not only from an individual company's perspective, but also from that of an entire economy (Figure 5.11). This proposition supports the value of the **JIT** (**just-in-time**) system. Some people say that JIT is simply transferring one party's inventory to another's and therefore it does not create real value to the company. But, if following the JIT principle means shifting inventory from a downstream to an upstream function as much as possible, we would put forth that it creates real value not only for individual companies, but also for the entire economy as a whole. Of course, JIT contributes to other more fundamental improvements, too, not just saving an inventory management cost.

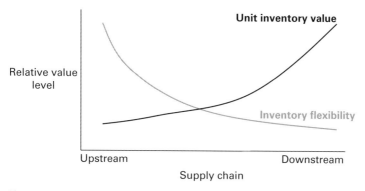

Figure 5.10 Inventory Value and Flexibility

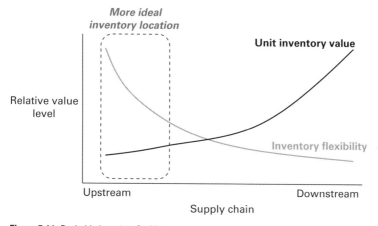

Figure 5.11 Desirable Inventory Position

(3) Flow strategy. How to manage the process flow is an important issue, which is also related to inventory management. Each process deals with both **physical flows** and **information flows**: physical goods such as raw materials, partly finished, and finished goods flow throughout the process, and also information about various aspects of production function flows through the process. Depending on the principal directions of such flows, we can identify two extreme process flow strategies: the **push strategy** and the **pull strategy**.

The **push system** has been widely adopted until recently. The primary motivation of the push system is to decouple the **stochastic interdependence** between individual processes (Figure 5.12). Suppose that a product is completed after going through two consecutive processes, P_1 and P_2. Each of the processes has a capacity of processing 100 units per hour. When both processes are performing normally, there is no need to worry about their stochastic interdependence. Now suppose that due to an unknown reason, P_1 suddenly becomes unable to function for an hour: such an unknown reason is of stochastic nature. If there is no inventory between the two processes, P_2 also has to stop for an hour until P_1 becomes functional again. But, if there is enough inventory to supply intermediate products to P_2 for at least an hour, then P_2 doesn't have to stop because of the stochastic disruption at P_1. In essence, the inventory decouples the stochastic interdependence between P_1 and P_2. Now assume that P_2 is failing due to a stochastic disturbance. If there is no inventory between the two processes, P_1 has to stop as well, until P_2 becomes functional again. Like in the previous situation, the inventory is decoupling the stochastic interdependence between the two processes.

Since the inventory acts as a buffer against stochastic irregularities between the processes, the upstream process P_1 does not have to worry about its downstream activity's condition, and vice versa. Consequently, there is little need to communicate between them, and the information flows unilaterally from the upstream to the downstream activity along with the physical flow of products. There are advantages and disadvantages in this system. The most important advantage comes from the stochastic **decoupling between processes**, which makes the process planning much easier. For example, since the inventory functions as a buffer between the processes, the upstream process doesn't have to take into account its downstream function's situation when planning its operations schedule. Therefore, the production scheduling is simple and straightforward from the perspective of the upstream process. The downstream process also views the inventory as a buffer that helps it plan its own production schedule without worrying about the **operability** of its upstream process. As a result, the entire production planning becomes efficient at least on the surface. There are disadvantages in the push system as well. First, retaining inventory involves diverse costs such as interest expenses to fund the inventory, warehouse expenses, obsolescence costs, and the like. Another more serious disadvantage is that the inventory might disguise critical problems in the system since it makes the processes work without any interruption. In many cases, such critical problems are fundamentally damaging the system's performance, but managers fail to identify their true sources due to the fact that the inventory is covering up. Consider that a pure JIT system eliminates inventory completely from the factory floor. Researchers point out that the JIT system enables the company to identify and rectify serious operations problems: its no-inventory strategy forces those problems to surface by themselves, and it makes them easy to find.

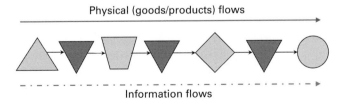

Physical (goods/products) flows

Information flows

= inventory.

Figure 5.12 Push System

Because of these strategic as well as economic reasons against stocking inventory, the **pull system** was developed (Figure 5.13). Like in the push system, the physical materials flow from upstream to downstream. But, information flows in reverse – from downstream to upstream. Consider the example system above. Under the pull system, P_1 does not start making products until P_2 says so – that is, it begins production only when it has received specific orders from P_2. Similarly, P_2 won't start processing until it has firm orders from its own downstream process – probably, the end-customer market. Because each process does not start producing until it actually receives a sign to do so from its immediate downstream process, there is little need for an inventory to exist between the processes. The pull system underlies the principles of JIT, which endeavors to eliminate inefficiency or waste through doing away with the inventory: without inventory on the shop floor, it becomes easier for managers to identify **root causes** of any process irregularity or malfunctioning. Like the push system, the pull system has its own demerits: the most serious problem in the pull system is concerned with a tight stochastic interdependence between the processes, which the push system is designed to circumvent. Since there is no inventory between the processes, when something is wrong at a single process, it risks stopping the entire system even when there might not be a real systematic deviation in the system. It is potentially damaging to the company, since it is very likely that unsystematic causes might affect the process in a random manner, which is beyond the control of any managerial efforts. If the entire system is stopped due to a **random cause**, it could be very costly to the company – the company cannot learn anything, even if it stops to learn.

As discussed above, each of the extreme systems, push or pull, has both advantages and disadvantages at the same time. This observation has motivated developing a balanced approach. A **contingent inventory** system is suggested to capitalize on the advantages of the two systems and to avoid their disadvantages. Figure 5.14 shows an example of the contingent inventory system. The contingent inventory system assumes 100 percent **inspection**, which is effective and fast enough to determine whether the product is defective or not in real time. Once the product is determined to be defective, the inspection system must also be able to tell whether the defect is triggered by a systematic – assignable – or random cause. Should the defective product be made due to an **assignable cause**, then the entire process must stop and management should search for the cause, that is, begin the **learning process**. On the contrary, if the defect is caused by random phenomena, then the process should not be interrupted.

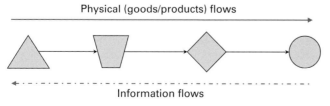

Physical (goods/products) flows

Information flows

Figure 5.13 Pull System

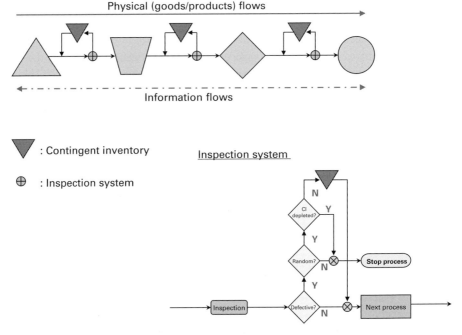

Figure 5.14 Contingent Inventory System

Therefore, the inspection system must perform two subsequent tasks: to determine whether the product is defective or not and, if it is, to decide whether it is caused by a systematic or just random phenomenon. To determine whether the product is defective requires the inspection system to be fast and effective in measuring the various attributes of the product and in comparing them with normal values. Then, how can the inspection system tell whether the cause is assignable or random? One way to tell is to keep a contingent inventory. For example, suppose the size of contingent inventory is n and the predetermined time length is T. Thus, a **contingent rule** would say that if the process produces defective products more than n units within the time period T, then we infer that the process is affected by assignable causes. How to determine n and T depends on probabilistic behaviors and relevant measures of the process in the past. The decision-maker can use **historical data** to determine the appropriate values of n and T for a certain level of confidence.

A primary objective of the contingent inventory system is to keep a minimum level of inventory, yet to avoid improper process stopping due to false alarms from random causes. Thus, the contingent inventory system helps the decision-maker to engage in **process improvement** since there exists only a small inventory, which does not conceal fundamental problems in operations to a great extent. In addition, it enables the decision-maker to avoid costly process disruptions by safely bypassing false alarms. Of course, the success of this system hinges on how to evaluate optimal values of n and T, "optimal" in the sense that these values reflect the decision-maker's attitude toward the risks assessed based on the historical stochasticity shown by the process.

(4) Forecasting. One of the most important objectives of SCM is to fulfill customer demand as much as possible. The firm can enhance its capability of accom-
plishing this goal by minimizing the **mismatch between supply and demand** –
making only what the market is actually demanding, i.e., supplying the exact
amount demanded. **Understocking** costs will occur when the supply is less than
the demand, whereas **overstocking** costs will occur when the supply is more than
the demand. Both understocking and overstocking are costly to the firm: understocking costs include lost sales and customer loyalty loss, and overstocking costs
include excessive inventory holding costs, potential markdown costs, and obsolescence costs.

How can the firm minimize the mismatch between supply and demand? One methodological issue is concerned with forecasting. **Demand forecasting** is predicting future
trends of demand for a particular product. The decision-maker uses the forecast data to
plan production and decide key decision variables. There are many forecasting methods,
which can be grouped into two large categories: qualitative forecasting methods and
quantitative forecasting methods.

Qualitative forecasting methods are based on subjective or individual judgments.
Suppose the firm introduces into the market a totally new product, for which there
is no historical data to analyze. Then, how can the firm plan for its production
quantity and marketing level? The firm must be able to forecast the future demand
for the product – how many units will be sold next month, quarter, and year.
Given no objective or historical data to work with, the decision-maker has no
other way except by relying on more subjective estimation. Perhaps, there are
experts inside or outside the firm, who can tell approximate figures of the
demand, or the CEO herself can make a personal assessment of the demand
based on her previous similar experiences. Another more formal, albeit still
subjective, method is to survey customers in the target market, by asking potential
customers whether they want to buy the product and, if they do, how many they
will buy, and so forth. Each of these approaches is a form of the qualitative
forecasting method. Note that we elaborate on a very important qualitative forecasting tool, the **Delphi method**, in a later section of this chapter.

On the other hand, there are more objective and structured forecasting methods
available as well. Virtually all of these quantitative methods are utilizing historical
data about the product in question or at least a product that shares much commonality
in terms of market experience with the product in point. Examples of **quantitative
forecasting** methods are **time series analysis** (moving average methods, exponential
smoothing, and so forth) and **regression analysis** for causal forecasting, to name
a couple.

Which forecasting methods should and can the firm use? This is an important
question for the decision-maker. One criterion to determine the appropriate forecasting methods is the product life cycle (PLC), that is, where the product in
question lies in its product life cycle. Figure 5.15 shows the relationship between
the PLC and relevant forecasting methods. When the firm introduces a new product

to the market for the first time, there is little information about how the market would respond to the product. With little or no previous information or data about the demand for the product, the firm can have only one option to estimate the characteristics of the market demand, i.e., using more subjective or judgmental methods. As the product enters the growth stage, the firm garners more information and data about the market's response to the product. As more historical and actual data points become available for analysis, the firm develops more capability for conducting sophisticated analyses, which utilize statistical as well as mathematical forecasting models. Therefore, as the product moves from introduction to growth and maturity in its PLC, the forecasting method changes from mainly qualitative to more quantitative and the decision horizon changes from relatively long term to shorter term. Finally, when the product reaches its decline stage, there are a few choices the firm can make. The firm might want to either exit from the current market or regenerate another PLC with a next-generation product. Should the firm decide to recreate the PLC by introducing a next-generation product, the relationship between PLC and forecasting methods is reiterated.

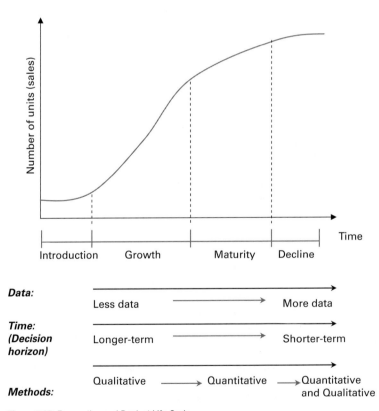

Figure 5.15 Forecasting and Product Life Cycle

5.3   Demand Uncertainty and Qualitative Forecasting

As we have discussed, inventory acts as a buffer against uncertainty, i.e., uncertainty increases inventory. Since inventory is closely related to cost, innovation, and learning, the firm must manage its inventory effectively by coping with demand uncertainty optimally, i.e., reducing the uncertainty as much as possible. Therefore, the firm's forecasting capability is vital. It is very important for the company to forecast the demand accurately, since the forecasting data are the key input to its production planning and scheduling. Wrong forecasting means severe uncertainty, which causes abrupt and frequent disruption in the production process, leading to quality failure.

There are two different types of demand uncertainty – aggregate level and product-mix level (Figure 5.16). **Aggregate level uncertainty** is about the overall product group or category such as passenger cars, ski parkas, bicycles, and the like. Let's focus on the uncertainty faced by an individual company. For example, consider an automobile company that manufactures and sells three passenger car models, A, B, and C. For coping with the aggregate level uncertainty, the company has to ask, *"How many passenger cars in total can we sell next year?"* Forecasting for the aggregate level demand calls for analyzing macroeconomic data such as income levels, population, interest rates, exchange rates, disposable incomes, and the like. It is usual to utilize some econometric methodology such as regression analysis. It is relatively easy to make an accurate forecast for the aggregate level demand, which changes rather slowly and/or predictably. Suppose that the company was able to sell 1 million units of passenger cars last year. Then, how many passenger cars can the company sell this year? In order to

Aggregate level uncertainty
- Forecasting using macroeconomic variables
    - ✓ method – econometrics
- Aggregate demand >> aggregate supply
    - ✓ capacity increase
    - ✓ "focused" strategy – refocusing the target market
- Aggregate demand << aggregate supply
    - ✓ capacity reduction
    - ✓ demand management – generating market demand
        - ❖ new product development, quality improvement

Product mix-level uncertainty
- Responsiveness is the key, assuming $D \approx S$ at the aggregate level
- Value of flexibility is very high
- Supply chain coordination tools employed
    - ✓ risk-based production planning, postponement
- Forecasting
    - ✓ abundant data available
        - ❖ Quantitative methods: regression analysis, time series analysis
    - ✓ no or very few data available
        - ❖ Qualitative methods: judgmental, market research, expert opinion (Delphi method)

Figure 5.16 Uncertainty Types and Forecasting Methods

answer that question, the company has to make a forecast based on such macroeconomic data as the gross domestic product (GDP) growth rate, exchange rate, interest rate, number of people who can afford to buy a car, and so on. Probably, the answer would be something like "5 percent increase over last year's demand, due to 3 percent increase in GDP and 2 percent depreciation of the currency." The change at the aggregate level demand from one year to the next is mostly on a smaller scale, e.g., 5 percent increase or decrease.

Compare the company's **supply capacity** with the **aggregate level demand**. If the aggregate demand is at least roughly equivalent to the company's capacity, i.e., the two are approximately balanced, there is no serious problem in terms of the firm's ability to cope with the aggregate level uncertainty. In contrast, what happens when the supply is much larger than the demand or vice versa continuously for an extended period of time? The most obvious action to be taken by the firm is to adjust its production capacity. If the demand is consistently much larger than the supply, the firm must consider increasing its capacity, unless it decides to serve only a small portion of the market. On the other hand, if the demand is consistently smaller than the supply, the firm must reduce its physical capacity so as to avoid unwanted overhead costs, unless it is willing to explore and develop new markets to increase the aggregate demand. That is, when there is a constant mismatch between aggregate demand and supply, to adjust capacity is more effective than to increase flexibility.

The other is the **product-mix level uncertainty**. Consider the automobile case again. Suppose the company estimates this year's aggregate demand for its passenger cars to be 1.05 million units. But, having an accurate forecasting for the aggregate level demand doesn't diminish the firm's worry about the uncertainty causing disruption and variation in its production. In order to properly plan and schedule its production, the company should know how many units out of the total 1.05 million passenger cars will be model A, B, or C. The product-mix level uncertainty is about the uncertainty involved with individual product types, e.g., model A, B, and C. The product-mix level demand can be much more sensitive to the most recent real-time factors or variables, which cannot be easily anticipated or expected long before they actually happen in the market, than is the aggregate level demand. For instance, a sudden trend or fad associated with a certain color or style may affect the consumer's mind so as to change her buying behavior, e.g., from model A to model C, at the last minute: usually such an abrupt change cannot be estimated or forecasted before it actually occurs and becomes visible. As such, it is more difficult for the firm to cope with the product-mix level uncertainty than the aggregate level uncertainty. That is, the product-mix uncertainty calls for the firm to respond quickly within a much shorter period of time.

Assuming that the firm achieves a balance between demand and supply at the aggregate level, its responsiveness or flexibility is essential to dealing with the product-mix level uncertainty. When we emphasize reducing the mismatch between demand and supply as one of the most imperative goals in supply chain management, it is about minimizing the mismatch at the product-mix level more than at the aggregate level. As a result, forecasting for the product mix is more difficult and challenging than for the aggregate demand. There are two different groups of forecasting methods, depending on whether the historical demand data are abundant or not. When abundant data are available, the firm can employ quantitative forecasting tools such as regression analysis and time series analysis. On the contrary, if no **historical data** for the product mix are available, the firm cannot but rely on more qualitative forecasting methods such as management judgment, market research, grass-root approach, expert opinion, and so forth. It depends on many strategic or qualitative factors to decide which specific methodology to use for qualitative forecasting.

Here, we want to focus on an **expert opinion** approach, i.e., the **Delphi method**, since it is a very powerful forecasting tool that objectifies subjective opinions of the experts. It is useful especially when the firm develops a completely new product, but there are no historical data available. The forecasting outcome derived from the Delphi method is a vital input to some of the strategic supply chain coordination mechanisms the firm can make use of to boost its flexibility, e.g., **postponement, risk-based production planning** (RBPP), and **vendor-managed inventory** (VMI): we elaborate further on these mechanisms in the ensuing chapters.

5.3.1   The Delphi Method

It is one of the most powerful qualitative forecasting tools, in particular when the firm develops an innovative product, for which little historical information and few comparable data are available. Figure 5.17 shows a conceptual structure of the Delphi method. We present the method's general procedure as follows:

(1)   to choose the experts to participate in the Delphi method, representing a variety of knowledgeable managers or employees in various independent market segments that cover the entire market the firm serves; to define the **stopping rule**, ε, so that the process is stopped if $\sigma/\mu < \varepsilon$ is achieved (note that μ is the mean and σ is the standard deviation of the experts' estimate for demand);

(2)   to put the experts in the same physical place so that the **face-to-face communication** and interaction are feasible and effective;

(3)   to explain rich details about the product by the champion of the product to the experts; for instance, such details as the philosophy of the new product (why to develop, i.e., motivation), complete elements of the product such as styles, colors, materials, and suppliers; after the first round, the developer or champion of the new product can explain further details about the new product, using the previous round's outcomes;

(4)   to let the experts discuss the product and its demand actively with each other to make their own forecasting (experts' brainstorming); after the first round, the experts can peruse and discuss the previous round's outcomes;

(5)   through a questionnaire, to obtain forecasts from all participants, including any premises, qualifications, and explanations about their subjective judgment for the forecasts, e.g., why they forecast that way; this must be an anonymous process, i.e., no one should know who estimates what and why;

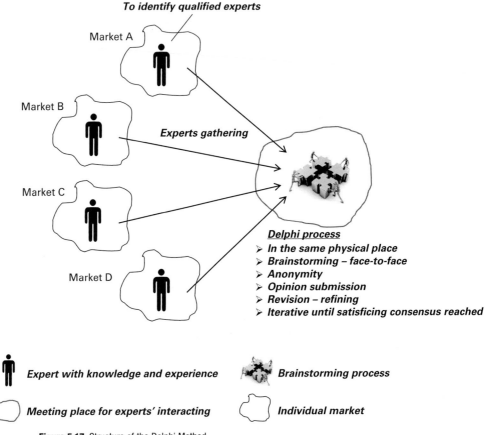

To identify qualified experts

Market A

Market B

Experts gathering

Market C

Market D

Delphi process
➤ *In the same physical place*
➤ *Brainstorming – face-to-face*
➤ *Anonymity*
➤ *Opinion submission*
➤ *Revision – refining*
➤ *Iterative until satisficing consensus reached*

Expert with knowledge and experience   *Brainstorming process*

Meeting place for experts' interacting   *Individual market*

Figure 5.17 Structure of the Delphi Method

(6) to summarize the results, including the mean (μ) and the standard deviation (σ) of entire expert forecasts for the new product's demand, plus thorough descriptive or qualitative explanations and reasons why each expert forecasts so;

(7) to test the stopping rule "Is the stopping criterion met?"; if $\sigma/\mu < \varepsilon$, stop the process and use the mean (μ) and the standard deviation (σ) of the new product's demand that are determined now; if not, move to the next step;

(8) to distribute the summary report (from Step 6) to the participants (i.e., experts); it is possible to refine the questionnaire, based on the most recent outcomes and distribute the updated survey form to the experts along with the summary report;

(9) go to Step 3.

We already mentioned that the Delphi method is a very powerful qualitative forecasting tool. How does it enable the firm to make an accurate forecasting, following the procedure above? As the Delphi method continues the iterative process of **brainstorming** and surveying, the variance (represented by "the standard deviation normalized by

Table 5.5 Rounds in the Delphi Method ($\varepsilon = 0.1$ Assumed)

Round (i)	Mean (μ_i)	Standard Deviation (σ_i)	Ratio (σ_i/μ_i)
1st	8,000	3,000	0.375
2nd	11,000	1,600	0.145
3rd	9,000	800	0.089

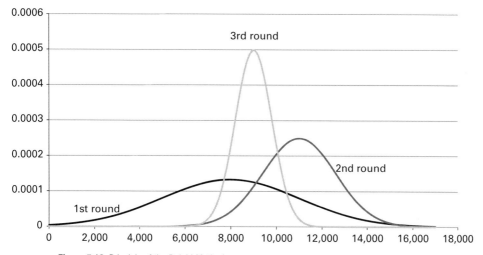

Figure 5.18 Principle of the Delphi Method

the mean") among the experts' forecasting is dwindling, i.e., $\dfrac{\sigma_1}{\mu_1} \geq \dfrac{\sigma_2}{\mu_2} \geq \ldots \geq \dfrac{\sigma_i}{\mu_i}$: the experts' forecasting converges to a consensus value. We infer that as the experts go through the brainstorming process using the summary forecast, they update and refine their own estimates by listening to others' reasoning and sharing their own ideas with other experts. This "listening-brainstorming-updating-refining" process might be the driving force behind the formidable effectiveness of the Delphi method.

Figure 5.18 shows the converging process of an example in Table 5.5. At the end of the first round of the Delphi method, the expert forecasting results in $\mu_1 = 8,000$ and $\sigma_1 = 3,000$, and therefore $\sigma_1/\mu_1 = 0.375$. Since σ_1/μ_1 is larger than the stopping criterion $\varepsilon = 0.1$, the process proceeds to the second round. The second round doesn't derive consensus and the process moves to the third round. Finally, $\dfrac{\sigma_1}{\mu_1} \geq \dfrac{\sigma_2}{\mu_2} \geq \varepsilon \geq \dfrac{\sigma_3}{\mu_3}$ holds after the third round and the Delphi method stops. Now the consensus outcome, $\mu_3 = 9,000$ and $\sigma_3 = 800$, is the forecasting result, which the company can use to plan and schedule its production of the new product.

How is the stopping rule $\varepsilon = 0.1$ determined? Usually the company can determine ε based on its experience in the past. Or sometimes it is possible to derive an analytical formulation to decide an optimal value. Whatever the case may be, ε is supposed to reflect the firm's **forecasting capability**, i.e., the higher the forecasting capability, the smaller the stopping rule ε.

5.4   Inventory, Innovation, and Learning

We already talked about various costs involved with inventory management. The high cost of keeping inventory is one reason why the company has to be careful about its inventory. But, we alluded to other factors that potentially make inventory critical to effective supply chain management. In this section, we discuss two such factors, i.e., innovation and learning, which are closely intertwined with inventory.

5.4.1   Inventory and Innovation Speed

Suppose there are two companies: one company currently has an inventory worth three times its monthly sales, i.e., three months' sales, and the other has an inventory worth only one month's sales. Assume that the two companies are comparable in every other aspect and have just developed new products that are exactly the same. How long does it take for the high-inventory company to be able to start selling its new product in the market? How about the low-inventory company?

Figure 5.19 shows the high-inventory case, i.e., it takes at least three months before the company can start launching its new products in the market, since it must sell its existing inventory first unless it can afford to write off the old products completely. On the other hand, the low-inventory company can speed up its new product introduction, i.e., it will be able to sell its new products in the market in one month (Figure 5.20). If the market is characterized with high uncertainty and/or fast technological innovation, the **time-to-market** can be a determining factor for competitive advantage: the faster the new product introduction, the stronger the firm's competitive advantage in the market.

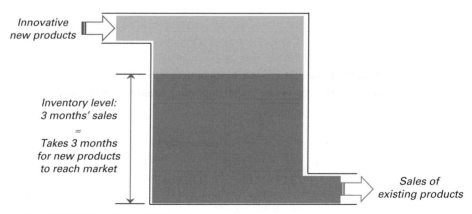

Figure 5.19 High Inventory and NPD Speed

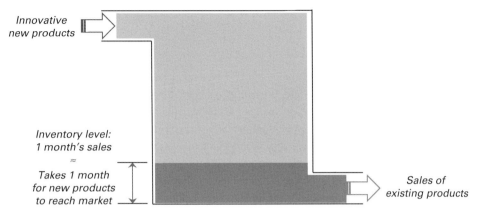

Innovative new products

Inventory level: 1 month's sales

≈

Takes 1 month for new products to reach market

Sales of existing products

Figure 5.20 Low Inventory and NPD Speed

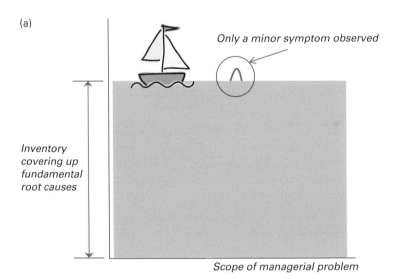

(a)

Only a minor symptom observed

Inventory covering up fundamental root causes

Scope of managerial problem

Figure 5.21 Inventory and Learning

5.4.2   Inventory and Learning

The other strategic role played by inventory is concerned with the firm's learning capability. In fact, it is the most important reason why the JIT system makes it a rule to eradicate inventory as much as possible. We use an analogy (Figure 5.21a). Suppose a ship sails on the ocean with a very high sea level, i.e., the water is full, which we analogize to a very high level of inventory. Because of the full water, the ship cannot see what is beneath the sea level, i.e., the water actually covers up whatever is below the sea level: it is comparable to a situation where a huge stock of inventory covers up the most serious causes of managerial problems so that the managers cannot see why those problems recur all the time.

(b)

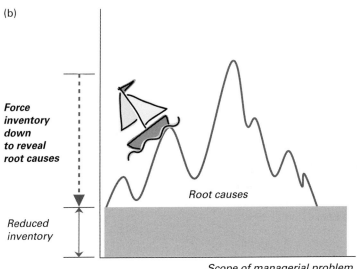

Force inventory down to reveal root causes

Root causes

Reduced inventory

Scope of managerial problem

Figure 5.21 (cont.)

In fact, the ship can observe only minor symptoms in the ocean, wrongly presuming that everything is fine or peaceful.

But, the ocean may not be such a nice environment. Suppose in fact there are massive rocks and reefs beneath the sea surface, all being concealed by the high water (Figure 5.21b). These are the **root causes** of the managerial problems in our analogy, which says that in order to enhance its learning (i.e., problem-solving) capability, the firm must eliminate redundant inventory, sometimes forcefully, if necessary. Only when the firm sees the root causes, can it start searching for solutions or cures to eliminate them. As such, inventory reduction must play a role in facilitating the firm's learning process.

Discussion Questions

1. Why does inventory occur? What is the role of inventory?
2. Explain blocking and starving in the production process.
3. What does "inventory decouples processes" mean?
4. What is supply chain inventory?
5. What is base stock or base inventory?
6. Why does a firm need safety stock?
7. What are the reasons for having a small inventory?
8. What are the reasons for having a large inventory?
9. When is it appropriate to use the EOQ model?

10. What are the principles for the newsvendor model?
11. What are the characteristics of the pull system?
12. What are the characteristics of the push system?
13. What is the contingent inventory system?
14. What is the relationship between product life cycle and forecasting methods?
15. What are the differences between aggregate level and product-mix level uncertainty?
16. What should the firm do if there is a constant mismatch between demand and supply at the aggregate level?
17. Explain the basic steps of the Delphi method.
18. What is the theoretical justification for the Delphi method?
19. Explain why and how inventory affects a firm's innovation.
20. Explain why and how inventory affects a firm's problem solving and learning.

案例 CASE STUDY 5.1
Kikkoman's Competitive Advantage

Kikkoman was initially founded in the mid seventeenth century in the small city of Noda, in Chiba prefecture, Japan. *Tamari* (or soy sauce using only wheat and no soybeans) production in the area had started in the sixteenth century, and it was in 1661 that the Takanashi family started producing soy sauce. A year later, the Mogi family started producing miso, a fermented product using similar ingredients to soy sauce. It was about 100 years later that the Mogi family also started making soy sauce, creating another branch, and in 1782 the name Kikkoman was used commercially for the first time. With time, more Mogi family branches started making soy sauce and the final eight families involved in Kikkoman were fixed in 1917 with the foundation of Noda Shoyu Co. Ltd.: six branches from Mogi, Takanashi, and Horikiri.

Kikkoman first ventured outside of Japan in the 1870s by participating in World Fairs in Vienna and Amsterdam. By 1879, they had registered their brand in California. They started by participating in fairs, showing local people that soy sauce was not only a Japanese sauce, but that it could also be enjoyed with a variety of other dishes that were not Japanese. The American public loved their sauce and soon Kikkoman was exporting bottled soy sauce to the US market. Their next step was to transition to ship in bulk and have it bottled locally. And then, in 1972, they established their first production plant abroad, in Wisconsin, United States. While it was mainly for the US market, it also served Canada and Latin America. Currently, North America accounts for 76 percent of Kikkoman's total sales. With a profit rate of 19 percent (compared to 2 percent in Japan), Kikkoman's early global expansion definitely played a major role in their current success.

Kikkoman is now a major player in the soy sauce market, both in Japan and abroad. They also operate the America-based Japan Food Corporation (hereafter referred to as JFC) established in 1969 and now export a diverse selection of Japanese food products all over the world. Across their sixty-seven group companies, they now have over 5,600 employees worldwide and achieved net sales of 343,168 million yen (approximately US$2.7 billion) for their fiscal year ending March 2015. But even though the current company has grown much beyond what the original founders would have imagined, some things haven't changed since the beginning: the way of making their original soy sauce and a particular rule that has certainly contributed to keeping the business successful. That is, every generation, only one child of each of the eight founding families, can join the business. Keeping power balance stable between the families and only allowing the most fitting individuals into the business has no doubt been a part of this continuing success story.

Kikkoman is currently the top player in the Japanese soy sauce market, with 26 percent of the share (32.5 percent if we combine it with Higeta, of which they acquired a portion in 2004). Their continued success as a family business can be partly accounted for by their location. Kikkoman was founded in Noda city, Chiba prefecture, not far from Edo (currently Tokyo). This area was a big production center for the two main ingredients of soy sauce: soybeans and wheat. Workforce was abundant in Edo, and transportation of raw ingredients and the finished product was made convenient by two nearby rivers, the Tone and the Edo. It is not a coincidence that two other old

Source: Developed and written by B. Kim. ©

companies that still remain and are currently also major players in the soy sauce market, Yamasa and Higeta, were also founded in Chiba prefecture.

Kikkoman soy sauce is entirely produced in house, with only four ingredients: water, salt, soybeans, and wheat. Unprocessed soybeans and wheat are bought in large quantities and stored on site at the factory. First, soybeans are soaked for a long period of time and then steamed at high temperatures. The wheat is roasted and crushed. Kikkoman Aspergillus, a type of fungus, is added to the mixture of steamed soybean and crushed wheat. After being cultured for three days in a highly controlled environment, it finally forms *koji*. It is then moved to a large tank to be mixed with a salty water solution to form *moromi*, which is to be fermented and aged for several months. When the *moromi* has aged sufficiently, soy sauce is extracted by pouring *moromi* into layers of fabric and squeezing out the sauce, first with the power of gravity and then mechanically for ten hours, in order to produce clear soy sauce. The raw soy sauce is left in a clarifier tank for three to four days to let the sediments drop to the bottom and soy oil to float to the surface. After being separated from these undesirable elements, it is heated in order to pasteurize it, but also to stabilize the quality of the soy sauce as well as adjust color, flavour, and aroma. It is then bottled (in either less than a liter, 1, 1.8, 2, or over 2 liter-sized bottles) to be sold. It should ideally be consumed within a year of its production for optimal taste and quality.

During this manufacturing process, two by-products appear: soy oil and cake, or *moromi* whose soy sauce has been squeezed out. The oil is used as fuel for the machines in the factory and the cake is sold to be fed to livestock. In 2014, Kikkoman was able to recycle 99.3 percent of all the by-products produced by its factories.

Over the last decade or so, Kikkoman has made tremendous efforts to optimize the efficiency of their delivery channels in Japan. They are now renowned for almost never having products run out of stock, while still maintaining a low inventory. The changes were prompted by the fact that, in 1993, the cost of logistics operations skyrocketed to over 10 billion yen (US$100 million) for a year. Before all of the changes they made, their system was as follows. Finished products were transported by truck, train, or boat from one of their three factories (Chiba, Hyogo, or Hokkaido) to a shipping center. From the shipping center, products could either go to wholesalers who would then directly sell to users, or go directly to a transfer center or warehouse. From the transfer center or warehouse, the product could then reach stores or wholesalers.

One of the most important things developed and instituted by Kikkoman to cope with the logistics issue was KOLS (Kikkoman Order Less System). The basic concept is to put all past order data online, and decide on the timing to ship out items with the help of these historical data. So, in short, Kikkoman went from a dispatch system based on current (e.g., fluctuating and/ or uncertain) orders to a dispatch system based on historical data and predictions. That is, KOLS was more logical and data-driven than the old system, which had been haphazard and myopic, relying on a rule of thumb without any systematic analysis. It works in three parts: KOLS-WP (Weekly Plan), KOLS-DEPO (Inventory), and KOLS-CRP (Continuous Replenishment Program).

KOLS-WP is the first step in Kikkoman's inventory management. Sales data is analyzed and a production plan is drafted. But, even if this is called a weekly plan, this step is repeated every day. An important thing for this to work is to have the most up-to-date information possible. If ordering data is entered in the system with a delay, products might become sold out in the meantime, so it is really crucial. Then comes KOLS-DEPO, which is keeping up with the exact inventory of products in all locations. Then comes KOLS-CRP. As small orders are made online, the data is updated automatically, which allows and aids the continuous replenishment program in a very systematic way. This helps in keeping the cost down. With better demand and inventory information across the markets (from KOLS-DEPO), KOLS-CRP enables the company to aggregate orders across stores and/or areas and plan deliveries in larger quantities without stocking-out between deliveries. For example, until now, a 4-ton truck would deliver every day (for 20 days a month), which would cost a total of 550,000 yen (US$5,500). If this could be cut down to a 10-ton truck delivering only eight times a month (through KOLS-CRP), the savings would be about 300,000 yen (US$3,000). As a matter of fact, this system developed by Kikkoman won a prize from the Japan Chamber of Commerce and Industry.

All these changes have been able to reduce Kikkoman's inventory quite successfully. In 2001, their total inventory was worth about 6.4 billion yen (US$64 million), but was reduced to about 4.9 billion yen (US$49 million) in 2007. Also, because the products they manufacture are perishable, selling them in time is a big issue. Thanks to its improvement in the logistics, Kikkoman is successful in that aspect and only very rarely has to discard products.

Questions
1. Draw the company's production process and the configuration of its supply chain.
2. What are the sources of Kikkoman's competitive advantage?
3. Why is it important for the company to reduce its inventory?
4. What measures did the company take in order to cope with the issues in inventory management?
5. How did the company's improvement in its logistics and supply chain management contribute to its competitive advantage?

案例 CASE STUDY 5.2
Is There an Optimum Level for Supply Chain Inventory?

James Jeong was the senior manager in charge of inventory at a Korean subsidiary of a global consumer electronics company headquartered in Brussels.[1] Over the last several years, while managing the inventory at the company, Jeong couldn't figure out whether there might be an optimal inventory level. That is, he had been asking questions like,

1. Is there an optimal inventory level?
2. Is the answer different among three different inventory types (i.e., raw material, work-in-process, and finished goods) in the supply chain?

To answer these questions, Jeong collected a massive amount of data and carried out an extensive analysis, using statistical tools. The first step was to develop a framework as shown in Figure 5.22: he was trying to explore how the current and the previous inventory could affect the sales, controlling the firm size and the demand trend, noting that the current inventory consisted of two parts, i.e., the firm accumulated inventory during the current period and the leftover inventory from the previous period became part of the current inventory. As such, if he wanted to understand the net effect (not confounded by the last period's leftover inventory) of the current inventory on the current sales, he would have to control the previous inventory by including it as a control variable. Similarly, he would have to control the current inventory when looking into the net effect (direct, not via the current inventory) of the last period's inventory.

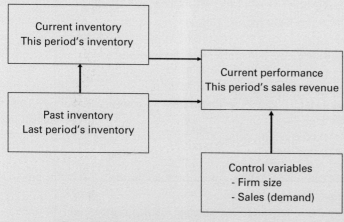

Figure 5.22 Research Framework

Source: This case is based on B. Kim, and S. Kim, "Inventory Types and Their Effects on Sales" (2016) 3(2) *International Journal of Inventory Research* 115–133. DOI: 10.1504/IJIR.2016.10001176. © 2016 Inderscience Publishers. Whenever necessary to make the case easy to read, most of the theories, equations, formulas, and references are omitted. Please refer to the paper for more details.

[1] This is a fictitious company.

Hypothesis. Jeong decided to develop testable hypotheses and reasoned as follows.

First of all, inventory bestows the firm flexibility to better cope with market demand uncertainty and thus has a positive effect on the sales revenue. On the other hand, it is possible that an excessive inventory, i.e., the leftover, in the previous period hampers the firm's ability to respond to the changing market demand and/or makes it difficult for the firm to introduce the new product to the market faster. As a result, an excessive inventory in the last period could affect the firm's current sales negatively. Because of inventory's dual effects, positive and negative, on the sales, there is an optimal level of current inventory, which maximizes the firm's current sales. In addition, these propositions laid out above are applicable not just only to finished goods inventory, but also to the upstream inventories such as raw material and work in process inventories. That is, in addition to the finished goods inventory, raw material and work in process inventories as upstream inventories in the firm's supply chain are strategically important variables to enhance the firm's sales. From the supply chain perspective, the firm must manage all of its supply chain inventories effectively to optimize its supply chain performances, one of which is the sales. Since all of the supply chain inventories are linked in a systemic way with each other, all of them are playing important roles in enhancing the firm's performance. For instance, if it is true that the finished goods inventory should be strategically important, then it must be also true that other upstream inventories are strategic.

Based on the reasoning detailed above, Jeong suggested the hypotheses as follows.

Hypothesis 1. There is a positive relationship between the current period's inventory and the current period's sales performance. That is, the larger the current inventory, the larger the current sales.

(a)   There is a positive relationship between the current raw material inventory and the current sales.
(b)   There is a positive relationship between the current work-in-process inventory and the current sales.
(c)   There is a positive relationship between the current finished goods inventory and the current sales.

Hypothesis 2. If the previous inventory's effect is separated from the current inventory's effect on the current sales (i.e., the current inventory is controlled), there is a negative relationship between the previous period's inventory and the current period's sales performance. That is, the larger the previous inventory, the smaller the current sales.

(a)   If the current inventory is controlled, there is a negative relationship between the previous raw material inventory and the current sales.
(b)   If the current inventory is controlled, there is a negative relationship between the previous work-in-process inventory and the current sales.
(c)   If the current inventory is controlled, there is a negative relationship between the previous finished goods inventory and the current sales.

Hypothesis 3. If the previous inventory's effect is separated from the current inventory's effect on the current sales (i.e., the previous inventory is controlled), there is a concave relationship between the current period's inventory and the current period's sales performance. That is, there exists an optimal level of current inventory for the current sales.

(a)   If the previous inventory is controlled, there is a concave relationship between the current raw material inventory and the current sales.
(b)   If the previous inventory is controlled, there is a concave relationship between the current work-in-process inventory and the current sales.
(c)   If the previous inventory is controlled, there is a concave relationship between the current finished goods inventory and the current sales.

The first two hypotheses combined suggest the current inventory has dual effects on the current sales. On the one hand, it enables the firm to meet the current demand more efficiently. On the other hand, it hampers the firm's effort to be more responsive to the changing market requirements, since the leftover inventory from the previous period has become part of the current inventory. By balancing these two effects together, controlling the previous leftover inventory, it is clear that there is an optimal level of current inventory, which helps the firm maximize its current sales.

Data and variables. Jeong used the Korea Information Service Value (KISVALUE) database, from which he selected 272 manufacturing firms listed in the Korean stock market indices, i.e., Korea Composite Stock Price Index (KOSPI) and Korea Securities Dealers Automated Quotation (KOSDAQ), as his sample. He collected 4,624 firm-year observations, i.e., data points, for the 272 firms in twenty-one different industries with Korea Standard Industry Code (KSIC) codes 10 to 32, covering the time period from 1996, when KOSDAQ was established, to 2012, the year for which the most recent data were available. That is, out of the entire manufacturing firms in KISVALUE, only 272 firms had existed during the time period. For the performance measure, Jeong decided to use SOA (sales on assets) in this study. He adopted the measure of inventory normalized by the company's average total assets.

Analysis methodology. To test the hypotheses, he used the panel data analysis since the data consisted of two dimensions, i.e., cross-sectional and time-series. With SOA as the dependent variable, Jeong developed four regression models: Model 1 to test Hypothesis 1, Models 2 and 3 to test Hypothesis 2, and Model 4 to test Hypothesis 3. The regression results are in Table 5.6. In addition to the independent variables, Jeong included several control and dummy variables to control various spurious effects.

Table 5.6 Regression Results

Independent Variables	Dependent Variable: SOA							
	Model 1		Model 2		Model 3		Model 4	
	Coefficient	p-value	Coefficient	p-value	Coefficient	p-value	Coefficient	p-value
Constant	−0.029	0.787	−0.030	0.769	−0.015	0.883	−0.016	0.880
RMI_t	0.657	0.003			1.518	0.001	2.554	0.003
$WIPI_t$	0.687	0.013			1.758	0.002	2.358	0.001
FGI_t	0.664	0.001			1.798	0.000	2.335	0.000
RMI_{t-1}			0.089	0.685	−1.057	0.026	−1.092	0.025
$WIPI_{t-1}$			0.331	0.148	−1.134	0.036	−1.140	0.031
FGI_{t-1}			0.091	0.623	−1.392	0.000	−1.347	0.000

Table 5.6 (cont.)

Independent Variables	Dependent Variable: SOA							
	Model 1		Model 2		Model 3		Model 4	
	Coefficient	p-value	Coefficient	p-value	Coefficient	p-value	Coefficient	p-value
RMI_t^2							−6.145	0.066
$WIPI_t^2$							−3.805	0.042
FGI_t^2							−2.748	0.053
SOA_{t-1}	0.707	0.000	0.719	0.000	0.720	0.000	0.711	0.000
Sales	0.000	0.438	0.000	0.658	0.000	0.547	0.000	0.393
Log (Size)	0.025	0.169	0.033	0.068	0.025	0.159	0.019	0.330
Time Dummy	Included		Included		Included		Included	
F (p-value)	258.72 (0.000)		237.68 (0.000)		252.85 (0.000)		235.41 (0.000)	
R^2	0.5979		0.5906		0.6066		0.6095	
Adjusted-R^2	0.5958		0.5885		0.6043		0.6070	

Note: RMI_{t-1} is raw material inventory in the previous period $(t-1)$; RMI_t^2 is $RMI_t \times RMI_t$; similar interpretations for other variables.

Conclusion and managerial implications. Jeong was pleased to see that overall the analysis results would support his hypotheses as well as reasoning quite strongly:

> On the one hand, inventory enhances the firm's sales (Hypothesis 1). On the other hand, too much leftover inventory dampens the sales (Hypothesis 2). In effect, the analysis strongly supports that there is an optimal inventory level (Hypothesis 3). That is, it is not always true that the larger the inventory, the better: the firm has to decide the appropriate inventory level, which is large enough to enable the firm to cope with the uncertainty in the current market demand, but not excessive in order to avoid any chances of being left over at the end of the current period.

In addition, Jeong was glad to confirm the perspective of supply chain inventory. That is, throughout the study, taking a supply chain perspective, Jeong examined three different supply chain inventories, i.e., raw material, work in process, and finished goods, simultaneously. For each of the three hypotheses, the analysis showed that the relationship between the inventory and the sales was valid for each of the three supply chain inventories.

Jeong realized that his study could suggest a few significant managerial implications as follows:

> The firm must manage its inventory as a strategic variable to influence its sales: it should try to find an optimal inventory level. In doing so, it has to consider all of the supply chain inventories at the same time: although it is possible that the finished goods inventory has the largest effect, other supply chain inventories such as raw material and work in process do have a significant effect on the sales as well. As a result, it is essential for the manager at the firm to take the supply chain perspective when designing an optimal inventory strategy.

Questions

1. Do you think that the analysis supports the statement "the current inventory enhances the firm's performance by providing more responsiveness for the current market demand"?
2. Do you think that the analysis supports the statement "the previous inventory dampens the firm's innovativeness and thus negatively impacts the firm's current performance"?
3. What is your answer to the question: *Is it always true that the more the inventory, the better the sales performance?*
4. What advice would you give to James Jeong, if you believe the analysis results are valid?
5. Do you think the analysis results in this study are counterintuitive? Why or why not?

CHAPTER 6

Logistics, Procurement, and Supplier Relationship

The final element of the structural dimension for designing an effective supply chain is the **transportation** or **logistics**, i.e., how to physically deliver the *best* materials (including raw materials, parts, semi-finished products, and finished products) to the *appropriate* customers, both internal and external. There are several factors to consider. The most important factor is quality, i.e., how to procure the finest materials that ensure high quality of the final product. This issue essentially involves identifying and selecting the best suppliers, i.e., from whom to procure such materials. Then the company should transport or deliver the materials to where they are required or can be utilized most effectively. Transportation costs and delivery timing are some of the critical factors the company should take into account when designing its logistic and **procurement** strategy. All of these issues inevitably make it crucial for the company to cultivate a strategic **supplier relationship**. In this chapter, we focus on the strategic aspects of logistics and procurement and how they interact with other essential elements of optimal supply chain management.

Key Learning Points

- Logistics is concerned with the physical delivery of materials (including raw materials, parts, semi-finished products, and finished products) to the appropriate customers.
- When determining an appropriate logistics option, the company has to take into account several factors such as *cost*, *speed* or *timing*, and *quality*.
- A make-or-buy decision is an important decision about *in-house operations (production)* versus *outsourcing*.
- Strategic outsourcing is different from contractual outsourcing in that it is based on a long-term commitment between the buyer and the seller; it requires the firms to develop a partnership, and therefore involves a high intensity of coordination between the partners for value-creating activities.
- A perception gap exists between the buyer and suppliers when the factors considered by the buyer as critical for an effective outsourcing partnership are significantly different from those perceived by the suppliers as critical. It is essential to effective supply chain coordination. That is, the larger the gap, the less effective the supply chain coordination.

- Supplier typology enables the firm to determine which supplier it should develop a strategic relationship with.
- It is prevalent that in a supply chain relationship, the retailer has a bargaining power much stronger than the supplier's. In order to overcome such an impasse, the supplier should try to develop innovation or globalization capability.

學 WISDOM BOX 6.1
Wisdom and Insights

Luxury Fashion Company and Supply Chain Management

Are supply chain management issues like outsourcing and supplier relationship critical to enhancing performance for a luxury fashion company at the highest premium segment of the market? By trying to answer this question, we could verify whether the key supply chain management principles we have learnt in this book are applicable to a wide range of markets as well as companies. The following excerpt is from an interview with a top designer and also top manager at a luxury fashion company, which is denoted as "**LC** (luxury company)" here.

What does quality imply to LC?

First, **quality** should mean **durability**. We need to make products that the customer can use for a long time. As such, we pay keen attention to raw materials like **fabrics** and other synthetic ones. But, materials have evolved over time. For instance, in the past, we didn't use polyester, but we do use it these days, since it is now good material.

Quality is also about excellence in **design**. We view design as a risky endeavor. But, design at LC is not driven by market demand or customers. The creative team is leading the design. Of course, sometimes, marketing function provides information about market trends, but the creative team plays the quintessential role in designing.

Quality also implies **service**. This is related to durability. LC products are made of very delicate materials. Although utmost attention is paid to ensure durability, sometimes it becomes necessary to fix the product. Except for cases requiring very simple repairs, all products needing services are shipped to our headquarters in Paris, where complete repairs are treated. We try to make sure that the services for our products are done perfectly, wherever the products are sold.

What are the overall characteristics of LC's supply chain?

LC has five in-house factories in France and several **contract manufacturers** in Italy for bags, glasses, and other accessories. There are about twenty outsourcing partners for manufacturing. We usually do not give a large volume to each outsourcing partner. Moreover, our request for high quality is quite demanding. Despite these, our suppliers are eager to work with LC. It probably reflects the unique characteristics of the luxury industry. In this industry, concepts are more important than volumes. A

Box continues

company like LC is powerful enough to lead the fashion trend and the market. Thus, working with LC itself gives the **outsourcing partners** prestige and visibility, which compensate for their hard work even for small orders. Regarding our **distribution channel**, we have our own LC stores, dispersed all around the world. A store manager is in charge of operating each retail store. Thus, our supply chain is highly integrated from manufacturing to distribution.

Like the integrated downstream supply chain, our design function is completely centralized in Paris. The creative team is in charge of design works in LC. As pointed out earlier, our creative team pays the keenest attention to the artistic attributes of LC products, not excessively driven by current market trends. But, in fact, as all of you already know, LC's creativity is coming from one genius "master designer." He is still active, but nobody knows what will happen to LC's design after him.

Despite its ultimate focus on artistic elements, the design function is not completely insulated from other supply chain functions. On the contrary, it is an integral element of our supply chain strategy. The creative team constantly provides guidance as well as advice to manufacturing plants and retail stores. For manufacturing, it provides guidance and advice regarding the best fabrics to use, suppliers who can supply the appropriate materials, and delicate production processes. For retail stores, it offers guidance and advice regarding the choice of products, display methods, and interior designs of the store. In this sense, the design or creative team drives the entire supply chain at a fundamental level.

Focusing on creativity and artistic design elements along with the concentrated supply chain, how do you deal with the issue of market responsiveness?

Although we say our design is driven by artistic talents, not by contemporary market trends, we do communicate with the market constantly as a way to enhance our **responsiveness**. LC usually runs fashion shows six times each year, four big fashion shows for the general public and two buyer shows for large commercial buyers. For about ten days during each fashion show, we get orders from the buyers. Based on such orders, we start pre-ordering fabrics. Having six fashion shows each year enables us to have quick cycles to be more responsive to the market demands. Of course, through the fashion show, we present to the customers our vision as well as direction toward artistic perfection for our products, and then we try to meet the customer's demand more responsively.

Without properly taking into account the market requirements when developing new concepts for new products, it seems like LC is using a "make-to-stock" system. But, it sounds a little bit strange that a company in the luxury industry uses a make-to-stock system. How do you respond to this statement?

Well, we do use a **make-to-order** strategy. But, it is only for the really rich customers. We estimate there are probably less than 300 customers across the world who can be categorized in this group. From the very beginning of the clothes-making process, we consult the customer about everything like fabrics, styles, designs, colors, and even

Box continues

accessories. Of course, our design team always tries to provide creative ideas and sometimes more ideal directions to these customers as well. Another market segment we serve is the "**ready-to-wear**" market. Here we use the "**make-to-stock**" system. That is, we make our products and sell them to the customers who want to buy them. In this market, through the creative team, LC exerts enormous leadership in defining the market trend itself. In a sense, we often educate our customers about the artistic beauty of LC products.

However, we want to make it clear that the make-to-stock system used by LC is very different from that adopted by companies in the mass markets. LC is in the luxury industry. As such, the kind of "ready-to-wear" market served by LC is still at the high end of the market. For instance, unlike most of the companies using the make-to-stock system, LC doesn't have large inventory at the end of the season. We use small batches and thus the volume is small. Should a particular product sell more than expected, we re-order during the same season. Sometimes we do have a very small inventory for basic items like simple blouses, which can be sold in the next season. But, even for such items, inventory rarely remains after the next season. In a very unusual case, we might have a really small leftover at the end of the season. We never move the leftover to outlets. First, we sell the leftover products to our employees at the cost. If there are any remaining unsold items, then we destroy them.

What is the biggest challenge faced by LC now?

LC is a company built on **creativity**. We're always concerned with how to create new ideas and new collections. In order to enhance our designers' creativity, we encourage them to be open-minded and curious about everything. Often our designers spend time on visiting exhibitions and museums, and participate in other forms of artistic activities. Since the creative designing is the key, we try to ensure that the creative spirits permeate through our organization. We emphasize communications, i.e., all of the parts in our organization get together physically or virtually to share ideas. Holding a fashion show is the most important means to achieve the goal.

Questions

1. How important is it for the company to manage inventory and procurement in terms of sustaining its competitive advantage?
2. How has the company's transportation or logistic strategy enabled the company to achieve its supply chain management goals?
3. What are the key factors or elements of the company's supply chain strategy? What forces have supported them and how?

6.1   Logistics

Logistics is the final element of the structural dimension in designing a supply chain: how to physically deliver the materials (including raw materials, parts, semi-finished products, and finished products) to the appropriate customers. Since we consider virtual delivery of information and data as part of the infrastructural dimension, logistics in this chapter largely involves physical objects. There are many delivery options available, e.g.: (1) land transportation that utilizes trucks or trains; (2) air transportation that employs airplanes; (3) sea transportation that uses diverse cargo vessels; and (4) albeit rarely used, others such as floating logs on a river.

When determining an appropriate logistics option, the company has to take into account several factors. There are three key factors, **cost**, **speed** or **timing**, and **quality**, which are related with each other. For instance, an expensive **transportation method** (e.g., airplane) is in general faster than an inexpensive one (e.g., train): there is a positive relationship between cost and speed. We can establish a relationship between quality and cost or speed. It is generally true that a high quality material is more expensive than a low quality one. Therefore, keeping an inventory of high quality material costs more than keeping an inventory of low quality material. Other things being equal, the company wants to keep a smaller inventory of high quality (i.e., expensive) material and utilize a faster (i.e., more expensive) transportation mode in case it needs the material urgently. Of course, as we alluded to before, these factors are also affected by other designing factors of the supply chain. For example, how to configure or connect supply chain functions can significantly affect cost and speed of a transportation or logistic option as well as the quality of supply. Keeping in mind that we should approach the issues of logistics, procurement, and supplier relationship in the context of broader supply chain management, we can discuss each of the logistics factors individually.

Rather than looking at the transportation mode separately, we consider it in light of the transportation cost. An expensive transportation option is in general a fast transportation means such as an airplane, whereas an inexpensive one is a relatively slow transportation means such as a train or cargo vessel. As such, we can relate the logistics issue with the inventory decision. Figure 6.1 suggests a simplified relationship between the two. For instance, if the unit inventory value (compared to its volume) is very high, it is costly to have a large inventory. Thus, other things being comparable, when the unit inventory value is excessively high, the firm wants to keep a small inventory and uses a fast transportation means whenever necessary – to meet an unanticipated demand. On the contrary, if the unit inventory value is low, it makes sense to stock a large inventory to deal with the market demand and use relatively inexpensive slow transportation options. As a result, there is a strategic fit between a high unit inventory value and fast transportation options and also between a low unit inventory value and relatively slow transportation means.

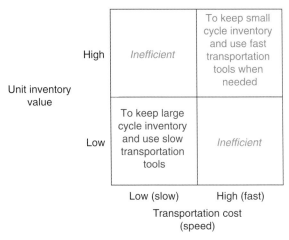

	Low (slow)	High (fast)
High	*Inefficient*	To keep small cycle inventory and use fast transportation tools when needed
Low	To keep large cycle inventory and use slow transportation tools	*Inefficient*

Unit inventory value

Transportation cost (speed)

Figure 6.1 Inventory and Logistics

IN-DEPTH CONCEPT 6.1
Minimization of the Total Procurement Cost

As discussed in the previous chapters, decisions on transportation or logistics are largely dependent on supply chain configuration and connection. More often than not, it is in turn necessary to take into account the long-term trend of transportation and logistics costs when determining the supply chain's configuration and connection. Like every other decision in supply chain management, the transportation and logistics decision is intertwined with other elements in structural and infrastructural dimensions. Nevertheless, to avoid a circular argument, we assume that the company has made an optimal decision on its supply chain configuration and connection, before tackling the issue of transportation and logistics. In fact, this approach makes sense, since the decision horizon for transportation and logistics is tactical, much shorter than that for configuration and connection. The company can utilize the transportation and logistics in order to deal with short-term contingencies in the supply chain.

Based on the assumption elaborated above, we discuss an example analytical method to solve the short-term transportation and logistics problem. Suppose that the company has five plants in five different countries, Korea (denoted as plant 1), Vietnam (2), China (3), Poland (4), and the United States (5). Further suppose that it procures raw materials from four suppliers in four countries, Korea (denoted as supplier 1), Vietnam (2), China (3), and Malaysia (4). Assume that the procurement cost reflects all the costs associated with the supply, e.g., including production cost, transfer price, transportation cost from the supplier to the plant, and all the other

Note that this is an advanced modeling method based on mathematical programming. Although we believe its managerial or conceptual implications can help you understand issues of logistics and procurement much better, we suggest you may skip this part unless you feel familiar with the subject. Please note that in our analysis chapter, we will explain a little more about the mathematical programming.

Box continues

related costs such as taxes, tariffs, and opportunity costs. In addition, for the sake of simplification, assume that the quality is fully taken into account when determining the **procurement cost** for each supplier. Therefore, the company's decision problem for a single period (i.e., a static decision-making problem for one period) is to minimize the total procurement cost while satisfying the demand for the materials at each plant. To solve the problem analytically, we set up a mathematical (transportation) model as follows:

$$Minimize \sum_{i=1}^{n} \sum_{j=1}^{m} c_{ij}x_{ij} = c_{11}x_{11} + c_{12}x_{12} + \ldots + c_{nm}x_{nm}$$

Subject to

$$\sum_{j=1}^{m} x_{ij} = x_{i1} + x_{i2} + \ldots + x_{im} \leq s_i \text{ for } j = 1, 2, \ldots, m$$

$$\sum_{i=1}^{n} x_{ij} = x_{1j} + x_{2j} + \ldots + x_{nj} \geq d_j \text{ for } j = 1, 2, \ldots, m$$

$$x_{ij} \geq 0,$$

where
- i: the index for supplier i, $i = 1, 2, \ldots$, n; n is 4 in this example, i.e., Korea is 1, Vietnam 2, China 3, and Malaysia 4;
- j: the index for plant j, $j = 1, 2, \ldots$, m; m is 5 in this example, i.e., Korea is 1, Vietnam 2, China 3, Poland 4, and the United States 5;
- x_{ij}: the procured amount of supply from supplier i to plant j;
- c_{ij}: the cost to procure one unit from supplier i to plant j;
- s_i: the supplier i's capacity;
- d_j: the plant j's requirement or demand.

  To demonstrate how to apply the analytical method to solving the procurement/transportation problem, we use an example, whose parameter values are in Table 6.1. In Table 6.1a, there is information about the procurement cost c_{ij} from supplier i to plant j. For instance, $c_{13} = 2$ implies it costs \$2 in total to procure one unit of supply from the supplier in Korea ($i=1$) to the plant in China ($j=3$). Table 6.1b shows the supplier's capacity and also the plant's requirement or demand. For instance, $s_1 = 200,000$ implies supplier 1 in Korea has a supply capacity of 200,000 units, while $d_2 = 150,000$ means plant 2 in Vietnam needs 150,000 units of supply. Now we can use an analysis software (such as the Solver Add-in tool in Microsoft Excel) to solve the decision problem.[1]

Box continues

[1] For more explanation, refer to Online Chapter 12 on analysis methods.

Table 6.1 Base Case

(a) Unit Procurement Cost Including Unit Supply Cost and Transportation Cost

	Plant				
Supplier	Korea (1)	Vietnam (2)	China (3)	Poland (4)	USA (5)
Korea (1)	$ 1.00	$ 3.00	$ 2.00	$ 4.00	$ 5.00
Vietnam (2)	$ 4.00	$ 0.50	$ 1.50	$ 5.00	$ 6.00
China (3)	$ 2.00	$ 2.00	$ 0.50	$ 3.00	$ 4.00
Malaysia (4)	$ 3.00	$ 2.00	$ 2.00	$ 4.00	$ 5.00

(b) Optimal Decision on Amounts from Supplier to Plant

Total Cost $ 3,425,000

	Plant					
Supplier	Korea (1)	Vietnam (2)	China (3)	Poland (4)	USA (5)	Supplier Capacity
Korea (1)	100,000	0	0	0	100,000	200,000
Vietnam (2)	0	150,000	150,000	0	0	300,000
China (3)	0	0	150,000	0	350,000	500,000
Malaysia (4)	0	0	0	200,000	50,000	250,000
Plant demand	100,000	150,000	300,000	200,000	500,000	1,250,000

If we apply the analysis method correctly, we get the optimal solution as in Table 6.1b, which suggests as follows:

- Korea plant should procure all of its requirement from the supplier in Korea;
- Vietnam plant should procure all of its requirement from Vietnam supplier;
- China plant should procure 150,000 units from Vietnam supplier and 150,000 units from China supplier;
- Poland plant should procure all of its requirement from Malaysia supplier;
- US plant should procure 100,000 units from Korea supplier, 350,000 units from China supplier, and 50,000 units from Malaysia supplier;
- then, the total procurement cost will be $3,425,000.

Of course, this optimal decision is only a static one, i.e., not a perfect "dynamic" solution. But, at least, it can be a starting point. In order to develop a realistic and implementable plan, the company should take into account other strategic or qualitative factors as well. Sometimes it has to make a decision for a **contingent event**, which was not properly anticipated or is quite uncertain in nature. A good analysis method should be able to accommodate these kinds of various contingencies and uncertainties.

To show an example of such flexibility, we consider a contingent case, where the procurement cost changes. Suppose that due to various reasons, the procurement cost

Box continues

from the supplier in China has changed so that the unit procurement cost from China to China changes from $0.50 to $1.50, while that to the United States increases from $4 to $7 as in Table 6.2a. Assume that the company can choose from two options to cope with this short-term contingency. The first option is to accept the procurement cost change and use the same supplier capacity. The other is to change a supplier's capacity.

Table 6.2 A Contingent Case

(a) Changes in Transportation Costs from the Supplier in China

Total Cost to Procure One Unit from Supplier to Plant

	Plant				
Supplier	Korea (1)	Vietnam (2)	China (3)	Poland (4)	USA (5)
Korea (1)	$ 1.00	$ 3.00	$ 2.00	$ 4.00	$ 5.00
Vietnam (2)	$ 4.00	$ 0.50	$ 1.50	$ 5.00	$ 6.00
China (3)	$ 2.00	$ 2.00	$ 1.50	$ 3.00	$ 7.00
Malaysia (4)	$ 3.00	$ 2.00	$ 2.00	$ 4.00	$ 5.00

(b) Option 1 – with the Same Supplier Capacity

Optimal Decision on Amounts from Supplier to Plant   Total Cost $ 3,875,000

	Plant					
Supplier	Korea (1)	Vietnam (2)	China (3)	Poland (4)	USA (5)	Supplier Capacity
Korea (1)	100,000	0	0	0	100,000	200,000
Vietnam (2)	0	150,000	0	0	150,000	300,000
China (3)	0	0	300,000	200,000	0	500,000
Malaysia (4)	0	0	0	0	250,000	250,000
Plant demand	100,000	150,000	300,000	200,000	500,000	1,250,000

(c) Option 2 – with the Capacity Increase of the Supplier in Korea

Optimal Decision on Amounts from Supplier to Plant   Total Cost $ 3,775,000

	Plant					
Supplier	Korea (1)	Vietnam (2)	China (3)	Poland (4)	USA (5)	Supplier Capacity
Korea (1)	100,000	0	0	0	200,000	300,000
Vietnam (2)	0	150,000	0	0	150,000	300,000
China (3)	0	0	300,000	200,000	0	500,000
Malaysia (4)	0	0	0	0	250,000	250,000
Plant demand	100,000	150,000	300,000	200,000	600,000	1,350,000

Box continues

The optimal solution for the first option is in Table 6.2b, where we observe significant changes in the procurement decision. The most notable one is that facing the steep increase in the procurement cost from China, the US plant now procures none from China, and instead increases its procurement from Malaysia fivefold and starts receiving the supply from Vietnam. It is intriguing to note that now the China plant gets materials only from the China supplier, which in turn changes its customer, i.e., from the US plant to the Poland plant. If the company accepts the new optimal decision in Table 6.2b, its total procurement cost will be $3,875,000, an almost 13 percent increase from the base case, where the procurement cost doesn't change.

Now suppose the company can choose the second option, which enables it to ask the Korea supplier to increase the capacity (e.g., reserved for the company) from 200,000 to 300,000. Further assume that the second option costs the company an additional $50,000 per period. Then, the key decision question is *Which option should the company choose?* To answer the question, we first need to get the optimal solution for the second option. Applying the same analysis, we get the optimal solution in Table 6.2c, which indicates that the total procurement cost is $3,775,000. Now which option is better for the company? If the company chooses the second option, the total cost including the extra cost is $3,825,000 (i.e., $3,775,000 plus $50,000), which is smaller than that of the first option (i.e., $3,875,000) by $50,000.

Based on the analysis outcome, we can conclude that the company should choose the second option. Of course, the conclusion is valid only when the company's objective is to minimize the total cost without considering any other strategic or qualitative factors. In fact, even if that is the case, our solution derived above cannot be perfect, since it is only a static one, based on lots of assumptions, many of which might eventually turn out to be invalid or unrealistic. Therefore, as we have emphasized many times, although it is always true to say a quantitative analysis is important, it should be regarded as the first step. With the concrete answers derived from the analysis, the company should take into account many other strategic and qualitative factors in order to reach the final decision. Yes, it is not an easy thing to accomplish. Making a timely decision is essential. Again, only a **learning organization** can handle all these complexities appropriately.

6.2   Supplier Relationship Management

Coordination is at the center of supply chain management. For effective logistics and procurement, coordination with suppliers is essential. As such, how to cultivate and retain good supplier relationships is the key. In this section, we discuss two vital issues in supplier relationship management, i.e., *strategic outsourcing* and *supplier perception*.

6.2.1   Strategic Outsourcing

A make-or-buy decision is one of the most important SCM decisions the company should make. In essence, it is a decision about *in-house operations (production)* versus *outsourcing*. To develop a framework to make such a decision, we should consider several factors or dimensions such as core competence, technological capability, and strategic importance of the product (e.g., part) the firm is trying to make the decision for.

We first want to define **core competence** for our use in this book. Figure 6.2 shows how we define the concept. A firm's core competence must be based on capability, which is difficult for a competitor to imitate, so that the firm has sustainable competitive advantage for a reasonably long period of time. This is the dimension of "**proprietary excellence** of the technological capability." Another fundamental dimension is concerned with the market demand. In order for the technological capability to enable the firm to enjoy sustainable competitive advantage, it must be consistent with the market demand – useful in making goods and services that are well demanded by the customers. If the technological capability is easy to imitate and/or non-value-adding, it has a low level of proprietary excellence. This kind of low-level technological capability creates little value for the firm regardless of whether it is consistent with the market demand pattern. Thus, it cannot be considered as "core competence." Suppose that the firm has a technological capability with high proprietary excellence, but its **fit with the market demand** pattern is relatively moderate. One might say that the firm has a sort of core competence in the sense that its competitor is not able to replicate the capability easily. But, strictly speaking, the firm's capability cannot be yet considered as core competence since it does not add much value to the firm.

In this case, whether the capability becomes the firm's core competence is dependent on whether the firm can refine or adjust its technological capability so as to apply it to make goods and services demanded by the market for a reasonably long period of time. In sum, the firm's true core competence must have high proprietary excellence and be compatible with the market.

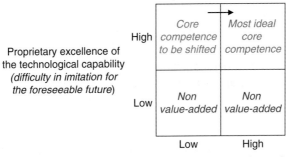

Figure 6.2 Definition of Core Competence

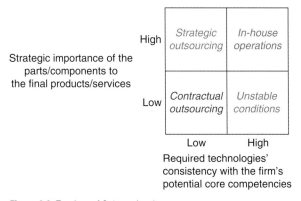

Figure 6.3 Typology of Outsourcing 1

Now suppose that the firm has to decide whether to make a certain part in-house or via outsourcing. In order to make a decision on this **make-or-buy** problem, the firm has to take into account two critical dimensions: *the strategic importance of the part to the final product the firm is making* and *the required technology's consistency with the firm's own core competence* (Figure 6.3). The first dimension, the strategic importance of the part to the final product, forces the firm to evaluate whether the part to be outsourced is a critical element in completing and/or enhancing the final product's value, including its functionality. The second dimension calls for the firm's assessing whether the technology necessary to make the part is consistent with the firm's potential core competence.

If the strategic importance of the part is high and the required technology is consistent with the firm's core competence, other things being equal, it is best for the firm to make the part in-house. It makes sense because firms had better outsource non-essential functions and/or activities when they want to focus on what they can do best, e.g., core competence. Therefore, if making the part is consistent with the firm's own core competence and the part itself is strategically important to the firm in that it is critical to enhancing the final product's real value, it is best for the firm to make the part in-house. On the contrary, when the required technology is not consistent with the firm's potential core competence, then it makes little sense to make the part in-house. However, we do not want to simplify the concept of outsourcing too much. Even when the required technology is inconsistent with the firm's core competence, the firm has to consider the other dimension's level – whether the strategic importance of the part is high or low. What does it mean for the part's strategic importance to be low? It can imply that the part is a **commodity** good – there are many companies that can make the part and the most important factor in determining the buyer's purchasing decision is the price. That is to say, the market for the part is a "**price-sensitive**" commodity market. When the firm buys a commodity product, it doesn't make sense to have a long-term relationship with the seller. Rather than such a relationship, the firm wants to find a seller that can guarantee the lowest possible price for at least a relatively short period of time. From the seller's perspective, too, it doesn't make sense for it to commit to a long-term relationship because it might be possible that tomorrow there would be another buyer, who is willing to pay more for the part than the firm does. This kind of myopic behavior will be prevalent since the key factor to determine the transaction is "cost or price," *not* technological factors, which would have required the business partners to commit to a long-term strategic partnership. As a result, when the required technology is not consistent with the firm's core competence, and at the same time, the strategic importance of the part is low, the best option available to the firm is to develop a **contractual outsourcing**. For a relatively short period of time, the contractual outsourcing does not require any strategic partnership between the buyer and the seller, and is guided mainly by the cost factors.

Strategic outsourcing would be the best option if the strategic importance of the part is high, despite its required technology not being consistent with the firm's core competence. Strategic outsourcing is different from contractual outsourcing in that it is in principle based on a long-term commitment between the buyer and the seller; it requires the firms to develop a partnership, and therefore involves a high intensity of coordination between the partners for such value-creating activities as new product development, market information-sharing, and production synchronization. Finally, the combination of low strategic importance and high consistency with core competence implies an unstable condition for the firm. It indicates that there exists a potential discrepancy between the firm's core competence and its value as perceived in the market. In a sense, the firm's core competence might have been identified incompletely or inappropriately. This kind of discrepancy requires a thorough re-evaluation of the firm's core competence.

There is another typology for in-house versus outsourcing. This model takes into account two dimensions: product characteristics and the firm's technological capability. The product characteristics are described as either "commodity" or "innovative." Other things being comparable, one would find a commodity product at a late stage of the product life cycle (PLC), whereas an innovative product is at an early stage of PLC. The firm's technological capability can be either high or low in a relative sense. Now we suggest a two-by-two matrix framework. Figure 6.4 shows that when the firm's technological capability is high and the product characteristics are innovative, then making the product in-house is the best option. On the other hand, when the product characteristics are of commodity and the firm's technological capability is relatively low, an opportunistic behavior might emerge – outsourcing or in-house, depending on contextual factors such as whether the firm has redundant production capacity, whether capable contract manufacturers are available in the market, and the like. When the product is commodity-like and the firm's technological capability is high, then it probably wants to outsource current product manufacturing, so as to concentrate in-house capacity on making products consistently with its technological capability.

Although the two models are supporting each other to a certain extent, the first model (Figure 6.3) offers a more systematic analysis of the make-or-buy decision: it is closely linked with the concept of core competence and thus more logical in relating key dimensions to actual cases. Nevertheless, the second model (Figure 6.4) has its own merit as well: the simplicity.

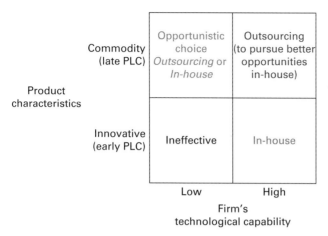

Figure 6.4 Typology of Outsourcing 2

6.2.2 Supplier Perception and Coordination

What happens when the necessary coordination fails in the supply chain? One of the biggest costs the supply chain partners have to pay when they fail to coordinate is the **bullwhip effect**, which we will elaborate in the next chapter. The bullwhip effect highlights *how a small change in the end-market demand distorts the perceived information and causes it to fluctuate more and more severely as it flows back from the downstream to the upstream in the supply chain*. This kind of **information distortion** occurs not because the participants in the supply chain are irrational, but paradoxically because they are very rational. In general, the managers try to avoid "**understocking**" more than "**overstocking**," since they don't want to disappoint their customers due to any stock-out. As such, they are inclined to have an extra **safety stock**, facing uncertainty in the customer demand; keeping an inflated amount of safety stock more and more as the information moves toward the upstream of the supply chain and makes ordering and producing more fluctuating. The problem is that their rationality fails to discern a fabricated risk from the true one. Figure 6.5 shows a simple example of the bullwhip effect: it depicts the patterns of ordering or production planning for the supply chain partners. It underscores that the fluctuation magnifies more and the **time-to-stability** (i.e., how long it takes to return to the normal state) becomes longer as the information reaches a more upstream activity, e.g., from the market demand, the distributor (or retailer), the manufacturer (or wholesaler), to the supplier. That is, the quality of the information deteriorates as it goes upstream: see the detailed definition and explanation of the **information quality** and its impact on the bullwhip effect in Section 2 of Chapter 7.

Perceptions in supply chain coordination.[2] What does it take for supply chain partners to coordinate? To answer the question properly, we need to focus on a rational or economic side. But, in reality, a softer side matters as well.

---

[2] Data based on B. Kim, K. Park, and T. Kim, "The Perception Gap among Buyer and Suppliers in the Semiconductor Industry" (1999) 4(5) *Supply Chain Management: An International Journal* 231–241.

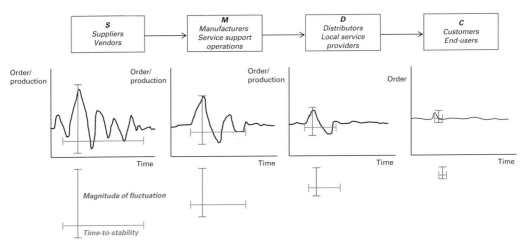

Figure 6.5 A Simple Example of the Bullwhip Effect

Firms are trying to concentrate on their core competence as a means to win competitive advantage amid fierce competition and rapid changes in the global economy. As such, it simply doesn't make economic or managerial sense for a manufacturing firm to do every production process in-house since doing so effectively prevents the firm from focusing on its core competence. Thus, outsourcing part of the internal production process to outside suppliers seems a viable option to the manufacturer who is aiming to develop strong core competence.

Outsourcing is an arrangement of cooperative inter-firm relationship, which should be based on mutual **trust** between partner organizations for improving performance of the inter-firm transaction. However, trust is a highly complex concept, difficult to define in an absolute sense. Trust is defined as the expectation that an actor:

(1) can be relied on to fulfill obligations;
(2) will behave in a predictable manner; and
(3) will act and negotiate fairly when the possibility of **opportunism** is present.[3]

In effect, the definition of trust is based on three components: **reliability, predictability**, and **fairness**. Now we can see the close link between trust and expectation, which in turn are deeply involved in understanding **perception**. We put forward another correlation between the inter-firm trust and perception gap, and suggest a large perception gap has a negative impact on the inter-firm trust. Thus, one can establish a causal connection between the perception gap and performance of the outsourcing transaction.

There is a **perception gap** between the buyer and suppliers when the factors considered by the buyer as critical for an effective outsourcing partnership are significantly different from those the suppliers perceive as critical. There can exist perception gaps among suppliers when their ideas about the critical factors differ significantly.

---

[3] A. Zaheer, B. McEvily, and V. Perrone, "Does Trust Matter? Exploring the Effects of Interorganizational and Interpersonal Trust on Performance" (1998) 9(2) *Organization Science* 141–159.

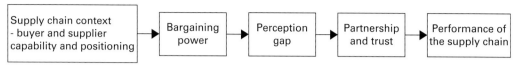

Figure 6.6 A Study Framework for the Perceptions in the Supply Chain

In this section, we examine the perception gap existing between the buyer and her suppliers and that among the suppliers. At a more detailed level, we would like to identify factors for which there exists a significant perception gap between the buyer and its suppliers, and among the suppliers themselves. Our premise is that knowing the factors associated with significant perception gaps enables the manager to explain why such perception gaps persist, and eventually to rectify them.

Perception gaps in a supply chain. Figure 6.6 illustrates the framework. First, there is the supply chain context, where the buyer and suppliers take on different positions in terms of access to alternative partners and capabilities. We argue that a specific supply chain context impacts on the bargaining power between the buyer and suppliers, and any imbalance in the bargaining position causes perception gaps among the partners. These perception gaps negatively influence the partnership or trust, and eventually affect the performance of the outsourcing relationship.

Bargaining power and perception gap. It is important to understand the relationship between these two factors. A couple of definitions of **bargaining power** are available: (1) the bargainer's ability to favorably change the bargaining set to influence the outcome of a negotiation; (2) one party's ability to win accommodations from the other party in a bargaining or negotiation situation. There are two sources of bargaining power: **context-based** and **resource-based**. The context-based bargaining power of one party comes from the availability of alternatives to itself. For instance, the bargaining partner who can access more alternatives has a larger bargaining power than its counterpart with few options. On the other hand, the resource-dependence theory postulates that the possession or control of critical resources constitutes power in an inter-organizational relation.

In this section, we discuss the perception gap in a specific context, where the single buyer (a manufacturer) outsources the production of key components to multiple suppliers. The number of buyers and suppliers involved in the supply chain is crucial in influencing the perception among the participants in the chain. We suggest three configuration types of outsourcing in the supply chain: (1) competitive-supplier outsourcing; (2) monopolistic-supplier outsourcing; and (3) complex-competitive outsourcing. This grouping is done from the buyer's (or manufacturer's) perspective. **Competitive-supplier outsourcing** assumes a supply chain where there are multiple suppliers competing with each other for supplying a (few) buyer(s), whereas there are multiple buyers that sometimes have to compete for obtaining quality supply from a (few) supplier(s) in the **monopolistic-supplier outsourcing**. Finally, we can consider a supply chain where there are multiple buyers and multiple suppliers who compete with each other in a complicated manner – this represents the **complex-competitive outsourcing**.

Key concepts. In order for the outsourcing partnership to survive, the supplier must have competent production capability. Although there are different ideas about what factors are important ingredients constituting the production capability, such differences seem insubstantial. For the production characteristics, we suggest four elements:[4] *price, quality, delivery (lead time)*, and *flexibility*. In addition, we integrate key elements of relational characteristics into four categories as follows:

- **Familiarity.** Suppliers might believe that having a good human/informal relationship (e.g., friendship) with the manager at the buyer firm could help them to win out-sourcing orders from the buyer company continuously. The variable *familiarity* captures such perceptions embedded in the suppliers.
- **Communication.** Suppliers as well as buyers would perceive that keeping an effi-cient "formal communication" channel with the buyer could help suppliers to win the outsourcing contract. To communicate efficiently, it is important to have an IT-related infrastructure in the supply chain.
- **Risk-sharing.** Since the business environment changes rapidly, suppliers as well as buyers could feel it necessary to have a kind of formal scheme to allow both partners to share the risks associated with environmental changes. For instance, buyers and suppliers might have to share the cost increases due to sudden changes in the price of raw materials, although such cost increases were not foreseen at the time of signing an outsourcing contract.
- **Long-term goal congruence.** For a collaborative relationship between buyers and suppliers to be sustainable, congruence in their long-term goals could be critical. Consider an example. It can be problematic if the buyer considers the outsourcing transaction as a temporary measure to save production cost, whereas suppliers regard it as a strategic venture. Because of this difference in their long-term perspectives, it would prove almost impossible for the partners in the outsourcing transaction to come up with a contract mutually profitable in the long run.

Propositions. Based on the framework outlined above, we suggest the following propositions, which can be tested against actual survey data:

1. Regarding the production and relational characteristics, the buyer has a priority, which is very different from that espoused by the suppliers as a whole.
2. The suppliers' perception that the relational characteristics are critical is much stronger than the buyer's.
3. Suppliers have significant perception gaps between themselves.
4. The most vulnerable supplier, having low production capability and a low-tech product requirement, perceives relational characteristics to be of greater significance than the other suppliers.

Figure 6.7 is one *example* of an expanded version of the preliminary framework in Figure 6.6. It shows that the specific supply chain setting forms a context-based

---

[4] W. Skinner, *Manufacturing in the Corporate Strategy* (New York: Wiley, 1978).

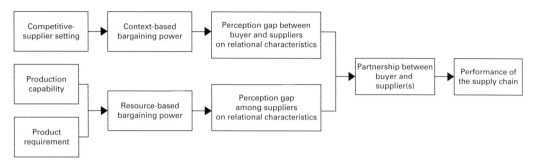

Figure 6.7 An Augmented Framework

bargaining power balance, which in turn affects the perception gap between the buyer and her suppliers: here a competitive-supplier setting is assumed. On the other hand, we argue that the suppliers' production capability along with the product requirement determines the balance of resource-based bargaining power that impacts the perception gap among the suppliers – e.g., as in the last proposition, a vulnerable supplier is the one having a low level of production capability and receiving a low-tech product requirement from the buyer. These propositions are designed to verify the framework in Figure 6.7. For an actual survey to test the propositions, refer to Case Study 6.1.

6.3 Supplier Typology

In Figure 6.3, we suggested different outsourcing strategies, depending on various factors such as the firm's own technological capability and the parts' required technology. Although it is important for a manufacturer to maintain a **strategic relationship** with its suppliers, this shouldn't imply that having a strategic supply chain relationship is always good and necessary. For example, if the parts supplied from its supplier require sophisticated technology that is difficult to find in the open market, it is critical for the manufacturer to maintain a strategic, long-term relationship with the supplier in order to ensure that the supply will stay stable and lasting. But, there can be an opposite situation as well. Suppose a part has become a commodity – it is easy to buy it in the open market and there are many suppliers that can make it economically and to a high quality. Under this situation, is it still necessary to try to develop a strategic partnership with the suppliers? The answer to this question is most likely "no." If there are many suppliers that make and sell the commodity product, the firm doesn't have to invest in building a partnership with the supplier. It would be better for the company to buy the product from the seller that offers the most competitive price. As this example highlights, it is important for the firm to select suppliers with which it wants to develop strategic partnerships. Developing a strategic partnership with a supplier often means that the company, e.g., the manufacturer, supports its supplier's innovation efforts and/or treats the supplier more favorably than other non-strategic suppliers. For example, the manufacturer orders from the supplier in a predictable manner, guarantees a minimum

Table 6.3 An Example Typology of Suppliers 1

	Innovator	Leader	Depender	Transactor
Supplier's competency	Technological leadership	• Dominant market share and cost advantage • Sustainable competitive advantage	• Cost advantage • Market leadership • Resource for investment	• Parts should be low-value adding • Low dependency on the company
Strategic guideline	• Be the largest customer to the supplier • Evaluate supplier's capability to maintain market leadership • Consider investing in the supplier	• Monitoring and evaluation to maintain long-term relationship	• Monitoring supplier's profitability • Exert bargaining power • Pricing based on learning curve	• Potential cooperation • Flexible relationships with many suppliers • Being concerned about economic change in the supply market

purchase amount, pays premiums as long as the supplier meets the quality standards, gives more preference to the supplier when there is a new business opportunity, and so forth.

Having a good supplier relationship is important to every company. It is particularly valuable to automobile companies. These companies have been trying to develop quality suppliers in strategically critical areas, i.e., for parts that are innovative and critical to the car's overall performance. Many global carmakers have their own frameworks to categorize suppliers and differentiate their supply chain strategies depending on the suppliers' characteristics. For instance, one carmaker categorizes suppliers into four groups – innovator, leader, depender, and transactor – and uses differentiated guidelines to deal with various suppliers (Table 6.3). The company views a supplier with technological leadership in the industry as the **innovator**, a supplier with dominant market share and sustainable competitive advantage as the **leader**, a supplier maintaining market leadership in terms of cost and resources as the **depender**, and, finally, a supplier supplying only low-value-adding parts as the **transactor**. Depending on the supplier's type, the company has specific guidelines for doing business with them. If the supplier is categorized as an innovator, the company will try to be the largest customer to that supplier, evaluate the supplier's capability so as to maintain its market leadership, and invest in the supplier's innovation activities. For a leader supplier, it tries to maintain a long-term relationship by frequent monitoring and

Table 6.4 An Example Typology of Suppliers 2

	Strategic Partner	Incumbent Relationship	Selected Competition	Competitive Bid
Description	Sustainable partnership for total cost reduction and supply-chain-wide innovation	Long-term relationship for cost reduction and successive improvement	Selected bidding based on product life cycle	Procurement through competitive bidding
Strategic goal	Strategic long-term partnership	Total cost minimization with extended partnership	Minimizing unit price and switch cost, considering product life cycle	Minimizing unit cost
Characteristics	Sharing long-term risk and profit	Long-term relationship with periodic reviews	Supplier's participation in product design phase	Spot transaction Supplier's participation in mass-production phase

evaluating. For a depender supplier, the carmaker suggests a pricing scheme that takes into account the supplier's learning curve, monitors the supplier's profitability, and sometimes exerts its bargaining power vis-à-vis the supplier's. Finally, the company wants to maintain flexible relationships with many "transactor" suppliers rather than to make a commitment to strategic relationships with them.

Another carmaker adopts its own framework to categorize suppliers (Table 6.4). It defines a supplier as a **strategic partner** when the company feels it is necessary to form a strategic relationship and share the long-term profits as well as risks with the supplier. An **incumbent relationship** is defined as a long-term relationship for cost reduction and continuous improvement. Although the relationship can be long-term, it requires periodic reviews by the carmaker. Cost minimization is the most important motivation for this type of supplier relationship. For the supplier categorized as **selected competition**, the company offers selected bidding chances by taking into account the PLC of the supply. Minimizing both the supply and switching costs is the primary motivation. Finally, in the competitive bidding relationship, the carmaker purchases its supplies through a competitive bidding or spot market transaction. The company's goal in this relationship is to minimize the unit cost.

Another carmaker is concerned about a similar problem: how to develop capable suppliers. The company wants to differentiate suppliers so that it could identify those with strategic importance to the company. Once strategic suppliers are identified, the carmaker will be willing to support them so that these strategic partners can innovate and grow with the company continuously. Figure 6.8 shows the framework with which the

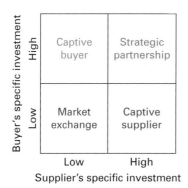

Figure 6.8 The Portfolio of a Buyer–Supplier Relationship

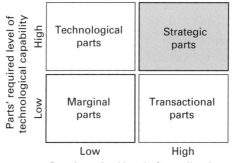

Figure 6.9 Categorization of Parts and Suppliers

company is able to categorize its suppliers. It categorizes suppliers depending on whether the relationship – the transaction between the buyer and the supplier – requires specific investments from the two parties. When such a relationship requires a significant amount of investment from both parties simultaneously, then the relationship is defined as a **strategic partnership**. On the contrary, if the relationship requires any such investments from neither the buyer nor the supplier, it is just **market exchange** – no recognizable relationship exists.

Although there are several useful models in the literature that it could adopt, the carmaker thinks it's better to approach this issue from a rather novel perspective. The problem begins with the fact that there are many automobile parts the carmaker has to deal with. Therefore, the company decides to establish a categorization model based on the parts' characteristics, rather than the supplier's characteristics directly. After conducting a thorough research, the company finally develops a framework consisting of two dimensions: *technological capability* and *coordination* (see Figure 6.9). The **technological capability dimension** represents factors related to technological competencies the parts' suppliers need to possess in order to meet the quality standards set by the company. On the other hand, the **coordination dimension** stands for factors related to the supply network's characteristics and the supplied parts' non-technical attributes. With these two dimensions, the company categorizes the parts into four groups: strategic, technological, transactional, and marginal.

The company's decision process flows as follows. First, it categorizes its parts according to the framework in Figure 6.9. Once the company knows what the strategic parts are, it identifies those suppliers who are capable of providing such parts to the company, and then it tries to establish a strategic partnership with them. The company will be willing to give more favor to the strategic partners and further support their efforts to innovate for their supplies.

6.4   Retailers' Domination

One potential pitfall that might dampen coordination in a supply chain is concerned with a severe imbalance in bargaining power among the supply chain partners. Since this issue is particularly prevalent in the retail industry, we focus on the industry as a case in point. In order to capitalize on economies of scale, retail stores are getting bigger and bigger. In fact, this increasingly becomes a sort of mantra in the retail business: it seems almost impossible to compete in the retail industry unless you are really big. There are pros and cons for this phenomenon of **mega retail stores**. Indeed, these mega retail stores return some of the savings they garner because of their size to customers. Or it might also be true to say that it is the customers themselves that ask the retail stores to size up and sell goods at bargain prices. Anyway, the huge pressure on cutting prices seems unstoppable. It is intriguing to note that a business magazine pointed out that Walmart's dominance creates problems – for suppliers, workers, communities, and even American culture.[5]

There are several reasons why the mega retailers' power has become so enormous. As the retailer becomes larger, in part because it wants to capitalize on the **scale economies**, its bargaining power grows more forceful as well. As Figure 6.10 shows, in the retail industry it is normal for there to be a multitude of suppliers or manufacturers that try to sell their goods to "only a few" mega retailers. In order to sell its products in great volume, a supplier cannot help but accommodate the big retailer's request to cut prices continuously: it is simply because there are few alternative outlets available.

Where does the customers' power to push the retailers to cut prices come from? There are several primary reasons, particularly in a fast-developing country. First, more customers have recently become wealthier and can now afford to buy cars. Therefore, they can drive to a distant store to buy groceries and other products, skipping small shops and traditional markets in their neighborhood. Although there are not many superstores in the market, still the competition among those big players hasn't been reduced. It is mainly due to the customers' enhanced mobility. The customers will drive to other superstores if the one near their homes doesn't offer competitive prices. Therefore, although one can say that the number of competitors in the retail industry has been

---

[5] A. Bianco and W. Zellner, "Is Walmart Too Powerful?" *BusinessWeek*, October 6, 2003 (cover story).

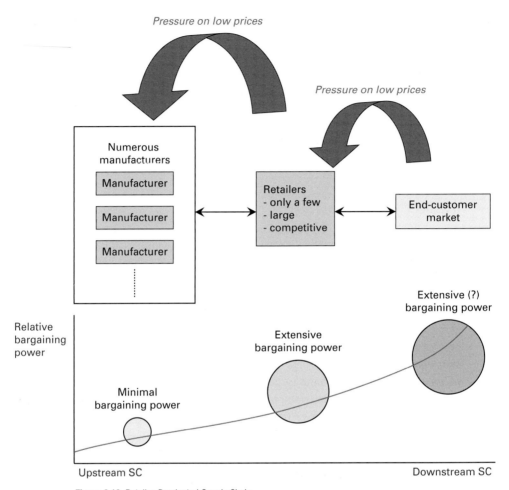

Figure 6.10 Retailer-Dominated Supply Chain

reduced, the real competition among the remaining mega stores is no less fierce than before. Moreover, the internet technology has equipped customers with another powerful weapon at their fingertips – the information about prices at different stores. Smart customers check the prices first through the internet and decide where to go shopping. Since the customers have the information and transportation means, they have more bargaining power vis-à-vis those retailers, even if the stores are mega-sized.

Many suppliers, or manufacturers that make and supply goods to the retailers, complain about the incessant and increasingly heavier pressures from the retailers on prices. We interviewed CEOs at the supplier companies in the food and beverage industry and some of them mentioned that unless the situation gets better soon, they cannot help but get out of the industry. As the Walmart case indicates, we believe this is a very serious situation that can be potentially detrimental, not only to the suppliers, but also to the economy as a whole. We fear that if suppliers are unable to cope with the heavy pressures to cut prices, some of them will be tempted to compromise the quality of their products and deceive the customers by covering this up. Then, the customers themselves will be the eventual victims. We put forward the view that it is very important for all of the supply chain partners to understand that any **sustainable partnership** in the supply chain requires each and every one of the supply chain partners to enjoy "fair and reasonable" profitability. Every participant must respect and try to guarantee other partners' fair shares of the value created through effective supply chain coordination. Maybe education is the only long-term solution to this kind of problem. But, there still remain several issues. Who will initiate such education? Who will pay for it? Will there be any enforcing mechanism? Although educating the supply chain partners about the importance of fair sharing and mutual understanding is vital not only for individual companies, but also for the economy as a whole, it may take some time for any initiative of education to earn enough support and momentum in the industry. It may be possible, very unfortunately, that the industry would be in an irrevocably deteriorating situation by the time the supply chain players realize the importance of fair sharing and mutual understanding as fundamental conditions for sustainable development in supply chain management.

Until such an industry-wide consensus on the issue is forged, are there any measures an individual supplier can take to weather the difficult time? In Figure 6.11, we suggest three feasible ways to overcome the retailer's excessive demand. For a supplier, the first and most important approach is to differentiate itself from others through **technological innovation**. The supplier must develop innovative products and/or innovate existing products so that the customers themselves demand and are willing to pay premium prices for these innovative products. Of course, this is the most effective yet most difficult way

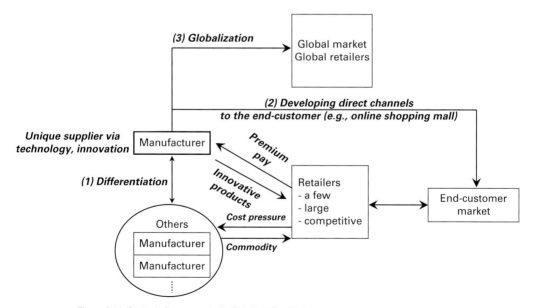

Figure 6.11 Strategic Responses to the Retailer's Domination

to overcome the retailer's unfair dominance. Nevertheless, the supplier must always try to stay technologically innovative. The second approach is to establish or find out direct **distribution channels** to the end-customers, i.e., distribution methods that bypass retail stores. Thanks to the advancement in the internet technology, it has become increasingly affordable to the suppliers, both small and large. These days, more suppliers establish their own internet home pages, where customers purchase the suppliers' products directly. One potential problem is the lack of variety. The customer usually cannot buy many different products at the same time from one supplier. There are, however, some effective ways for the suppliers to overcome this obstacle.[6] The third and final strategic response is to globalize into foreign markets and initiate business with global retailers. Having additional alternatives always enables the company to retain an enhanced bargaining power vis-à-vis its customers as well as competitors. In fact, **globalization** has been the most important growth strategy for strong and competitive companies, both large and small.[7]

Discussion Questions

1. All of the design factors for supply chain management are related to each other. In particular, there is a close relationship between inventory and logistics. Explain the relationship in detail and why the company should consider inventory and logistics simultaneously.
2. Explain the main differences between strategic outsourcing and contractual outsourcing.
3. Why is there a perception gap between a buyer and its suppliers? Why is it important for the buyer to manage the perception gap properly? Is it also important for the suppliers to understand the perception gap? Explain why or why not.
4. What are the primary objectives for the company to develop its own framework to categorize its suppliers? What might be the pitfalls of such a framework? What should the company do to avoid such pitfalls?
5. Suppose that a company (e.g., a supplier of a powerful retailer) is in a weak bargaining position vis-à-vis the retailer. What are the probable causes for such a problem?
6. Consider the company mentioned in Question 5. What are the strategic choices the company should make in order to overcome such an impasse?

---

[6] For instance, refer to the adaptive channels in Chapter 8.
[7] H. Simon, *Hidden Champions of the 21st Century: Success Strategies of Unknown World Market Leaders* (London: Springer, 2009).

Let's consider an actual case, for which a survey is conducted to test the propositions based on the framework in Figure 6.7. Our context in Figure 6.12 delineates the supply chain, which involves a buyer and its four suppliers. That is, it is a competitive-supplier outsourcing case, where the suppliers are competing with each other to better serve the monopolistic manufacturer, i.e., the buyer. Thus, the buyer has more bargaining power, which is context-based, since it has more alternatives than the suppliers have (Figure 6.13).

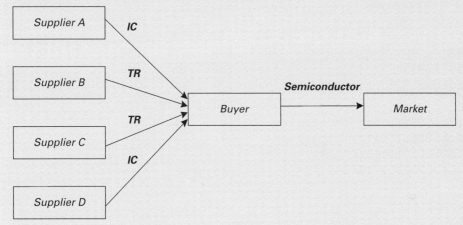

Note: IC = integrated circuit; TR = transistor; these are the parts supplied by the suppliers to the buyer company.

Figure 6.12 A Competitive-Supplier Outsourcing Setting

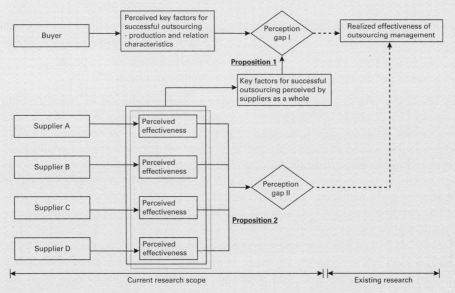

Figure 6.13 Study Propositions

Source: Developed and written by B. Kim. ©

Case companies. In order to test the propositions, we surveyed four suppliers transacting with the single buyer. Table 6.5 summarizes the suppliers' profile. Suppliers A and D supply integrated circuits (IC) to the buyer, while B and C supply transistors (TR). It is determined that IC requires a higher technological capability than TR does. From the buyer's perspective, it would be easier to find an alternative supplier for TR than for IC. In the next section, we show how to evaluate the supplier's production capability by analyzing the survey data from the buyer company. The outsourcing relationship represents the period during which the supplier has engaged in the outsourcing transaction with the buyer.

Table 6.5 Profile of Suppliers in the Sample

Supplier	A	B	C	D
Product	IC[1]	TR[2]	TR	IC
Technological requirement of product[3]	High	Low	Low	High
Production capability[4]	Low	High	Low	High
Total number of employees	9,000	800	340	450
Firm size[5]	Large	Large	Small	Small
Outsourcing relationship (years)	9	10	4	5
Number of managers surveyed	16	16	16	16
Average tenure of managers (years)	7.0	6.3	3.5	4.8

Notes:

[1] Integrated circuit.
[2] Transistor.
[3] IC requires more high technology than TR.
[4] Evaluated by managers at the buyer firm, using Duncan Test at 10 percent.
[5] Informal categorization based on number of employees.

The buyer company is a large semiconductor manufacturer in Korea, enjoying about 20 percent market share in the 16 M DRAM market worldwide. We surveyed sixty managers in the buyer company, each having been involved in the outsourcing activity with the four supplier companies for several years out of their average tenure of 8.83 years at the company.

Summary of survey results. For the relational characteristics, managers at the buyer company assume a priority from communication, long-term goal congruence, risk-sharing, and familiarity in that order. It is somewhat striking to see that the pattern of prioritization by the suppliers mirrors that of the buyer except for a minor difference: this is also true even if we look at the prioritization among both production and relational characteristics at the same time. This observation leads us to reject the first proposition, concluding that in contrast to our proposition, the priority set by the buyer is very much consistent with that by the suppliers as a whole. As a result, we conclude that there might not be much difference between the two partners (i.e., suppliers and the buyer) when perceiving the importance of factors in a simple prioritization.

However, we did find a significant difference when comparing the extent of perception by the two partners. In Table 6.6, we compare the extent of perception asserted by the suppliers as a whole with that by the buyer for each of the production and relational characteristics. Except for price and risk-sharing, average responses by the suppliers are higher than those by the buyer, and the differences are statistically significant, indicating that the suppliers perceive both production and relational characteristics as more critical than the buyer does. This outcome supports the second proposition.

Table 6.6 Perception Gap between Buyer and Suppliers

Characteristics	Individual Factors	Average Responses by Suppliers	Average Responses by Buyer
Production	Price	6.4688	6.5167
characteristics	Quality	6.7500*	6.4333
	Lead time	6.2656*	5.7833
	Flexibility	5.7031*	5.2333
	Average	6.2969*	5.9917
Relation	Familiarity	4.2656*	3.6667
characteristics	Communication	5.7344*	5.3167
	Risk sharing	4.6406	4.5833
	Long-term goals	5.5781*	4.6667
	Average	5.0547*	4.5583
Sample size		64	60

Notes:

* significant at 5 percent.

The survey was performed using a 7-point Likert scale.

Perception gap among suppliers. Now we want to take a look at the perception gap among the suppliers. Our focus shifts from the perception gap between the buyer and suppliers to that among the suppliers themselves. Thus, a question arises as to how to differentiate them. We decided to use two dimensions: suppliers' **production capability** and the **product requirement**. These seem to best reflect the resource-based bargaining power in the current research context. Product requirement is imposed by the buyer on the supplier, which is the technological requirement of the product outsourced to the supplier by the buyer. Based on the suppliers' profile, it is determined that suppliers A and D supply products that require a higher technological sophistication, whereas suppliers B and C supply products requiring a lower level of technology. We assume that the product requirement is an important dimension because it captures, to a certain extent, the buyer's expectation about the supplier's outsourcing competence or the supplier's own perception of the buyer's expectation.

Another important criterion related to, yet distinct from, the product requirement is the supplier's production capability, as evaluated by the managers at the buyer company. For consistency, the same items of production characteristics are used to appraise each supplier. As mentioned already, we asked sixty managers at the buyer company to evaluate each of the four suppliers in terms of their production characteristics: price, quality, lead time, and flexibility. Using the Duncan pairwise test, we ordered the four suppliers according to their production characteristics in Table 6.7. Combining the results for four items of production characteristics, we derived a composite rating that suggests suppliers B and D have higher production capability than suppliers A and C.

Table 6.7 Supplier's Production Capability Evaluated by the Buyer

| Supplier | Elements of Production Capability | | | | |
	Price	Quality	Lead time	Flexibility	Composite
Supplier A	II	I	I	II	**II**
Supplier B	I	II	I	I	**I**
Supplier C	II	II	I	I	**II**
Supplier D	I	II	I	I	**I**

Key:
I – high capability;
II – lower capability.
Note: Using the Duncan test, significant at 10 percent.

Figure 6.14 graphically shows the grouping of the four suppliers by production capability and product requirement. Note that suppliers A and B are larger (in terms of firm size) and have enjoyed the outsourcing relationship longer than suppliers C and D have. Although not intended originally, this distinction enables us to control potentially confounding effects. From the perspective of an economic transaction, suppliers A and B could be regarded as having more bargaining power vis-à-vis the buyer than other suppliers, possibly because of their larger size and longevity of outsourcing relationship with the buyer. In a similar vein, supplier D can be viewed as having a solid bargaining power since it is evaluated as the most competent among the four suppliers by the customer. As a result, supplier C seems to lie in the weakest position in terms of bargaining power, compared with the rest of the suppliers.

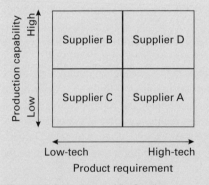

Figure 6.14 Categorization of the Suppliers

The results reported in Table 6.8 support the third and fourth propositions. The supplier in the best bargaining position, supplier D, perceives only one factor, i.e., communication with the buyer company, as the most important for successful outsourcing partnership, while those at the next level in terms of their bargaining power, suppliers A and B, perceive long-term goal congruence in addition to communication as the most critical factors. Quite interestingly, the most vulnerable supplier, supplier C, seems to perceive all of the relational characteristics as equally important in maintaining the successful outsourcing relationship. Figure 6.15 summarizes the results presented in Table 6.8.

Table 6.8 Individual Supplier's Prioritization

Supplier	Suppliers' Prioritization of Relation Characteristics
Supplier A	Comm. (5.69) L-T Goal (5.44) Risk share (4.75) Familiarity (3.94) ←——— I ———→ ←——— II ———→ ←— III —→
Supplier B	L-T Goal (5.88) Comm. (5.69) Risk share (4.63) Familiarity (4.44) ←——— I ———→ ←——————— II ———————→
Supplier C	L-T Goal (5.75) Comm. (5.63) Familiarity (5.19) Risk share (5.13) ←——————————— I ———————————→
Supplier D	Comm. (5.94) L-T Goal (5.25) Risk share (4.06) Familiarity (3.50) ←— I —→ ←——— II ———→ ←——— III ———→

Note: Using the Duncan test, significant at 10 percent.

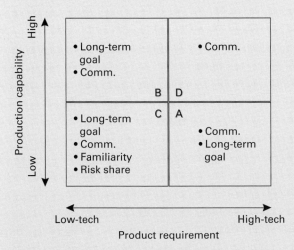

Figure 6.15 Relational Characteristics Emphasized by Each Supplier

Conclusions. From this study, we are able to infer: (1) it is true in general that there exists a significant perception gap between the buyer and her suppliers; and (2) a vulnerable supplier (possibly due to less production competence) perceives relational characteristics as more critical than do those in a better bargaining position (possibly due to either larger firm size or higher production competence).

This is an important verification. It enables the buyer company to understand that its suppliers might have very different perceptions about what factors are important for an effective and lasting outsourcing partnership. This knowledge helps the buyer to deal with each supplier in a more appropriate and tailored way. On the other hand, a supplier, especially the one in a vulnerable position, can redirect its resources from concentrating on relational characteristics (which are not critical from the buyer's perspective) to enhancing production characteristics and thus production capability. Once each partner figures out each other's bargaining position and competence, they can reach a fair contract of outsourcing that can nurture a productive partnership.

Questions

1. What factors or forces determine the bargaining power balance between the buyer and its suppliers?
2. Why does the most vulnerable supplier perceive all of the "relational characteristics" to be equally important? What does it mean?
3. Why is it necessary for the buyer company to understand that there might exist a perception gap between itself and its suppliers?

案例 CASE STUDY 6.2
The Importance of Sustainable Purchasing and Supply: OPITO

What would happen if Christmas trees were not available until Easter? How would you feel if you tried to buy a coffee at your favorite high street café only to be told they had run out of coffee beans? Making sure the key components that a business or service relies on are available when needed is the responsibility of the purchasing role.

Purchasing and supply – also known as procurement – may appear to be a "hidden" function in many organizations. In fact, procurement is a highly strategic role, whether the organization is manufacturing or service-orientated, in the public or private sector, for profit or not. Procurement is complex. It covers the full supply chain from contracts (negotiating) and procurement (purchasing) to logistics (storage/distribution).

All businesses need inputs in order to be able to operate. These might be physical inputs, such as raw materials, like engine components for a car manufacturer. They may also be service-based, such as specialist engineering consultancy when trialing new technology or distribution services for a high street retailer. It is vital that inputs not only meet the required quality and reliability standards, but also that they are competitively priced.

Effective purchasing. Purchasing and supply focuses on sourcing, pricing, and buying the right things at the right price and right time in order to deliver a service or product. Effective purchasing can help an organization to reduce costs, maintain quality, and manage the levels of risk in its supply chain. The scale or importance of the item is relative to the level of risk to the business. Missing coffee beans will affect the day's profits; getting the wrong size of engine for a car could close down the production line.

OPITO and CIPS. For the oil and gas industry with its high levels of risk, the Chartered Institute of Purchasing and Supply (CIPS) is providing training to improve the efficiency and effectiveness of purchasing and supply. OPITO, the focal point for skills, learning, and development in the oil and gas industry, undertook a labor market survey of the industry which identified a sector-wide skills shortage. Oil & Gas UK then undertook a supply chain survey. This showed that there is both a current shortage and a likely future need for purchasing and supply chain specialists in the oil and gas industry.

CIPS and OPITO are therefore working together to promote career opportunities and develop specialized training to meet this need. This case study explores the role of purchasing and supply in the oil and gas industry.

The purchasing and supply role. Every business, from an NHS hospital to the biggest brands in the world such as Coca-Cola or McDonalds, needs supplies. Purchasing may involve the day-to-day necessities like photocopier paper, soap and towels for washrooms, or service support for IT equipment. However, the purchasing role also covers high-tech or large-scale equipment for major projects such as the building of an aircraft carrier or the Olympic stadium, as well as the skills required to operate it.

Purchasing and supply roles therefore require high levels of skill. CIPS is the professional body which aims to promote the highest standards of excellence in purchasing and supply management

Source: Reprinted with permission from Business Case Studies LLP.

across all industries. It provides these through its professional qualifications program, focused training and education, and by rigorous assessment procedures.

Adding value to the business: Those involved in purchasing and supply are in a position to consider every stage of a business's processes, from raw materials to waste management. This "helicopter view" can help a procurement manager to spot ways of making efficiencies or opportunities to improve the quality of products or services bought. They can see not just internal impacts, but also what is happening in the external environment and the marketplace. This can help to generate new ideas to add value to the business, identify how it can increase competitive advantage, or improve sustainability.

An example of the vital nature of the role relates to when BP needed to manage the supply chain of emergency goods following the Deepwater Horizon oil spill in the Gulf of Mexico in 2010. The supply chain team had to source everything from mealworms to feed wounded birds, to booms to prevent the oil spreading further, to dispersant materials to remove the oil. The challenges included finding sufficient quantities of emergency goods at very short notice, as well as trying to keep budgets under control.

Supporting innovation: Procurement managers are also involved in researching suppliers in new markets and developing new and innovative procurement methods to improve effectiveness. They also agree and manage service level agreements (SLAs). An SLA is a contract that specifies standards, timings, and payments for the supply, along with penalties for missing targets. It sets out the responsibilities and expectations for both the business (the buyer) and its suppliers. A key element of the SLA is ensuring that the price quoted by suppliers will not be subject to change, thus affecting the purchasing budget.

Longer-term purchaser and supplier relationships can provide stability and add value to both parties. The purchaser may be able to get the best possible terms and prices or a supplier may "go the extra mile" for the business in an urgent situation. This type of collaboration builds trust between buyer and supplier, which might enable a just-in-time relationship, where both parties hold minimum stock and so reduce costs.

Purchasing and supply in oil and gas. The oil and gas industry is divided into the "upstream" and "downstream" operations. Upstream involves exploring for oil and gas and extracting it safely. The downstream part of the industry is concerned with refining, distribution, and sales.

The supply chain: The oil and gas industry has very long supply chains. Many companies may be involved in supplying the materials, components, and services at different stages and across the various processes involved in extracting, refining, and distributing oil and gas. Procurement becomes even more important in this type of global operation. A company such as BP sources services and supplies from many different countries. These range from mechanical and electrical parts to professional services such as project management or legal expertise for drawing up contracts.

Reliability is a crucial factor in supply, in terms of both quality and timing. If supplies are of poor quality, delivered late, or cost more than was agreed, this will affect productivity and profitability. If production is delayed or faulty products need to be scrapped, this can reduce profits. Poor quality inputs could also affect the safety of the process – a major consideration in the oil and gas industry.

For example, to help improve safety and quality of supply, BP is introducing safety performance indicators into contracts of suppliers involved in high-risk activities. Suppliers who do not meet these standards may be removed from contracts. As part of this safety focus, BP is also planning to reduce use of agency staff in procurement roles and boost its in-house expertise in supply chain management.

"Make or buy": An important decision for many businesses is whether to carry out a particular part of its process itself ("make") or buy in the components or expertise it needs. This decision might depend on, e.g., whether the skills and capacity are available in-house, whether there is a need for high security of supply, or whether it is simply cheaper to outsource.

For example, an oil company could choose to rent or own an oil platform. If it rents, its costs are limited to the rental period, with repairs and maintenance being the responsibility of the owner. Buying outright might cost more initially, but the company has the benefit of the asset. However, it also has the issues and costs of maintenance and, ultimately, disposal. Purchasing managers work with operational managers to consider these issues and find the most cost-effective and efficient solution for the business.

Sustainable procurement. Other key factors to consider when choosing a supplier include their ability to respond quickly to changing customer needs and how well they can help toward meeting a business's sustainability goals.

CIPS offers a structured online audit process to help purchasing managers map their organizations' purchasing systems against best practice. This enables them to assess how energy efficient and sustainable their purchasing processes are.

Benefits of sustainable sourcing: Sustainable procurement is a high-profile matter for businesses today. It can help save money, reduce waste, improve competitiveness, and build a business's reputation. As part of their sustainability programs, many oil companies have invested in local transportation networks or built schools. They provide jobs and, by sourcing supplies locally, help to develop the local economy. The global oil industry has a responsibility to the countries in which it operates to manage its operations as sustainably as possible. A purchasing manager might want to consider whether the supplier behaves responsibly, e.g., adhering to ethical standards or sourcing raw materials in an ethical way.

For example, Shell is working with its existing suppliers to implement the Shell Supplier Principles. These set out the minimum standards which Shell suppliers need to meet. These include using energy and natural resources as efficiently as possible to minimize impact on the environment and covering health and safety issues.

Efficiency: Other aspects of sustainable business include managing waste effectively and reducing the company's carbon footprint. This can be improved by choosing suppliers who also take their responsibilities toward environmental impact seriously. For example, Marks & Spencer made £70 million of efficiency savings during 2010/11. Alongside reductions in waste and packaging and increased energy efficiency, the company is working with suppliers to reduce carbon emissions in the supply chain by improving efficiency of deliveries.

Roles and skills. Although engineering and technical roles are crucial in the oil and gas industry, oil companies also require lawyers, accountants, geologists, electricians, plumbers, crane drivers, mechanics, divers, and designers.

Roles in purchasing and supply cover all levels, from operational ones such as buyers and store managers, to strategic ones such as in supply chain analysis or strategic sourcing, so there are opportunities for everyone.

Entry levels vary. Many people join oil and gas companies after having worked in other industries. Some young people join the industry straight from school; others after a college or university course. For example, Hannah has a degree in mathematics and economics.

> I wanted a career that would offer variety and challenge. As a purchasing manager, I have both. My job has given me a detailed knowledge of different parts of the oil and gas industry, plus a significant amount of responsibility.

Procurement in action: Graeme is a group procurement and supply chain manager with over twenty-five years' experience in the industry. With an engineering background, he did not originally consider purchasing and supply as a career, but got a taste for the challenges of the procurement role when he spent six months in the job as part of his degree.

> The procurement process in oil and gas is complex, with a key reliance on safety. In addition, some of the materials we use in this industry are highly specialized, which can mean long lead times for purchase. However, the engineers or companies needing the materials expect very quick responses, so management and forecasting to anticipate their needs is highly important.

People involved in purchasing need business knowledge and the ability to analyze markets. CIPS provides six levels of qualifications for the procurement and supply profession across the world. All UK qualifications are Ofqual (the Office of Qualifications and Examinations Regulator) accredited and appear on the Register of Regulated Qualifications. Students may start a CIPS qualification with no entry requirements.

Steve is head of global procurement and supply chain management at Prosafe, a leading owner and operator of oil and gas rigs.

> Procurement is a highly strategic role. The oil and gas industry supports the whole world economy, from the fuel in vehicles to plastic paperclips. My company provides oil companies with accommodation vessels, which are like floating hotels. Deliveries might reach a platform only once a week, so every last detail from wi-fi access and toilet paper to all the operational and engineering requirements has to be in place, at the right time, in the right quantity and quality. Young people may not be aware of how interesting it is to work in purchasing and supply chain roles – there is no "standard day." I love it and I believe the job I do makes a difference.

Muhib is a procurement specialist at BP. He sources both equipment and services and deals with contracts that range in value from £1 million to £60 million. His role includes careful assessment of the effectiveness of each supplier to ensure BP is getting value for money. This is a great responsibility and it may involve deciding whether or not to change supplier. This is a major decision, as it carries potential risk to the company and the continuation of its operations.

Purchasing and supply is a powerful and highly responsible role, dealing with high value contracts. The real satisfaction I get is from seeing what I do make a huge difference. I really enjoy my job and see my long-term future career in this industry.

Conclusion. Well-managed procurement ensures that supplies of the required quality are available at the right time, place, and cost. Supply chain managers help to:

- reduce costs and improve profitability – bulk buying can provide economies of scale;
- reduce waste by selecting inputs that generate less waste (and also lower costs);
- manage demand, e.g., through just-in-time supply;
- improve cash flow by securing favorable prices and payment terms;
- improve efficiency by making sure suppliers hit deadlines; and
- improve the competitiveness of the business by seeking out innovative products and services to add value.

In the oil and gas industry, where safety is a central concern, effective management of purchasing and supply is a vital role. Its procurement managers need to have good people skills, sound common sense, commercial and business skills, and the ability to communicate appropriately at all levels.

OPITO and CIPS are working together to ensure that the industry has the relevant training and qualifications programs to meet the long-term needs of the oil and gas industry.

Questions

1. What is the strategic role of purchasing and supply?
2. What are the important characteristics of purchasing and supply in oil and gas?
3. What are the key factors that affect the firm's decision on "make or buy"?
4. What is sustainable procurement?
5. Why is sustainable procurement important to enabling the company to be competitive in the market?

Part III

Infrastructural Dimension of Supply Chain Management

CHAPTER 7

Supply Chain Coordination

In this chapter, we discuss key issues related to decision-making for effective supply chain management. In the previous chapters, we covered basic decision-making factors for SCM, i.e., elements of the structural dimension such as configuration, connection, inventory, and logistics, by looking into the detail of each element: how to define each of them and to understand their dynamics, how the CEO as the key decision-maker can manage these elements effectively, and how they interact with each other to influence the performance of the supply chain. In this context, we now elaborate on fundamental characteristics of **supply chain coordination** as the **infrastructural dimension**: why and how supply chain partners should coordinate with each other, how much intensity of coordination is needed for effective SCM under specific situations, what are the essential conditions for sustainable supply chain coordination, and what are the possible mechanisms to facilitate **sustainable coordination** between the supply chain partner companies.

Key Learning Points

- The infrastructural dimension of supply chain management is coordination, i.e., how the supply chain partners coordinate with each other for such intangible rudiments as informational and behavioral factors.
- Some of the prominent areas for supply chain coordination include information-sharing (especially, information about market demand), collaboration on new product development and R&D, and other joint decision-making (e.g., joint marketing decision).
- Sustainable supply chain coordination requires two conditions, system-wide optimization (coordination must increase the total profit for the entire supply chain) and individual fairness (each supply chain partner's profit must increase in the foreseeable future).
- Lack of information-sharing between supply chain partners could cause the bullwhip effect, which increases inventory throughout the supply chain and thus significantly decreases the profit of not only each supply chain partner, but also the entire supply chain.

> • When there exists a strategic relationship between supply chain partners (e.g., a manufacturer and its supplier), it is not unusual for the manufacturer to support the supplier's innovation effort. Coordination for innovation, if implemented properly, can maximize the value creation for the supply chain as a whole.

學 WISDOM BOX 7.1
Wisdom and Insights

Essence of Supply Chain Coordination

What are the essential characteristics of supply chain coordination? We attempt to get an answer to the question by summarizing our interview with a top manager at BMW, one of the best carmakers in the world.

How can you characterize the supply chain management of the BMW Leipzig?

We have a very complex supply chain, which deals with more than 500 suppliers, many of them for **JIT** delivery. The complexity mainly comes from two sources. First, since we want to accommodate as many different features as possible for our customers, the number of possible combinations of the cars' configurations is enormous. Some people estimate it can be 1,017 in theory. The sheer number of alternative configurations itself poses a great challenge to our SCM. Second, we allow our customers to change their orders as short as 6 days prior to the assembly line. It poses another big burden on our suppliers, who should deliver supplies on a JIT basis. We request our suppliers to accommodate changes in our orders made as short as 4 days before delivery.

It is usual to have a very complex supply chain in the car manufacturing industry. But, the BMW Group supply chain is much more complex due to its strategy to customize individual cars for individual customers. We want to customize cars as close to 100 percent of the customer's request as possible. For instance, in the US market, 90 percent of the orders are placed by dealers, who specify great details of car features and configuration after consulting with the actual end-customers.

As alluded to already, BMW's operations and supply chain strategy seems to pose many difficult challenges to its suppliers. From the suppliers' perspective, why do they want to work with BMW? That is, what motivations do the suppliers have to coordinate with BMW?

That's a difficult question. Although BMW was rated "the best car manufacturer" in the world, it is a relatively small company and thus doesn't have a huge buying power. Like any other carmaker, BMW also tries to reduce its purchasing cost as well. Nevertheless, we're doing business with really strong and good suppliers. It's not easy to explain why and how that's possible. Well, we believe that's mainly because we treat our suppliers as real partners in creating value for our customers. For

Box continues

instance, we involve our major suppliers in R&D activities for developing new products like gearboxes, interior modules, and the like. It is based on our understanding that almost 70 to 80 percent of our important innovations have been derived from our suppliers. We have an innovation center in Munich, where one can see very intensive **R&D coordination** between BMW and the suppliers. It is not just for simple information-sharing, but real collaboration to develop core new products. We don't subsidize the suppliers in return for their participation in the R&D and new product development. Instead, BMW tries to compensate them by offering steady orders and reasonable purchasing prices after the new product development is completed. More importantly, we think the suppliers can get some intangible benefits from coordinating with BMW. Working with the most technologically advanced company like BMW itself enables the suppliers to improve their own technological capability essential for them to create their own values for their customers, e.g., possibly carmakers other than BMW.

Questions
1. Do you think BMW's coordination with its suppliers is sustainable? Please list reasons why you think so and why not.
2. Is it easy for other companies to emulate BMW's supply chain coordination strategy? Explain why and why not.

7.1   Infrastructural Dimension: Coordination

In addition to the structural dimension, there is another key dimension, i.e., the **infrastructural dimension**, which the decision-maker has to take into account when designing an effective supply chain. Elements of the structural dimension are primarily related with physical flows, requiring some form of physical assets such as facilities, products, mechanical tools, and the like. On the contrary, the infrastructural dimension consists of only one element, **coordination**, which deals with intangible rudiments such as informational and behavioral factors.

7.1.1   Definition of Coordination

A formal definition of coordination comprises several key concepts: (1) coordination involves more than one party, organization, or entity; (2) it implies that these parties, organizations, or entities work together to accomplish their mutual, common goals or objectives; (3) it cannot be done unilaterally, i.e., all of the involved parties must agree to work together, e.g., to plan, communicate, collaborate, arrange, or adjust, whenever necessary.

Supply chain partners coordinate with each other in numerous areas. Suppose that a manufacturer and its key supplier have formed a **strategic relationship** over time, e.g., the relationship is strategic in that the supplier has been engaged in the new product development process at the manufacturer's site, and the manufacturer has supported the supplier's **quality** improvement effort to a great extent. They probably share R&D facilities, streamline the IT infrastructure between them to facilitate the transaction information flow and to share demand information, and fund R&D projects jointly. As a result, coordination is a joint activity involving two or more decision-making entities – firms or organizations – that endeavor to accomplish common goals or objectives through that activity. In addition, we would say that a substantive coordination must be based on a strategic relationship between the supply chain partners.

As alluded to, there are many different types of coordination. Table 7.1 lists a few of them. The first and foremost area of supply chain coordination is in sharing of information on market demand for the product, market conditions, competition and competitors in the market, technology and its trend, and the like. That is, the supply chain partners share such information to achieve their common goals, e.g., enhancing the profit of the supply chain as a whole. Another important area is concerned with new product development along with R&D. Of course, supply chain partners might conduct joint R&D, not necessarily specifically linked with new product development, e.g., R&D for quality improvement of the current product. More comprehensively, any incremental or radical improvement in the supply chain can be coordinated between the supply chain partners as well. Another stylized application of coordination is collaborative planning, forecasting, and replenishment (CPFR). **CPFR** aims to maximize the product and/or service availability for customers and simultaneously minimize inventory as well as logistical costs. All related partners in the supply chain must work together and share their information and capability with each other in order to maximize the benefit of CPFR in terms of planning for and fulfilling the customer requirements. Although IT (information technology) can be a key to successful implementation of CPFR, it is more than a simple collection of technological tools: it calls for close coordination between supply chain partners and as such is part of managerial philosophy. In addition, there are many areas in managerial decision-making, for which the supply chain partners need to coordinate with each other to create common value throughout the value chain. It is obvious that some of the areas in Table 7.1 are overlapping each other. Nevertheless, each of the areas in Table 7.1 deserves a full and independent interest from supply chain managers.

Table 7.1 Areas of Coordination

- sharing of information on demand, market, competition, technology, and the like;
- collaborative new product development;
- collaborative R&D;
- collaborative quality improvement and other incremental improvements;
- collaborative planning, forecasting, and replenishing; and
- collaborative decision-making in such areas as marketing, financing, new market entry, workforce, and the like.

We have already mentioned that the real value must be created at the interaction point between the market and the supply chain system. Therefore, in order to create value, the participants in the supply chain must coordinate with each other in performing value-creating activities such as new product development, innovation, and quality improvement. In essence, through such coordination, the decision-maker must be able to design the structural elements – configuration, connection, inventory, and logistics – so as to optimize the supply chain performance. In the previous chapters, we have discussed performance measures for effective SCM, where we put forth that services associated with the product constitute the logistical, informational, and organizational supports for the core product in order to help the customer to start utilizing the product faster, more reliably, and more efficiently. A **quick response system** is one of these services the firm needs to provide to the customer in order to improve the supply chain's total performance. Coordinating product designs and logistical decisions must buttress such services as quick and accurate response systems, which must flexibly cope with the changing needs of the market quickly in terms of response time or accurately in terms of matching supply with demand. These capabilities – quick and accurate response capabilities – can't be achieved by one of the supply chain partners unilaterally. These capabilities can be nurtured only when all of the supply chain partners work together – coordinate with each other – to harmonize their value-creating activities. For example, consider an automobile supply chain, where Hyundai Motor is the assembler. Hyundai wants to design a product mix to accurately respond to the changing market demand. Since the market demand changes constantly, Hyundai probably has to revise its product mix plan from the end of the previous sales season to the beginning of the new models' sales season. However, even if Hyundai wants to match its supply with the market demand as accurately as possible, it cannot accomplish its goal effectively unless the suppliers are willing to accommodate Hyundai's constantly changing production scheduling and ordering of the parts. In effect, Hyundai's accurate response is not something it can unilaterally achieve. Now suppose that Hyundai wants to quickly respond to an unusual request from the market. For instance, customers suddenly require a particular car model, far exceeding the company's original forecast. In order to grab the extra profit, Hyundai should increase the production of the car heavily demanded by the market, but unfortunately it doesn't have enough materials to make the car to meet the market demand, because its original forecast did not anticipate this kind of sudden surge in demand. In this case, it is essential for Hyundai to get high-quality materials from the suppliers much faster than when dealing with usually anticipated demand. Therefore, quick response capability is not something Hyundai can exert without fully committed supplier collaboration. In sum, supply chain coordination is an indispensable force to enable the supply chain partners to enhance such critical capabilities as quick and accurate responses, which must be regarded as a **channel capability** rather than an individual capability.

Coordination intensity. There are different levels of coordination between supply chain participants. As Figure 7.1 and also Figure 3.7 show, there are intra-functional

- Intra-functional coordination: coordination between the components of each functional organization, e.g., coordination within manufacturing function (process design ↔ cutting ↔ assembling)

- Inter-functional coordination: within individual firms, e.g., coordination between manufacturing and marketing

- Inter-organizational coordination: between channel participants

Figure 7.1 Level of Coordination

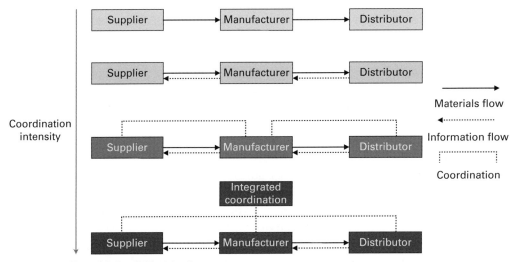

Figure 7.2 Coordination Intensity

or inter-functional coordination, and intra-firm or inter-firm coordination. The simplest form of coordination is intra-firm intra-functional coordination, which can be accomplished by individuals at the same company's functional department. Coordination could evolve over time – from intra-firm intra-functional to inter-firm inter-functional coordination. As the coordination level heightens, its complexity also increases.

There is another way to look at the coordination level – **coordination intensity**. Figure 7.2 shows the increasing intensity of coordination. The lowest intensity level is perhaps the case where there is virtually no coordination between the supply chain participants: it is also consistent with a pure push system. The next level is comparable with a situation where information flows from downstream to upstream, so that a certain amount of information-sharing is unavoidable. Similarly, this is comparable to a pure pull system. The next higher level is the case where two consecutive supply chain partners, e.g., the supplier and the manufacturer or the manufacturer and the distributor, coordinate with each other to accomplish mutually beneficial goals. Note that this level of intensity requires much more than just sharing information about market demand.

Such coordination enables the supply chain partners to achieve far more superior performance via coordination than that without any sincere coordination between the partners. In general, this level of coordination intensity is involved with such sophisticated collaborating activities as new product development, quality improvement of the existing product, new market opportunity identification, collaborative R&D, or marketing activity. The most intensive coordination encompasses the entire supply chain system, not just neighboring supply chain partners. Thus, this level of supply chain coordination assumes an integrated entity that oversees the system-wide coordination to ensure achieving best outcomes from the perspective of the supply chain as a whole. But, this integrated entity doesn't have to be a real, say legal, entity as long as it has influence over supply chain partners to coordinate resource allocation and related decision-making processes. For example, consider a supply chain in the automobile industry, which consists of suppliers, a car assembler as the manufacturer, and car dealers as the distribution function. In many such cases, the assembler has the biggest bargaining power. Leveraging this bargaining power, the manufacturer might be able to take the role of integrating coordination throughout the supply chain without establishing an independent formal organization to do the task. If this arrangement works effectively, it exemplifies a situation where there exists an integrated entity to oversee the system-wide coordination, even if there does not exist any separate legal entity to assume the role.

Fundamental conditions for sustainable coordination. So far, we are convinced that coordination is essential in enhancing the performance of the supply chain system as a whole, through improving such channel capabilities as quick response and accurate response. In reality, however, there might exist a very delicate issue. Reconsider the example of an automobile supply chain, where the assembler has the biggest bargaining power; in fact, this is in general a typical situation in the real world. Should there be no intervening forces, the manufacturer would be tempted to appropriate most of the benefit from coordinating channel capabilities to satisfy the customer's demand quickly and accurately. One can raise a serious question: *Why do firms coordinate?* This question becomes particularly more critical to supply chain partners who are not "dominating players" in the supply chain, unlike the automobile assembler in the above example.

We would like to suggest two fundamental conditions for **sustainable supply chain coordination** among supply chain participants. Sustainable coordination implies that the supply chain participants are committed to such coordination with a strategic perspective, i.e., from the long-term viewpoint. Therefore, sustainable coordination could overcome short-term difficulties as long as the supply chain partners believe that there is a reasonably high likelihood for the two fundamental conditions to prevail at least in the near future.

The two fundamental conditions for sustainable supply chain coordination are (1) **system-wide optimization** and (2) **individual distributive justice** or fairness. Figure 7.3 depicts the two conditions. Consider as before a simplified supply chain consisting of supply, manufacturing, and distribution functions. Let π_s denote the profit for the supply function when there is no supply chain coordination. We make π_m and π_d denote profits without supply chain coordination for the manufacturing and

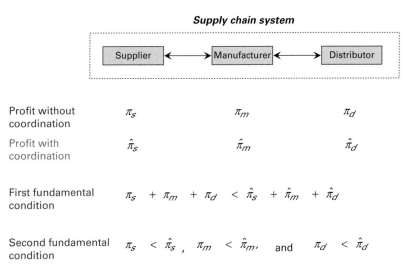

Figure 7.3 Two Fundamental Conditions for Sustainable Supply Chain Management

the distribution function, respectively. Now we use a variable with a hat to represent the profit for each supply chain partner, when there is supply chain coordination – i.e., $\hat{\pi}_s$, $\hat{\pi}_m$, and $\hat{\pi}_d$ respectively for supply, manufacturing, and distribution.

The first fundamental condition is **system-wide optimization**. In order for the supply chain partners to participate in the supply chain coordination in the long run, it must be stably held that the total profit for the supply chain system as a whole should increase due to such coordination. Hence, $\pi_s + \pi_m + \pi_d < \hat{\pi}_s + \hat{\pi}_m + \hat{\pi}_d$ must hold firmly in the long run.

The second fundamental condition is **individual distributive justice** or fairness. In order for such coordination to be sustainable in the long run, it is not enough to make sure that the system-wide profit must increase specifically due to the coordination among the supply chain participants. What if most of the benefit is appropriated by the dominant firm in the supply chain? Suppose a situation where a supplier and a manufacturer form a supply chain and the manufacturer is the dominant player. Further, suppose that the supply chain system as a whole creates value in that the system-wide profit with coordination is larger than that without such coordination. However, using its stronger bargaining power, the manufacturer grabs most of the increased profit. There might be an extreme situation where the supplier's profit even deteriorates. Thus, the manufacturer enjoys increased profit at the expense of its supply chain partner. Should there be no alternative business opportunities for the supplier in the short run, the supplier can't do anything but stick to the unfair supply chain relationship. However, this kind of maltreatment will be tolerated only as long as there does not exist any other alternative for the supplier – the supplier finds the supply chain relationship with the manufacturer unfair and will look for other business alternatives as much as possible. While searching for a new business partner, the supplier can't pay necessary attention to the quality improvement for the existing products which it is currently supplying to the manufacturer. On the contrary, if the supplier is actively participating in the supply chain coordination, it will be able to grab more share and eventually have its profit far exceeding the pre-coordination level. Even if the supplier can afford to be more tolerant of "the unfair manufacturer-dominating situation" in the short term, it must have the belief that the situation will improve soon enough. Thus, the second fundamental condition requires that $\pi_s < \hat{\pi}_s$, $\pi_m < \hat{\pi}_m$, and $\pi_d < \hat{\pi}_d$.

One can point out that the second fundamental condition contains the first, i.e., should the second fundamental condition be held, the first condition holds automatically. Algebraically it is a correct argument. But there is a time sequence between the two conditions – the supply chain partners look up the first condition to decide whether the coordination is worthwhile in the first place, then consider the second condition after a certain period of coordination has passed. Using the second condition as the initial criterion is like setting too challenging a hurdle and probably makes it very hard for the supply chain coordination to start at all. Even applying the first condition without any room would be too strict; e.g., in order to get such coordination started, it would suffice for the supply chain partners to believe that, in the near future, the first fundamental condition will prevail. Once the supply chain firms agree on the high likelihood that the first condition will eventually hold, they will be willing to coordinate even if the second condition is a little violated at least for the initial period of coordination. However, in order for the coordination to be sustainable in the long run, the supply chain participants should have consensus on the likelihood that the second fundamental condition will be realized in a reasonably short period of time.

7.2   Inventory and Information Quality

Now let's consider inventory in the context of information-sharing, one of the most important coordination areas between supply chain partners. As discussed in Chapters 3 and 5, inventory is one of the key structural dimensions for effective supply chain management. We defined inventory as a buffer against uncertainty. Inventory is one of the most important managerial variables, primarily due to its financial ramification: in general, inventory is one of the biggest elements in a company's financial statements; it is estimated that the annual **inventory management cost** (including all tangible and non-tangible, e.g., opportunity, costs needed to manage inventory per year) is about 25 to 40 percent of the inventory value, depending on various conditions of different industries. In the previous chapters, we briefly sketched the relationship between inventory and uncertainty: generally speaking, the larger the uncertainty, the more the inventory; in addition, $uncertainty \approx \dfrac{1}{information}$, i.e., the more information the firm has, the less uncertainty it must face.

Building upon the discussion in the previous chapters, here we focus on **information quality** and inventory's strategic roles in the SCM context. There is a phenomenon called the "**bullwhip effect**," where the **information distortion** grows exponentially as the information moves upstream in a supply chain (Figure 7.4).

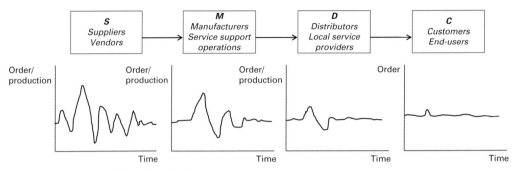

Figure 7.4 Information Distortion

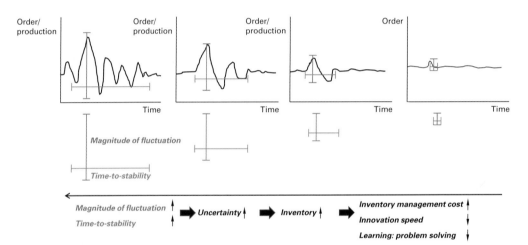

Figure 7.5 Consequences of Information Distortion

Figure 7.5 shows what happens as the information moves backward from the market to the supplier: as the information flows backward, the ordering or production amount fluctuates more severely, i.e., the magnitude of fluctuation becomes larger and the time-to-stability becomes longer; the **time-to-stability** measures how long it takes for the ordering or production to return to a normal state. More fluctuation means more uncertainty, which in turn requires the firm to have more inventory. As discussed in the previous chapters, more inventory means the firm has to pay more inventory management cost. In Figure 7.5, there are two more consequences of the increased inventory, i.e., slower innovation speed and less learning, which we deliberate after defining and examining information quality (Figure 7.6).

Information quality. This measures how accurate the information is. That is, the more accurate the information, the higher the information quality. Similarly, the higher the information quality, the lower the uncertainty faced by the company. Information quality is a function of two factors: first, a physical or psychological distance between

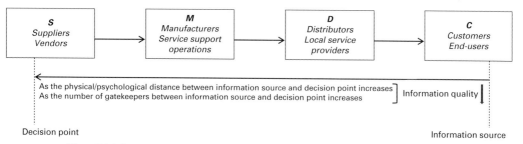

Figure 7.6 Information Quality

the **information source** (where the information originates, i.e., the end market in the example) and the decision point (where the decision must be made, e.g., distributor, manufacturer, or supplier); and, second, the number of **gatekeepers** (i.e., supply chain members or partners) between the source and the decision point. Conceptually, we put forth a plausible relationship as follows: $IQ \approx \dfrac{1}{D \times G}$, where IQ stands for the information quality, D for the physical or psychological distance, and G for the number of gatekeepers. That is, the information quality decreases as the distance or the number of gatekeepers increases.

7.3 Coordinating Innovation

In the previous section, we discussed two fundamental conditions for sustainable coordination (Figure 7.3). Coordination in SCM can be sustainable only if all the parties involved in the supply chain should benefit from such coordination at least in the foreseeable future. One of the most important such benefits is that from coordinating innovation, e.g., an innovation project, between the supply chain partners. Before discussing an example of innovation coordination in detail, we define innovation more formally.

Innovation typology. There is an important typology that divides innovation into two types: product innovation and process innovation. **Product innovation** is concerned with improvements that enhance the product's value to the customer such as progress in design, functionality, quality, aesthetics, and the like. On the contrary, **process innovation** includes improvements in the production process that enable the company to make the product more efficiently. In many cases, process innovation makes it possible to mass-produce the product at low costs. There is a relationship between the two types of innovation and the PLC (product life cycle): see Figure 7.7. During the early PLC, product innovation is much more important and frequent than process innovation: since the product is novel, it is not yet fully known how to make the product efficiently. Moreover, during the early phase of PLC, innovative consumers are the primary customers and they are willing to pay high premiums as long as the product satisfies

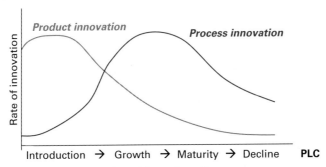

Figure 7.7 Product Innovation and Process Innovation

		Overturned core concepts	
Linkage between core concepts and components	Changed	Architectural innovation	Radical innovation
	Unchanged	Incremental innovation	Modular innovation

Reinforced   Overturned

Core concepts

Figure 7.8 A Typology of Innovation

their quest for innovation. As the market matures, however, the market size expands and more people buy the product. Therefore, in the late phases of the PLC, price competition becomes fierce and companies seek ways to make the product more economically. Process innovation becomes crucial in helping the companies compete in the mature market.

Another renowned typology categorizes innovation according to two dimensions:[1] whether the core concept of the product is reinforced or overturned; and whether or not the linkage between the core concept and other components is changed (Figure 7.8). The **core concept** is the backbone of the product in point. Consider an automobile's engine. A core concept of the engine is concerned with the power source – e.g., whether the engine is powered by internal combustion using gasoline or an electric battery (for an electric vehicle). The core concept of the product usually defines the product's fundamental characteristics and shapes the customers' perception of the product's true value to them. In general, the core concept is directly related to the product's essential functionality.

But, a product comprises more than the core concept. For instance, the automobile engine doesn't just consist of an internal combustion or electric system. In order for the engine to perform appropriately, it must have additional components or parts

---

[1] R. M. Henderson and K. B. Clark, "Architectural Innovation: The Reconfiguration of Existing Product Technologies and the Failure of Established Firms" (1990) 35(1) *Administrative Science Quarterly* 9–30.

surrounding the core concept. Therefore, how the core concept is linked with its surrounding components is another key dimension in defining the innovation type. Innovation is radical when both the core concept and its linkage with key components are changed simultaneously. A **radical innovation** is essentially a new invention of a product or process. Innovation is modular when the linkage remains the same, whereas the core concept is overturned (**modular innovation**). When both the core concept and the linkage are reinforced rather than overturned, the innovation is called an **incremental innovation**. Sometimes there is innovation that accommodates an efficient change in the linkage between the core concept and the linkage, while leaving the core concept intact. Such innovation is called an **architectural innovation**.

This typology can be applicable to both product and process innovation at the same time. It also highlights that innovation doesn't always have to be something radical: an incremental or architectural innovation is equally important and has a significant impact on the firm's performance improvement as the radical innovation does. We can also see a potential interrelationship between the core-linkage typology of innovation and the PLC. In the early phase of the PLC, it is more likely to find a radical innovation, i.e., a new invention. As the PLC matures, the innovation path probably moves toward either a modular or an architectural innovation. Finally, as the PLC enters the decline stage, the primary innovation pattern will be of incremental innovation. Whether the innovation path goes through the modular or the architectural innovation will depend on the basic characteristics of the industry or the company in point. It is important to see that the decision-maker must be aware of the close interplay between the innovation path and the PLC.

Coordinating innovation. Now, consider a case where a manufacturing company coordinates innovation, e.g., an innovation project, with its supplier. We suggest a specific context as in Figure 7.9. The manufacturer helps the supplier innovate by giving some financial aid – for example, a subsidy. Through such an innovation, the supplier can improve its productivity or quality of its product, which is supplied to the manufacturer. With either productivity improvement or quality improvement, the supplier can afford to provide its product to the manufacturer at a lower cost. The manufacturer's innovation subsidy returns to the manufacturer as a form of

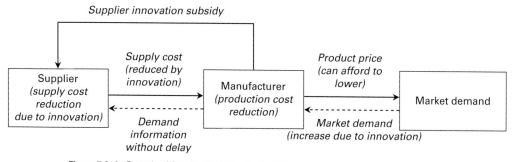

Figure 7.9 An Example of Coordinating Innovation in SCM

reduced supply cost or better quality of the supply. First, as the supply cost decreases, the manufacturer itself becomes more capable of producing its final product at a lower cost and eventually can afford to sell the product in the market at a more affordable price. The customers will be willing to buy more of the product from the manufacturer as the price goes down while its quality remains intact. Or as the supply quality becomes better without cost increase, the manufacturer's own product quality improves with the same price and the customers are more willing to buy the manufacturer's product. Increased sales through either way, other things being equal, implies increased profit for the manufacturer, which in turn makes it easy to support the supplier's innovation activity.

The case described above is of a virtuous cycle. But, as in most cases of system dynamics, there is no guarantee that such a virtuous cycle should always happen. As such, there is an important question: *Under what circumstances can coordinating innovation between the manufacturer and the supplier be beneficial to the two partners at the same time?* As already alluded to, such an innovation contributes to the manufacturer and the supplier simultaneously only when it creates real value to the market so that the customers are willing to pay more premiums or buy more. In the previous section, we also put forth that as the PLC evolves, the type of innovation that can create value in the market changes as well. At the early phase of the PLC, the product innovation is more valuable, whereas the process innovation becomes more critical as the PLC moves to the maturity and decline stage. Applying the second typology, we postulate that at the early phase of the PLC, a radical innovation can be more valuable, and as the PLC evolves, either a modular or an architectural innovation, and eventually an incremental innovation, should become more valuable.

Combining the arguments so far, we summarize what kind of innovation the firm should focus on when coordinating with its supply chain partners as the PLC evolves. Figure 7.10 shows such a relationship. Returning to the example about the coordination between the manufacturer and the supplier, we suggest that the two partners should focus more on a product innovation (more consistent with radical innovation) when their PLC is at its relatively early stage, and as their PLC enters the more mature and declining stage, the focus should shift to a process innovation (more consistent with incremental innovation).

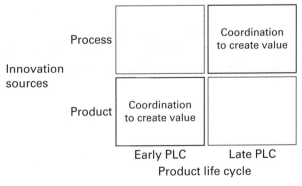

Figure 7.10 Coordinating an Innovation and PLC

IN-DEPTH CONCEPT 7.1
A Simulation Case Study for Coordination and Decision-Sharing

Coordination between supply chain participants can contribute significantly to enhancing profitability for each participant. Consider a supply chain relationship between a manufacturer and its supplier, which is strategic and long-term. Then, the two supply chain partners cooperate with each other on multiple operations activities. Let's focus on the coordination between the manufacturer and its supplier on both current products' quality improvement and new product development. By enhancing the product quality, the manufacturer will be able to sell more of the existing product on the market and thus earn more profit. In turn, the supplier can also expect to become more profitable since the manufacturer should buy more from the supplier. This is the primary motivation on the supplier's part to coordinate with the manufacturer for quality improvement. Assuming that the relationship between the two will last for a long time, the supplier and the manufacturer would find it necessary to collaborate on developing new products for future profit generation. An issue faced by the supplier is how to allocate its resources, available for such collaboration, between improving current operations (for quality improvement) and developing a new product in collaboration with the manufacturer. The manufacturer, likewise, will face the same question, albeit with different decision factors. Since they have to allocate their *present* resources between *current* operations and *future* possibility, they are facing a trade-off decision. Figure 7.11 describes this situation. In short, the question is *how to coordinate how much to spend on each of the activities over time*. One would be able to answer the question by determining the relative profitability of the activities, which must take into account future as well as present profit streams, uncertainty involved in the new product development, and the characteristics of the market demand.

Coordination requires **joint decision-making**, either explicit or implicit, between the supply chain partners. Thus, the **bargaining power balance** between the two decision-makers becomes an important issue, e.g., how to share the decision-making process between the manufacturer and its supplier or how to set a performance goal aligned for both partners. In essence, our primary question is: *How does the structure of the decision-making process (as a coordination process) affect each supply chain partner's profitability, and thus the sustainability of the strategic supply chain relationship itself?* Here, we consider three different types of the decision-making process structure: *manufacturer-dominating*, *supplier-dominating*, and *balanced*. Under the manufacturer-dominating decision-making structure, the manufacturer has complete control over the supply chain relationship. On the contrary, the supplier-dominating decision-making process sets up an objective function to take into account the supplier's profitability only. Finally, the balanced decision-making process takes into account both the supplier's and the manufacturer's profit optimization.

This section helps us understand the underlying mechanism of supply chain coordination. We would like to suggest, however, that you skip most of the technical discussion on simulation if you are not familiar with the methodology. Please note that in the analysis chapter, we explain the basics about the simulation methodology.

Box continues

Which decision-making process enables the supply chain partners to achieve the best outcome? In order to answer the question, we look into the detailed dynamics of resource allocation by both the supplier and the manufacturer.

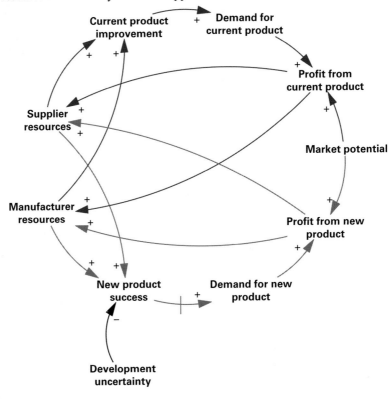

+: positive influence; –: negative influence; : delayed effect

Figure 7.11 Influence Diagram

Case company. The case company in this study was a major telecommunications company in Korea, Company S. The company was dominating the Korean telecommunications industry. As of 2003, its market share of the Korean mobile telecom market was over 50 percent. Although it was the largest player in the market, it was also one of the most active contributors to technological innovation in the industry. For instance, it helped the entire industry to move from analog to digital technology.

Among its many suppliers, Company S retained a strategic partnership with one major supplier for a long time. The supplier was *not only* supplying key parts to the company, *but also* helping it to improve the quality of its product based on the analog technology in the market. While Company S was the dominant player in the analog-based telecom market, it also recognized that the dominant design in the future would be based on digital technology. Thus, when the company started developing a new product using digital technology, it realized that coordination with its major supplier was critical, particularly during the transition from analog to digital. The company needed prototype

Box continues

parts and materials for the new product development from the supplier. Thus, the relationship between the company and its key supplier developed into a strategic one.

During such collaboration on both quality improvement and new product development, the company allowed the supplier's voice to be heard to a certain extent. The supplier was not just a passive "provider" of parts and materials, but was allowed to play an active role in operations and designing activities, albeit not to the full extent. Such cooperative decision-making between the two partners resulted in some managers at the company becoming concerned about inefficiencies in the process: they implied that excessive supplier interference with the decision-making would result in suboptimal resource allocation and lower performance. It was not an easy question, *whether it could be better to have the supplier participate in the decision-making process* or *whether such balanced decision-making would lead to an enhanced financial performance.* Allowing the supplier to participate in the decision-making process was related to the balance of bargaining power between the manufacturer and its supplier in the supply chain collaboration. For instance, if Company S accommodated more feedback as well as input from its supplier into its decision-making on quality improvement and new product development, the supplier's bargaining power would increase and vice versa.

Focusing on the period of technology transition, we developed a system dynamics simulation model that described the dynamic interaction between the company and its supplier as accurately as possible. To develop a realistic model, we interviewed key managers at both Company S and its supplier, and also observed their actual decision-making processes.

Technical Note 7.1 Simulation Rules

Resource pooling. Part of each company's sales revenue is earmarked for quality improvement and new product development. We use 30 percent in our model, based on our observation that each company has earmarked 25 to 30 percent of its sales for the two activities.

Resource allocation rules. When each company allocates its earmarked resources between quality improvement and new product development, it compares the potential benefits of the two activities. When it makes a resource allocation decision, it estimates the marginal value of improving quality and also the marginal value of new product development effort, and compares these two values. The resources are allocated to each activity proportionally.

Quality improvement dynamics. The quality of the existing product is improved by the efforts of the manufacturer and/or the supplier. In addition, a decreasing rate of return is adopted – the quality improvement dynamic is concave.

NPD dynamics. We employ a project management routine, which is widely used in the literature. The routine encompasses such dynamic equations as workflow, rework, rework discovery rate, and fraction of completion.

Box continues

Market demand dynamics. Before the new product is completed, the market demand for the existing product is determined by the overall attractiveness of the existing product. However, once the new product development is finished, the company estimates the attractiveness of the new product along with that of the existing product, and compares them to determine the relative attractiveness in order to calculate the relative demand for the two products. The attractiveness of each product is determined by two factors: *quality* and *price*.

Pricing policy. After observing the actual data, we use a decreasing pattern of price over time. During the early period of the PLC, the price is relatively high, but it decreases over time in order to attract more customers in the market.

Learning effects and production cost dynamics. The variable cost to produce the new product, as well as the existing one, is affected by the learning curve effect. We use a 5 percent learning rate for both companies.

Model verification and simulation. The first step in our simulation was to calibrate, or verify, our model against the real-world data in order to see whether the model was realistic in the sense that it could replicate what had happened in the market reasonably well. Figure 7.12 shows the result of such calibration, using the actual sales data from the company. It shows that our simulation model was good enough to describe what actually happened in the market.

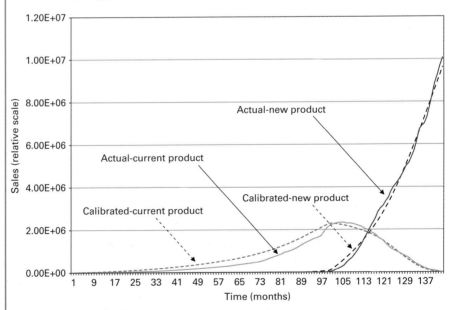

Figure 7.12 Model Verification

Before proceeding to the what-if analysis, we discuss some of the key outcomes from the calibration. Figure 7.13 shows the profits of the calibrated dynamics: the

Box continues

manufacturer enjoyed more cumulative profit than the supplier did. In fact, the supplier's cumulative profit picked up only after the new product was successfully developed in the ninety-seventh month. On the contrary, the manufacturer (Company S) enjoyed a significant level (vis-à-vis the supplier) of cumulative profit from the very beginning. We contend that given the case setting, the manufacturer was able to earn a significant portion of profit from quality improvement of the existing product early on and also from the new product, whereas the supplier was getting more profit from the new product development rather than the quality improvement activity. Note that the total profit is the sum of the manufacturer's and the supplier's profits.

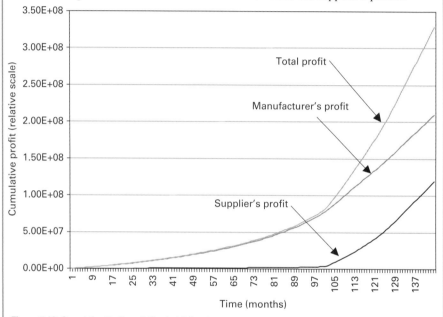

Figure 7.13 Cumulative Profits – Calibrated Estimates

The what-if analysis. Our primary objective was to determine how variations in the structure of the decision-making process affect the collaborative performance. Three types of decision-making process structures were considered: manufacturer-dominating, supplier-dominating, and balanced. We varied the weight structure of the objective function to represent the three types and estimated the profits by utilizing the optimization function in the system dynamics simulation, that is: (1) the manufacturer-dominating case, where we used an objective function to maximize only the manufacturer's cumulative profit at the end of the decision time horizon; (2) the supplier-dominating case, where the objective function was to maximize the supplier's profit only; and (3) the balanced case, where the objective function was to maximize the sum of the profits for both the supplier and the manufacturer at the same time.

Figure 7.14 shows the manufacturer's cumulative profits for the three different scenarios: the cumulative profit was maximal when the objective function was to

Box continues

optimize the manufacturer's profit only. The cumulative profit was minimal when the objective function took into account the supplier's objective function only. We can make similar arguments from the supplier's perspective in Figure 7.15. One striking observation is that the supplier's cumulative profit became increasingly negative when its profit objective was not reflected in the decision-making process at all, i.e., when the manufacturer made the decision to its own advantage at the expense of the supplier's.

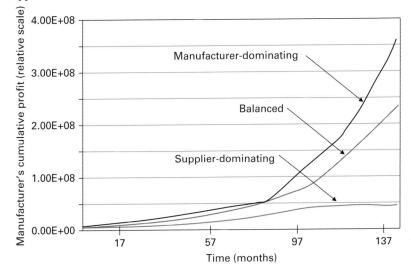

Figure 7.14 Manufacturer's Profits as Decision-Making Sharing Changes

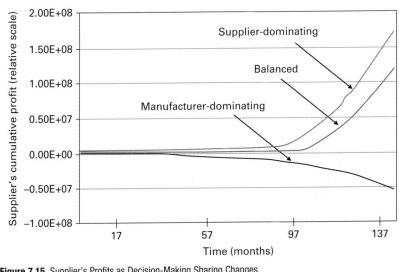

Figure 7.15 Supplier's Profits as Decision-Making Sharing Changes

Box continues

Figure 7.16 shows the total profit dynamics for the three decision-sharing scenarios. Possibly except for a very short period of time, throughout the decision time horizon, the balanced decision-making process produces the largest total profit.

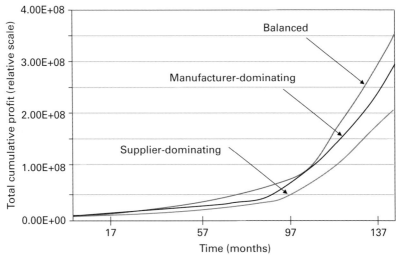

Figure 7.16 Total Profits as Decision-Making Sharing Changes

We summarize the results in Table 7.2. From the perspective of the manufacturer's own profit, the best is the "manufacturer-dominating decision process," whereas from the supplier's perspective, the best is the "supplier-dominating decision process."

Table 7.2 Summary of Changes in Profits

DMP* Player	Estimated Actual (Calibrated)	Manufacturer-Dominating	Balanced	Supplier-Dominating
Manufacturer	210 MM**	356 MM	233 MM	37 MM
Supplier	119 MM	–58 MM	121 MM	169 MM
Total	329 MM	298 MM	354 MM	206 MM

Notes:

* DMP – decision-making process;

** MM – million in relative scale.

The critical question is *whether either of the dominating cases would be sustainable in the long run.* A short answer to the question is "no." The second column ("estimated actual") of Table 7.2 represents the profits the manufacturer and the supplier would have earned, given the present market conditions; the calibrated profits are those the supply chain partners would have earned without deliberately influencing the decision-making balance.

Box continues

To the manufacturer, the best is to make a decision on its own, wielding 100 percent of the bargaining power during the decision-making process, i.e., the manufacturer-dominating case. But, this is not acceptable to the supplier: should the supplier accept the deal, its cumulative profit would have changed from 119 million to –58 million in the relative scale. On the other hand, should the supplier wield 100 percent bargaining power during the decision-making process, the manufacturer's profit would have changed from 210 to 37 million. Again, it is not an acceptable deal to the manufacturer. Finally, the only "acceptable" alternative to the "estimated actual" case is the balanced decision process. Not only is the total profit the largest among the four scenarios, but also each individual player's profit becomes larger. The manufacturer's profit increases from 210 to 233 MM, while the supplier's increases from 119 to 121 MM. Thus, the balanced decision process satisfies two fundamental conditions for sustainable supply chain coordination: (1) system-level optimization – the total profit after coordination should be larger than that before such coordination; and (2) distributive justice or fairness at the individual level – each participant's profit should be larger than that before such coordination.

We can apply the concept of **bargaining zone** to the period after about the 110th month in Figure 7.16. After this month, the profitability of the balanced decision process surpasses that of the others. Should the decision time horizon be longer than 110 months, the manufacturer and the supplier could find the balanced decision process more attractive than when either one dominates the decision process completely. Therefore, there is room for them to bargain with each other to strike a mutually beneficial and acceptable arrangement in sharing the decision-making process, as long as they have long-term perspectives.

Implications. Our simulation result indicates that the balanced decision-making process engenders the best outcome, which is sustainable and acceptable to both players in the supply chain. The result from the study suggests important managerial implications. As the managers at the case company expressed, there might exist a delicate concern over collaboration with other partners in the supply chain. For instance, the managers at the manufacturing company were concerned about potential inefficiencies that might be caused by the supplier's excessive interference in their decision-making process for resource allocation. In a real-world situation, managers might be tempted to wield an excessive power in their decision-making process, i.e., to be the dominating player in the supply chain. But, the case study presents a strong *empirical* evidence against such an inclination. It implies that a decision-making process dominated by one party in the supply chain isn't sustainable – such an arrangement can't be acceptable to other parties in the long run. In a more practical sense, for example, a decision process dominated by the manufacturer without taking into account the supplier's profitability might eventually cause the manufacturer's own profitability to be reduced significantly. This is primarily due to the manufacturer using the supplier's resources first before using its own resources when it has full power to make resource allocation decisions over not only its own resources, but also

Box continues

the supplier's – thus either wasting some of the supplier's resources or using them for non-value-creating activities. All these combined would cause inefficiency to the supply chain as a whole. The case study indicates that the collaborative decision-making in a supply chain creates more value at the system level, i.e., from the entire supply chain's perspective. How to share the additional value created through such collaboration is also an important issue, which deserves further empirical and theoretical studies in the future.

Questions
1. Why is the balanced decision-making generating the best outcome? Please offer a logical explanation based on the case study.
2. What factors should the supply chain partners take into account when they decide how to allocate the increased supply chain profit due to the coordinated decision-making?

Discussion Questions

1. What is coordination? Suggest a formal definition of coordination.
2. Where should the supply chain partners coordinate? That is, what are the areas where coordination is needed or most valuable?
3. Define sustainable coordination. What are the fundamental conditions for sustainable coordination?
4. What is the bullwhip effect in supply chain management? What causes the bullwhip effect? Suggest how to overcome the phenomenon.
5. What is information quality? What factors determine it?
6. What is the relationship between the bullwhip effect and information quality?
7. What is the relationship between product innovation and process innovation in the context of product life cycle?
8. Define architectural innovation and radical innovation. What are the criteria you use to define such innovations?
9. What might be the relationship between innovation coordination and product life cycle?
10. Evaluate a statement that coordination is beneficial to the supply chain partners. Is the statement always valid? If not, under what conditions is it invalid or questionable?

案例 CASE STUDY 7.1
Value of Coordination at UNIQLO

We try to understand how UNIQLO perceives the value of supply chain coordination by reviewing the interview with a top manager at the company.

How do you define the mission for UNIQLO? UNIQLO's brand mission is to become a global fashion brand to help every customer wear high-quality, low-price casuals. More specifically, UNIQLO aims to provide our customers with highly fashionable, high-quality basic casuals at the lowest possible prices whenever and wherever they want. In effect, UNIQLO endeavors to be the "Global #1 Casual Brand," by studying our customers incessantly and maximizing efficiency through low-cost management and direct integration of manufacturing with sales.

How can UNIQLO achieve high quality and low price at the same time? First and foremost, from the early stage of product development and design, we try to make sure that our product meets not only the customers' fashion-related requirement, but also their expectation about an appropriate price. Once a new product is designed, we ask our manufacturing department to calculate the expected manufacturing cost. If the expected cost warrants an appropriate price, i.e., a price acceptable to our customers, we go ahead with production. Otherwise, we try to reduce the cost further until it satisfies our criterion.

There are two main elements determining the manufacturing cost: labor and raw materials. We are saving labor costs by producing our products in places like China and Southeast Asian countries, where the labor costs are still relatively low. Currently we're making 60 to 70 percent of our products in China and the remaining in Southeast Asia or Eastern Europe. We have about seventy outsourcing plants as our key business partners, and are dispatching master team members to the local plants for active technological support. Master team members are retired experts with over thirty years' experience in the fashion and textile industries in Japan. Their mission is to transfer advanced technologies to our outsourcing partners and help them improve their quality and process management throughout the manufacturing processes. Although these outsourcing partners are not part of UNIQLO, they're strategic partners, who work with us very closely as if we're under the same roof. In fact, almost 70 to 80 percent of our partners have been working with us for ten to twenty years and over time have developed close relationships in terms of partial ownership sharing and transaction activities. Once UNIQLO clothes are made in the outsourcing plants, most of them are shipped to destination markets through sea, only 2 to 3 percent being shipped via air.

We believe that the quality of raw materials determines the quality of clothes significantly. Also, the stable supply of raw materials is critical. We collect information from the market and industries, based on which we develop and supply materials by working with R&D, merchandising, and material planning teams along with our production plants in China. In addition, we try to develop new materials through strategic alliances with raw material suppliers. For instance, we worked with one of our strategic partners, Toray Industries, and developed the "Heat-tech" garment, a functional new material that has superior attributes such as comfortable body fit stretch and heat protection.

Source: Revised from B. Kim, "Quality Goals and Supply Chain Strategy in the Fashion Industry" (2013) 16(2) *Qualitative Market Research: An International Journal* 214–242. DOI: 10.1108/13522751311317602. © 2013 Emerald Publishing.

Another example is Kaihara Corporation. The company is the world's best denim manufacturer and also UNIQLO's strongest strategic partner, who has been supplying UNIQLO with high quality denim at surprisingly reasonable prices ever since UNIQLO opened its first ever urban store in Tokyo's trendy Harajuku area in 1998. For natural materials like wool and cashmere, our expert team with twenty to thirty years' experience visits actual farms in countries like Mongolia and Nepal, and directly makes deals so as to minimize the cost. Moreover, in order to secure a stable supply, we sign contracts with suppliers about two to three years ahead of the time we actually need the raw materials. Again, our expert team works on both developing new suppliers and managing the existing ones.

What is UNIQLO's primary target market? What is UNIQLO's strategy to be competitive in the target market? Our direct competitor in the fashion industry, Zara, is focused on young people in their 20s and 30s. But, UNIQLO tries to position itself as a family brand covering from teenagers to customers in their late 30s. Zara tries to compete in the market through design and pattern diversification. On the contrary, UNIQLO seeks to appeal to the customers by offering diverse choices in colors and materials. For example, almost 60 to 70 percent of UNIQLO designs are basic clothes, with the remaining 30 to 40 percent being fashion-trendy products. Unlike other competitors that bring five to ten different colors to the market, however, UNIQLO offers clothes in ten to twenty different colors. In addition, we develop functional materials such as Heat-tech and leverage them to win over customers. As such, we pay much attention to new material development, where lots of relevant teams in the company get involved. That is, teams in charge of design, marketing, merchandising, and material get together and do intensive brainstorming. After the active discussion, the CEO makes a final decision for critical issues. After gathering key information about the market trend and customer preferences, UNIQLO holds meetings for new material and product development four to six times each year.

What is UNIQLO's operations strategy regarding inventory management, forecasting, production planning, and so on? Inventory management is important to every company. UNIQLO is no exception. In fact, we make an extra effort to manage inventory, aiming to have zero left over at the end of the sales season. The first step is to try to minimize the mismatch between supply and demand by simultaneously establishing marketing, store operations and sales, and inventory plans before placing raw material orders. Currently, we don't have a formal centralized control tower for such coordination. Each department or team reports its plan as well as assessment to the chairman and CEO, who makes the final commitment based on the consensus among submitted plans and assessments. That is, we're using an informal coordination process, where the chairman is closely involved. Once the plan is finalized and implemented, we trace inventory at each SKU level. Based on the inventory tracking, we either place additional orders for those under-stocked or offer price discounts for those over-stocked so as to minimize the leftover inventory at the end.

We have to do thorough pre-planning because we need to place initial orders in large quantities in order to enjoy economies of scale. Our strategic outsourcing partners are willing to accept a wide range of "initial" orders. For instance, we can place an order of 6 or 26 million fleece jackets as long as it is made once at the beginning of the production cycle. In that sense, we have a very high level of volume flexibility. However, we don't place additional orders once the initial order is placed. There is only one exception, i.e., we allow an additional order for core products with a strict condition that it is within 5 percent of the initial order. Of course, from UNIQLO's own perspective, it is more profitable to place additional orders after observing the market. But, it could destroy the trust between UNIQLO and our strategic suppliers regarding the integrity of the original contract. Moreover, we may not be able to enjoy economies of scale for the additional orders, i.e., the unit cost for an order of 1,000 is certainly more expensive than that of 10,000.

In principle, we had a "Help yourself!" rule for our store operations. That is, our store employees don't provide close services to the customers, who are supposed to find what they want to buy. However, we realized that we cannot ignore cultural attributes unique to individual country markets such as China and Korea. Therefore, in certain markets, our store employees spend 50 percent of their time on helping customers at the store. For instance, we do fitting for jeans for free as part of our complimentary services to our customers.

Why do the outsourcing partners cooperate with UNIQLO in order for the company to achieve high volume flexibility? What is their true motivation? The question is indeed very critical to understanding the fundamental sources of UNIQLO's competitive advantage. But, I feel a little embarrassed to say that there is no grandiose secret here which other competitors cannot replicate. To sum up the essence of our competitive strategy, it is the "trust" we build with our strategic partners. In particular, we have been committed to building trust regarding the risk involved with unwanted inventory. Suppose one of our competitors places an order of 10 million units and its outsourcing plant produces and delivers the order as requested. The company then sells the clothes in the market, but unfortunately 5 million units are unsold and become leftover inventory. Do you know what usually happens in the industry? The company returns the unsold clothes to the outsourcing partner for a refund. In this example, the fashion company doesn't take any risk related to leftover inventory. In fact, 100 percent of the risk is borne by the outsourcing company. Assume that the fashion company has bigger bargaining power and so the outsourcing company has to accept the deal. Now think about the next season. The fashion company anticipates a huge surge in the demand and wants to reserve a large capacity from its outsourcing partner. But, what do you think the outsourcing company's reaction would be? After experiencing the terrible situation when 100 percent of the risk is forced to be on the shoulders of the supplier, it is not very difficult to see that the outsourcing partner is much less willing to cooperate with its client, the fashion company.

UNIQLO's strategy is exactly the opposite. If we place an order of 10 million, then we will pay for all of the 10 million units no matter what happens, i.e., whether the leftover is 1, 5, or 9 million. We take full responsibility for the risk associated with ordering. Once we have made the promise and kept it, our strategic partners start to trust UNIQLO firmly and are always willing to accommodate our orders with the highest priority. Of course, in order to continue retaining this much trust, we always try to make sure that our initial forecasting is extremely accurate. Developing new and innovative materials is closely related to strategy, since our forecasting can be more accurate if we can generate the demand more actively by marketing innovative materials.

Now you may see the **virtuous cycle** in place. We develop innovative materials and colors which appeal to the target customers. Through these active initiatives, our forecasting can be very accurate and our sales volume becomes large. Believing in our forecasting accuracy, we place a large order and can afford to honor our promise to our suppliers, taking full responsibility for absorbing any market risk. In turn, trusting our commitment, our strategic outsourcing partners accommodate our large orders, which are sometimes fluctuating in volumes. With this unwavering support from our suppliers, we can deal with uncertainty in the market demand and maximize sales without serious mismatch between supply and demand. Now we make a healthy profit in the market and increase our market share. As we grow, we open new stores in diverse areas and as a result our ability to sense the market improves. Our forecasting ability increases and our potential customer base expands. With all these positive forces and outcomes, we become even more capable of honoring our promises to our strategic partners. Now the virtuous cycle continues.

Questions

1. Is it possible to pursue two goals, quality improvement and cost reduction, simultaneously? How has UNIQLO been able to achieve them together?
2. What was the role played by the company's coordination with its supply chain partners in achieving the goals at the same time?

案例 CASE STUDY 7.2
Coordination between Verizon and Samsung

The mobile phone industry is one of the most challenging business environments around, with just a handful of large powerful customers and competing suppliers, extremely short product life cycles, and an extensive and complex distribution network. Despite these challenges, Verizon and Samsung together successfully implemented collaborative planning, forecasting, and replenishment (CPFR) capabilities – a multi-million-dollar opportunity for both companies. It is an insightful example, since building collaborative relationships between customers and suppliers can be fraught with challenges, i.e., many companies struggle with a lack of trust and interest in improvement that precludes them from developing a winning partnership.

Economic background and timing of Samsung getting Verizon to agree to CPFR. In 2008 to 2009, the United States was being affected by the subprime mortgage crisis and also a recession. During this tough economic time period, many companies were focused on their cash reserves and cutting costs. Like many other companies during that period, Verizon experienced a reduction in revenue and sales and had to focus more on cost savings. Verizon was under pressure to reduce its inventory levels by one week in a cost-cutting move. In fact, one of the biggest cost savings Verizon could initiate was managing its inventory levels.

In order to save money on their inventory levels, Verizon decided that it was time to partner with Samsung on CPFR and other supply chain initiatives. The only inventory that Verizon carried was handsets, as the other core parts of their business were all virtual (content, subscriptions, etc.). So, reducing handset inventory would be a major win for Verizon.

Characteristics of mobile carriers. Verizon rejected Samsung previously due to importance of in-stocks. Verizon was not concerned with managing inventory as much as the CE (consumer electronics) retailers that Samsung did business with. With Verizon, Samsung was much more focused on handset sales and managing inventory, whereas Verizon was more focused on its contracts, monthly airtime, and content. For wireless carriers, handsets being out of stock affected not only the handset sale, but the sale of contract, monthly airtime, and content. A handset being out of stock at Verizon impacted much more on the bottom line than if a TV was out of stock at Best Buy. This being the case, being overstocked on handsets made more economic sense to Verizon. The US recession in 2008 to 2009 helped Samsung to get their foot in the door at Verizon with CPFR.

The challenge. In 2007, G. S. Choi, the current CEO of Samsung Electronics, transferred to Samsung Telecommunications from the company's Consumer Electronics group. After building a highly collaborative and successful relationship with US retailer Best Buy, he was interested in replicating this model with the US telecom carrier, Verizon. At the time, the telecommunications group had no sharing of data with Verizon and it was operating in a culture of supplier as servant. The company wanted a more collaborative relationship and had made prior attempts, which were rejected by the Verizon team. Frank Fermo (Purchasing

Source: Revised from S. Aronow, "Case Study: Award Highlights Success of Verizon-Samsung CPFR Journey," Gartner Operation Excellence Series, Case ID: G00224201 (published online August 17, 2012). © 2012 Gartner, Inc.

Manager for Samsung Telecommunications at Verizon), who had been involved with the Samsung account for more than eight years, noted that, "early on, there were some confidentiality concerns at Verizon around sharing future sales volumes with handset makers."

Then, two things happened that significantly accelerated the progress. The first was that Mr. Choi spoke with the CEO of Verizon, Mr. Lowell McAdams, and highlighted millions of dollars in cost-saving opportunities available to both companies if they instantiated CPFR. The other was a burning platform created by the mounting financial crisis in 2008.

There were significant hurdles to clear for the CPFR effort to work. Verizon wanted to lower inventory levels and also maintain 100 percent in-stock performance from Samsung. Samsung wanted an improved sales forecast from Verizon that would lower their inventory requirements. Product life cycles were short, so the team needed to pay attention to channel inventory and product transitions. According to Mr. Schrader (Senior Program Manager for Supply Chain Management and CPFR at Samsung Telecommunications), "previously, there was a lot of gaming, tied to optimizing local metrics instead of trying to deal with the volatility." Samsung shifted its focus from what was sold into the channel to taking action based on actual inventory in the channel. "Culturally, this was hard to do, particularly when Sales was trying to hit their end of quarter goals." The reality in the old model was that Verizon was pushing out sales orders anyway based on excess channel inventory. Another strong motivation for Samsung to reduce inventory was the risk of obsolescence driven by extremely short (6 to 9 months) product life cycles. After two months of aging, Samsung typically used aggressive discounting to move inventory off the shelves. Mr. Fermo also highlighted the importance of managing these short product life cycles and said that, "Verizon's first step toward supplier collaboration was sharing weekly new product introduction (NPI) forecast data. Once Verizon saw the value of suppliers' improved responses, the ice was broken for sharing additional data."

Approach. A joint workshop approach was used to design the new process and tools. The program ran pilots and iterated the design based on learning along the way. The goal was a simplified planning process. A lean approach was followed, including a boundary condition that no additional work could be added for Verizon employees.

A key output of the design was an improved method for calculating vendor-managed replenishment (VMR) purchase order proposals. They started with Verizon's sales forecast and netted out open sales orders and inventory goals at each DC (distribution center). From there, they moved from static to dynamic replenishment ratios for determining delivery amounts to regional DCs, based on actual sell-through amounts. After the CPFR team implemented this VMR capability and achieved significant inventory reductions, they presented the results to the Verizon management team. The response was positive and was accompanied by a request for even more improvement.

The team recognized that the entire channel from the manufacturing shop floor to retail point of sale was not balanced. A holistic, one-company plan (OCP) was the next step. With VMR, inventory targets had been reset at the customer DC based on product life cycle rules of thumb. Now, with OCP, inventory targets were reset across the entire supply chain to balance it out.

Implementing VMR was a necessary prerequisite, since there would have been too much volatility across the channel without that capability.

With a solid foundation in place, the objective was now to have as lean an entire channel as possible to support Samsung's aggressive (6 to 9 months) product life cycles at Verizon's expected service levels. Under OCP, differentiated inventory targets were set at the SKU-DC level based on product life cycle position and DC type (customer or vendor). Inventory targets were lowered incrementally over time until they hit resistance on the ability to maintain target service levels.

Results. The two partner companies were able to achieve several key performance goals:

Unit forecast accuracy: Forecast accuracy, measured by comparing actual demand at the SKU-DC level to a 4-week average sell through forecast, improved from below 50 percent to above target levels of 80 percent within one quarter. A significant part of this improvement was Verizon shifting its planning cadence from a monthly to a weekly frequency.

Incremental decreases in inventory: Samsung improved its ability to get the right mix of products into the right DCs with a more precision planning process. According to Mr. Schrader, "this was the first time he had seen Samsung 'weaponize' CPFR against its competition" in that it had the infrastructure to support this capability, whereas other handset suppliers did not. Over the course of three months, Samsung stabilized the VMR process and took inventory holding and obsolescence/write-off levels down significantly without negatively impacting service levels.

Improved on time delivery: Verizon's improved demand forecast accuracy allowed Samsung to make huge improvements to its on-time delivery performance, as measured by an On Time Right Quality metric. At the time, Verizon used a Days Late measure of total days away from its Requested Dock Date. The expectation was near precision delivery, not +/− 2 days like other customers. Prior to the CPFR program, Samsung was consistently over a week late compared to the target level of 1 day late. Today, they easily beat that measure.

Reduced trucking costs: One side benefit generated by the new VMR purchase order proposal was that the calculation drove full pallets and truckloads for a lower average shipment cost per unit.

Process automation: Sales orders and DC inventory balancing, previously done on spreadsheets, was automated, saving time for Verizon. It was important to note that the new process took time to develop and iterate. There were eleven meetings before both the executive and working levels of both companies bought in to the joint business plan.

Improved market share for Samsung: There was now a joint collaborative culture around continuous improvement based on Verizon's confidence in Samsung's doing OCP with Verizon. As a result, Samsung's market share of Verizon's handset business significantly increased. Once OCP was implemented, Verizon expected other suppliers to hit the same performance levels and, when they couldn't, Samsung captured additional share.

Table 7.3 shows the improvements made in both partners' operating performance as a result of implementing CPFR capabilities.

Table 7.3 Improvements in Verizon's and Samsung's Operating Performance

Key Performance Indicator	Period 1	Period 2	Period 3	Period 4
Verizon channel inventory	Baseline	69% of baseline	56% of baseline	49% of baseline
Samsung channel inventory	Baseline	60% of baseline	60% of baseline	60% of baseline
Sales forecast accuracy	47.5%	62.0%	84.2%	Hit target level of 80% within one quarter
On-time right quantity misses	Baseline	40% of baseline	27% of baseline	Hit target level of 1/8 of baseline

Lessons learned. Top managers at the two companies were able to learn valuable lessons from their endeavor to implement CPFR. Mr. Schrader noted that over time they discovered that there needed to be value statements tailored for both the executive and working levels. For instance, going to the working level and saying "we'll save you millions of dollars in supply chain cost" when this could create days of extra work would be unacceptable. Likewise, talking to executives about the advantages of dynamic DC balancing "would have their eyes rolling back in their heads."

The original design worked well for mid-life products, but did not account for anomalies found during other stages of the product life cycle nor those driven by promotion planning. As a result, the team modified the design to set up variable weeks of inventory at DCs that accounted for regional promotions as well as the channel fill and ramp-up associated with product introduction and ramp-down for end-of-life. They also noted that carrier channel fill for Verizon's roughly 2,000 branded stores behaves differently from the fill for the extended channel. For instance, more inventory was required for Walmart when factoring in the layout of their points of sale and DCs. Mr. Fermo noted that "product EOL (end of life) management has definitely improved over time and continues to be an ongoing challenge due to the extremely short life cycles of mobile devices."

When it comes to business process improvement, the "devil is often in the details." For the Verizon-Samsung team, this was certainly the case. The original planning process started with the requested customer dock date (RDD) and backward scheduled production and shipment to the previous work week, but did not specify the exact date it needed to ship out. At the time, packaged goods deliveries took three days to air ship from Korea to US-based DCs. From there, they were transported to local customers. As a result, if an order was shipped out from Korea on the Saturday of the previous week, the RDD goal would be missed. The new design took delivery lead times to the DCs into account. The team also implemented a local packaging center that sent kits to customer order and then back-scheduled off orders to the exact day needed.

While in the end the team reached an effective joint design, Mr. Geklinsky (Director of Verizon's Supply Chain Management) felt that "after the initial push and as interim goals were met, the team could have maintained its cadence and depth of focus on collaborative design to reach the best design more quickly."

The team could not have implemented OCP without first laying down foundational VMR capability. Mr. Schrader advised other companies to "not try to skip steps in maturing their CPFR capability, but show the business benefits of VMR first to sell the broader value statement." His team had to progress based on a step-wise improvement in capabilities on both sides. They wanted to put in more capabilities sooner, but simply weren't ready.

Reflection. The relationship and capability between Verizon and Samsung improved over time to the benefit of both companies. Mr. Geklinsky saw both sides identifying ongoing opportunities and noted that "with a foundation built on trust and support, we'll continue to make strides in meeting both sides' objectives through the alignment of business goals and rhythms."

When asked about concerns that competitors would adopt these practices to gain competitive advantage against Samsung, Mr. Schrader responded that, "right now they don't have the foundation to implement these more advanced capabilities. To use an analogy, I can watch Tiger Woods play golf, but it just doesn't turn out the same way for me. Everyone has a different planning process in the telecom industry. These improvements stuck at Verizon due to the pre-selling done with senior management and the right environment at both companies to implement the capabilities."

Frank Fermo commented that "he appreciates the effort and resources dedicated by the Samsung Team to make the CPFR process a win for both companies. Candidly, the tools enable the process, but it is people collaborating that really make the process work."

Questions

1. What motivated Verizon and Samsung to decide to start CPFR?
2. What were the most serious challenges faced by the two companies in implementing CPFR successfully?
3. How were the two companies able to overcome such challenges?
4. What were the key success factors for implementing CPFR by the two companies?
5. Is it easy for other companies to adopt the strategy carried out by Verizon and Samsung? Why or why not?
6. Suggest general pieces of advice you want to give any partner companies that are considering collaborative projects together.

CHAPTER 8

Strategic Tools of Supply Chain Capability

In this chapter, we discuss crucial strategic tools the firm can use to coordinate its supply chain. As discussed in the previous chapters, coordination is the quintessential force for effective supply chain management, which is the most important part of **supply chain capability**, i.e., the company's ability to coordinate with its partners sharing the same value chain. In Chapter 7, we suggested a few critical areas of **supply chain coordination**, one of which is new product development. That is, the supply chain partners often find it indispensable to coordinate with each other to develop a new product or service successfully. Thus, we elaborate on **new product development** as an essential area of supply chain coordination.

Another essential area of supply chain coordination is **information-sharing** between supply chain partners. The most important information is concerned with the market demand uncertainty. That is, the supply chain partners coordinate with each other to cope with the market demand uncertainty. In this chapter, we delve into several supply chain strategies designed to enable the supply chain partners to deal with the market demand uncertainty in order to maximize value creation. Specifically, we discuss such strategic tools as **vendor-managed inventory (VMI)**, **postponement**, **accurate response systems**, and **product-mix flexibility**. In addition, we consider **channel strategy** as a relevant area for supply chain coordination.

These strategies constitute the supply chain capability, which is derived from proactive and sustainable supply chain coordination among the partner companies sharing the same value chain. Of course, there are many more tools out there than discussed in this chapter. Our objective, however, is not to enumerate all of them, but to find out key common attributes of those strategic tools in order to provide a set of generalizable principles that enable the supply chain partners to attain superb supply chain capability.

Key Learning Points

- Supply chain management (SCM) is closely linked with product life cycle (PLC) in that as the product evolves following its life cycle (e.g., from being innovative to being functional), its associated supply chain should also evolve from a (relatively more) responsive to an (relatively more) efficient one.

- As time-based competition has intensified and responsiveness has become more requested in the market, cross-functional team (CFT) approach has emerged as an effective methodology for new product development.
- The company must conduct a thorough cost-and-benefit analysis to determine whether the CFT approach is better than a more traditional "sequential" approach for its new product development.
- The most essential goal of vendor-managed inventory (VMI) is not saving inventory management cost, but getting direct access to information about market demand in order to optimize production planning and the product's responsiveness.
- Postponement is a strategic supply chain management tool to enable the company to implement mass customization.
- Accurate response systems (e.g., risk-based production planning) help the company to effectively deal with product mix uncertainty in the market.
- Flexibility is the driving force behind the company's ability to be responsive to the changing market demand. But, it is not a purely technical concept. In fact, it is a managerial principle, depending on how to design the process and manage the workforce creatively.
- Coordination should be extended to the company's channel strategy.

學 WISDOM BOX 8.1
Wisdom and Insights

Making "Positives" Dominate "Negatives"

Zara is one of the most profitable fashion companies in the world. It is well known for its great **responsiveness**. Research has identified a few critical factors that have driven the company's success over the years. *What makes the company a role model of supply chain management?* We have found it interesting (and also important) that some of the company's success factors seem counterintuitive. For instance, it is common sense or well-accepted wisdom that keeping **in-house capacity** can damage the firm's flexibility because of the high **overhead cost** associated with retaining the physical facility. As such, many researchers have proposed that the firm should use **outsourcing** in order to be more flexible and also to reduce the overhead cost. On the contrary, Zara keeps a large capacity in-house, possibly larger than that of any other company in the global fashion industry. Zara's large in-house capacity seems pretty much counterintuitive, considering the company's stellar performance. Should it be counterintuitive?

Box continues

Every managerial decision always involves two consequences, one positive or desirable and the other negative or undesirable. It is true for the in-house manufacturing capacity. Keeping a sizable in-house capacity could imply two things for Zara simultaneously (Figure 8.1). On the one hand, as research shows, keeping a large in-house capacity increases overhead cost, which in turn increases the company's overall cost and eventually reduces the profit. There is, however, another chain of consequences. In contrast to the negative cycle, it also creates a positive one, i.e., in-house capacity actually enhances the firm's manufacturing flexibility and thus its responsiveness, which increases sales and finally the profit itself.

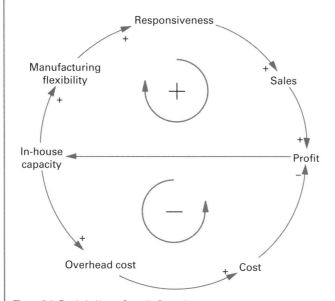

Figure 8.1 Zara's In-House Capacity Dynamics

Similar to in-house capacity, keeping a **centralized distribution center** (DC) poses the same challenge to the company (Figure 8.2). If a global company tries to minimize its logistic cost, it seems reasonable to have distribution centers dispersed across the globe to be closer to local markets. On the contrary, Zara has a centralized DC structure, i.e., its major distribution centers are centralized in Spain. Like the in-house capacity, this centralized DC structure poses two different dynamics to the company. As mentioned above, there is a negative cycle: the centralized DC structure causes excessive logistic costs, which reduce the company's end profit. For instance, suppose Zara produces clothes in Spain and it also outsources a portion of production to its outsourcing partner company in China. If the company had a distribution center in China, it

Box continues

would locally store the clothes produced in China and ship them to the end-consumer markets (e.g., Korea or Japan) directly whenever necessary. But, since Zara runs centralized distribution centers, it has to ship the clothes produced in China to the DC in Spain first, and then ship them out to end-consumer markets whenever necessary. Shipping in to the centralized DC first and shipping out to end-consumer markets later on could cost twice as much as under a decentralized DC structure. Similar to the in-house capacity case, of course, there is another cycle, which is positive for Zara. Since the demand at a local end-consumer market (e.g., Japan) could be very different from that at another (e.g., Korea), it is very important for Zara to strike a balance across the different local markets. That is, the company has to coordinate its production as well as supply in a way that achieves the balance among the end-consumer markets, in order to minimize the mismatch between demand and supply on a global scale. It can be very difficult for the company to achieve that level of coordination, unless it has very accurate and reliable information throughout its global supply network. The centralized distribution centers provide the company with high **information transparency** much better than that under a decentralized DC structure. Such high information transparency enables the company to make a better product mix decision, which in turn enhances the firm's market responsiveness and eventually increases sales.

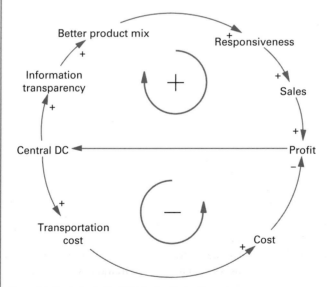

Figure 8.2 Zara's Centralized Distribution Center Dynamics

We can combine these two dynamics together as in Figure 8.3, which shows complicated dynamics consisting of both positive and negative cycles, i.e., **reinforcing** and **balancing loops**. As mentioned before, every managerial

Box continues

decision engenders two different effects simultaneously, one positive and the other negative. Then, what determines whether the decision is good or bad for the company? Let's consider the in-house capacity case. Is it good or bad? The correct answer to this question is "both!" In fact, it all depends on how the company implements the strategy. A successful company can make its positive cycles dominate the negative ones, whereas a failed company is unable to control its negative cycles, which – when left alone or uncontrolled – eventually dominate the positive cycles.

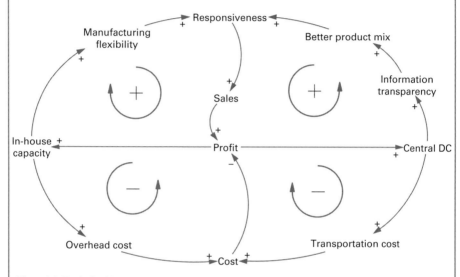

Figure 8.3 Zara's Combined Dynamics

How can a company make its positive cycles dominate the negative ones? This is where the firm's integrating capability becomes essential. In Figure 8.4, we explicitly include the integrating capability in the company's in-house capacity dynamics. A successful, i.e., high-performing, company invests part of its profit in developing its **integrating capability** to coordinate and communicate throughout its supply chain. With its enhanced integrating capability, the company can better utilize its in-house capacity, by coordinating through its retail stores, suppliers, designers, production plants, and distribution center in order for the company as a whole to be faster in accommodating the changing needs or requirements of the market. In effect, its **learning capability** enables the **positive cycle** of the in-house capacity to move increasingly faster, i.e., reinforces the **positive dynamics** to become a continuous, **virtuous cycle**. Similarly, the company can leverage its integrating capability to slow down the **negative cycle** caused by keeping the in-house capacity. With its strong integrating capability, the company can improve its process capability to reduce the overall overhead costs, including the set-up or changeover times: the integrating

Box continues

capability enables the company to coordinate among many functions and activities within the manufacturing system and between its suppliers and in-house production. Figure 8.5 graphically depicts the logic underlying Zara's high performance despite some counterintuitive strategic decisions.

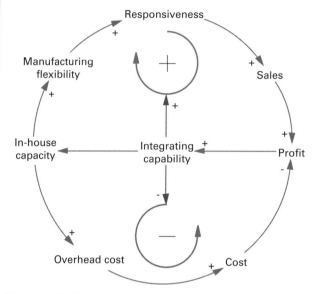

Figure 8.4 Role of Integrating Capability

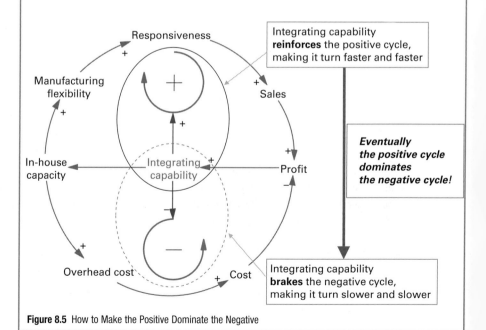

Figure 8.5 How to Make the Positive Dominate the Negative

Box continues

A summary of the above is as follows. First, every decision generates two effects, one positive or favorable and the other negative or detrimental for the company. As such, whether the decision helps the company perform better or worse depends on how the company implements its strategy. The key is its integrating capability. If the company develops its integrating capability strongly, it can make the positive effects dominate the negative and eventually improve its performance. It can even overcome difficult problems and bring about significant counterintuitive achievements.

Questions

1. Do you agree with the statement that every decision engenders two effects, positive and negative, simultaneously?
2. How has Zara been able to implement counterintuitive (e.g., different from some of the common wisdom in published research) strategies successfully?

8.1   New Product Innovation

In order to create value sustainably, a company must develop and launch new products continuously. Once a new product is developed, it must grow or evolve through its product life cycle. As we defined in Chapter 1, the value life cycle encompasses both new product development and product life cycle. In effect, the company's new product development must support and be driven by its supply chain strategy.

8.1.1   Product Life Cycle and Supply Chain Management

The PLC (product life cycle) consists of four stages – introduction, growth, maturity, and decline – through which a product or technology evolves over time. The exact shape and/or slope of the PLC depend on various factors of the market where the product or technology belongs. For instance, the semiconductor industry has a product life cycle much shorter than that of the shipbuilding industry. There are several explanations. Perhaps the **innovation cycle** – the time period in which a new innovation occurs – might be different. The semiconductor industry has an innovation cycle much faster than that of the shipbuilding industry. This difference reflects the different market characteristics as well. Customers of the semiconductor industry have a much faster budget cycle and/or feel more competitive pressure than those in the shipbuilding industry. In effect, one would say that the clock-speed of the value chain in the semiconductor industry is much faster than that in the shipbuilding industry. The **value chain clock-speed** measures how fast the product or technology moves through its value chain on average. Despite its reliance on numerous factors for its shape and speed, the PLC offers a framework robust enough to be applicable to virtually every type of product or technology.

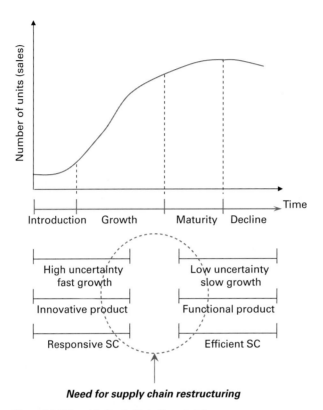

Figure 8.6 PLC and Its Supply Chain Characteristics

Although the exact shape and slope might be different, the fundamental nature of the PLC seems remarkably consistent across different industries. In the early stage of the PLC, i.e., the introduction stage, information and data about the product are scarce. This is obvious since the product is new to the market and thus the company has not been able to accumulate enough market experience. As the sales of the product increase, i.e., the product enters the growth stage of the PLC, the company gathers an increasing amount of information and data about the market. When the company doesn't have enough information and data about market demand, it faces high uncertainty since uncertainty is the opposite of having information: uncertainty is a relative, not an absolute, concept. As Figure 8.6 shows, the company has to cope with a high level of uncertainty and the uncertainty subsides as the product moves along its PLC.

When a new product starts its PLC, it needs to be an **innovative product**. Otherwise, there is no reason for the market to buy it. An innovative product must provide more value to the customers than other existing ones, i.e., it has $\dfrac{Performance}{Price}$ much higher than that of the existing and competing products. Because of this innovative trait, the new product enjoys more premiums in the market than other products do. But, as the demand for the new product increases – the product moves to the growth stage – its premiums shrink since more competing products become available in the market. It is increasingly likely that the product becomes a commodity product. Although the exact speed can be different across different products, every product transits from an innovative to a **functional product** as it travels along its PLC.

How should the supply chain reflect this change in the PLC? As the product's basic trait evolves from being innovative to being functional, the supply chain must also change from a responsive to an efficient one. That is, a **responsive supply chain** must be flexible enough to accommodate diverse market demands and cope with high uncertainty in the market. For a responsive supply chain, appropriate performance measures include high product quality, enhanced product differentiation, high customer satisfaction derived from the company's responsiveness, and so forth. The relationship between the strategic partners of a responsive supply chain has to be compatible with these performance objectives. On the other hand, an **efficient supply chain** is designed to cope with a relatively stable market environment affected by low uncertainty – it is compatible with the functional product. When the PLC enters the maturity stage, the competition in the market revolves around the price of the product – cost competitiveness becomes the determining factor. Therefore, an efficient supply chain must be structured to make the product more cost-competitive. For instance, in order to do this, the company might have to utilize outsourcing wisely, focus on process control to save production costs and/or reduce defects, and so forth. The relationship between supply chain partners might have to change as well. To maintain a responsive supply chain, the relationship between the manufacturer and its supplier needs to be strategic, long-term, and based on mutual trust. On the contrary, a typical relationship between the supply chain players in an efficient supply chain might be myopic, short-term, and discretely transaction-oriented.

It is clear that the supply chain has to change as the PLC evolves over time. In that sense, the supply chain strategy must be dynamic and systemic.

8.1.2   New Product Development Process

The concept of **time-based competition** was widely heralded in the early 1990s. In fact, the concept reflected the competitive characteristics during that time, when "how fast to introduce new products in the market" determined the company's competitive advantage. As such, companies tried to find ways to speed up their new product development processes. One of such approaches, **concurrent engineering**, emerged in the engineering side: it proposed that the firm should perform multiple tasks simultaneously, not sequentially, in a bid to minimize the project lead time. A similar concept was developed in management areas, i.e., **flexible new product development** (flexible NPD), which not only emphasized "performing tasks concurrently or simultaneously" like the concurrent engineering did, but also underlined "effective communication and coordination among managerial functions." More recently, the concept of the **cross-functional team** (CFT) approach has become more widely used, which is essentially equivalent to the flexible NPD process.

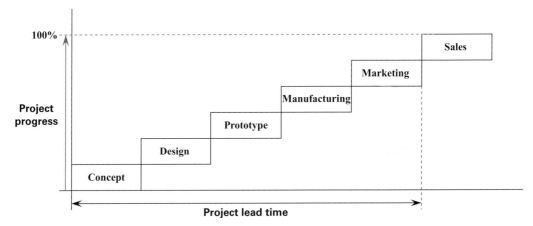

Figure 8.7 A Traditional Approach to Project Management

Concurrent engineering. As the basic principle, we want to discuss the fundamental features of concurrent engineering first, which is also a project management method. Figure 8.7 shows the traditional approach to project management. In general, to complete a project, multiple functions at the company should get involved. The traditional or **sequential method** requires each function to get involved in a sequence (Figure 8.7). It is likely that the "concept" function initiates the project, then "design" is done in accordance with the concept. After the design, a "prototype" needs to be constructed, then the "manufacturing" function starts getting involved in the development process in earnest, e.g., checking the engineering feasibility of the design or concept, identifying and arranging appropriate supplies to deliver materials required to make the new product, and the like. The "marketing" function starts gathering more information about the detailed market demand as well as channel options. And, finally, the "service" function gets involved in developing a strategy (e.g., structuring a service network, writing a formal service manual, so on) for after-sales services tailored to the new product. Which specific stages or functions should be included in the project lead time depends on the detailed attributes of the project, but in this section, we include activities up to marketing in the project lead time. As in Figure 8.7, the traditional approach proceeds monotonically from concept to marketing and sales one by one – in a strict sequence.

On the contrary, the concurrent engineering approaches project management very differently (Figure 8.8): it is equivalent to the flexible NPD or CFT approach in management. It allows (in fact, urges) stages or functions to overlap with each other. For instance, under the concurrent engineering approach, the company starts the design stage even before it completes the concept development stage. Similarly, building a **prototype** can start before the design or even before the concept stage is done. This kind of **overlapping** is allowed (or even encouraged) for manufacturing and marketing functions, too.

Why should the firm try concurrent engineering? What are the benefits of concurrent engineering compared with the **traditional approach**? The first and most important motivation for concurrent engineering is to reduce the project lead time. As Figure 8.9

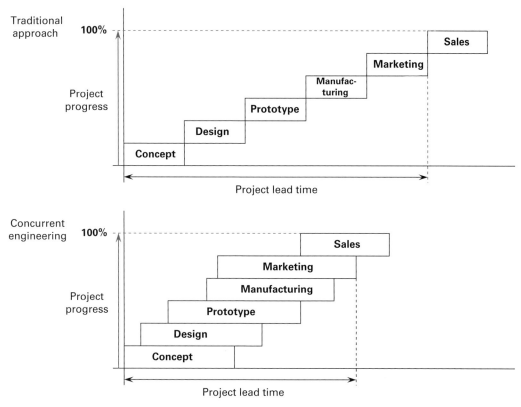

Figure 8.8 The Concurrent Engineering (CFT or Flexible NPD) Approach

shows, the **project lead time** can be reduced significantly. Reducing the new product development lead time, e.g., is critical to staying competitive in the market, where the "time-based competition" becomes increasingly more evident. Where does this benefit come from or how is it possible for the company to reduce the lead time? This lead-time reduction comes from the fact that the company performs multiple activities simultaneously. If one looks at the project at a particular point in time, only one activity is being performed when the traditional approach is adopted. On the contrary, under concurrent engineering, multiple activities are concurrently performed at a particular point in time – several activities are overlapped. Performing several activities simultaneously requires an **integrated team**, comprising managers as well as employees from various areas of the company that are actually involved in the project, e.g., departments in charge of concept development, design, prototype, manufacturing, marketing, and so forth. In effect, this integrated team takes care of the project from its conception to completion.

Although the lead-time reduction is the most visible achievement of concurrent engineering, there are other subtler, yet equally important, benefits as well. Potential quality improvement and cost reduction are such benefits. As Figure 8.10 depicts, the flexibility to fix serious flaws in the new product development is very high in the early stages of the project. This flexibility decreases rapidly as the project proceeds to its production stage.

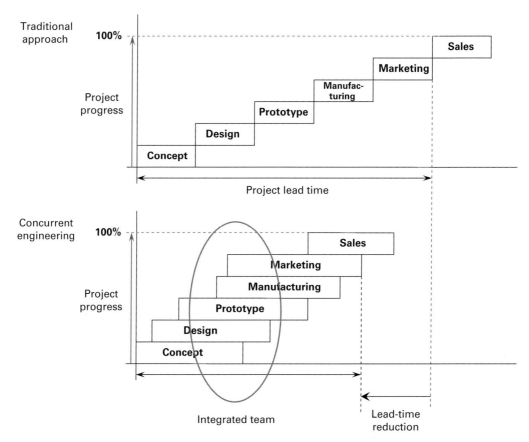

Figure 8.9 Benefits of Concurrent Engineering (1)

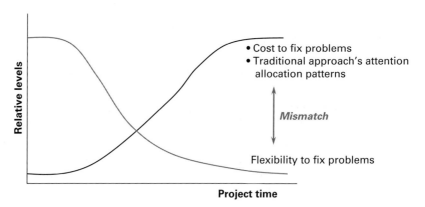

Figure 8.10 Benefits of Concurrent Engineering (2)

Suppose a carmaker designs a new passenger car incorrectly, but fails to fix the problem at the design stage. The prototype is made assuming the design is correct, and the planning for manufacturing starts presuming the prototype is the right one. However, since the design is flawed in the first place, the manufacturing stage cannot go as planned. In general, serious flaws in the earlier stages are uncovered in the latter stages such as manufacturing. When serious problems are discovered in the manufacturing stage, it is usually too late to apply fundamental measures to fix the problem completely. Should the traditional approach be adopted, the project would have proceeded too far to go back to the drawing board again. It is simply too costly. Facing this difficulty, an ordinary company usually decides to be satisfied with settling down with just "ad-hoc solutions" to cover up the problem rather than solving it completely. But, when the company believes it has to implement this kind of **ad-hoc solution**, it is also tempted to disguise it from the customers. Even worse, some companies try to sell their products even if they know the products are defective, at least potentially serious if not outright dangerous. This strategy to cover up the fundamental problem might work for a short period of time, but it cannot be sustainable.[1] In fact, the cost of dealing with defects found out by the customers in the market is much higher than that of fixing them before they leave the company's plant in the first place.

In effect, the concurrent or CFT approach enables the company to minimize the mismatch between the managerial attention allocation pattern and the flexibility to fix problems in new product development by identifying and highlighting the potentially serious problems early in the process. That is, the CFT approach forces the manager to pay more attention to early stages in the new product development process. It essentially aligns the management's attention allocation pattern with the changing pattern of problem-solving flexibility.

In concurrent engineering (i.e., flexible NPD process or CFT approach), workers and managers from all the necessary functions work together from the beginning, and thus it becomes more effective to identify potential problems and develop affordable methods to solve them early on. For example, since the design people work with those in manufacturing from the outset, they pay more attention to manufacturing possibilities – whether the products embodying their design can be manufactured in the company's own production plant. Similarly, the marketing people can input their knowledge about the market into the design or even concept development stage, so that the product's concept and design are consistent with what the customers actually want. In essence, an effective integrated team can enhance the project quality and, at the same time, save costs involved with solving problems often found too late in the project process.

So far, we have focused on the benefits of concurrent engineering. If the concurrent approach offers only the benefits, it seems natural that every company should adopt the approach. However, it doesn't make sense because every activity involves both costs and benefits at the same time. Having said that, what are the biggest costs of implementing concurrent engineering? What are the most serious obstacles to implementing concurrent engineering? Most of the costs involved with concurrent engineering are due to the increased need for **communication**. Figure 8.11 simplifies the communication patterns in the two approaches. In the traditional approach, the communication moves rather

---

[1] Refer to the recent scandal in the car industry: Volkswagen tried to cover up its diesel car's pollution emission – see www.nytimes.com/interactive/2015/business/international/vw-diesel-emissions-scandal-explained.html?_r=0.

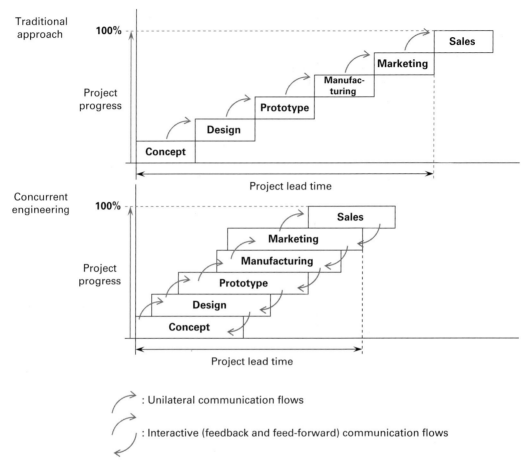

Figure 8.11 Communication Issues in Project Management

straight, from the early stage to the latter unilaterally – without any **feedback communication** between activities. On the contrary, concurrent engineering requires incessant
feedback and feed-forward communications, not only between adjacent activities, but
also between distant activities simultaneously. One can say that the figure simplifies the
communication patterns too much and, in reality, there might be a certain level of
feedback communication even in the traditional approach. Perhaps such an argument
has a valid point. Despite a slight simplification, however, we estimate that the required
amount of communication in concurrent engineering can be much larger than that in the
traditional approach, perhaps by as much as fifty times. In order to process huge amounts
of communication effectively, the company must have a robust infrastructure to support
the data and information flows that such a huge communication need requires.
In a similar vein, the company must have an organizational structure, including reporting
relationships among managers, which must support and be consistent with the infrastructure to process the communication constantly. In effect, it is not a simple task to
implement concurrent engineering successfully. It requires the company to review all of

its existing business processes, such as communication patterns, IT infrastructure, organizational structures, and resource allocation mechanisms. Because of these complex potential risks, some people say that a failed implementation of concurrent engineering causes **concurrent chaos** in the organization. Successful implementation of concurrent engineering can be a daunting task, yet we know that the benefits can be potentially significant enough to offset such huge costs.

8.1.3   Comparative Analysis: CFT versus Sequential Approach

So far, we have compared two approaches to new product development (NPD), i.e., traditional (sequential) and concurrent engineering. We also stated that flexible NPD or cross-functional team (CFT) approach is equivalent to, but also more managerial than, concurrent engineering – hence, we use the terms like flexible NPD and CFT approach in lieu of concurrent engineering. In this section, we want to elaborate on the primary differences between the two contrasting approaches, i.e., sequential and CFT, in great detail by highlighting the advantages and disadvantages of the approaches more thoroughly.

We redraw the sequential approach and the CFT approach in Figure 8.12, which is essentially the same as Figure 8.8 except that the after-sales function is included in the

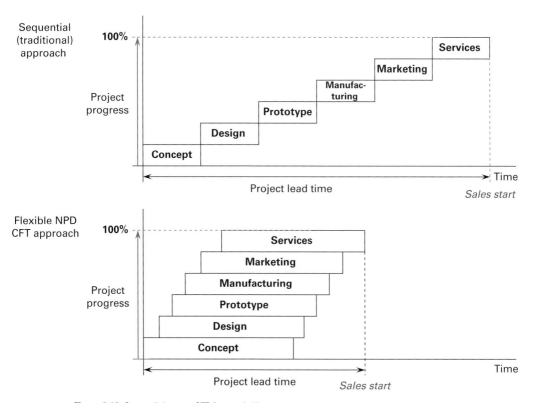

Figure 8.12 Sequential versus CFT Approach (1)

Table 8.1 Sequential versus CFT Approach to NPD

	Traditional/Sequential	Flexible/CFT
Fundamental characteristics	✓ Involving one function at a time ✓ One-directional (upstream to downstream) communication	✓ Multiple functions simultaneously ✓ Constant feedback and feed-forward

Advantages	✓ Simplicity
	✓ Simple accountability ↑ (?)
	✓ Most of the CFT's disadvantages
		✓ Lead time ↓
		✓ Problem-solving capability ↑
		✓ Risk exposure ↓
		  ➢ Incorporating "changing customer requirements" ↑
		  ➢ Incorporating "cutting-edge technological innovation" ↑
		✓ As a result, product quality ↑

Disadvantages	✓ Most of the CFT's advantages
	  ➢ Lead time↑
	  ➢ Risk exposure↑
	  ➢ Problem-solving capability ↓
		✓ Concurrent chaos; confusion; complexity ↑
		  ➢ Communication load ↑
		  ➢ Coordination cost ↑
		✓ Resource waste, duplication ↑
		✓ Accountability ↓ (?)
		✓ Employee exhaustion ↑
		  ➢ Employee morale ↓ (?)

Key issues to be resolved	✓ Cognitive → Behavioral → Performance
	  ➢ Incentive alignment for "cognitive → behavioral"
	  ➢ Infrastructure support for "behavioral → performance"	

NPD process as the last step of the project and the sales start after the service element is fully taken into account. Table 8.1 summarizes the fundamental characteristics, advantages, disadvantages, and key issues to be resolved for the two approaches.

Fundamental characteristics. Before discussing the basic attributes, it is necessary to note that when a function or activity is involved in the NPD process, it does not always imply that the firm actually performs that function or activity. For instance, when the manufacturing function is involved in the process, it means that the managers from the manufacturing function are participating in the NPD process, rather than they are physically making the product; in fact, the actual manufacturing must continue as long as the market demands the product, long after the NPD process ends.

There are two fundamental characteristics of the sequential approach. At a particular point in time, only one function or activity is involved in the process (Figure 8.13). As a result, communication is one-directional, i.e., from an upstream to a downstream

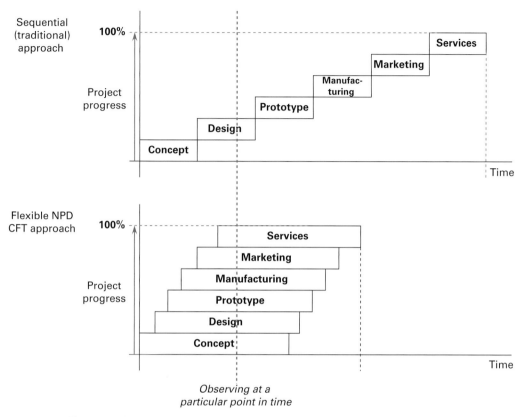

Figure 8.13 Sequential versus CFT Approach (2)

activity. These two characteristics are due to the basic structure of the sequential approach.

On the contrary, for the CFT approach, multiple functions or activities are interacting with each other at a particular point in time, which necessitates constant feedback and feed-forward communication among the involved activities. **Feedback** is the communication from a downstream to an upstream function. **Feed-forward** is different from feedback in that once the upstream function receives the feedback from its downstream partner, it revises or refines its original instruction (i.e., communication contents) and re-communicates it to the downstream function. That is, constant feedback and feed-forward mean continuous, iterative, and closed-loop communication, as well as flows of information and data among the functions or activities.

Advantages of the sequential approach. One of the key advantages of the traditional approach is its **simplicity**. Since only one function or activity is involved at a time, it is simple and straightforward to manage and communicate. Sometimes simplicity implies heightened **accountability**: it is simple to determine who is responsible for what, since each function or activity is performed independently of others. Simplicity also means little confusion or complexity among the project members and therefore might reduce any coordination cost and resource duplication. Although simplicity renders accountability in general, it may not be that straightforward: project members in the sequential approach might thrust the responsibility on others by finger-pointing and making excuses, unless they feel strong *esprit de corps*.

Advantages of the CFT approach. The CFT approach enables the firm to reduce the project lead time and thus to be more competitive in the time-based competition. It is also possible for the firm to enhance its **problem-solving** capability. For instance, in the sequential approach, when the design is seriously flawed so that the existing production system is unable to make the product in conformance with the design, such a problem cannot be identified until the manufacturing function discovers it. But, even if the manufacturing function recognizes the problem, it is not easy to fix it fundamentally under the sequential approach. Note that the fundamental solution is to go back to the design step and rectify the problem from scratch. Unfortunately, there are several obstacles in the sequential approach which make it difficult to take such an action. First, there might be some **organizational resistance** to such a method: the design function is unlikely to accept its responsibility for the problem. Even if the design function is less resisting, there still remains a practical issue, i.e., it cannot fix the problem completely, perhaps because those involved in the project have left the function or are now involved in different projects with little memory or record about the project associated with the problem. Another potentially grim situation is that it is too late to go back to the design stage, since the new product launch is due very shortly. Facing all of these difficulties, the firm might be tempted to settle down with a quick-fix, **ad-hoc solution**, e.g., hammering or cutting the parts to assemble them by force, which ultimately causes quality fiasco. In sharp contrast to the sequential approach, the CFT approach can identify any manufacturing problem early in the process, because the manufacturing function is involved in the NPD process early on and communicates constantly with other functions, including the design; therefore, problem identification occurs early on and, as such, it is much easier to fix the problem. This is consistent with the notion of **design for manufacturability**, which requires the design function to design the product, not only from its own aesthetical and user-friendly perspective, but also from that of the manufacturing, so that the design can be effectively realized in the manufacturing process.

These days, the concept of "design for manufacturability" is expanded to the entire value life cycle, not just product life cycle or supply chain alone. For example, **design for serviceability** and **design for recyclability** are fast becoming critical. Figure 8.14 shows a simplified value life cycle from concept and design, manufacturing, actual use and maintenance by the customer, to the end of the product's life cycle, when the product is recycled. If "design for manufacturability" is a notion important to the company, "design for serviceability" is key to the customer's satisfaction with the product or service while he or she uses it. As in Chapter 3, one of the essential dimensions of quality is **serviceability**, i.e., the ease, convenience, and effectiveness of maintenance services, including repairs and regular

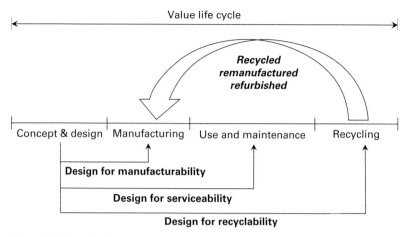

Figure 8.14 Design for Serviceability and Recyclability

maintenance check-ups, while the customer is using the product or service sometimes even after the warranty period is expired. As such, "design for serviceability" implies that the company should design its product and service in a way that results in the most effective after-sales services for the customer. One example is to adopt a modular design concept so that when a part of the product is broken or needs to be repaired, the part itself can be isolated from other parts of the product and replaced with a new one without disassembling the whole product, in order to minimize the time and cost required for the maintenance service. Of course, the company should find a way to design its product or service not only for heightened serviceability, but also for other quality dimensions, such as performance and aesthetics.

As consumers as well as governments pay an increasing amount of attention to environmental issues, sustainability is becoming an essential managerial subject. Recycling is an integral part of supply chain sustainability, which emphasizes minimizing the negative environmental impact of products and services. Although "design for recycling" is not currently required by consumers or governments, it will soon be a strong competitive advantage for the company to develop its product or service to ensure it can be recycled in the most effective way. That is, if the company can design its product so that it can be recycled easily and efficiently after its life cycle is completed, it will be able to enjoy competitive advantage in the market, which is sensitive to the environmental causes. For instance, the company should design its product based on **modularity** so that in the end it can be dismantled easily and also without damaging other individual parts, which can be reused for new products or services. Again, the success of "design for recyclability" depends on the firm's ability to develop new products or services in a way to achieve not only recyclability, but also other quality dimensions such as performance, aesthetics, and even serviceability, in addition to the manufacturability. Implemented prudently, the CFT approach can help the company attain its design expertise in order to realize "design for manufacturability, serviceability, and recyclability" simultaneously without excessively compromising other important quality dimensions.

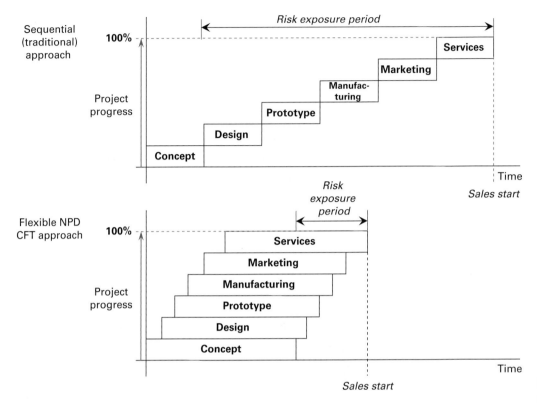

Figure 8.15 Risk Exposure of NPD Process

Another key benefit of the CFT approach is related to the concept of **risk exposure**, i.e., exposure of the NPD process to market and technological uncertainties, which makes the firm vulnerable to changes in customer requirements, as well as new technological breakthroughs in the market. Figure 8.15 shows the risk exposure period, i.e., how long the firm is exposed to the market and technological risks. In this section, we propose that it is the period from the moment the concept of the new product is frozen to when the shipping of the new product to the market starts. The term "**freeze**" implies "an act to stop the process so that no further changes are allowed." For example, "**concept (design) freeze**" means a time or action point, from which no changes to the concept (design) are allowed. In Figure 8.15, the risk exposure period of the sequential approach is much longer than that of the CFT approach, indicating that the sequential approach is much more vulnerable to the market and technological risks than is the CFT approach. That is, the CFT approach can better incorporate recent changes in customer requirements and the newest developments of technological innovation into the new product than the sequential approach can. These make the new product developed through the CFT approach much more competitive in the market. All of these advantages result in improving the product quality and customer's utility derived from the product.

Disadvantages of the sequential approach. Major disadvantages of the sequential approach are basically those opposite to the advantages of the CFT approach. That is, the sequential approach has a longer lead time, lower problem-solving capability, and larger risk exposure. As a result, it is likely that the quality can be subpar.

Disadvantages of the CFT approach. Despite its strengths, the CFT approach is prone to some serious disadvantages, unless managed effectively. Since it involves multiple functions at the same time, **organizational complexity** rises due to an increased communication load, which leads to a higher coordination cost. Under this approach, duplication or repetition of the same activity may occur, which causes resource waste. It is also more likely that the project members feel exhausted due to complex coordination with other multiple functions simultaneously and such feeling could damage employee morale in the long run.[2]

So far, we have considered the pros and cons of each of the NPD approaches. In reality, however, it is reasonable to expect that a company chooses an approach which combines or mixes the two methods, i.e., sequential and CFT, to a certain extent. For instance, it is possible for a company to use the CFT approach with less or shorter overlapping between functions, which is more comparable with the sequential approach. For the sake of simplicity, however, let's suppose that the company has to choose only one of the two approaches. Which one is better? The answer depends on the specific condition or context where the company is doing business. From Table 8.1, we know the biggest benefit of the CFT approach comes from its ability to respond effectively to changes in customer requirements and technological breakthroughs. In other words, the value of the CFT approach increases as the market as well as technological uncertainty intensifies. What about the cost to implement the CFT approach? Most of the implementation costs are internal, i.e., incurring inside the company and therefore depending on the internal structural and infrastructural conditions of the company. As such, under normal conditions, one can expect that the cost to implement the CFT approach doesn't vary much as the external uncertainty changes. The situation described above is depicted in Figure 8.16, which is conducive to the **cost-benefit analysis** for the CFT approach. Now return to the question, *Which approach should the company choose?* Figure 8.17 hints at an answer to the question. That is, conceptually it is possible to find an uncertainty level below which the CFT approach is not desirable, i.e., the cost is larger than the benefit. For instance, if a company is in an industry, which is largely stable and stagnant, it might not be necessary to apply the CFT approach, paying the expensive

---

[2] The communication load required for the CFT approach is said to be as much as fifty times more than that for the sequential approach. For the sake of clear explanation, consider a simple example where there is an NPD project team, consisting of ten functions. Assume that we can measure the communication load by analyzing how many times the functions communicate with each other. Since for the sequential approach there are only two functions involved simultaneously, the number of communications at a particular point in time is one. On the other hand, since for the CFT approach each function needs to communicate with the other nine functions at the same time, the total number of communications is $_{10}C_2 = \dfrac{10 \times 9}{2 \times 1} = 45$. Therefore, the communication load for the CFT approach is increased by almost fifty times.

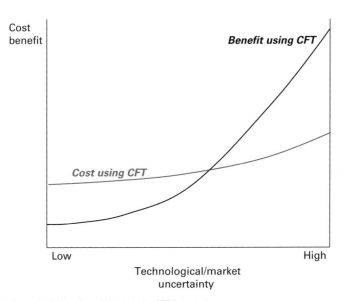

Figure 8.16 Cost-Benefit Analysis for CFT Approach

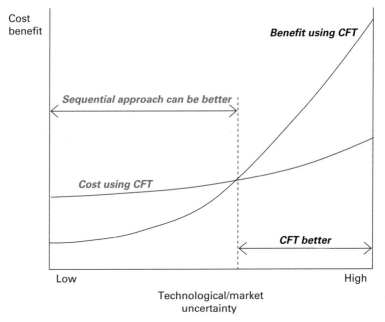

Figure 8.17 Comparative Cost-Benefit Analysis

costs. If there is little uncertainty in the market, the company had better try the sequential approach, which might perform as well as the CFT approach, but with much less cost. Of course, in order to make a definitive decision, the company should do a similar cost-benefit analysis for the sequential approach.

Figure 8.18 Cognitive and Behavioral Changes Required

Implementation of the CFT approach. Suppose that the company has undertaken a thorough analysis and concludes that it is desirable to apply the CFT approach. What should the company do to ensure a successful implementation? There exists a chain relationship from cognitive, behavioral, to performance (Figure 8.18).

Whenever an organization introduces a new technology or change within itself in a bid to improve performance, the first thing it must do is to make sure that every member, manager, or employee of the organization understands and wholeheartedly accepts the technology or change, firmly believing in its effectiveness. This is the **cognitive change**, which requires communication and commitment from the top management. For instance, the company's CEO should communicate the message (e.g., why it is critical to adopt the technology) to the members of the organization and show her sincere commitment to the technology. Only then will the managers and employees truly perceive and accept the importance and value of the technology.

But, ensuring the cognitive change in every member of the organization is one thing, and making everyone behave consistently with her cognitive belief is another. Without **behavioral change** among its members, the organization cannot fulfill the promise of the new technology to its fullest extent. What must be done to bring about the desired behavioral change among the managers and employees? The foremost mechanism is an **incentive alignment**, which convinces everyone in the organization that behaving consistently with knowing (i.e., cognition) pays off. Note that incentives don't just have to imply monetary compensation. There are many non-monetary, i.e., **intrinsic**, incentives, such as personal interest, enthusiasm, honorary recognition, and other emotional elements.

Finally, even if the organization is successful in changing its members' behavior in accordance with their cognitive acceptance, however, it is not sufficient to improve performance. There must be an effective **infrastructural support** to link the behavioral change with substantive performance improvement.

The CEO's role in implementing the CFT approach. Consider a company that determines to implement the CFT approach. The company's CEO communicates with her employees consistently and intensively so that they are convinced of the importance and effectiveness of the approach. Although there is cognitive change among the employees, however, the CEO cannot see any substantial behavioral change. That is, it is clear that every employee believes in the effectiveness of the approach, but not many work hard to coordinate with others from other functions or departments. Without continuous coordination among multiple functions, the CFT approach cannot be successful. The CEO soon finds out why her employees don't behave consistently with their belief: the current compensation system relies heavily on individual performance with little incentive for coordination with each other. Hence, the CEO completely overhauls the incentive system, which now gives a much larger weight to the multi-functional coordination, i.e., a big portion of the employee's compensation is now linked with the employee's work as a member of the CFT project. The new incentive system emphasizes team performance, not an individual one. After aligning the incentive system with the goal, it is now clear that the employees behave consistently with their belief, e.g., they are eager to coordinate with those from other functions or departments in the CFT project. Despite the desired change in behavior, however, the CEO doesn't see any significant improvement in performance at the firm level. After searching for a clue, the CEO finds out why. It turns out that the employees do not have the most efficient tools to enable them to communicate and coordinate with each other. Only when the CEO installs the infrastructure powerful enough to support the communication and coordination among the CFT members, the employees' behavioral change eventually brings about a significant improvement in performance.

This example highlights the role that the CEO must play in successfully implementing a new technology such as the CFT approach. The CEO has to motivate managers and employees to believe in the new system and behave accordingly with their belief by aligning the incentive system and providing ample support for coordination and communication.

8.2   Coordination to Deal with Market Uncertainty

So far, we have focused on the firm's internal coordination, e.g., coordination among multiple functions within the same company. In order to maximize its value creation, the firm has to coordinate with other companies that share the same value chain. In this section, we delve into some of the coordination mechanisms for the company to deal with market uncertainty. These mechanisms are part of the firm's critical supply chain capability.

8.2.1   Vendor-Managed Inventory (VMI)

Vendor-managed inventory (VMI) is a supply chain arrangement where the customer's inventory inside their own premises is managed by the vendor, not the customer itself. The basic structure of VMI is shown in Figure 8.19.

Consider an example where LG Electronics (LGE) is the customer and LG Display (LGD) is the supplier: for the retailing industry, another example is that E-Mart (a retailer) is the customer and CJ (a food company) is the vendor (Figure 8.19). LGD supplies TFT-LCD panels to LGE, which manufactures and sells TVs by assembling the required parts, including the TFT-LCD panels. More specifically, LGD delivers its TFT-LCD to the warehouse at LGE, i.e., inside the premises of LGE. Whenever LGE manufactures a TV set, it retrieves one TFT-LCD panel from its warehouse.

Table 8.2 Advantages and Disadvantages of VMI

	Vendor	Customer

+	✓ Direct access to demand info ↑
	   → Info Quality ↑ → Disruption ↓
	   → Production planning ↑
	   → Productivity ↑, quality ↑, inventory ↓
	✓ Sales ↑
	✓ Relationship with customer ↑
		✓ Inventory costs ↓
		✓ Sales ↑

−	✓ Inventory costs ↑	✓ Flexibility in choosing appropriate vendor ↓ ✓ Information leakage ↑
☞	✓ Inventory ownership issue – related to the bargaining power balance ✓ Information grade – relationship	

Key: ☞ – key issues that must be resolved.

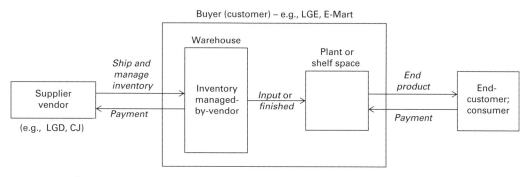

Figure 8.19 VMI Structure

Assembling other parts along with the panel at its plant, LGE completes and sells the TV to the end-customer, who can sometimes be a retail store like Walmart. Under the VMI relationship between LGE and LGD, the inventory at LGE's warehouse is managed by LGD, not by LGE. What are the advantages and disadvantages of VMI from the customer's standpoint or from the vendor's? That is, it is indispensable to understand the motivation as well as the cost from each partner's perspective in the VMI relationship, in order to implement the strategic arrangement successfully (Table 8.2).

The customer's perspective. VMI offers at least two significant benefits to the customer: one is the reduced inventory management cost, and the other is the increased sales. It seems obvious for the customer to pay less for the inventory since it is managed by the vendor: VMI minimizes any complexity involved with inventory management for the customer. In fact, it is known that the retail industry is one of the first pioneers to adopt VMI: it looks reasonable, since the industry is usually characterized by complexity due to an enormous number of products a retail store has to manage. Under the VMI arrangement, the retailer is free of the headache to monitor the inventory constantly. Another major benefit, increased sales, is possible due to the vendor being much better at preventing any stock-out of its products, since it pays thorough attention to its own products only.

On the other hand, there are two major disadvantages. First, the customer might lose some flexibility in changing its suppliers or choosing a better supplier over the one which currently has the VMI relationship. That is, in exchange for possible cost saving and increased sales, the customer might have to take the risk of being locked in the relationship with the vendor having the VMI relationship. It may cause a particularly damaging impact if the industry is prone to fast technological changes and the competition among suppliers is fierce. Another problem is concerned with proprietary **information leakage**. In order to be effective, VMI calls for close coordination and information-sharing between the customer and its vendor. Unless the relationship is tightly monitored, such close information-sharing might lead to the leakage of the proprietary information or knowledge owned by the partner companies. Suppose a hypothetical example where the vendor has established the VMI relationship not only with the customer, but also with the customer's competitor in the same industry. Through the VMI arrangement, the vendor probably has access to the information or knowledge proprietary to the customer. Then, it is not unimaginable that the vendor is tempted to share that proprietary information with the customer's competitor under certain circumstances. That is, the customer has to constantly monitor the VMI relationship in order to minimize the risk of leaking its proprietary information and knowledge to its competition.

The vendor's perspective. The most important motivation for the vendor to engage in the VMI relationship is to have direct access to the end-customer's demand information. By managing the customer's inventory, the vendor in effect bypasses its immediate customer (i.e., that in the VMI relationship) in reaching out to the end-customer or market and has direct access to the demand information, sometimes on a real-time basis. As a result, the **information quality** is enhanced sharply, because the distance is shortened and the number of gatekeepers between the source and the decision point is reduced. Heightened information quality means reduced uncertainty faced by the vendor, which in turn implies little disruption in production and better production-planning capability. All these improvements enable the vendor to increase its productivity and product quality, along with its own internal inventory being cut sharply. That is, there is a significant positive repercussion of the direct access to the end-market demand information. Another benefit is that the vendor can expect its sales to increase due to the same reason causing the increase in the customer's sales. Finally, the vendor can retain a strategic relationship with the customer, which has a favorable long-term ramification.

On the other hand, the vendor must take the burden of managing the inventory inside the customer's warehouse. Sometimes the inventory management cost can be excessive. As such, the vendor must conduct a comprehensive cost-benefit analysis to compare the advantages and disadvantages of undertaking the VMI relationship before making a final decision.

Two issues to be resolved. There remain two issues which both the customer and the vendor in the VMI relationship had better consider fully and be prepared for. The first is concerned with the ownership of the inventory at the customer's premises. Whose inventory is it legally? This issue is critical since it determines who is responsible for the inventory losses, e.g., damages, thefts, decays, obsolescence, and the like. Because of the risk of such losses, each partner doesn't want to own the inventory. For instance, the customer wants the vendor to have the ownership and pays the vendor only for those units it actually uses, e.g., assembles or sells. Therefore, it depends on the balance of bargaining power between the customer and the vendor who should take the burden of owning the inventory: in general, it is likely that the one with weaker bargaining power is forced to own the inventory legally. The second issue relates to one of the customer's concerns, i.e., the potential leakage of proprietary information or knowledge. Unless such a concern is reasonably resolved, the customer may not be actively involved in the VMI relationship and thus it becomes difficult to implement VMI effectively. One way to minimize such a worry would be to define information grades and to assign an appropriate grade to each vendor in the VMI relationship. For example, the customer may define the information grades as follows: Grade A (the highest), B, C, D, and E (the lowest); that is, Grade A is for sharing all information and data, including the consumers' buying patterns/behaviors, relating to the vendor as well as its competitors on a real-time basis . . . Grade E is for sharing delayed (i.e., not real-time) information and data on the sales volumes and prices of the vendor's products only. Then, the customer has to decide which information grade to grant to which vendor, perhaps based on its prior business experience with the vendors. Here, the contract theory can play an essential role.

Sometimes VMI partners, especially the vendors, complain about the ineffectiveness of VMI in the real world. But, most of the complaints are based on a serious misunderstanding regarding the true value and motivation of VMI. Many companies seem to believe that the essential benefit of VMI is to save costs or increase sales, often ignoring the most fundamental principle of VMI. That is, the greatest value of VMI is coming from the direct access to the end market's demand information, which in turn improves the information quality significantly and thus eventually enhances the firm's capability. Only when the partners completely understand the true value as well as motivating principle of VMI, will they be able to reap the benefit of VMI to the fullest extent.

8.2.2   Postponement

As Figure 8.20 indicates, there exists an inverse relationship between production volume and customization. As the company increases its production volume, it becomes more difficult for it to customize its products (or services) to the specific needs of its customers. Likewise, as the company increases its customization level, it becomes

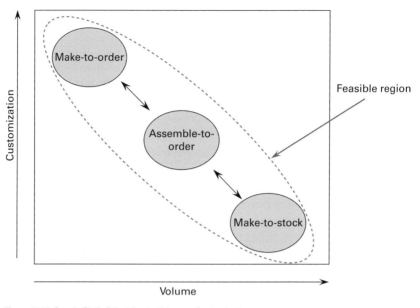

Figure 8.20 Supply Chain Principles by Volume x Customization

harder for it to produce its products (or provide services) in mass quantities. **Make-to-stock** is the supply chain strategy, according to which the company mass-produces its products without fully taking into account customization. It is compatible with the **push system** in inventory control. The other extreme is the **make-to-order (make-to-build)** strategy, under which the company tailors its product to the specific needs of its customer and therefore cannot afford to mass-produce the product. Again, it is compatible with the **pull system** in inventory control. In between these two strategies is **assemble-to-order**. The primary difference between make-to-stock and assemble-to-order is that the latter does care about the customer's need and incorporates it into the final product. On the other hand, it differentiates itself from make-to-order by limiting the options of customization to a few choices. Hence, the assemble-to-order strategy offers only limited customization, as opposed to the full customization of the make-to-order strategy, which enables the customer to get involved in the production process early on in order to have a wide range of alternatives.

Recently, **mass customization** has become a key strategic concept. But, as Figure 8.21 shows, mass customization is contradicting the usual wisdom in published research. Mass customization is a terminology consisting of two incompatible words: "mass" and "customization." By definition, customization implies something that is tailored to a small and select group of people, thus excluding the possibility of serving the mass market. The reason why the concept of mass customization emerges is closely related to the rapidly increasing competition in the market, which requires better customized services at affordable prices. In order to be competitive in this global market, therefore, it is essential for the firm to pursue the goal of full mass customization. One way to implement the strategy is to utilize "postponement."

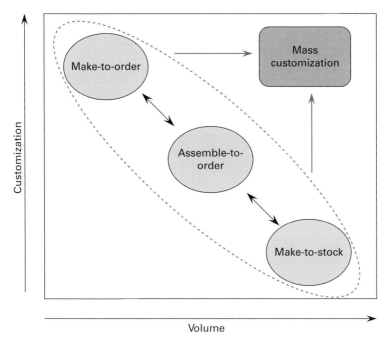

Figure 8.21 Positioning of Mass Customization

Principles and benefits of postponement. We first elaborate on the basic characteristics of postponement. For example, consider a company that produces multiple product types: A, B, and C. As Figure 8.22 shows, the company will sell to the market the three types of products when the sales season starts. Since it takes time to produce the products, the company needs to start its production well ahead of the sales season.

Although the final products can be quite different from each other, all of them are based on a certain platform, so that it is possible for the three products to share a common production line, at least during the initial production phase. The point at which the **common platform** can no longer be utilized and each product must start using a particular production line is called the **product differentiation** point. The first half of Figure 8.22 shows a more traditional case, where the individual products are differentiated early on – the product differentiation point occurs early in the production period. The basic strategy of **postponement** is to delay the product differentiation point as much as possible. Consequently, this strategy requires retaining the common platform for a longer period of time: postponing the product differentiation point is made possible by increasing the portion of the common platform throughout the production process.

Pros and cons of postponement. The first and most important benefit is the increased capability of matching the firm's supply with market demand. How is this possible? Figure 8.23 succinctly describes the logic. As the starting point of the sales season approaches, more information about the market demand composition becomes

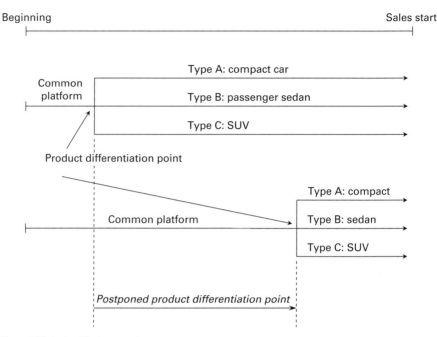

Figure 8.22 Logic of Postponement

available. This information tells us about how the final market demand will be divided among the product types. For instance, suppose that the total market demand for the products as a whole is 1,000. Then, how many units of the 1,000 will be for product type A, B, or C? Figure 8.23 shows the related probability distributions. In the early phase of the production process, the company lacks accurate information about the market demand and therefore the probability distribution looks widely spread – it has a high standard deviation and thus is associated with high uncertainty. But, as the company accumulates more information about the detailed market demand structure, the uncertainty level faced by the company diminishes – the forecast for the market demand composition becomes sharper and more reliable.

If the traditional approach without postponement should be adopted, the decision-maker would find it difficult to decide how to divide the production capacity into three different product types since she doesn't have enough information. Therefore, the likelihood that the production composition decided in the early production phase matches the market demand composition in the end cannot be high. In Figure 8.23, there is an example. Suppose that the actual demand realized is Type A = 200, B = 300, and C = 500. Since the company lacks reliable information at the early production phase, it cannot help but base its decision only on the available information at that point, which is, e.g., to produce 300 of Type A, 500 of B, and 200 of C. Thus, the total mismatch between the supply and the actual market demand will be 600. This is the likely scenario we can imagine when the traditional "early product differentiation" method is adopted. Now, suppose the company uses the postponement strategy, and therefore can afford to

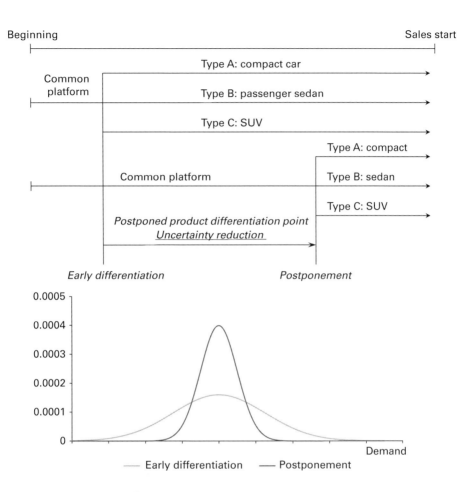

Figure 8.23 Uncertainty Reduction Due to Postponement

- Example: demand forecast
  (Mismatch is the difference between actual demand and mean estimate)

Product Type	Early Differentiation		Postponed Differentiation		Actual Demand
	Production (Mean Value)	Mismatch	Production (Mean Value)	Mismatch	
A	300	100	250	50	200
B	500	200	320	20	300
C	200	300	430	70	500
Total mismatch		600		140	

delay its product differentiation until the late production phase. At the postponed product differentiation point, the company would have more accurate information about the final market demand composition: based on the accurate information, it decides to produce 250 of A, 320 of B, and 430 of C, resulting in the total mismatch of 140, an almost 77 percent reduction in mismatch between supply and demand. The primary benefit results not just from reducing the mismatch. While postponing the product differentiation point until the company has more information about the market demand, the company becomes more capable of customizing its products to the end-customer requirements, i.e., customers' diverse needs. As such, the example we've just mentioned demonstrates how the postponement enables the company to implement the mass customization strategy.

The postponement strategy is particularly effective when the total size of the market demand is known, but how the total demand will be divided into different product types is not very clear. The example in Figure 8.23 uses such a case, where the total demand is relatively easy to forecast, but the composition of the product types, i.e., the **product mix**, is highly uncertain. It is also a realistic condition. For instance, it is known to be relatively easy for a carmaker to forecast how many passenger vehicles (as a whole) will be sold in the following year, but extremely difficult to forecast how many of the total demand will be product type A, B, or C.

Why it is difficult to implement postponement. So far, we have primarily discussed the benefits of postponement: it is an effective tool in realizing mass customization. If postponement offers only the benefits without costs, it is obvious that every company has to utilize it. But, the reality is not that straightforward. As Figure 8.23 visualizes, in order for the company to use it effectively, it is essential for the different product types to have much **commonality** – i.e., share common parts and/or a common platform to a great extent in the production process. Making different product types share a common platform is not a small task. It requires creative thinking. More practically, the post-ponement strategy requires enhanced **modularity** in product and process design. The company probably has to redesign its product and process so that the different products can be processed until a sufficiently late phase of production, using the common platform. In addition to these internal efforts for modularity, the company has to pay keen attention to its relationship with suppliers, who will have to redesign their own product and process in order to be compatible with their customer's modular product and process. For example, suppose Hyundai decides to fully implement the postponement policy and replace existing designs with the modular product design and modular process design. Due to this change, probably key parts inside its Sonata, e.g., the engine components, should be retrofitted. Then, MOBIS, its key supplier, would have to refit its engine module for Sonata. It is very important for Hyundai to commu-nicate with MOBIS about why it is necessary to coordinate such changes simulta-neously. Without a strong strategic partnership, Hyundai would find it difficult to convince MOBIS about the rationale behind the changes.

In sum, the postponement can help the company implement the mass customization strategy and enhance its capability of reducing the mismatch between supply and demand, but it also requires the company to develop modular product design and modular process design and also to establish strategic partnership with its key suppliers. It implies that a successful utilization of postponement needs a concerted effort from the supply chain partners. In this sense, postponement is another channel or **supply chain capability** which can be fully accomplished only when the relevant supply chain partners work together, i.e., coordinate with each other.

8.2.3   Accurate Response Systems

An **accurate response system** is another principle of SCM. Its primary objective is also to minimize the mismatch between supply and demand – to accurately respond to the market demand changes in order to match its production decision with the demand pattern in terms of volume and product mix (Fisher *et al.*, 1997). In effect, some of the key elements of an accurate response system have already been discussed while studying the postponement strategy.

Consider an automobile case. In the automobile market, there is usually a starting point of a sales season: automobile companies have target sales timings for their new models. For instance, the 2016 Hyundai Sonata was introduced for the first time to the market in early September 2015. Thus, the sales season of the 2016 model of Hyundai Sonata started in September 2015. In order to start selling Sonata from September 2015, Hyundai had to begin assembling the cars as early as in January 2015 or even October 2014.

When the first production of the 2016 Hyundai Sonata started in early 2015 or late 2014, Hyundai probably didn't have accurate information about how many Sonatas would be demanded in September 2015. What made the matter more complicated was that Hyundai was making not just Sonata, but other car models, such as Grandeur, Avante, and SUV as well. Suppose that the sales seasons for these models also start at the same time, i.e., September, every year. Then, when Hyundai plans its production for the next season, it has to decide how many units of each model to make with the limited production capacity. The product mix decision has to be made early in the **production–sales cycle**.

Let's consider the example in Figure 8.24. The sales of new models will start in September next year. But, the production must start in November this year since Hyundai has a plant with a capacity of 100 cars (any type) per month and the company cannot idle its plant until it has more accurate information about the market demand. The company expects to get highly accurate information during the auto show to be held in Seoul in April next year. It is usual for potential buyers to place orders for specific car models during the auto show and such orders are reasonably binding, i.e., they are firm orders. We assume that the expected total market demand for the three models is about balanced with the company's total production capacity available for the ten months from November this year to August next year: both of them are about 1,000 cars combining the three models together.

Depending on how much information about the market demand (in particular, the demand mix) the company has, production capacity is divided into two: **speculative capacity** and **reactive capacity**. When the company has to make products without sufficiently accurate information, the capacity is a speculative capacity, whereas when there is accurate information available, it becomes a reactive capacity. In essence, the division between speculative and reactive is a relative, not absolute, concept. For instance, with the same physical capacity, a company can have more reactive capacity than other companies do, should it be able to gather the market information earlier than others. For our Hyundai example, the production capacity

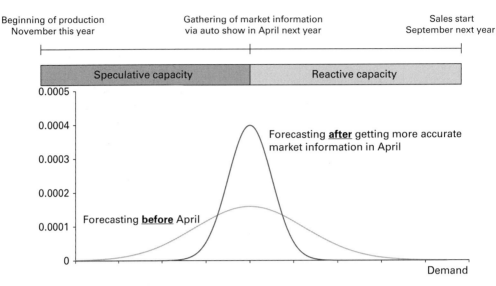

• Average and standard deviation of demand for each car type

Product Type	Before Getting Accurate Market Information		After Getting Accurate Market Information		Actual Demand
	Mean	Standard Deviation	Mean	Standard Deviation	
A – Avante	300	50	250	40	200
B – Sonata	500	200	320	30	300
C – SUV	200	300	430	90	500
Total mismatch	600		140		
Capacity available		500		500	

Figure 8.24 Accurate Response System – Speculative versus Reactive Capacity

the company can utilize from November this year to March next year is a speculative capacity since the company doesn't have accurate information about the market demand mix. On the contrary, the capacity available to Hyundai from April constitutes the company's reactive capacity. This demarcation is determined by when the company gathers the accurate information about market demand – the auto show in April next year.

Now return to the example in the table in Figure 8.24. In November this year, Hyundai has to decide how many cars of each type it has to make using its speculative capacity, i.e., before gathering the additional market information in April. Now look at the three types of car: "A" refers to the Avante model, B refers to the Sonata model, and C refers to the SUV model. Based on the historical demand information, as well as market survey outcomes, the company estimates the mean and standard deviation for each product's demand from September next year. The standard deviation represents the market demand uncertainty for the car type. According to the example, Avante has the least uncertainty associated with the market demand: it has the smallest standard deviation compared to the mean demand among the three types. On the other hand, SUV seems to be very uncertain, implying that its market demand is hard to forecast. At first glance, Sonata seems to have medium-level uncertainty compared with the other two. The size of speculative capacity is 500 cars regardless of the car types. Now Hyundai has to decide which models it has to plan making before April. Since the demand for Avante looks certain, it seems less risky to produce Avante even before getting additional information. On the other hand, the high uncertainty associated with the SUV's market demand implies that the chances are high that the market demand for SUVs will change significantly after April's auto show. Then, how should Hyundai plan its speculative production? Assuming that other conditions and factors remain the same or comparable, it makes more sense to produce Avante mainly by using the speculative capacity, while most of the Sonata and SUV production needs to be planned on the reactive capacity. Of course, it may not be wise to use the entire speculative capacity in making Avante only. Even if Avante has the least uncertainty, it still has a certain level of uncertainty, which must also be taken into account. Likewise, although the demands for SUV and Sonata seem quite uncertain, they also have a certain level of certainty. Therefore, an ideal production planning on the speculative capacity would look like making 250 of Avante, 150 of Sonata, and 100 of SUV. Of course, this is just an example, based on an intuitive judgment. Indeed, there exist more analytical methods that can help the company find optimal answers to this problem. Discussing such technical issues in detail is beyond the scope of our current discourse. However, it should be valid to say that the simple principle mentioned above underlies most of the analytical methods. Once the April auto show is finished, Hyundai would have more and better information about market demand composition.

Suppose that the information in Figure 8.24's table has the updated data. Hence, according to the accurate information from the auto show, Hyundai now believes that the mean demand for Avante will be 250, for Sonata 320, and for SUV 430. Since the company has already produced 250 of Avante using the speculative capacity, it probably doesn't want to make more Avante. Instead, the production plan to use the reactive capacity would be to make 170 of Sonata and 330 SUVs. In the end, the total mismatch will be 140: the company should have produced 50 Avantes fewer, 20 Sonatas fewer, and 70 SUVs more. Even if accurate response systems are applied, it is not possible to completely eliminate the mismatch. But, still the chances are that the magnitude of mismatch can be significantly reduced!

Hyundai's example sheds light on a regular matching relationship between the capacity characteristics and the product uncertainties. Figure 8.25 shows such a relationship. Other things being comparable (or remaining unchanged), it makes sense to use the speculative capacity for making products with low uncertainty, whereas it seems better to use the reactive capacity for making products with high uncertainty. Again, there are more sophisticated and analytical methods to determine exactly how many of each product should be scheduled using which type of capacity. Although as mentioned already we don't get into that level of detail, the reasoning outlined so far should give the company sufficient insights to understand how it should approach this kind of issue.

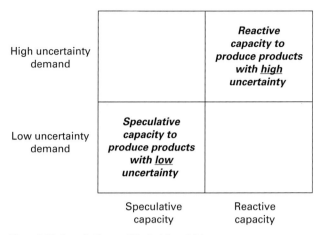

High uncertainty demand		*Reactive capacity to produce products with <u>high</u> uncertainty*
Low uncertainty demand	*Speculative capacity to produce products with <u>low</u> uncertainty*	
	Speculative capacity	Reactive capacity

Figure 8.25 Capacity Type and Product Uncertainty

Levers to increase the firm's reactive capacity. The terminology used in this section is a little misleading. In general, people would relate the word "reactive" to "passive," "slow," or even "inflexible." But, in the context of accurate response systems, reactive simply implies that the decision-maker *reacts* to the more accurate information, and the capacity planned after this information is collected is the *reactive* capacity. In fact, between speculative and reactive capacity, the reactive one is more flexible in that the company can *flexibly* adjust the production quantities of various products in a way to reflect the newly gathered information. Therefore, other things being equal, a unit of reactive capacity should be more valuable than a unit of speculative capacity. Therefore, the company generally tries to increase its reactive capacity.

There are several levers the company can utilize to effectively increase its reactive capacity (Figure 8.26). The company can have more "effective" reactive capacity by reducing the set-up times and/or using smaller batch sizes. If it takes less time to change from making one model to making another, the company will have more time to actually make products. Thus, the shorter **set-up time** means more capacity. A batch means the size of production that needs to be started and finished together within a relevant time range. For example, if the **batch size** for Sonata is 100, the company can make Sonata only in multiples of 100, e.g., 100, 200, 300, and so on. Consider the example in this section, where the production plan to use the reactive capacity would be to make 170 of Sonata and 330 of SUV. But, suppose that the batch size for both vehicles is 100. Then, the company probably cannot make 170 or 330 cars. Instead, it may have to make 100 Sonatas and 400 SUVs, or 200 Sonatas and 300 SUVs. Either option will cause the mismatch between demand and supply to grow. It is obvious that the company will have more flexibility and therefore increase the "effective" capacity if the batch size is 10 rather than 100.

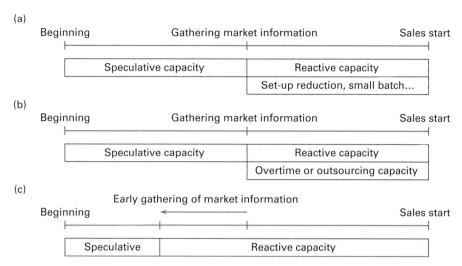

Figure 8.26 Ways to Increase Reactive Capacity

Although these two approaches – reducing the set-up times and reducing the batch size – are useful in increasing the reactive capacity, they are also applicable to other general situations. These two methods are general approaches to increase the effective size of capacity under most operations contexts. Another generic approach is to use overtime and/or outsource part of production to other companies. How effective this approach can be depends on whether the company is maintaining a strategic partnership in its supply chain. In this sense, the firm's ability to implement accurate response systems is a supply chain capability that must be supported by other partners in the supply chain.

Finally, the more direct and perhaps more demanding approach is to gather accurate market information early. As alluded to already, the categorization of speculative *versus* reactive capacity is not an absolute concept. It is a relative definition. We call capacity "reactive" when we use that capacity after getting more accurate information. Should the company find effective ways to gather such information much earlier than now, it will have more reactive capacity, which is more valuable than the speculative capacity. It is always possible for the company to gather information earlier, but there is no guarantee that such information is better and more accurate; merely gathering information early is not enough. In order to reap the benefit of earlier information gathering, the company must be able to maintain the high quality of information, i.e., it should not compromise the information quality while gathering the information early. A possible way is to give an incentive to the buyer, who places a concrete order early. Consequently, the issue of accurate response systems relates to the firm's overall capability to deal with the market uncertainty including its ability to make a reliable forecasting, ability to design and implement an incentive system to motivate the customer to provide more dependable information, ability to plan and coordinate with its supply chain partners effectively, and the like.

8.2.4   Product-Mix Flexibility: Value and Structure

While discoursing the structural dimension of SCM in Chapter 4, we briefly discussed flexibility as the firm's ability to cope with uncertainty. It is possible to group demand uncertainty into two types – aggregate and product mix. In this section, we focus on the product-mix level uncertainty and examine how flexibility helps the firm deal with the uncertainty.

Process flexibility or **product-mix flexibility** is the firm's ability to appropriately adjust its product mix as the market demand changes. Suppose a company operates four plants, A, B, C, and D, to manufacture four different products, a, b, c, and d. If the firm doesn't have any process flexibility, i.e., it has **zero flexibility**, each plant can make only one type of product. In contrast, when the firm has perfect process flexibility, i.e., **100 percent flexibility**, each plant can make any of the four different products in any combination if necessary. In between these two extreme cases, i.e., zero and 100 percent flexibility, is **partial flexibility**, which enables all or some of the plants to make two or more different product types. We ask two questions: What is the **value of flexibility**, i.e., how can the firm define the value of flexibility? How much flexibility, e.g., partial or 100 percent flexibility, does the firm need?

Regarding the first question, Jordan and Graves[3] put forth the value of flexibility as defined by two factors, expected sales and utilization, both of which are desirable performance measures. That is, the larger the expected sales, the better; the higher the utilization, the better.

To answer the second question, consider an example in Figure 8.27: currently, each plant has the capacity to make 1,000 units of one product type only, i.e., the firm has zero process flexibility; the market demands 800 units of product a, 1,200 units of b, 1,400 units of c, and 600 units of d. At the current state, the firm achieves expected sales (s_0) of 3,400 units and a utilization (u_0) of 0.85. Let's examine two different strategies the firm can take, one with changing capacity and the other with increasing flexibility.

Strategy to adjust capacity. In order to increase expected sales or utilization, the firm can adjust its capacity. Suppose the firm adds more capacity in a bid to increase the expected sales: now each plant has an increased capacity to produce 1,200 units, but still doesn't have flexibility so that each plant can make only one product type. Assuming the demand pattern remains the same, the firm now achieves increased expected sales (s_+) of 3,800 units, but the utilization (u_+) is decreased from 0.85 to 0.79. Now, consider the opposite decision: the firm cuts the capacity, hoping to increase utilization. If each plant's capacity is reduced to 800 with the demand intact, the firm achieves a higher utilization (u_-) of 0.94, but the expected sales (s_-) decrease to 3,000 units. Although highly hypothetical, the simple example demonstrates that the firm may not overcome the trade-off between expected sales and utilization by adjusting its capacity only.

---

[3] W. C. Jordan and S. C. Graves, "Principles on the Benefits of Manufacturing Process Flexibility" (1995) 41 (4) *Management Science* 577–594.

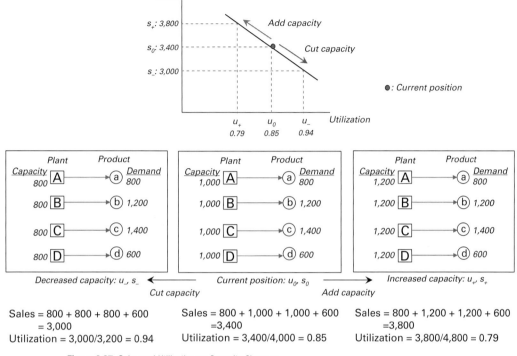

Figure 8.27 Sales and Utilization as Capacity Changes

Strategy to increase flexibility. What happens if the firm decides to deal with the situation by improving its flexibility? Figure 8.28 describes an example of partial flexibility: the firm improves flexibility for plant C and D only so that now plant C can make two product types, b and c, while plant D can make c and d. If the firm indeed implements such an improvement without altering the current capacity, it will be able to attain expected sales (s_F) of 3,800 and a utilization (u_F) of 0.95, both of which are improvements over the values, i.e., 3,400 and 0.85, respectively, at the current state. It is important to note that the firm can mitigate the trade-off between expected sales and utilization by improving flexibility; as the firm improves its flexibility, the curve defining the relationship between expected sales and utilization is expanding outward in a convex shape as depicted in Figure 8.28.

Returning to the second question, how much flexibility is needed? For the particular example discussed above, if the firm adds a little more flexibility, it can attain full expected sales, i.e., 4,000, and also a perfect utilization, i.e., 1.0: for instance, this can be done by allowing plant A to make product b in addition to a. Although this arrangement is also partial flexibility, it is higher "partial flexibility" than the one presented in Figure 8.28. What about the complete, i.e., 100 percent, flexibility, which enables each plant to make any combination of four product types? In fact, the perfect flexibility doesn't perform better than the "higher" partial flexibility mentioned above. That is, in

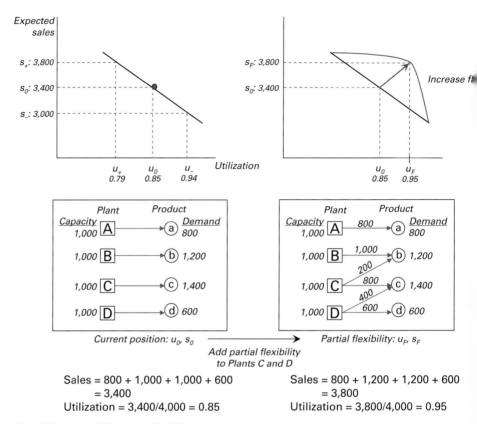

Figure 8.28 Sales and Utilization as Flexibility Increases

many cases, partial flexibility is as good as **perfect flexibility**. Considering the extra costs, which are sometimes excessive, to accomplish 100 percent flexibility, however, it is more effective or economical for the firm to design partial flexibility into its supply chain, in order to achieve a result as good as that attained through perfect flexibility.

Discussion Questions

1. How does the uncertainty associated with the demand for a product change as the product evolves through its product life cycle? How should the firm's supply chain strategy cope with such a change in uncertainty?

2. What is the concept of "time-based competition"? How did the concept affect the firm's new product development strategy?

3. Define the "cross-functional team (CFT)" approach to new product development. What are the main advantages and disadvantages of the approach?

4. How might the CFT approach minimize the mismatch between the managerial attention allocation pattern and the flexibility to fix problems in new product development?

5. Define "design for serviceability" and "design for recyclability." Why are these concepts going to be critical in the near future?

6. How can a company decide whether the CFT approach is better than other approaches?

7. What should the company do to make a transition from the cognitive to the behavioral change in the organization? Answer this question in the context of implementing the CFT approach.

8. What are the pros and cons of VMI (vendor-managed inventory) from the vendor's perspective?

9. Where do the benefits of postponement come from? What are the fundamental conditions for implementing the postponement strategy?

10. Explain how the accurate response system enables the company to achieve responsiveness.

11. What are the differences and similarities between postponement and the accurate response system?

12. Explain why there is a trade-off between expected sales and capacity utilization in the context of process flexibility.

13. How does a partial flexibility help the firm achieve as much benefit as the full flexibility does?

14. What are the key factors to determine the level of a firm's flexibility?

案例 CASE STUDY 8.1
Using Supplier Relationships to Serve Customers Better: Marks & Spencer

To compete in today's modern retail environment, an organization depends more than ever on its ability to develop business opportunities as and when they arise. A key element in developing a business strategy is for decision-makers to build on the unique elements which help that organization to do well.

Understanding and building on this capability is particularly important in ensuring that the core strengths and competencies of the organization not only fit the business environment, but also help to develop it further and faster than its competitors. This strategic capability to respond to changing conditions will help counter threats to the organization's development.

Marks & Spencer (M&S) aims to become the world's leading volume retailer with a global brand and global recognition. Its unique retailing formula has already enabled the company to enter a large number of markets around the world. M&S owns no factories and does not make the goods which are sold in its stores. The core competence at the heart of this formula, which provides many advantages over competitors, is that of the supplier relationship.

All organizations have to obtain resources in order to provide goods and services. This is known as the supply chain. M&S has a policy of buying and dealing directly with suppliers. This partnership spans the whole supply chain, including producers and raw material suppliers. It is a symbiotic relationship – the organizations work together and depend on each other for success. The strength of these relationships has provided M&S with many advantages over its competitors. These advantages, in turn, lead to benefits for customers, such as better product quality, value, availability, and constancy of supply.

This case study focuses on how this special relationship with the supply base enables M&S to serve customers better. The lingerie market will be used as an example.

Market position. When looking at an organization's competitive position, it is important to understand the opportunities that exist within a market, as well as other competitive threats. A market can be defined as: *"a collection of individuals and organizations who are actual or potential buyers of a product or service."* The market environment in which organizations compete is usually known as the micro-environment. This refers to all the factors that influence an organization's activities in a market, such as changes in the needs and expectations of customers, as well as patterns of competition.

Lingerie is a market which incorporates both core and fashion products – changing consumer trends and tastes influence the type and nature of products produced and required. As a result, organizations must constantly develop new product concepts in response to customer demand. If an organization does not meet these demands and expectations, it will fail. For a company like M&S, building on one year's product successes presents a challenge for the following year, while products which have been less successful will leave gaps to fill and areas to develop.

Decision-makers at M&S cannot afford to be complacent when developing goods for such a market. Sound judgment, experience, and entrepreneurial flair are all required to understand the complex cycle of the fashion market.

Source: Reprinted with permission from Business Case Studies LLP.

The lingerie market in the United Kingdom is worth more than £1.75 billion. M&S has a 40 percent share of this market and is, therefore, a clear market leader. However, the improved performance of competitors and new entrants to the industry mean M&S must strengthen its position. Consolidating a market position is concerned with strengthening and further developing that position – it does not mean standing still. Competencies, such as mutually advantageous supplier relationships, must be continually developed to improve competitive advantage.

Integration of the supply chain. The common objectives for M&S and its suppliers are to:

- increase sales;
- minimize stocks;
- minimize commitment; and
- maximize flexibility.

The key to doing this has been to manage, or integrate, the supply chain so that both M&S and its suppliers are working toward the same business objectives. Communication is therefore important between all parts of the chain to ensure that the differences between demand from customers and the suppliers' ability to meet such demand can be minimized.

Developing supplier relationships: M&S's ability to respond quickly to changing customer needs lies with mutually advantageous relationships developed with suppliers throughout the supply chain. Many of the suppliers have seen their businesses grow alongside that of M&S. The strength of these relationships and the mutual trust and support each provides is a critical element for the development of each business.

An important element in managing this supply chain is "fairness." Working closely with a limited number of suppliers involves helping each of them to meet their own business aspirations, but not at the expense of other key suppliers. The starting point for managing the supply chain is to coordinate M&S's business strategy with each of the suppliers' business plans. This will provide the structure and direction for each supplier to follow.

M&S's strategic objectives are to develop all new products so that they:

- fully satisfy the customer in terms of comfort and fit;
- are available at the required time;
- are clearly specified so that they can be launched into any manufacturing site; and
- provide the maximum benefits permitted by each design.

The beginning-of-season strategy meeting provides suppliers with the opportunity to discuss their expectations with M&S, such as the areas of business they would like to grow. It also enables M&S's decision-makers to provide suppliers with a realistic assessment of where they need to develop. Discussions at this stage may broach issues such as how to encourage others to take their products further forward and how to spread knowledge.

At the heart of this process is integrity. It is important that all parties are dealt with in a fair and equitable way which sustains relationships to provide long-term business opportunities and developments.

Supplier strategy: For many lingerie suppliers, M&S is often their main customer. These relationships are interdependent – M&S depends on the capabilities of its suppliers to help meet customer requirements. If M&S is successful in meeting the needs of its customers, then the suppliers will also reap the benefits and rewards.

Planning a business strategy with suppliers helps to provide a clearer brief for all parties involved in the process of supply. Interim meetings provide a useful opportunity for suppliers to provide feedback from trade fairs and discuss trend predictions. Much of the information provided for these meetings is market-driven. Working with suppliers enables M&S to combine its own experience with that of suppliers to identify new product ranges which will fit in well with other existing product ranges.

Meetings with suppliers help to provide a clear structure for the range of products at an early stage. They also identify key issues, e.g., which fabrics to use, technical priorities, and establishing the number of products which will be bought for that season. It is important that potential problems are foreseen and solved. More detailed meetings earlier mean less crisis management later.

Meetings also involve discussions on the development of the previous season's products so that priorities can be established for the forthcoming year. This might include:

- sales patterns;
- trends in the market and fashions;
- color palette and theme boards;
- yarns, fabrics, trims, and components; and
- the general shape, fit, and direction of the range.

The buying process. Members of the buying team work with either primary suppliers who manufacture garments or secondary suppliers who provide the fabrics as part of the range-building process. By working with suppliers throughout the buying process, M&S's contribution to the finished product is all encompassing. The buying team comprises the following:

1. **Selectors** work closely with M&S's design group and suppliers, and are responsible for offering choice to customers and delivering it into stores on time. Doing this involves considerable research in order to keep up to date with the latest trends.
2. **Merchandisers** are responsible for profitability. Their role involves negotiating prices, estimating the quantities needed, sales analysis, and scheduling the production with manufacturers and suppliers.
3. **Technologists** develop and monitor specifications and quality control systems. They act as technical advisors to the selectors and merchandisers, as well as to manufacturers. They also work on long-term projects with secondary suppliers which provide the business with advances in manufacturing and fabrics.

Nicola Lewis is a selector for M&S. She began working for the company after leaving university. Beginning her career in Stores, she has now moved into the Buying Group. Nicola helps to compile a well-balanced range of products which will appeal to M&S's core customer base, but which also has plenty of newness to move the range forward. Managing the supply base involves two buying cycles based on two seasons, Autumn and Spring. It involves working up to 18 months ahead.

Developing and cementing relationships with suppliers is central to Nicola's role as a selector at M&S. Working in a fast-changing business environment with a broad mix of personalities and characters, she feels that by building relationships that encourage people to be individuals, they become a source of creativity and innovation. Working with suppliers provides Nicola with independence and empowerment to manage a project. It also involves being a member of a team focused on meeting customer needs.

Fabric suppliers come from across the world. Discussions enable designers to share their ideas and discuss innovations in a way which helps them to become more competitive. After careful analysis, which involves assessing the design, production viability, and cost, white sealing takes place. This is the preselection of prototypes which meet the criteria with the intention to buy.

M&S selectors, merchandisers, and technologists then work with each supplier to help prepare products to meet the high standards necessary for the stores. This involves the following:

- **first fit**, which provides information and measurements establishing the base size for the style;
- **pre-production** meetings to discuss production viability of M&S standards and confirmation of packaging details;
- **test lots**, which confirm the viability of patterns, as well as make-up methods and standards;
- **grades**, which approve dimensions and fit of sizes identified; and
- **wearer trials**, which assess the performance of garments in customer use (the fit, fabric, trims, colors, and labels are all important for this final stage of development).

Courtaulds Textiles is a large textile company which, as a major supplier, has had a relationship with M&S that goes back more than fifty years. Staff at Courtaulds Textiles work closely with those at M&S through shared goals and values. If a product range is successful for M&S, then Courtaulds Textiles will also reap the rewards.

Courtaulds Textiles believes that M&S's demands for excellence have helped it to become a better manufacturer. Working with staff at M&S has led employees at Courtaulds Textiles to recognize that the customer is constantly looking for newness.

This has stimulated investment and innovation, which has in turn fueled the market toward technological and scientific development. At the same time, wider policies such as quality and environmental standards have helped Courtaulds Textiles to become a better business.

Standards and quality. Green sealing the product is the term used when the product is bought and owned by M&S. It is the standard used to authorize bulk production. To meet the stringent requirements for M&S, products must be the very best that design, technology, and manufacturing can achieve. This provides real, practical benefits for the final customer.

Specifications and standards are established which enable everybody involved with the garments to understand the requirements. Monitoring specifications, standards, and quality involves working closely with suppliers, with cooperation throughout the supply chain.

- Specifications are those aspects of a product which can be realistically measured or assessed, such as the quality of raw materials used, product dimensions, and product performance.

- A standard is a physical example agreed between a customer and a supplier.
- Quality refers to the individual characteristics of each product that enable it to satisfy customers. For an organization like M&S, quality is particularly important in providing a framework which enables M&S products to develop a competitive advantage over rivals.

One important link in the relationship between M&S and Courtaulds Textiles is the exchange of electronic data using Electronic Data Interchange (EDI). Courtaulds Textiles helped to develop the system with M&S. The system transfers information, such as prices, images, and product details, between each organization's computer systems.

Another key development has been the increased use of video-conferencing, which, by linking garment suppliers and raw material suppliers to M&S, has helped to improve communication and reduce lead times.

Conclusion. As the leading company in lingerie retailing, M&S has set benchmarks for the whole industry to follow. Although the company has a large market share, it faces fierce competition from other top retailers.

The key element in furthering its competitive advantage has been the development of strong supplier relationships. Through management of the supply chain, M&S has clearly differentiated its activities within the industry to create a dynamic and responsive lingerie business which recognizes people as a source of innovation.

Questions
1. Characterize M&S's business objectives as well as its competitive market position.
2. Define "integration of the supply chain" from the company's perspective. How important is it in enabling the company to be competitive in the market?
3. Describe the company's buying process in detail. Does it help the company to be competitive in the market? Why or why not?
4. What are the potential benefits of linking the company's information system with its suppliers?

CHAPTER 9

Innovation and Technology

Technology consists of knowledge, procedures, and devices, both conceptual and physical, and is also a mechanism used for **problem solving**. **Innovation** is often defined as **new combination**. Therefore, technological innovation is new combination of knowledge, procedures, devices, and problem-solving mechanisms. It has been touted as the biggest force driving economic development and prosperity. Technological innovation has also enabled the company to achieve highly sophisticated coordination with its supply chain partners. Since coordination is at the center of supply chain management, it is true to say that most of the recent development in SCM can be attributed to technological innovation, especially **internet-based technology**. As such, in this chapter, we review important technological innovations that have been closely related with improvements in operations and supply chain management. Our fundamental premise is that technology cannot be understood independent of organization, i.e., technology and organization must interact with each other and evolve together in order to accomplish an optimal result from technological innovation. It should be valid for supply chain management as well. We elaborate the premise from the learning perspective covered in Chapter 2.

Key Learning Points

- Technological innovation is "new combination of knowledge, procedures, and devices, both conceptual and physical, and also a mechanism of problem solving."
- Creativity is the driving force behind technological innovation.
- A disruptive technological innovation replaces the old technology and starts a brand-new technology life cycle, which may not be tangent to the old technology life cycle, i.e., there is a huge discontinuity between the two. It is so dramatic that it changes any existing rules of competitive advantage in the market.
- Contrary to the disruptive technology, an incremental technological innovation is a continuous improvement of the old, existing technology.
- Technological innovation shrinks the product life cycle, which in turn causes technological innovation to occur faster.
- Technological innovation has had impacts on supply chain management significantly over the years.
- Fidelity is the level of structural and infrastructural congruence between the development environment and the implementation environment. In order to

achieve the performance improvement by implementing the technological innovation as expected, the company must maintain a high level of fidelity between the two environments.

- Mutual adaptation or co-evolution of technology and organization is the most effective way to apply new technology to an existing organization.
- An innovation system is a dynamic framework, consisting of culture, top management, organization, and process.
- In new product development, the top management's role is to define the feasible direction when it becomes necessary to set up a milestone.
- To make the "failure-is-accepted" culture possible, the company should have a knowledge management system that enables it to learn from its failures.

學 WISDOM BOX 9.1
Wisdom and Insights

Can We Teach Creativity?

Schumpeter defined innovation as new combination. Confucius discussed a similar concept (Figure 9.1), "Revitalize the old to know the new, then you are truly a teacher!" A literal translation would say, "If you warm the old so as to know the new, you deserve to be a teacher!" What did he mean by "warm the old" or "revitalize the old"? Some interpret it as "learn from the old knowledge, people, events, and things." Although we agree with the interpretation in general, we believe what Confucius meant is larger than that. We would say that in order to know the new, we should first make the "old knowledge, people, events, and things, which are largely dormant at the present time" relevant to the present by warming or revitalizing them, e.g., shuffling the status quo or making a new combination of them. Therefore, Confucius defined "innovation (to know the new)" as "to revitalize the old (to make a new combination of the old)."

溫故而知新 可以爲師矣
Revitalize the old to know the new, then you are truly a teacher!

Figure 9.1 Confucius's View on Innovation – a Free or Truthful Translation

Technological innovation is "new combination of knowledge, procedures, and devices, both conceptual and physical, and also a mechanism of problem solving." Then, what is behind technological innovation? **Creativity**! Creativity is much related to the human capacity to think differently or outside constraints such as conventions, traditions, norms, and institutional boundaries. There are two different types of creativity, **artistic creativity** and **business creativity**. Think about great artists like Beethoven, Mozart, and Picasso. They all embodied creativity. How about Apple's Steve Jobs? Many people often said that Jobs was a role model of creativity. Are these two examples of creativity the same? Most likely, the answer is "No." We postulate that

Box continues

the former is "artistic creativity," while the latter is "business creativity." These two types of creativity share commonalities, e.g., both are rooted on the human capacity or ability to think differently or out of the box and both are making or creating things, tangible or intangible, invaluable to human society. Despite these important similarities, however, they are also quite different from each other.

What are the main differences between the two types of creativity? First, artistic creativity never puts forth **commercialization** as its ultimate goal, whereas business creativity should pursue it as the most essential objective. In fact, without a commercial success, business creativity means very little. As such, business creativity usually targets a mass market for commercialization: of course, one can say that there is indeed certain business creativity that tries to serve a niche market, e.g., luxury fashion customers, but still such a case is effectively focusing on a "relatively" mass market, compared to that for pure artistic creativity. A corollary following the first arguments is about a due date. Artistic creativity is not constrained by a due date, whereas business creativity must meet a due date, e.g., a commercial launching date. For example, Apple should plan its launching date for an innovative product like iPhone on a global scale, i.e., when to introduce the new iPhone to which market around the globe. In fact, how to arrange the new product launching dates across the world affects the company's commercial success and eventually its profitability. On the contrary, a great artist like Beethoven or Picasso pays little attention to the time constraint. For example, Picasso could have completed a masterpiece in a day or never been able to complete a simple picture in ten or twenty years, i.e., it could have taken as long as he would have wanted. The time was just not a factor for him! In a similar vein, artistic creativity rarely tries to get a fast or quick outcome, whereas business creativity prefers a fast or quick result as long as other conditions like a minimum quality are not severely compromised.

Another big difference between the two creativities is concerned with **teamwork**. In general, an artist is a solo player, who thinks, works, and creates alone as a free, unattached soul. On the contrary, business creativity should be supported and carried out by a group of individuals, i.e., a team. We already learned how important it is for the company to form a cross-functional team to develop an innovative product. Artistic creativity is rooted on individual ingenuity, say a genius, whereas business creativity can be embodied only by a team consisting of individuals with diverse backgrounds and capabilities.

All of these critical differences are summarized in Table 9.1. So what? One question we want to ask is, *"Is it possible to teach creativity?"* It depends! Considering all of these differences and unique characteristics, it seems very clear that we CANNOT teach artistic creativity beyond a certain very limited level. But, then, how about business creativity? To a much larger extent, we hope and also believe that we can teach business creativity as long as we can garner appropriate ingredients such as the right people, effective leadership, and optimal sets of resources and incentive mechanisms. After all, a great company should know how to make "creativity" a part of everyday business, not a special case.

Box continues

Table 9.1 Comparison between Artistic Creativity and Business Creativity

Attribute	Artistic Creativity	Business Creativity
Commercialization goal	No	Yes
Mass market	No (a small, sophisticated one)	Yes (should appeal to the masses)
Due date	No	Yes
Fast outcomes?	No (not in general)	Yes (quick market result)
Individual ingenuity	Yes (prerequisite)	Yes, but only one factor
Teamwork	No (not usually)	Yes (mostly)
Teachable?	No (not in general)	Yes (possibly)

Questions

1. Is it possible to integrate artistic creativity and business creativity? What should the company do in order to accomplish such an integration?
2. Some say innovation is "connecting the dots." What does this mean?

9.1 Disruptive Technological Innovation

There is an important concept in defining technology, i.e., continuous versus disruptive technological innovation. Like a product life cycle, technology evolves or develops along a technology life cycle (Figure 9.2). That is, technology follows a path from an initial or introductory stage, growth, maturity, to declining stage. Once it reaches the declining stage, the technology faces a few possible fates, much like a product does. It may disappear completely, i.e., it becomes so obsolete that it can no longer perform any valuable function. It may prolong itself, i.e., although it becomes old, it may still be creating value, possibly because a new technology does not yet function economically enough to replace the old sufficiently. The last possibility is that a significant technological innovation occurs, replaces the old technology, and starts a brand-new technology life cycle. If the new technological innovation is so dramatic that it changes any existing rules of competitive advantage in the market, the new technology life cycle may not be tangential to the old technology life cycle, i.e., there is a huge discontinuity between the two. Such a technological innovation is a **disruptive technological innovation**. The gap between the old and the new technology life cycle is a **competence-destroying discontinuity**, which implies that the difference or gap between the two technologies is so large that any existing rules or principles valid under the old technology are no longer applicable in the market dominated by the new technological innovation.

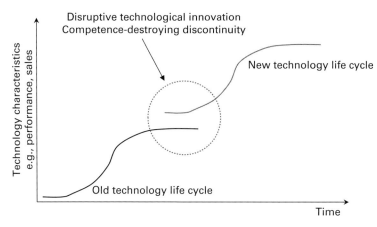

Figure 9.2 Disruptive Technological Innovation

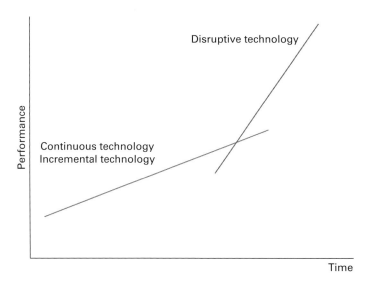

Figure 9.3 Incremental versus Disruptive Technological Innovation

Contrary to the disruptive technology, an incremental innovation is a continuous improvement of the old existing technology. For an **incremental technological innovation**, it is possible to predict the improvement speed or path, since the performance improvement rate is consistent with the previously valid one. In Figure 9.3, there are two linear lines, one with a smaller slope, which increases gradually, and the other with a larger slope, which increases steeply. The "gradually increasing" line depicts an improvement path of incremental technological innovation, whereas the "steeply increasing" line shows an improvement path of discontinuous or disruptive technological innovation. The big difference between incremental or continuous technology and disruptive or discontinuous technology is concerned with the

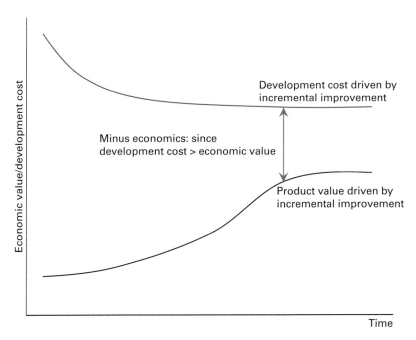

Figure 9.4 Product Value and Cost

improvement rate, i.e., the slope of the linear line. The disruptive technology is called "disruptive," since its improvement rate is much larger than that of the previous "incremental" technology. That is, the disruptive technology's improvement rate is so drastically large that it is so much better than that of the existing technology and nullifies the current rules of competition, which have been a norm under the present "continuous" technology.

How can a disruptive technological innovation be embodied? Technology is embodied in either a product or a service. Consider an example in Figure 9.4, where there are two curves: one depicting an evolutionary path of the development cost to make the product and the other showing an evolutionary path of the product's value or utility from the customer's perspective. Note that these evolutionary paths are driven by incremental or continuous technological innovation. The case in Figure 9.4 implies that the true economic value of the product is negative. That is, the product does not have any value from the market's standpoint, since the production cost is larger than the economic value derived from the product throughout the relevant time horizon, although the gap between the two becomes narrower due to the incremental innovation or improvement, which is not big enough to close the gap completely.

Then, what does a disruptive technological innovation mean in this case? Disruptive technological innovation can have an impact in two areas – product value and cost. Figure 9.5 shows a case where a disruptive technological innovation enhances the product value significantly and thus makes it economically viable for the company to produce the product. On the contrary, a disruptive technological innovation can also

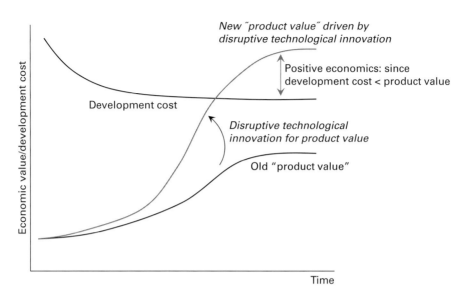

Figure 9.5 Disruptive Technology for Product Value

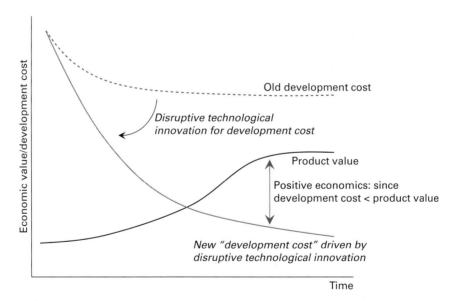

Figure 9.6 Disruptive Technology for Development Cost

reduce the production cost so significantly that it makes it economic to produce the product (Figure 9.6). **Product innovation** is concerned with technological innovation to enhance the product value, while **process innovation** is concerned with technological innovation to reduce the production cost. Both types of technological innovation can play an important role in making it economically viable to produce and sell the product in the market.

9.2   Technology and Supply Chain Management

Although innovation can be succinctly defined as "new combination," we would like to have a more detailed definition, which can guide the manager's decision more practically. From a managerial perspective, innovation should be improvement that enables the company to stay at an irreplaceable "competitive" position in spite of constant and incessant threats from competitors in the market. As discussed earlier in this chapter, such an innovation can be either incremental or disruptive. What do we mean by an **irreplaceable competitive position**? Being irreplaceable is being difficult or even almost impossible for others to imitate, while being competitive implies having a strong and potent competitive advantage vis-à-vis competitors.

Why is it more useful for us to define innovation in such a way? By defining innovation as improvement that helps the company stay at an irreplaceable competitive position, we can avoid too much focus on the "newness" of innovation. Consider a few cases. Many people would agree that Apple (www.apple.com) is an innovative company, probably because it has constantly developed "new" products such as iPod, iPad, and iPhone. That is, Apple is an ultimate role model of innovation. Then, how about **Klais**? In fact, not many people readily recognize the name "Klais," which has been the world's best organ manufacturer for more than 130 years (www.orgelbau-klais.com). The company has handcrafted organs with the utmost precision and quality, which have never been challenged in the market. Nevertheless, people might hesitate a little in saying the company is an innovator, mostly because the company has been making only one product, the organ, for over a century, i.e., it has never developed a "new" product. Our definition of innovation (staying at an irreplaceable competitive position), however, enables us to call a company an innovator even without creating new products or services all the time. That is, as long as the company successfully makes an effort to improve in order to stay at the superlative competitive position for a long period of time, it does deserve to be called an innovator.

As such, our definition of innovation is more comprehensive and encompassing than the succinct "new combination" is. On the one hand, it acknowledges an innovative company like Apple, which is creating new products all the time through **radical innovation**, i.e., a radical new combination of existing resources or materials, processes, and capabilities. On the other hand, it also views a company like Klais as an innovator, which has been constantly improving and perfecting its current products or services in order to stay at the forefront of competition in the market.

9.2.1   Technology and PLC

Technological innovation is one of the most important forces that shape the competition dynamics in management. It is also closely related to supply chain management. The most conspicuous relationship between technological innovation and SCM emerges via the PLC. Figure 9.7 shows a product life cycle and its associated **price premium curve**. As the product matures, its potential (say, bargaining power) to charge the

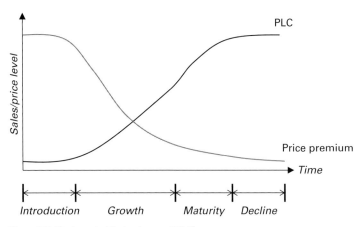

Figure 9.7 The Impact of Technology on PLC (1)

customer a higher price decreases. For example, when the product is first introduced to the market, it might be a new and improved product, from which the customer can enjoy unique and/or enhanced utility and satisfaction different from that derived from old or existent products. Therefore, the customer is willing to pay a high price in order to buy and consume the new product.

But, as the market grows, more competitors enter the market and intensify the competition, which pushes down the price curve. In fact, another explanation is equally convincing. In order to grow in the market, the firm has to make its product attractive or appealing to more customers: the easiest or perhaps most effective way to do so is to reduce the price. These two explanations are complementary in essence. Competitors enter the market when they see premiums enjoyed by the early entrants. In order to compete in the given market, they probably have to compete on price and thus drive the price down. Or in order to stay in the crowded market, firms have to make their products appeal to more customers by reducing their prices. There are two dynamics interacting simultaneously. On the one hand, the fierce competition drives the price down. On the other hand, the firm's desire to grow pushes the price down. It is pointless to differentiate one force from the other: they are combined to shape the price curve. As the product enters a more mature stage, it becomes a sort of commodity, which in general cannot exert any pricing power. Therefore, as the product passes through the mature and decline stages, the price premium curve tumbles to the bottom.

These days, it seems in general that the PLC has shrunk. Figure 9.8 shows what it means to have a **shrunken PLC**. In fact, we are seeing a **shortened PLC**; other things being equal, the product reaches its mature and decline stages much faster than before. Why has the PLC been shortened? Studies point out technological innovation as the primary cause. As the technological innovation becomes frequent and dynamic, the company can more afford to offer its customers lower prices and thus the price premium curve shrinks first. As the price curve shrinks, it actually brings the PLC down with it. Figure 9.9 shows such a mechanism.

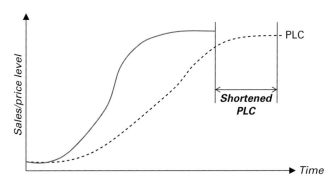

Figure 9.8 The Impact of Technology on PLC (2)

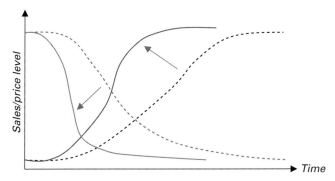

Figure 9.9 The Impact of Technology on PLC (3)

Of course, the true reason that the PLC has been shortened could be more than just such a technological innovation. The more basic question would be, *Why should there be any technological innovation in the first place?* First, maybe the customers themselves have become so much more sophisticated that they demand products with features that can be made from more advanced technological innovation. Or the fierce competition among the incumbents and the entrants in the market forces the companies to compete in R&D and therefore the technological innovation is fueled by such hyper competition. Another plausible explanation can be simpler: there has been technological innovation because there *can* be technological innovation. That is, such innovations have been in large part by-products of general scientific advancements in the economy and society: the companies are simply given opportunities to utilize such technological advancements in making their commercialized products. Finally, some people want to find a solid explanation inside the manager's mind. They regard a manager as an entrepreneur at heart. The manager is born to pursue innovation in her life. As an entrepreneur, she wants to make her company grow in the market and the natural way to make sure that this happens is to pursue technological innovation relentlessly.

To us, all of the explanations above point out the same thing: market competition, the manager's propensity to grow, and technological innovation are all combined to force

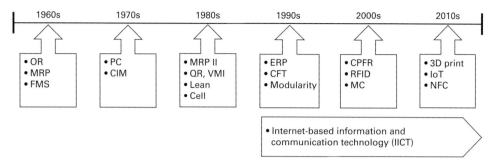

Figure 9.10 Evolution of SCM Technology and Key Concepts

the shortening of the PLC, and the shortened PLC in turn makes the dynamic interplay among these forces even mightier. So far in this section, we have established how the technological innovation affects the PLC. Based on our discussion in the previous chapters, one should be able to see how the changes in the PLC caused by technological innovation could have a huge impact on the strategic decisions the firm has to make for effective supply chain management.

9.2.2   Evolution of SCM Technology and Key Concepts

As discussed above, technological innovation has been closely linked with development in supply chain management. Although the technological innovation for supply chain coordination has proliferated more recently, say in the 1990s, we review the evolution of technological innovation from the 1960s, when technological tools for operations management started emerging more formally (Figure 9.10). Note that we consider *not only* purely technical or technological tools, *but also* more managerial or conceptual methodologies as part of technological innovation. For a more structured review, we divide the time line into six epochs, each lasting roughly ten years (Table 9.2).

1960s. This is the period of "**scientific methodologies**" applied to management. First, OR (**operations research**) methodologies were developed and fully applied to operations management. Many tried to solve optimization problems in inventory and routing or transportation. In 1964, **MRP (material requirements planning)** was introduced. It focused on topics like production planning, scheduling, and inventory control. As manufacturing flexibility was perceived as critical for coping with market uncertainty, **FMS (flexible manufacturing system)** was developed and patented in 1965.

1970s. This is the time period when the computer became an integral part of management. Computing power multiplied in the 1970s. As the PC (personal computer) or desktop computer became widely utilized, almost a revolutionary change occurred in management, in particular, every aspect of operations such as design, analysis, control, and the like. In this period, **CIM (computer integrated manufacturing)** was fully

Table 9.2 SCM Technology and Key Concepts

Period	SCM Technology and Key Concepts
1960s	• OR (operations research) methodologies applied to operations management • Focused on solving optimization problems in inventory and routing or transportation • In 1964, MRP (material requirements planning) introduced, focused on topics like production planning, scheduling, and inventory control • FMS (flexible manufacturing systems) patented in 1965
1970s	• PCs (personal computers) or desktop computers widely utilized in every aspect of operations, such as design, analysis, control, and the like • CIM (computer integrated manufacturing) fully developed for automation in manufacturing • CAD (computer-aided design)/CAM (computer-aided manufacturing)
1980s	• MRP II (manufacturing resource planning) to optimize planning of all resources for a manufacturing company • QR (quick response) system to reduce lead time, improve quality, and reduce cost • VMI (vendor-managed inventory) to cope with high uncertainty in the market demand • JIT (just-in-time) system and lean manufacturing recognized and adopted by companies in the United States • Lean manufacturing or lean production from the Toyota Production System (TPS) to eliminate any waste • Cellular manufacturing as an essential part of TPS, such as JIT and lean manufacturing system
1990s	• Internet-based or internet-driven information and communication technology (IICT) • ERP (enterprise resource planning) to connect every process throughout its value chain – the transformed outgrowth of MRP II • Due to time-based competition in the 1990s, a concurrent engineering or a cross-functional team (CFT) approach to developing a new product • Modular production system (MPS), modularity as an alternative to the traditional design concept
2000s	• CPFR (collaborative planning, forecasting, and replenishment) to reduce supply chain inventory (i.e., inventory stocked throughout its supply chain) and increase sales considerably • RFID (radio-frequency identification), a tiny electronic device comprising a small chip and an antenna, containing a few thousand bytes of data and information about the product or service where it was attached • Mass customization – customization in large scale
2010s	• 3D printing, a third industrial revolution with a huge impact on supply chain management • Internet of Things (IoT) to connect physical objects or devices and let them communicate with human beings and with each other to make an intelligent decision • NFC (near field communication) – a set of communication protocols for device communication within a very short distance

developed and it contributed significantly to automation in manufacturing. **CAD (computer-aided design)** and **CAM (computer-aided manufacturing)** were part of CIM.

1980s. A more advanced or sophisticated version of MRP was developed, i.e., **MRP II (manufacturing resource planning)**, whose objective was to optimize planning of all resources for a manufacturing company. Whereas MRP dealt with "materials" only, MRP II proactively did financial planning in addition to operations planning and developed a capability to deal with uncertainty, e.g., to conduct scenario or what-if analysis.

As the market responsiveness became more important (especially in areas like the fashion industry), the concept of the **QR (quick response)** system was developed to reduce lead time, improve quality, and reduce cost. Similarly, companies like Walmart began using **VMI (vendor-managed inventory)** to cope with high uncertainty in the market demand.

As Japanese companies started dominating the global manufacturing sector, Japanese management principles like the **JIT (just-in-time)** system and **lean manufacturing** became recognized and adopted by companies in the United States. The concept of lean manufacturing or lean production came from the **Toyota Production System (TPS)**, which was formally developed by the Japanese carmaker Toyota. It was a managerial philosophy that tried to eliminate waste which did not add any real value for the manufacturing system. Although it was first developed much earlier, in the 1980s **cellular manufacturing** was technologically advanced as an essential part of TPS, such as JIT and the lean manufacturing system. The central unit of a cellular manufacturing system was the cell or work cell, where process flows were organized by families of parts or end-customers. For instance, the cell consisted of diverse or dissimilar equipment and machinery in order to manufacture related or similar parts and products, following identical or linked routings.

1990s. A significant breakthrough in technological innovation very much relevant to supply chain management occurred in the 1990s. It was the internet! The **internet-based** or **internet-driven information and communication technology (IICT)** changed virtually everything in business as we knew it. In order to connect every process throughout its value chain, the company adopted **ERP (enterprise resource planning)**, which was the transformed outgrowth of MRP II.

As the technological innovation accelerated, which further shrunk the product life cycle, it became more important for the company to develop its new product faster by coping with uncertainty in the market more effectively. **Time-based competition** in the 1990s motivated the company to adopt a **concurrent engineering** or a **cross-functional team (CFT)** approach to developing a new product.

To respond rapidly to the changes in the customer's requirements, the company had to change its design principle. In this context, **modularity** emerged as an alternative to the traditional design concept, which underlay the **modular production system (MPS)**. Applied effectively, MPS enabled the company to shorten the development lead time, reduce the cost, and enhance the serviceability, i.e., make it easy to undertake maintenance of the product/service. ERP certainly helped the company to accomplish all of these.

2000s. Supply chain management became the source of competitive advantage. Thus, one of the most important goals of technological innovation was to achieve supply chain coordination efficiently and effectively. In particular, a significant issue was how to integrate all the decision-making throughout the supply chain from the supplier to the distribution function. **CPFR (collaborative planning, forecasting, and replenishment)** was significantly improved and implemented to integrate supply chain functions. Implemented optimally, CPFR enabled the company to reduce its supply chain inventory (i.e., inventory stocked throughout its supply chain) and increase sales considerably.

Although it failed to prove its full potential, **RFID (radio-frequency identification)** was once thought to revolutionize supply chain management. It was a tiny electronic device comprising a small chip and an antenna, containing a few thousand bytes of data and information about the product or service where it was attached. Since it also functioned as a unique identifier of the product or service, it was expected to improve inventory management significantly. As alluded to above, it was unfortunate or unexpected to some that RFID never had a chance to be commercialized sufficiently to demonstrate its full gamut of applicability. There were several explanations. Some pointed out potential users' or customers' ill-founded fears or misunderstandings. Others blamed some technological limitations of RFID. Whatever the true reason behind the lukewarm performance of RFID, it was clear that few organizations wholeheartedly accepted it.

As it became increasingly important to satisfy constantly changing customer needs or requirements, customization was gaining an ever-growing momentum. But, this time it was not just customization, but customization on a large scale. That is, **mass customization** was now perceived as a core competitive advantage and a great number of technological innovations specifically focused on it.

2010s. Design is the core of new product innovation. CAD was a computer-aided design tool which helped a human designer to complete her design ideas more efficiently. That is, CAD assisted the designer to draw lines and shapes more accurately on a blueprint, i.e., a two-dimensional plane. Now suppose that a designer or even just an ordinary customer has an idea about a new product, say a coffee mug. She only has an idea – no manufacturing capability. But, she wants to have a physical product of her own coffee mug. She wonders if there is a printer (much like a color printer we use in everyday life) which can manufacture the coffee mug exactly as she imagines. That is, such a printer is not simply "printing" a drawing or document, but "manufacturing" a physical object or product according to the design instructed by the designer or customer. It is the concept of the **3D (three dimensional) printer**! It has a vividly descriptive name, "**additive manufacturing**," i.e., it makes the object or product one layer at a time until the final object or product is completed. If this concept is connected with internet-based technology, the potential change to the market can be enormous. For instance, a customer in Korea wants to buy a BMW, but she doesn't want to buy an existing model. In fact, she has fantasized about her own dream car, which she designs. If the 3D printing is perfectly implementable, she transmits her dream car design to a BMW factory in Germany and the BMW plant builds the car exactly as she wants, using the company's 3D printer. Is it possible? Yes, many experts believe this kind of story is not just a fairy tale. We do think it will be fully executable in the near future, probably closer than anyone imagines. Then, the most ideal form of mass customization can be materialized! Some go further in saying that the 3D printing could open up a third industrial revolution and have a huge impact on supply chain management.

Think about another interesting case. You have a large refrigerator at home. Usually, it is stocked with a number of foods, e.g., milk, juices, meats, vegetables, fruits, condiments, and so on, many of which are perishable. Because you are a busy person, you often forget about the "best before" date for your precious foods and therefore waste them. You think it would be great if the refrigerator could talk to you, e.g., it tells you about the foods it stores and their expiration dates, reminds you of which foods should be reordered, and suggests which foods you should eat this morning by taking into account the freshness of the food, your dietary needs, and your health. It would be even better if your refrigerator could talk to your smartphone so that they decide which foods should be reordered when and where. That is, if it was possible for machines like the fridge, audio system, home theater, heating, lighting, and smartphone to communicate with you and even each other, your life would be much better or happier! No wonder such development can have a huge impact on supply chain management, by enhancing efficiency, eliminating waste, ensuring safety, and strengthening coordination. Imagine a factory where all of the machines and equipment can communicate with each other and also the managers. At such a factory, the manager can discover bottleneck processes and fix them swiftly, recognize operational hazards early on and root out safety problems, have accurate information about the inventory level and make an optimal procurement decision, and allocate the workforce more effectively to exactly where it is most needed. The **Internet of Things (IoT)** is the embodiment of the concept or technology which connects physical objects or devices and lets them communicate with human beings and with each other to make an intelligent decision.

Conversion of traditionally separate industries was envisioned even in the 1990s, when the internet was born in earnest. In particular, some anticipated that telecom companies would soon become competitors of banks and credit card companies. Such a prediction seems widely materialized these days. An increasing number of people live a wallet-less life nowadays. For instance, you don't need cash or plastic (i.e., your traditional "plastic" credit card) to pay for your coffee, lunch, taxi, or movie ticket. You just need your smartphone equipped with **NFC (near field communication)** technology,[1] a form of contactless technology. NFC is a set of communication protocols which make it possible for an electronic device like a smartphone to communicate with another device within a very short distance, e.g., 10 centimeters or less from each other. Some say NFC is an advanced form of RFID or it is an application area of IoT. It is clear that NFC has the potential to make a significant change to the way in which supply chain participants have been transacting, e.g., the transaction and payment mode.

[1] See http://nfc-forum.org/.

9.3   Awareness, Alignment, Appreciation: Triple-A SCM

Technological innovation has helped the manager to enhance supply chain performance. Here we ask, *"Which specific development stages of supply chain management has the technological innovation influenced?"* Rather than focusing on functional areas of supply chain management, we are more concerned with the development stage of SCM. We put forth that a company's supply chain management develops or grows in three stages, i.e., awareness, alignment, and appreciation.

- **Awareness:** Any effective supply chain management should be based on **awareness**. That is, everybody in the organization, from a field worker all the way up to the CEO, should acknowledge the importance of effective supply chain management and cherish the value of coordination with both internal and external partners of the supply chain. Only when everybody involved is aware of the fundamentals of SCM can the company design and try to implement its supply chain strategy.
- **Alignment:** The essential success factor of SCM is effective coordination between supply chain partners. Coordination should be supported by mutually beneficial goals or objectives of the supply chain participants. That is, it cannot be accomplished unless the entire supply chain partners share a common goal or objective to a great extent, i.e., there should be **"goal alignment"** throughout the supply chain. If the supply chain partners share the common goal, they are willing to coordinate with each other even when doing so compromises their myopic profitability.
- **Appreciation:** We already discussed the importance of sustainable supply chain coordination. One of the most critical factors to sustain this coordination is a reasonably fair sharing of coordination benefit. How should we make sure that every supply chain partner who has participated in coordination receives her fair share of contribution? It is obvious that the first thing the company should do to answer the question is to measure the performance improvement due to coordination and estimate how much each supply chain partner has contributed to coordination. It is the stage of **"appreciation."** Albeit seeming simple, performance measurement in a fair and accurate manner is an extremely difficult task.

We call this the **"triple-A stage model"** of SCM development. It can be an "iterative or continuous" feedback process as shown in Figure 9.11. Once the company reaches the "appreciation" stage, it should not stop there, i.e., it should not be complacent with its own achievement. Rather, the company should move to another round of "awareness." That is, it should identify new areas or sources of potential improvement and try to mobilize all of its members to understand why it is necessary to remove any obstacles or problems getting in the way of achieving the improvement and garner their awareness. Then the development cycle continues. Note that whenever the company moves toward another round of the triple-A cycle, it accumulates more knowledge and experience about its supply chain management and thus improves its own learning capability. As the triple-A process continues, the company becomes more competitive in creating value through supply chain management.

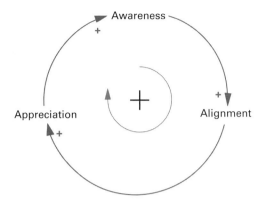

Figure 9.11 Triple-A Supply Chain Management

Our essential premise is that technological innovation has contributed to each of the supply chain development stages, i.e., awareness, alignment, and appreciation. For instance, many of the communication technologies helped the company to enhance its members' awareness of the value of effective supply chain management, i.e., to motivate the members to pay more attention to successfully implementing the supply chain management strategy. Similarly, many tools and technologies have been developed and utilized for goal alignment. For instance, most of the internet-based technological innovation has enabled the company to coordinate with its supply chain partners by aligning their incentive systems and goals together. Several of these technological innovations in turn have helped the supply chain partners understand each other's true contribution and made it possible for them to find an appropriate profit sharing. An internet-driven ERP connecting all the supply chain partners can be a good example of technology that has contributed to appreciation, i.e., it has enabled the company to accurately assess the incremental value due to supply chain coordination and find a systematic scheme to share it among the supply chain partners according to their relevant share of contribution.

9.4   Technology and Organization

Successful implementation of technological innovation is critical to enhancing a firm's competitive advantage. The place where new technology is tested and developed is called the "**development environment**." It can be the company's R&D center or factory floor. The place where the company applies the technology is called the "**implementation environment**," which is in general the company's manufacturing facility. Once the technology is developed in the development environment, it is transferred to the implementation environment.

Fidelity is the level of structural and infrastructural **congruence** between the development environment and the implementation environment (Figure 9.12). For example, if the structural condition consisting of physical factors like machinery, equipment, facility, materials, parts, and the like at the development environment is similar to or congruent with that at the implementation environment, we say there is a high level of

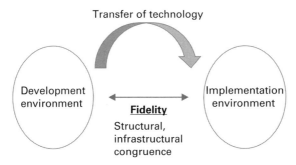

Figure 9.12 Fidelity between the Development and Implementation Environments

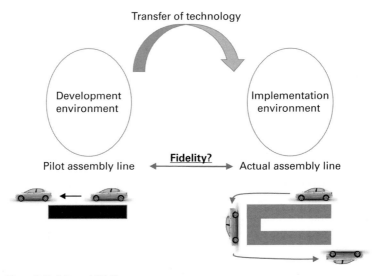

Figure 9.13 Failure of Fidelity

fidelity between the two environments. Similarly, if the infrastructural condition consisting of virtual elements such as organizational chart, communication system, information-sharing and decision-making mechanism, organizational culture or norms, education and training, compensation system, managerial philosophy, and the like at the development environment is similar to or congruent with that at the implementation environment, we say there is a high level of fidelity between the two environments. We would probably be able to define a composite measure of fidelity between the two, encompassing both structural and infrastructural conditions simultaneously.

Why is it important to keep fidelity between the two environments? Consider an example of a carmaker in Figure 9.13. The company has a recently completed, cutting-edge R&D center. It had been developing a new process technology, which it expected to improve performance at its assembly line significantly. When the company completely developed the new technology, it transferred it to the assembly line located almost 100 miles away. Once the technology was fully transferred from the R&D center to the assembly line, the company was excited about a "potentially" huge performance improvement, which was optimistically anticipated. But, unfortunately, what awaited the company was not the boosting of performance, but quite the opposite, i.e., some violent deterioration of performance. What was happening? The company was at odds with the actual outcome, i.e., it couldn't understand why. For the next several months, the company was embarking on a soul-searching mission: Why did the technology that looked so promising at the R&D center (i.e., the development environment) turn out to be a fiasco on the actual assembly line (i.e., the implementation environment)? After months of agonizing fact-finding, the company concluded that there was a lack of fidelity between the two environments. More specifically, the company found out that there was a huge discrepancy between the physical structures of the assembly line. The R&D center was using a pilot assembly line, which was brand new and much more automated and advanced than the actual assembly line running at the manufacturing plant. Therefore, the company was unable to integrate the technology that was developed and optimized for the development environment with the actual manufacturing environment. That is, the lack of structural fidelity between the development and implementation environments caused the technology to fail in the actual manufacturing setting. After realizing the problem, the company completely overhauled its R&D center in order to restore the fidelity with the actual production environment. It then tried to redesign the technology and finally successfully implemented it in the real manufacturing plant.

9.4.1   Mutual Adaptation of Technology and Organization

Even if we understand the concept and its importance of fidelity, however, it still remains unanswered *how to explain the phenomenon more systematically*. To answer the question, we need to define another essential concept, "**the gap between technology and organization**." When a new technology is introduced to an existing organization, it rarely fits with the existing condition, both structural and infrastructural. We call the level of incongruence between technology and organization a "gap" between the two. This gap causes malfunctioning of the technology in the organization. That is, as long as the gap is not closed sufficiently, the technology cannot accomplish its potential performance in the organization.

Consider an example where a company tries to implement new technology in its own organization. Why does it want to do so? One of the most important reasons why a company applies new technology to its management is because it wants to enhance its performance. That is, performance improvement is probably the number one objective in technology implementation. Such an expectation can be depicted as in Figure 9.14, where the company expects the new technology to improve the performance rapidly from the very moment it is introduced into the organization, i.e., at t_1. Unfortunately, however, the actual outcome is usually different from the expectation. Contrary to the expectation, many companies actually experience performance deterioration following the implementation of new technology (Figure 9.15). In effect, this counterintuitive phenomenon, i.e., **performance deterioration**, is due to the gap between technology and organization. Extending our discussion on fidelity, we postulate that the gap is caused by the discrepancy between the environment of technology development and that of organizational implementation. As such, structural and infrastructural conditions associated with the gap are comparable with those related to the fidelity.

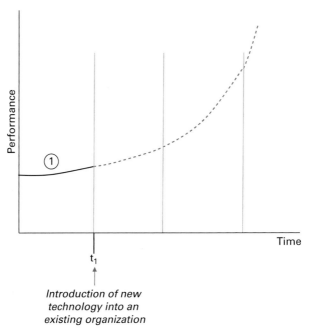

Figure 9.14 Performance Expectation of New Technology

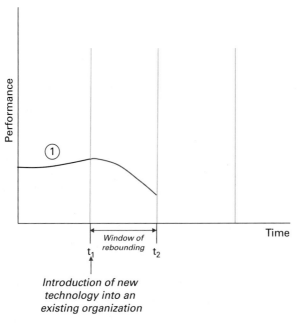

Figure 9.15 Actual Performance Result of New Technology

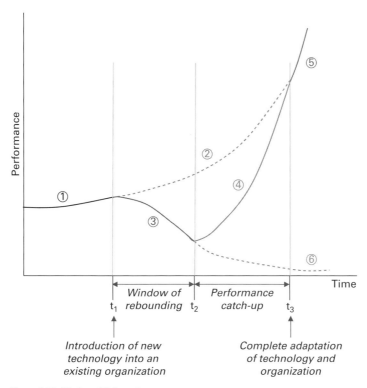

Figure 9.16 Window of Rebounding

The larger the gap between technology and organization, the more difficult it is for the company to enhance its performance with the technology. Therefore, the company should endeavor to close the gap as fast as possible. What if the company is unable to close the gap on time? We conceptually define the "**window of rebounding**" as the time period during which the company must close the gap sufficiently to reverse its performance deterioration, i.e., to start improving the performance by utilizing the new technology inside the organization. It is the period between t_1 and t_2 in Figure 9.16. But, what happens if the company fails to reverse the course of performance deterioration during the window of rebounding? If the company cannot overcome the impasse of performance deterioration, it is very likely that the company loses momentum to start improving. This is the path consisting of ①–③–⑥ in Figure 9.16, where the company becomes so helpless that it almost gives up any attempt to improve its performance and the performance deteriorates continuously. On the contrary, if the company tries its best and eventually finds an effective way to rapidly close the gap so that it can change the course of performance deterioration before the end of the "window of rebounding," the company can enhance the performance quickly and significantly so that it catches up with the level of performance expected when the new technology was first introduced into the organization. It is the path of ①–③–④–⑤ in Figure 9.16, where the company closes the gap sufficiently during the window of rebounding so as to start a rapid performance

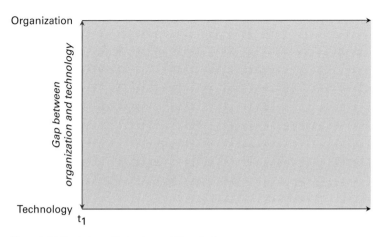

Figure 9.17 Gap between Technology and Organization

catch-up and eventually achieves the level of performance it did expect from the new technology. That is, the company has learned a very effective way to improve the performance using the technology and finally catch up with the anticipated performance level during the "**performance catch-up**" period – $t_2 \sim t_3$ in Figure 9.16.

The complete reversion of performance deterioration and eventual catch-up with the original expectation between t_1 and t_3 as in Figure 9.16 result from the company's effort and capability to rapidly close the gap between technology and organization. In fact, this is the **adaptation** or **fidelity-restoring process**.

Let's first *conceptually* depict the gap between technology and organization as shown in Figure 9.17. There are three types of adaptation process between technology and organization. First, the company can close the gap by adjusting or adapting the existing organization to the new technology. For instance, suppose the company wants to introduce an ERP system to its organization, expecting that it can enhance its operations performance significantly with the new technology. Since it is usual that an ERP system is designed and developed by an external software vendor, however, initially there is a great deal of discrepancy between the ERP system (new technology) and the organization in terms of structural and infrastructural aspects. Given a huge *structural* and *infrastructural* gap between the ERP and the existing organization, the company cannot improve its performance through implementing the ERP system. Maybe the structural condition under which the ERP was developed is very different from that in the organization. It is also possible that the ERP assumed a particular communication flow, an infrastructural factor, which is quite different from the communication system currently employed in the organization. Due to both structural and infrastructural differences, the gap between the ERP and the organization exists. The first way to fix the problem, i.e., to close the gap or level of discrepancy, is to change structural and infrastructural conditions of the organization in order to make them consistent with those underlying the ERP system. For example, the company probably should replace its existing machinery and/or equipment with those that are more compatible with the ERP system. It might further want to change its organization chart, communication mechanism, and even culture or norms so that they

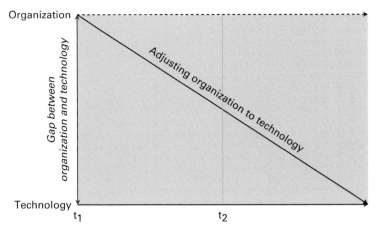

Figure 9.18 Adaptation of Organization to Technology

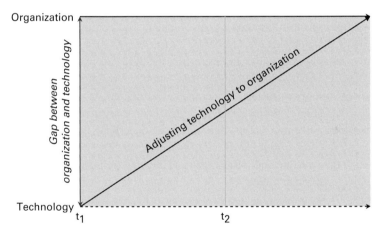

Figure 9.19 Adaptation of Technology to Organization

become more compatible or consistent with those embedded in or assumed by the ERP system. It is called the "**single adaptation of organization to technology**" (Figure 9.18).

Another way to close the gap is to adapt the technology to the organization. Consider the ERP case again. Believing that its organization has been driving its success in the past, the company wants to keep the organization intact. Therefore, rather than adjusting its organization, the company asks the software vendor to change the ERP codes so that the structural and infrastructural elements of the ERP system become more congruent or compatible with those of the organization (Figure 9.19). Similarly, it is the "**single adaptation of technology to organization**."

Of course, in theory these two "single" adaptation methods can help the company to close the gap between technology and organization. But, what is more important is not whether or not the company can close the gap, but *how fast* the company can achieve it. As in our discussion about "window of rebounding" and "performance catch-up period" in Figure 9.16, how fast the company can reverse the performance deterioration is imperative

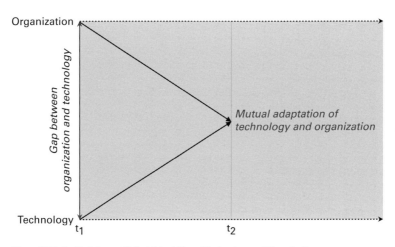

Figure 9.20 Co-Evolution or Mutual Adaptation of Technology and Organization

in determining whether the company can eventually succeed in achieving the full potential of the new technology in time, i.e., before it's too late. As such, the company should close the gap as rapidly as possible. In this regard, the third "adaptation process" can have an advantage. As opposed to the "single" adaptation, we call it the **mutual adaptation of technology and organization**.[2] Under mutual adaptation, on the one hand, the company tries to make appropriate changes to its organization's structure and infrastructure so that they become a little more compatible with those underlying the technology. And, on the other hand, it works with the software vendor (e.g., the ERP developer) to make suitable changes to the structure and infrastructure of the new technology, until the gap between technology and organization can be completely or at least sufficiently eliminated (Figure 9.20). We propose that the third approach, i.e., the mutual adaptation of technology and organization, is the best shot of closing the gap in time (i.e., before it's too late or during the window of rebounding period) in order to accomplish the originally expected performance improvement. If the company has a commitment to the mutual adaptation process, it has to pay attention to "thorough preparation" before actual implementation of the new technology in the existing organization. That is, the company should plan ahead about how to make what changes to the structure and infrastructure of both technology and organization, probably from the moment when it decides to introduce and implement a new technology in the organization.

9.5   Innovation System for Sustainable Innovation

At the beginning of this chapter, we discussed two different types of creativity, i.e., artistic creativity and business creativity. Although we may not teach artistic creativity, we can teach managers business creativity. In fact, business creativity should be part of a normal

[2] D. Leonard-Barton, "Implementation as Mutual Adaptation of Technology and Organization" (1988) 17(5) *Research Policy* 251–267.

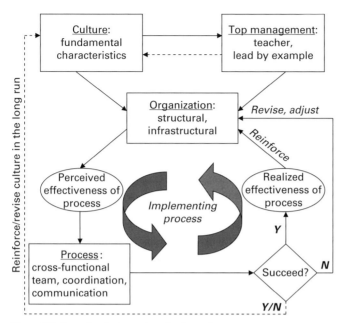

Figure 9.21 Innovation System as Learning Dynamics

management process. That is, innovation should be viewed as an integral element of management. Should innovation be part of management, there must be a system which makes sure that innovation occurs in a continuous and predictable manner. In published research, many have suggested key dimensions of such a system. Among those diverse suggestions, we put forth a generalizable set of essential dimensions that consist in an **innovation system**. The set comprises four pillars, i.e., culture, top management, organization, and process. These four factors are linked with each other in a feedback closed loop (Figure 9.21).

The company's culture constitutes its fundamental characteristics, which can either facilitate or constrain its activities, initiatives, functions, and decision-making patterns. In effect, the culture defines the company's comprehensive boundary or context, within which the members of the organization behave, think, grow, make decisions, interact with each other or outside stakeholders, and so forth. That is, it defines or designates the norms the members of the company are expected to accept as their guiding principles inside the organization. Considering the potentially great influence of culture on every aspect of the company, we can say that there are certain characteristics or attributes of culture which are more conducive to creativity or technological innovation. For instance, it is well studied and documented in published research that an informal (as opposed to formal or excessively hierarchical) culture is more compatible with creativity: but, it is vital to note that "informal" should not imply "lack of discipline." In fact, a strong culture is both informal and disciplined, i.e., the *legitimate* authority, which we expand upon below, is well respected and honored. In addition, creativity or technological innovation is expected to flourish under the cultural environment that cherishes or encourages such elements as mutual respect, continuous learning and improvement, open and free communication, and personal growth or sense of self-actualization among the members of the organization. Another essential attribute of culture is to allow or accept failure. In fact, the success rate of an innovative idea is very low: some people estimate it hovers around 5 percent on average, although this largely depends on industry-specific factors. If we accept the 5 percent success rate, it implies it is necessary to overcome nineteen failures in order to accomplish one success on average! If a company insists no failure is accepted, then it cannot expect any innovation from its employees, who are undoubtedly discouraged by the "failure is unacceptable" slogan and thus cannot make any serious attempt to innovate. No failure, no innovation! It is as simple as that. Therefore, creativity or technological innovation is stimulated by the culture that encourages its members to challenge the status quo and accepts a failure as a result of such an innovative attempt.

Given the cultural boundary, top managers must try to design and develop an organization that is capable of creating and innovating constantly. In fact, they have to demonstrate strong leadership that is consistent with creativity and stimulates technological innovation. But, their authority should not be derived from a formal, i.e., legal, status, position, power, or force. It must be rooted on and driven by moral or ethical integrity. An ideal top manager must lead the organization by example, i.e., she should become a teacher for the organization's members. What is the essential role of a teacher? The teacher does not admonish her students for the sake of punishment. Whatever she does has only one goal: to help her student to learn and grow as an independent individual. That's exactly what we expect the top manager to do in the company, i.e., to help and challenge people to learn, solve problems, innovate, and finally create value, not through an authoritarian command and control, but acting herself as a role model and teacher. In effect, an essential virtue of the top manager is to show her strong commitment to leading the company into the direction set by the company culture. Finally, the top manager should put a knowledge management system in place. This doesn't mean sophisticated technical stuff like a huge database. Rather, it should be part of the company's management philosophy, which systematically records detailed data and information (including the decision-making logic) about every innovation project, not only successful, but also failed, and enables the manager to retrieve them whenever needed. Recall that the ideal company culture should allow employees to fail, i.e., a failure should be accepted in the culture. On the one hand, it makes sense since the company cannot always succeed in innovating. On the other hand, accepting and even encouraging failure might not be plausible since the company is not a charity or non-profit organization. Unless the company can find a way that turns the failure into something valuable, "failure is accepted" is just a "great-sounding" motto with no sustainable meaning to the company. Consider the pharmaceutical industry. In that industry, we often hear of news that a pharmaceutical company has developed an innovative drug, the sales of which could reach multi-billion dollars in the global market. What might be more interesting is that the blockbuster drug was actually derived from a big failure in the past! That is, what the company learned from its failed project has made it possible to quickly develop the megahit drug. It is a great example of turning a failure into the foundation for a success! If the company can develop a system that helps it learn from its failure and apply that knowledge to another technological innovation (e.g., a successful new product development), then the cost incurred by the failure is not a total waste, but a valuable tuition paid by the company for its learning. We put forth that the culture that accepts or allows failure can have a true meaning or be sustainable only when the company puts in place a knowledge management system that enables it to learn from the failure for even greater new technological innovation. This is the essence of the knowledge management system, to which the top manager must pay attention.

Although the corporate culture forms a boundary within which the top manager must make a decision, it is also possible and sometimes usual for the top manager to make a big impact on the company's culture, albeit very slowly and most likely in the long run. As such, the direction of influence is bilateral as in Figure 9.21.

Within the comprehensive boundary defined by culture and top management, the company should design the detailed organization. For example, how to structure or organize jobs, tasks, duties, functions, and so forth, who and how to hire for the jobs and tasks, how to develop a protocol or norm for communication and coordination among the employees and also with the external stakeholders, and the like. In essence, through organizing, top management can define the relationships within and around the company in a stable and predictable way. For example, creativity or technological innovation is more compatible with an organization that promotes more diversity among its members (including workers and managers), applies cross-functional teams for innovation projects, and has less hierarchy.

Process is concerned with actual implementation. That is, it consists of specific activities, steps, tools, and methods used to realize the technological innovation, e.g., developing an innovative new product. Brainstorming or deep immersion of thinking, an attribute of process, is regarded as one of the most important factors for successful innovation. Some companies use prototype as a communication tool, not just a perfunctory step before completing a final product. In fact, prototype has been widely used as a tool to visualize the work-in-process project.

Figure 9.21 shows the dynamic relationship among these four pillars, i.e., culture, top management, organization, and process. Although culture and top management have a significant lasting impact on organization and process, the direction of influence is not always unilateral. That is, as the innovation continues through the "organization – process" cycle, i.e., the implementation process, sometimes it happens that the rules or principles defined by the culture and top management seem to conflict with the actual conditions set by the market, i.e., the environment. If such a phenomenon is just short-lived, then there would be no significant change to the current system. But, if such conflicting repeats or becomes magnifying, then it signals that something is wrong in the current norms, i.e., rules or principles defined by the culture and top management. As these signs of something big breaking down continue and multiply, it becomes increasingly obvious for the company to make a change to its own culture and even top management. Once the new fundamental market forces or conditions are properly taken into account, i.e., the culture and top management acknowledge and accommodate them, new culture and top management emerge and the dynamic cycle regenerates and continues until another unwavering conflict with the market or environment occurs.

In sum, the innovation system is a tightly linked mechanism of a **dynamic feedback loop**. As such, one cannot extract one factor or pillar from the whole system and apply it to a different environment, hoping it enables the innovation spirit to flourish there. For instance, consider a company, Firm H, that has a very strict formal hierarchy, not allowing any failure. It probably has top management that is accustomed to top-down command and control and a severely authoritarian management style. Facing a sluggish growth, Firm H wants to revitalize innovation inside its organization. With help from a consulting company, it has finally decided to introduce the cross-functional team (CFT) approach to its new product development process. Any guess about the outcome? It is very likely that the company cannot reap the benefit of the CFT approach unless it makes appropriate changes (consistent with the principles underlying CFT) to its culture and top management. The CFT approach can work best when the communication is freely done and the members are encouraged to try new things without the fear of being penalized if they fail, and the like, i.e., under the culture and top management philosophy that are quite different from those at Firm H. If the company is really serious about innovation, it should start with building a culture and top management that are consistent with stimulating creativity and technological innovation in a sustainable way.

9.5.1   Role of Top Management versus Knowledge Workers

Since top management should play the central role in building an environment for creativity and technological innovation, let's consider its role more thoroughly. We call non-executive managers and employees (i.e., all the members who are not in top management at the company) "knowledge workers," who actively participate in innovation projects and have a certain level of authority to make a resource allocation decision at the company. That is, a **knowledge worker** is an employee who can make an independent decision within a boundary set by top management.

For an example, let's consider a specific context of new product development. We already postulated that the top manager must play a role as a teacher in order to instigate creativity and technological innovation in the organization. Then what is the main difference between the top management's role and the knowledge worker's role in new product development? To develop an innovative new product, it is imperative to start with a wide range of new ideas about the product and its target market. Why? Since a priori it is not possible to predict exactly what kind of product the market will like the most, the company should initially contemplate many probable alterative designs or models in order to boost the probability of success. Then, *who has the best information and data leading to such ideas?* It is the workers and employees that have the most relevant ideas, since they are likely to have the closest connection, interaction, or relationship with the customers in the market. If the organization has knowledge workers with various backgrounds, they generate diverse ideas, all pointing to different directions or solutions (Figure 9.22). As such, during the initial stage of new product development, it is essential to encourage knowledge workers to freely suggest new (sometimes crazy) ideas and engage in thorough brainstorming among themselves to test each of the offered ideas and to search for better alternatives. They are expected to devote their knowledge and experience fully to the process. What about the top management? During the initial stage, the top manager must not intervene in the regular development process like intense brainstorming and let the knowledge workers do

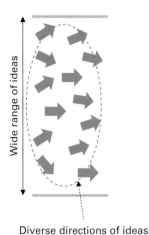

Diverse directions of ideas

Figure 9.22 Role of Top Management versus Knowledge Workers – the Initial Stage

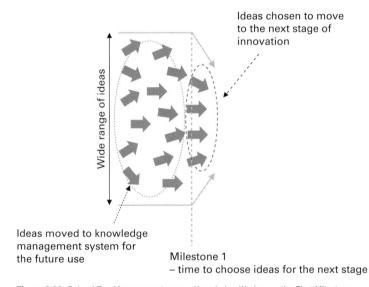

Ideas chosen to move to the next stage of innovation

Ideas moved to knowledge management system for the future use

Milestone 1 – time to choose ideas for the next stage

Figure 9.23 Role of Top Management versus Knowledge Workers – the First Milestone

their best. She can give them broad guidelines and/or advice if asked: note that the range of ideas (allowed to be freely explored by the knowledge workers) in Figure 9.22 is defined by the top manager in the first place. That is, the knowledge workers' freedom, latitude, authority, and uninhibited explosion of innate creativity should be guaranteed, challenged, and instigated during the initial stage of new product development.

Recall that one of the prominent differences between artistic creativity and business creativity is concerned with a due date. That is, all business creativity cannot help but abide by the set due date for launching into the market. It practically implies that the chaotic state of "crazy ideas all pointing in different directions" cannot go on forever. There should be a point when it is said, "enough is enough," i.e., when the company should decide which ideas should stay or go (Figure 9.23). It is a **milestone** for choosing the ideas or alternative designs, which should be saved and moved to the next stage in the development process. It has to be the role played by the top manager. That is, the top manager must decide when is the best timing for the milestone and take an appropriate measure to enforce it. Once the top manager determines the milestone and chooses those ideas that move to the next stage, her decision and choices are accepted and honored by the knowledge workers without even a second thought. This is also an example of corporate culture which is informal, but disciplined at the same time.

In Figure 9.23, we see that there are two different types of ideas, i.e., one group of ideas that are selected by the top management and moved to the next stage for further consideration and the other not selected for the next step. What happens to those ideas or designs that are terminated at the milestone? Will they be scrapped and thrown into the garbage? Recall the concept of "**knowledge management system**" when we discussed "top management" as one of the pillars for an innovation system. The knowledge management system is not necessarily a physical apparatus, but a management philosophy that enables the company to preserve its failure experience and turn it into a source of new knowledge and insight for future innovation. Only when the company has this system working can it promote the culture that accepts and encourages failure for future innovation. Again, it is one of the vital roles of the top management to design, develop, and optimally implement the knowledge management system.

The process described above can continue through the next milestones (Figure 9.24 and Figure 9.25) until the company finally chooses or completes its new product

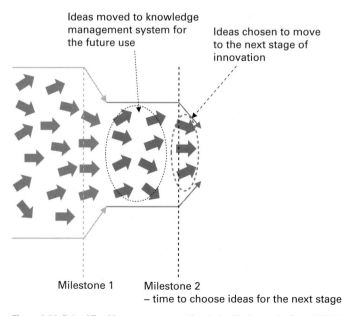

Figure 9.24 Role of Top Management versus Knowledge Workers – the Second Milestone

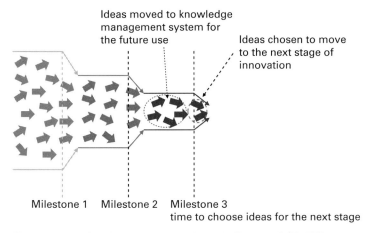

Figure 9.25 Role of Top Management versus Knowledge Workers – the Final Milestone

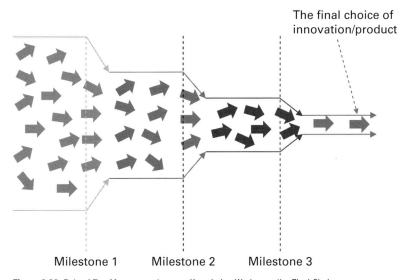

Figure 9.26 Role of Top Management versus Knowledge Workers – the Final Choice

(Figure 9.26). To assume the role of a teacher, the top manager must not interfere with the daily decision-making by the knowledge workers, who in turn should commit to perfecting the project with their own diverse knowledge and experience, but must honor and follow the milestone decisions eventually reached by the top management. Of course, it is possible for the top manager to participate in the operations (i.e., daily, functional) activities of the development project, only if and when she defines herself as one of the knowledge workers, not as a teacher.

The Principle of "Threaded Pearls"

Recall Case Study 7.1 "Value of Coordination at UNIQLO" in Chapter 7. Using the case as a role model, we would like to develop a principle for effective supply chain management. The principle is consistent with an old Korean proverb, "Three buckets of pearls are not a jewel, unless they are threaded together!" Even without delving for a formal interpretation, we can grab at least a rough implication of the proverb, i.e., "integration is the key!" We would like to suggest calling this the **"principle of threaded pearls"** or "principle of unbroken links in a supply chain."

Principle of unbroken links in a supply chain. A supply chain with unbroken links is the state where every link or connection between partners in the supply chain is connected effectively, i.e., coordination between any two companies or participants in the supply chain is implemented optimally. The "principle of unbroken links in a supply chain" postulates that the supply chain performs superbly only when it has no broken link between any two partner companies. We elaborate on this principle by conducting the cause-and-effect analysis of UNIQLO in several steps.

> **Step 1**: UNIQLO has achieved high profit since it has high sales and low cost. Low cost makes it possible to charge low prices, which in turn support high sales (Figure 9.27a and b).

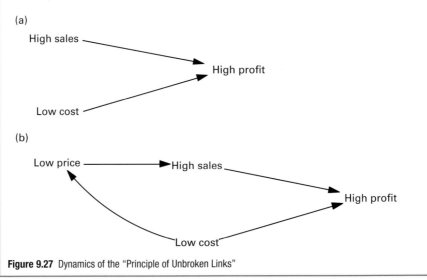

Figure 9.27 Dynamics of the "Principle of Unbroken Links"

Box continues

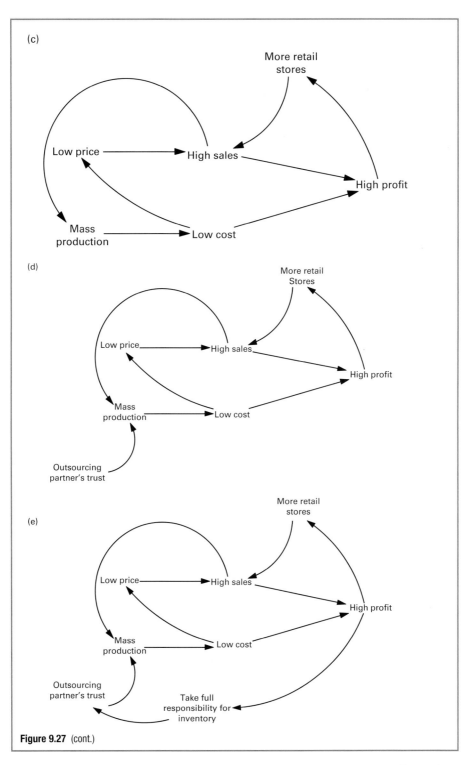

Figure 9.27 (cont.)

Box continues

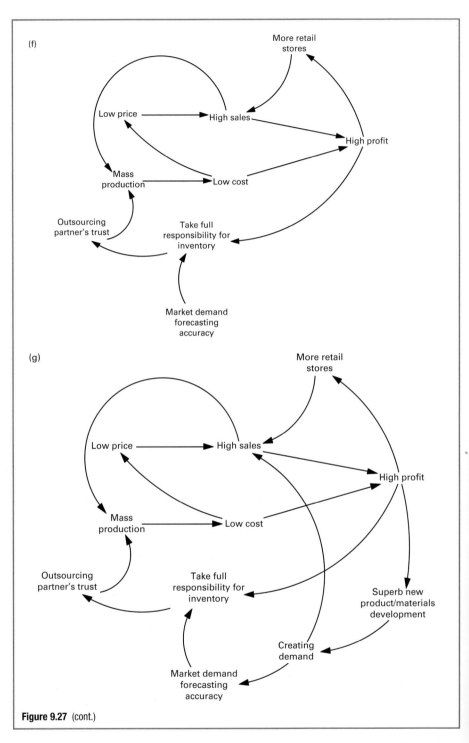

Figure 9.27 (cont.)

Box continues

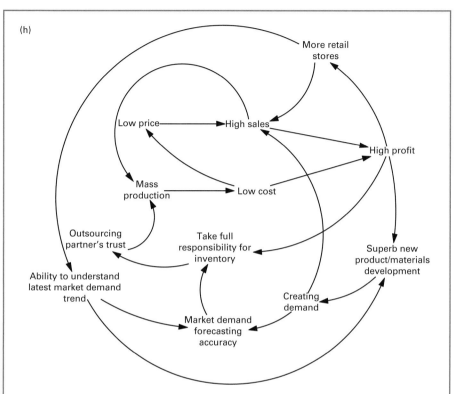

(h)

Step 2: High profit helps UNIQLO open more retail stores, which support high sales. High sales enable UNIQLO to mass-produce, which again lowers the cost (Figure 9.27c).

Step 3: One of the most important forces for the company's mass production is the coordination with UNIQLO's outsourcing partners, which is impossible without trust between them and UNIQLO (Figure 9.27d).

Step 4: How can UNIQLO build trust with its outsourcing partners? It takes an enormous commitment on the part of UNIQLO, i.e., the company has to take full responsibility for inventory. For example, UNIQLO makes a commitment to paying its outsourcing partners for the entire order it places, regardless of whether or not the company can sell it completely in the market. Experiencing this level of commitment by UNIQLO, the outsourcing partners are willing to make their own commitment to supplying whatever amount and whenever UNIQLO orders. With such commitment from its outsourcing partners, in turn, it becomes possible for UNIQLO to achieve a great deal of volume flexibility, one of the company's most significant competitive advantages. In fact, UNIQLO's high profit makes it easier for the company to make its commitment (Figure 9.27e).

Step 5: However, high profit alone cannot explain UNIQLO's commitment to building up the trust with its outsourcing partners. It requires UNIQLO's ability to make an accurate forecasting for market demand. Such forecasting ability must be backed by the company's capability of creating market demand, which in turn calls for the company's ability to develop new products and materials continuously. Superb new product and material development must be funded with high profit. By creating market demand, UNIQLO can also increase its sales (Figure 9.27f and g).

Box continues

Step 6: In fact, both market demand forecasting accuracy and superb new product/ material development are made possible by the company's ability to understand the fundamental trend of the latest market demand. These are cultivated by UNIQLO through leveraging its many retail stores, i.e., utilizing its retail stores as the field posts to sense and gather the latest information about the changes in customer requirements and tastes and also technological breakthroughs (Figure 9.27h).

As the UNIQLO executive mentioned, there is no secret to the company's success. In fact, when we look into each one of the company's success factors individually, they all look so simple and straightforward. There seems to be nothing other competitors cannot easily imitate. Then, how is it that no other companies have been successful in duplicating UNIQLO's strategy effectively? Here is the principle of unbroken links in a supply chain!

It is deceptively simple for a company to have a few strong and effective links among many in its supply chain. But, it is extremely difficult for the company to have all of the links well connected, i.e., to coordinate all of the links in the supply chain strongly and effectively, supported by mutual trust and commitment among the partners. UNIQLO is a legendary company that has grown from a local mom-and-pop store to a truly global fashion company over the course of about thirty years. Only when we fathom the principle of unbroken links in a supply chain will we be able to learn important insights from UNIQLO's strategy.

Questions
1. What are the primary sources of UNIQLO's competitive advantage?
2. Are there any potential weaknesses in UNIQLO's strategy?
3. How has technological innovation helped the company to be competitive?
4. Is it difficult for other competitors to emulate the company's strategy? Why or why not?
5. Can you suggest other additional factors that can be included in the cause-and-effect dynamics of UNIQLO? You might want to draw your own cause-and-effect diagram.

Discussion Questions

1. What are the major differences between artistic creativity and business creativity?
2. Define disruptive technological innovation. Is it an absolute concept or a relative concept?
3. Explain the relationship between technological innovation and product life cycle.
4. What are the significant technological innovations in the 1990s that are closely related to supply chain management?
5. Suggest several technological breakthroughs in the 2010s that are likely to have a great impact on supply chain management.

6. Define the triple-A supply chain management development stages. What is the relationship between technological innovation and the triple-A model?

7. Define fidelity between the development environment and the implementation environment. Why is it important to have "fidelity"?

8. Explain the concept of "mutual adaptation of technology and organization." Suggest an actual example where the concept can be highlighted.

9. What are the most striking differences between the role of top management and that of knowledge workers in new product development?

10. Explain the concept of "threaded pearls" or "the principle of unbroken links in a supply chain." How does this concept relate to "integration" in supply chain management?

案例 CASE STUDY 9.1
Integrated Information Systems: See the Whole Picture (Canon)

An independent research organization recently examined the work practices of 1,501 companies in six countries. They found that disorganized work practices within these business organizations wasted time equivalent to an average of ninety-eight working days each year for every person employed. In terms of employee productivity, the United Kingdom came out the worst.
On average, people were working effectively for only 48 percent of the time. Poor organization was largely responsible. Prominent within this poor organization were inadequate systems for managing information and communication.

Information and communication technologies (ICT) help modern organizations to be better organized and to meet their objectives more effectively. Good ICT solutions enable an organization to:

- handle much larger quantities of information and other resources;
- achieve much higher accuracy levels (make very few mistakes);
- reduce the costs of all their processes; and
- improve the services offered to internal and external customers.

This case study illustrates ways in which organizations like schools and businesses can become more efficient by integrating their ICT effort. This may well require them to call on the services of an integrated ICT provider who can help such organizations to control costs and to reap the benefits of utilizing IT systems and multi-functional devices in an integrated way.

Schools can benefit directly by using modern information management systems that save and release staff time. Society also stands to gain; students who become familiar with good information management practice while at school are better equipped to become effective members of the future workforce.

The Canon story. Canon was founded in Japan in 1933, and first made its name in the 1930s as a producer of cameras. It became associated with high levels of innovation and product development, and in 1964 it branched out to produce the Canola 130, the world's first ten-key electronic calculator.

During the 1960s, Canon became a truly international company, with exports accounting for 50 percent of sales. In 1968, the company moved into photocopying and by the mid-1970s Canon was producing laser printers. During the 1980s and 1990s, the company continued to innovate, developing high-grade computer systems and more sophisticated cameras, copiers, and digital imaging systems.

Increasingly, the company has focused on developing environmentally friendly technologies, producing recyclable copiers and other equipment.

Today, Canon is known for providing state-of-the-art integrated IT and office solutions, as well as top-class photography and imaging systems. In the United Kingdom, Canon is an industry leader in imaging products and services for digital environments, both in the office

Source: Reprinted with permission from Business Case Studies LLP.

and at home. Canon's technology is designed to enable companies and individuals to achieve their goals – an objective which is encapsulated in the company's "You Can" philosophy.

Operating the core business. Companies which set out, through their products and services, to help other companies become and remain efficient operators need to be at the forefront of innovation and good practice themselves.

Canon prides itself on the research that it carries out into developing new technologies. It has research centers located in Europe (e.g., France, the United Kingdom), the United States, and Japan.

The company operates in a highly competitive environment. It recognizes the importance of managing its processes in ways that ensure that its new products come to market quickly, are to the highest technical specifications, and can be competitively priced.

Key to this is Canon's appreciation that a good information management strategy is an essential component of business success. Today's businesses are faced with a mass of documentation, e-mails, and other paperwork circulating around them. Canon has developed skills and technologies to take control of this potential information overload, the know-how to manage it, and the ability to share it throughout the organization and beyond.

Canon has used its technology, understanding, and systems integration skills to help improve its own business processes – aiding it to become more efficient, more productive, and more profitable.

Because it understands the important contribution of information and communications systems to effective working, Canon is well placed to help other organizations improve their own information management systems. With its history of technological innovation in the fields of state-of-the-art integrated IT and office and imaging systems, Canon seeks to continually provide solutions that best meet customer requirements.

For today's digital, networked offices, this means providing a range of information technology and communications solutions built around a core set of digital products.

Strategic management. Strategic management involves making long-term plans that are clear and well thought out, rather than simply reacting to problems when they arise. In business, we make a distinction between a reactive organization and a proactive one. The proactive organization is the one that plans ahead. Unfortunately, many UK companies are forced to operate in a reactive way – particularly in the area of developing an information management strategy. The problem is that, as companies grow, they need to deal with their customers in more complex ways – and their current information management systems need to be updated. Some add individual components to their existing systems (helping them to maximize the value of their previous investments), while others will start from scratch. Whichever route a business takes, it makes sense to think strategically, and particularly to examine ways of integrating the various compatible components of information systems, e.g., copiers, computers, and printers. Many organizations have the correct equipment, but may not be using it as effectively as they could; others – such as Oaks Park High School in Essex, where Canon has built an advanced ICT network for use by teachers and pupils – are able to build solutions from the ground up.

The whole picture. The key to successful information management is to link together the various components of an information system. For example, once connected, a central copier replaces a host of desktop printers. Also, within a properly integrated system, staff can access fax services direct from PCs.

Information management is all about helping people to carry out their daily work in a more streamlined and efficient way. A well-integrated information system will ensure that staff:

- spend less time on contributing/seeking/extracting/retrieving data;
- undertake fewer tasks when handling information;
- generate less paper-based data; and
- have access to a system that is secure and protects confidentiality where necessary.

Let's look at how this can happen within an integrated system. Suppose that a school's business studies teacher – Joe – urgently needs to order a new textbook that has just been published and reviewed.

1. Joe e-mails the school office to request an electronic copy of an order form.
2. Joe completes the electronic order form and e-mails it to the Head of Department for approval.
3. The Head of Department having given approval, Joe prints off a paper copy of the order as a record, and forwards the electronic document to the school office, which must see all purchasing orders.
4. The school administrator has a query about the exact ISBN of the book, so contacts Joe via a virtual private network (VPN). The VPN automatically forwards both the document and the call.
5. Joe clears up the query and automatically sends a final copy of the order to a printer in the office. Office staff are able to send off the order (electronically) to the bookshop and to place copies of the order in the appropriate central electronic and card files.

When the book arrives, the information system's software can, in a matter of seconds, record the acquisition, make the payment, debit the appropriate accounts, and update stock records.

If the system was not integrated, every stage in the process would be more complicated and prone to error. For example, Joe would need to make multiple paper copies of his order, which he would have to personally deliver to his Head of Department and the School Office for signatures. He would have to visit them at a time when they were not busy, and a letter would need to be sent with the order.

There is a good chance that at some stage the order would be left waiting for a long period on someone's desk, and there is a fair chance that important information might be missed out or lost in the process. In contrast, an integrated system takes out the delay, uncertainty, and waste of resources involved in information handling.

Information handling: providing the solutions. The elements of an information management system are as follows:

- **Peripherals** – black and white and color copiers, laser and bubble jet printers, scanners, and faxes.
- **Networks** – servers, PCs, cabling, firewalls, etc.
- **Document management** – software which supports the products and offers users the ability to scan, file, and retrieve documents while saving valuable storage space.

As a major provider of these solutions, Canon has played a significant role in helping a range of business and non-business organizations to develop better information management systems. It has also developed a tailored suite of ICT solutions for the education market. These are designed to keep costs down and minimize teachers' administration time, therefore allowing them to concentrate on their real job.

The aim is to equip educational establishments with a business-level ICT infrastructure that not only meets the organization's own needs, but also contributes to producing the workforce of the future. With such a system, schools are able to enhance their students' ability to learn, practice, and hone their information management skills. For example, with the right infrastructure in place, students could access the school's website remotely from home to help with their homework. This site could even contain lesson notes to assist parents/caregivers in supporting the learning experience.

Many schools operate within severe budgetary constraints. One solution, therefore, is to lease rather than purchase outright. Buying outright ties up resources that could better be used for other educational purposes, thus using a significant portion of the head teacher's equipment budget. Increasingly, schools recognize leasing as the best solution for hiring hardware such as computers and other essential equipment like copiers.

Schools are relatively large organizations and, as such, are able to benefit from economies of scale, including technical economies. Technical economies stem from using more sophisticated techniques to reduce costs. Proactively developing an information management system based on the latest peripherals, document management systems, and voice data is a good example of using technical economies of scale for better financial management.

Economies of scale are the advantages of doing something on a large rather than small scale. Economies of scale lower the unit cost of production. For example, producing 1,000 high quality copies of a school prospectus on a modern dedicated in-house copier is much cheaper (per copy) than ordering 100 copies of the prospectus from a local printer.

Conclusion. Sophisticated information and communication technology systems contribute to the efficient running of organizations. An integrated system such as the one outlined above enables all of the separate parts of the organization to pull in the same direction. Canon has a long history of providing appropriate technological systems to businesses. The company is now helping educational organizations to operate in a business-like way through the development of strategically focused information management systems.

Questions
1. Characterize the competitive environment faced by Canon.
2. What are the key benefits an organization can reap by integrating its information and communication technologies (ICT)?
3. How would you define a "well-integrated information system"? What might be the key benefits a well-integrated information system can offer to an organization?

Part IV

Sustainable Value Chain Management

CHAPTER 10

Global Supply Chain Management

Global supply chain management (**G-SCM**) is about managing business activities in the supply chain, which is configured and coordinated on a global scale. Thanks to ever-increasing **globalization** among small and medium-sized enterprises, as well as large multinationals, it has rapidly become an important issue in management. Despite its perceived importance, however, G-SCM remains an area that has not been systematically researched to give a sense of "integration" as an important management issue. In this chapter, we present an integrating framework, i.e., a **process model of global supply chain management**, which contains most of the key G-SCM issues and subjects in a systematic way so that individual study outcomes accumulate, rather than disperse. Moreover, the framework will help managers to plan their global supply chain strategy more systematically. After introducing the framework, we delineate its key elements in detail.

Key Learning Points

- From the supply chain management perspective, we define globalization as managing business activities, or value chain activities, configured and coordinated on a global scale.
- The process model of global supply chain management is based on two dimensions: time and scale/scope.
- There are four essential time epochs in globalization, i.e., pre-entry, entry, post-entry, and exit or transition.
- The scale/scope dimension is a set of strategic variables for which the global company has to develop detailed choices and plans during the globalization process.
- The learning propensity model (LPM) encompasses the learning principles which underlie the process model. There are two additional methodologies, market-based learning and risk containment analysis, based on the learning propensity model.

學 WISDOM BOX 10.1
Wisdom and Insights

Breaking an Impasse through Creating New Links

How fast should we globalize? This is one of the most challenging questions the CEO of a global company should contemplate. Although growth itself cannot be the ultimate goal of globalization, however, it is certainly an important stepping stone for sustainable globalization. Suppose a company tries to grow in the global market through expanding its supply chain and thus enhancing its presence. As shown in Figure 10.1, the company initially expects a **reinforcing cycle** between **globalization effort** and **global expansion**. That is, as it makes an effort to globalize, the company can expand its supply chain and further its global presence, which in turn ensure that the company can afford to make more effort to globalize. Such an initial expectation can be depicted in Figure 10.2: as the company's globalization effort intensifies, its global expansion and presence also increase continuously.

Figure 10.1 Initial Cause-and-Effect Dynamics

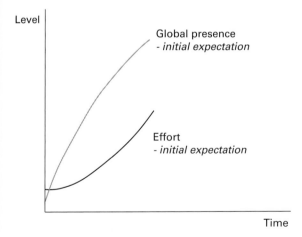

Figure 10.2 Initial Expectation about Input and Output

Box continues

However, the simple dynamics in Figure 10.1 do not describe the reality precisely. In fact, there is another dynamic cycle running with the company's **globalization strategy**. Figure 10.3 shows more realistic dynamics: in addition to the reinforcing loop between globalization effort and global expansion, there is a **balancing loop** consisting of global expansion and the current state of global capacity, i.e., whether the global capacity exceeds the company's capability to manage its global operations. As long as the global capacity is within the boundary of the company's global capability, the company can grow and amplify its presence in the global market as it increases its effort level devoted to globalization. Soon enough, however, the company realizes that it hits a point after which it cannot grow further as it has so far, even if it makes much more effort to globalize (Figure 10.4). It is the point where the capacity starts exceeding the capability, i.e., the company's current capability is no longer strong enough to manage the company's global capacity effectively: the constraint in Figure 10.3 has become "*binding*" and the company is now facing an impasse!

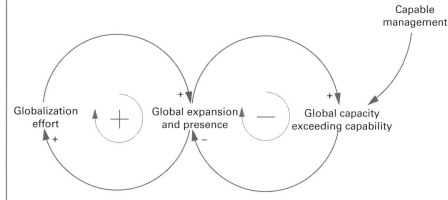

Figure 10.3 Actual Cause-and-Effect Dynamics with an Impasse

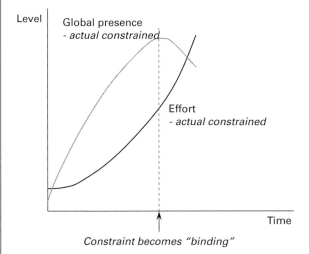

Figure 10.4 Actual Outcomes of Input and Output

Box continues

Is it possible for the company to escape from this impasse? The first step to finding an answer is to understand why it has to face such a stalemate in the first place. A close examination of Figure 10.3 reveals what determines the company's global capability. That is, its capable management or managerial capability decides the level of capability to enable the company to manage its global operations. As such, the only way to **break the impasse** faced by the company is to relax the **binding constraint**, i.e., to make the company's capability bigger than its global capacity by developing its managerial talent or capability further. Conceptually, the company can accomplish this by creating new links to the existing dynamics. Figure 10.5a shows how to break the impasse by **creating new dynamic links** to the existing dynamics in Figure 10.3: via its global expansion and presence, the company has to increase its sales, which in turn should be translated into increased profit; it should invest a significant portion of the increased profit in management development, e.g., through education, training, and other programs to nurture its managers and their managerial capability, which in turn amplify the company's global capability and relax the capacity constraint. If the company succeeds in designing this new "reinforcing cycle" by creating new links (Figure 10.5b), it can get over the impasse and grow and expand in the global market continuously (Figure 10.6).

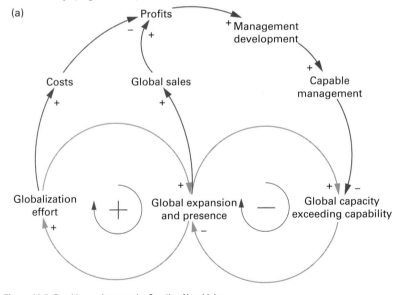

Figure 10.5 Breaking an Impasse by Creating New Links

Box continues

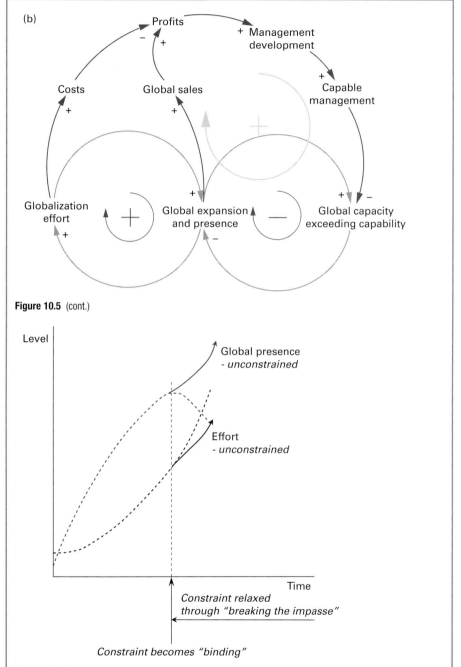

Figure 10.5 (cont.)

Figure 10.6 Unconstrained Outcomes of Input and Output

Although the conceptual logic "breaking the impasse by creating new links" seems clear and attractive, there is a caveat. It cannot succeed unless the newly created "reinforcing" cycle is fast and strong enough to dominate the existing negative, i.e., "balancing," cycle. In effect, whether this "creating new links" strategy is successful

Box continues

or not depends on how well the company manages the reinforcing cycle consisting of increased profit, management development, and managerial capability. In all probability, the company should have an integrating capability to make the reinforcing faster and stronger continuously.

Questions

1. Why does the company face an impasse that prevents it from growing further in the global market?
2. Explain the logic of "breaking an impasse by creating new links."
3. What does it take for the company to break the impasse successfully?

10.1   Globalization from a Supply Chain Perspective

Thanks to increasingly globalized competition, it becomes almost futile to try to make a distinction between G-SCM and domestic SCM. The basic principles discussed in the previous chapters are applicable to both global and domestic SCM. In this chapter, therefore, we focus on how the issues of globalization and global management are related to the subjects delineated so far, rather than consider global SCM as a new and stand-alone concept from scratch. More specifically, we want to develop a framework that systematically organizes key issues in SCM so as to help managers to design their globalization strategy from the SCM perspective.

There have been numerous studies on global supply chain management, but it is not easy to see the underlying connection among those studies. We define global SCM as *managing business activities, or value chain activities, configured and coordinated on a global scale*. It has rapidly become an important issue because of the tremendous forces driving globalization in the world economy. Despite its *perceived* importance, however, G-SCM remains an area that has not been *systematically* studied. As such, there appears to be an explicit phenomenon that although there are quite a few studies related to G-SCM in published research, there does not seem to be a systematic framework that can encompass these diverse studies as a whole so as to give them a sense of integration as an important management area, rather than just a collection of loosely associated individual investigations.

In this chapter, we present such a guide, a **process model for global supply chain management**, which we believe has the potential to alleviate the deficiency pointed out above. It comprises two dimensions: *time* and *scale/scope/speed*. In essence, it contains key decision factors for global SCM in a dynamic time sequence. It defines important decision variables (related to the scale, scope, and speed of global SCM) at each of the key decision timings (according to the time dimension). For instance, the framework can help managers to answer the following questions:

- How should the global company design its global supply chain at the time of entry to the foreign market?
- How much scale/scope should the company pursue for its global supply chain as its experience about global operations accumulates? And how fast should the company do this?
- How should the company determine when to exit from the market and/or whether to move to another?

10.2 Dynamic Decision Factors for Globalization

As we discuss later, the underlying theory for the process model is the **learning propensity model (LPM)** in the dynamic learning theory. The model defines and integrates various subjects and issues in global operations management according to two dimensions: *time* and *scale/scope/speed*.

A logical way to define the time dimension is to divide the decision horizon, using "entry time" as the focal point. Table 10.1 summarizes critical points in the time dimension along with their important decision factors. There are four essential time epochs in globalization, i.e., pre-entry, entry, post-entry, and exit or transition.

Time epochs:
① **Pre-entry – global conceptualization** – deals with the strategy issues a global company must take into account before actually entering the global market, i.e., during the pre-entry stage.

Table 10.1 Time Dimension and Decision Factors

Timing	Decision Factors
Pre-entry	Globalization motivation
	• Market saturation/attractiveness, competitive reaction
	• Efficiency, risk diversification, learning/innovation
Entry	Entry mode
	• Target country (market): cultural difference
	• Resource commitment, profitability potential
	• Value chain configuration and coordination
Post-entry	Growth/expansion strategy
Going-concern	• Scale, scope, speed (3S)
	• Vertical versus horizontal growth/expansion
	• Corporate culture, corporate DNA
	• Localization
Exit	Industry life cycle – new market opportunity
	Strategic trade-offs – resource opportunity cost

② **Entry – global initiation** – focuses on strategic factors for the global company when it actually enters the global market, i.e., at the entry point.

③ **Post-entry – global operations** – delineates the most dynamic implementation issues the global company needs to peruse when it designs its global expansion strategy, i.e., during the post-entry period.

④ **Exit** or **transition – global restructuring** – provides useful guides and insights for the firm when it faces a mature or declining market, product, or technology, i.e., strategic considerations at the point of transition such as regeneration, sustaining, or exit.

The other dimension is a set of strategic variables for which the global company has to develop detailed choices and plans, i.e., scale, scope, and speed, during the globalization process (Table 10.2). The strategic factors or variables such as key issues and subjects of G-SCM can be studied in the context of each time epoch defined above. For instance, when designing its G-SCM, the company must take into account many strategic factors, which might have different implications as well as characteristics, depending on the specific globalization stage, and thus require different strategic focuses.

The scale, scope, and speed as strategic factors are as follows:

1. Generic strategic factors: These are strategic and conceptual elements such as globalization motivation, global market entry mode, global expansion, global transition, and so on.
2. Structural factors: These are structural factors related to the global company's configuration and coordination mechanism, including issues of strategic alliances.
3. Strategic operations factors: Strategic tools and application methods related to global supply chain or global manufacturing network management are, in essence, part of the structural factors. However, considering their importance for successful globalization, they deserve to be identified as an independent dimension. Some of the examples that we have already discussed in the previous chapters include process flexibility, postponement, risk-based production planning, and the like.

10.2.1   Pre-Entry Period: Global Conceptualization

This is the time period before the company enters a global market. During this period, the company should plan and prepare for its globalization. One of the most important issues at this stage is to answer why the company tries to globalize, i.e., whether globalization is vital or not, by defining its **globalization motivation**. Unless the company has a definite motivation, it might find it difficult to stay the course during the ensuing globalization process. In effect, a strong "globalization motivation" enables the company to pursue a consistent strategy for effective globalization. The firm should regard globalization not as a fad, and therefore it globalizes after proper analysis of the logic behind the globalization drive.

Only when the firm can justify its globalization bid strategically can it define the basic building blocks with which it will design a more detailed strategy at a later stage. For example, the firm needs to start thinking about the potential strategic implications of its

Table 10.2 The Process Model for Global Supply Chain Management

Globalization Process	Global Conceptualization — Pre-Entry	Global Initialization — Entry	Global Operations — Post-Entry	Global Restructuring — Transition
Generic strategic factors for globalization	■ Globalization history ■ Globalization motivation ■ Country capability (organizing principles) ■ Administrative heritage	■ Entry mode (cultural, economic, political distances)	■ Global expansion strategy (globalization speed)	■ Transition strategy (regeneration, remaining, exit)
Structural factors for globalization – global network management	■ Defining/designing configuration and coordination	■ Forming strategic alliances (JV, green field, acquisition) ■ Implementing configuration and coordination	■ Managing strategic alliances (including subsidiaries)	
Strategic operations – global supply chain management (G-SCM)	■ Defining/designing G-SCM	■ Implementing G-SCM	■ Managing/improving G-SCM - Flexibility - Tech management - Postponement - Risk-based production planning - Localization	
Overarching theoretical foundations		Learning propensity model • *Dynamic learning* • *Market-based learning* • *Risk containment analysis*		

global supply network by measuring the pros and cons of different scale–scope combinations. It is necessary to take into account several conceptual elements such as globalization (or internationalization) history, the impact of the organization's administrative heritage on its globalization, country capability and its impact on understanding the dynamics of global competitive advantage, and the like.

Globalization motivation. A company can use globalization to gain competitive advantage. For instance, the company might try to gain "**efficiency**" by moving its manufacturing to a less developed country, where it can capitalize on relatively cheap labor and/or have a better access to inexpensive raw materials or other necessary supplies. It is also possible for the company to be able to diversify by globalizing. That is, investing in different areas on a global scale helps the company gain "**risk diversification**." For example, suppose the company has its manufacturing plants in China and the United States. Further suppose that the two countries face different industry as well as market cycles and thus experience dissimilar characteristics of risk, so that one country's economy might be booming, while the other's is in decline. Then, the company's overall market risk can be controlled, since the two countries' risks offset each other. Finally, the company can gain "**knowledge** and **learning**" by globalizing. Sometimes a company in a less developed country sets up a research center in a developed country. Certainly, the company tries to achieve neither efficiency nor risk diversification. Rather, it endeavors to gain more sophisticated knowledge and learn about the market and/or technology.

There are more "competition-driven" reasons, too. For instance, the company might have to pursue globalization as a "**competitive reaction**" to its competition. When its strong competitor enters a certain global market, the company also has to enter the market to react to its competitor's move, even if currently it does not expect to gain any competitive advantage. A similar strategy is "**strategic pre-emption**." For instance, the company might decide to enter a global market to pre-empt its competitor's entry, i.e., even if the competitor does not have any presence in the market.

There are "market-related" factors as well. The company has to try to globalize when the domestic market is fully saturated so that it is no longer possible to grow in the domestic market (domestic **market saturation**). Sometimes, even if the domestic market is not fully saturated, the company might want to move to a global market, when the foreign market offers much better opportunities, e.g., it is much easier or more efficient to grow in the foreign market (foreign **market attractiveness**).

10.2.2   Entry Point: Global Initiation

Once the firm has clearly identified its globalization motivation and contemplated the building blocks of the global strategy, it is ready to enter a particular global market. At the point of initiating globalization, i.e., the entry point, the firm has to decide its entry strategy: there are at least three key decision-making areas at the entry point, i.e., target market, entry mode, and value chain.

Target market. Which market should the company enter as part of its globalization? One of the foremost criteria to select a target market relates to the market's **economic potential** (i.e., profit or growth) and **learning potential** (i.e., knowledge about market and technology). Obviously, the most ideal target market is that with high economic potential and also high learning potential. Since such a market (i.e., with both high market and high learning potential) can be rare, we would regard a market as ideal or of strategic importance when it has at least one potential high, e.g., high market with moderate learning potential or high learning with moderate market potential.

How fast should the company enter an ideal target market or a market of strategic importance? It depends on the company's overall ability, which consists of knowledge and experience about the market, as well as its managerial capability relevant to globalization. If the company's ability is strong (i.e., extensive knowledge and experience, plus strong management capability), it can enter the ("strategically important") target market rapidly (**rapid entry**). Otherwise, it should enter it more gradually in a step-by-step or phased way, e.g., perhaps through forming a joint venture with an able local partner (**phased entry**). What if the market is not ideal currently, but seems to become strategically important in the foreseeable future? The company should approach such a market in a more opportunistic way (**opportunistic entry**), only when it has strong ability. For instance, the company might want to make a small investment in the market (e.g., to set up a small marketing or sales branch), observe the market development trend, and accumulate knowledge and experience about the market. It can increase its commitment when the market's potential develops significantly so that it becomes strategically important. If the market currently has little potential and the company's ability is frail, the company should not try to enter it, but try to grow its capability perhaps by focusing on its domestic operations.

It is also necessary for the company to take into account various types of difference between its home and the foreign country when evaluating the foreign market's attractiveness. It is in general that the larger the difference, the more difficult it is to enter the foreign market successfully. As such, when the company has decided to enter an ideal foreign market, but the difference between its home and foreign country is huge, it must pay keen attention to how to overcome the obstacles due to the difference: it should probably design a global strategy that enables it to prepare for resolving the problems prior to entering the market. There are at least four types of such a difference (i.e., distance), each of which comprises the following factors:

1. cultural distance – language, social norms, religion, ethnic and social networks;
2. economic distance – differences in consumer incomes, natural resources, human resources, infrastructure;
3. geographic distance – physical remoteness, common border, transportation and communication links; and
4. administrative distance – shared monetary or political association, political relationship, colonial ties.

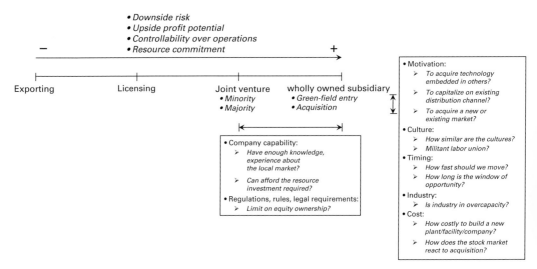

Figure 10.7 Entry Mode Decision

Entry mode. At the entry point, the company must decide how to enter the foreign market, i.e., the entry mode it should take. Which specific entry mode the company has to take depends on several key factors, e.g., the level of controllability the company desires to retain, the level of potential profitability the company can appropriate when the market is booming, and the level of resource commitment the company can afford to make. If the company wants to have a high level of controllability over its global operations, which is in turn consistent with a high level of appropriative profitability when the economy is booming, the required level of resource commitment is also high. It is also true that the larger the investment and commitment, the higher the **downside risk**, i.e., the risk the company should take when the market is in downturn.

There are four different types of entry mode (Figure 10.7): as it changes from simple exporting, licensing, and joint venture to wholly owned subsidiary, each of resource commitment, controllability over operations, upside profit potential, and downside risk increases. Nowadays, it is a widely held view that substantive globalization is achieved through either a **joint venture** or a **wholly owned subsidiary**. Depending on the ownership extent, there are two types of **joint venture (JV)**: it is a **majority JV** when the company controls more than 50 percent of the JV; otherwise, it is a **minority JV**. If the company owns 100 percent of the business entity in the foreign country, it is its "**wholly owned subsidiary**." The company opts either to build a new business from scratch (**green-field entry**) or to acquire an existing one (**acquisition**). There are two questions the company should ask before making a final choice about its entry mode. *When is it better or necessary to choose a joint venture over a wholly owned subsidiary?* Suppose that the company has decided to choose a wholly owned subsidiary. *Then which method, green-field entry or acquisition, should the company choose?*

There are at least two criteria to use when answering the question about joint venture versus wholly owned subsidiary, i.e., the company's capability and legal requirements such as regulations and rules. First, the **company's capability** is concerned with its level of **knowledge and experience** about the local (foreign) market and its amount of **resources** available for the local (foreign) market. If the company does not have enough knowledge and/or experience about the local market, there is a high risk associated with entering the market alone. In this situation, the company had better get help from a local partner, i.e., a joint venture partner, which can provide the company with economic, social, legal, and even cultural advice. Similarly, if the entry into the foreign market requires a huge amount of resources, the risk involved with the entry goes up sharply as well. In general, one company finds it difficult to invest significantly in entering a market: this is particularly true when the company lacks the necessary experience of and knowledge about the market. In this case also, it is better for the company to share the burden with a partner (not necessarily a local one) to reduce the required amount of resource commitment. The other is concerned with **legal requirements**, such as government regulations and rules. To do business in the local (foreign) market, the company should know the legal system in detail. For instance, the legal system in China is very unique and different from those common in most Western countries. In this situation, the company can find it useful to have a local partner who is very knowledgeable about the legal system in the local market. In this case, a joint venture can be a preferred form of entry mode. There is a cultural aspect as well. Let's consider an example. It is well known that the "**guanxi** (关系)" is very important in doing business in China: *guanxi* means "relationships or connections." It applies *not only* to private businesses, *but also* government regulations. For instance, in order to abide by the government regulations, sometimes it is necessary to capitalize on the *guanxi* with government officials. As such, without having a reasonable level of *guanxi* with government officials and/or business partners, the company might find it hard to do business efficiently in China. One way to overcome such deficiency is to find a capable local partner who maintains an extensive *guanxi* with the government officials and local business counterparts alike.

To determine whether it is better to start from scratch (i.e., a green-field entry) or to acquire an existing business (i.e., an acquisition), we consider five factors, i.e., motivation, culture, timing, industry, and cost. First, it depends on the company's **motivation** for globalization. If the company wants to acquire advanced technology in an existing company or to capitalize on an existing distribution channel to access the market, it might have to enter the foreign market through acquiring an existing firm, i.e., an acquisition is better than a green-field entry. Another criterion is concerned with corporate **culture**. In fact, it is well known that the cultural difference between firms in a merger and acquisition (M&A) is probably the number one reason why the M&A fails. When the company's corporate culture is very different from that of a potential M&A target in the foreign country, the company probably has to opt for a green-field entry, i.e., to enter through setting up a new business from scratch. **Timing** is also a key factor to consider. Suppose that the company sees a strong business opportunity in the foreign market for the next two years, but it would take three years to build its own business. In this situation, what should the company do in order to seize the opportunity? It is obvious that a green-field entry would make the company's entry too late! That is, it must globalize through an acquisition. In general, the window of opportunity, i.e., how long the market opportunity lasts, is a very critical "timing" issue. **Industry characteristics** in the foreign market are significant as well. If the industry already suffers from overcapacity or is fully saturated, it is unlikely that a green-field entry produces good results for the company. Finally, the company should take into account **cost** factors. *Is a green-field entry costlier than an acquisition?* The answer to this question depends on several economic conditions or factors, e.g., general construction costs, stock market premiums, and the like. Depending on the country's overall industrialization and/or labor market, it can be less or more costly to build a new business from scratch. If the stock market in the foreign country is very efficient, the company probably has to pay premiums when its intention to acquire a listed company is announced. As such, it is not easily generalizable whether a green-field is less or more costly than an acquisition. Therefore, the company must take into account all of the relevant factors when deciding the entry mode, in particular, between a green-field and an acquisition.

Value chain configuration and connection. At the entry point, the company also has to make a long-term decision on its value chain configuration and connection. As we defined in the previous chapters, configuration is about how to spread or locate value chain activities physically or structurally. **Global configuration** is the configuration done on a global scale. Once the configuration is decided, the company has to make a decision on connection, i.e., how to link and/or communicate the dispersed functions or activities effectively. All of the important factors and logics we have discussed about configuration and connection in the previous chapters remain valid for global config- uration and connection. The only difference is that now the company has to make a decision by taking into account additional factors relevant to the foreign market or context on a global scale.

10.2.3   Post Entry as a Going Concern: Global Operations

Once it is in the foreign market, the company has to plan how to sustain itself there as a going concern. In effect, the company has to develop its **growth and expansion strategy** in the global market. There are three dimensions to the growth and expansion strategy, i.e., scale, scope, and speed. **Scale** is concerned with the size of global operations, e.g., global capacity of production, R&D, procurement, and the like. The company has to decide an optimal scale of its global operations. Of course, it depends on many factors, such as the company's knowledge and experience about the global market, its resource availability, and so forth. **Scope** is about the range of global operations, e.g., whether the company has globalized its production function only or several functions, including marketing and R&D. **Speed** is concerned with how fast the company can grow or expand its global scale and scope. In effect, *how fast the company can globalize* is a function of the company's managerial capability for globalization, e.g., whether the managers are capable of managing or controlling the scale and scope of the company's global operations. Although a large physical capacity enables

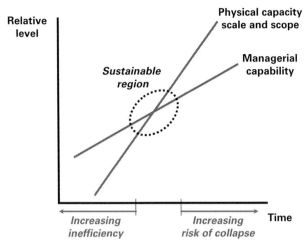

Figure 10.8 How Fast to Grow

the firm to realize economies of scale, it can impose a severe organizational strain on the firm at the same time. Managing an extensive global manufacturing network requires a high level of managerial capability. When the firm's organizational or managerial capability is overused, it can be ruptured, leading to the firm's own collapse under the heavy burden of globalization. Figure 10.8 shows such a situation. There is a caveat, though. When its physical capacity is far less than what its managerial capability can manage, the company might suffer inefficiency.

From the value chain's perspective, there is also an issue of **expansion direction**, i.e., vertical expansion *versus* horizontal expansion and across countries *versus* within a country. The company can pursue a **vertical expansion** strategy by expanding its value chain activities vertically, e.g., from manufacturing to marketing, R&D, procurement, and so forth. A **horizontal expansion** is expanding the scale and/or scope of a given value chain activity. For instance, the company can increase its manufacturing capacity in the current location from 1 to 2 million units per year or build another manufacturing plant in a different location in addition to its existing one. From a geographic perspective, the company might opt to expand its scale and scope **across different countries** or **within the same country**. Of course, when deciding its global expansion strategy, e.g., *vertical versus horizontal* and *across countries versus within a country*, the company has to take into account many important factors, which we have already touched on.

Finally, these days no company can ignore the importance of the **cultural issues** it faces if it wants to stay and flourish in the global market as a going concern. In fact, it is well known that cultural difference is one of the major reasons for failures in globalization, especially when the company's culture is very different from or incompatible with that in the foreign country or those of the companies it has to interact with in the foreign country. As such, it is critical for the company to understand and try to assimilate itself into the culture of the foreign country.

The process to adapt or assimilate itself into the foreign country's culture is often compared to the company's **localization**. That is, it is important for the company to adapt its **corporate DNA**, i.e., **culture**, to that of the local, i.e., foreign, market. Although it is not always easy to achieve complete localization, once the company localizes its management, managers, and the way it conducts business in the foreign market, this surely becomes a very strong competitive advantage. One criterion to test the level of the company's localization is to see whether the customers in the foreign country view the company as a domestic one, e.g., a true member of their local community, rather than a foreign company that is simply transferring the profit from them to its own country of origin.

10.2.4   Exit or Transition from the Global Market: Global Restructuring

As there is a right time for the company to enter the global market, there certainly exists a right time to exit from it. Facing the market or industry maturity, the company has in general three paths to choose from: to exit from the market/industry for good (to go out of business); to regenerate its PLC via technological innovation and secure its leadership position (to create or move to another PLC); and to stay in the market/industry as long as it is possible to earn profit to cover its variable costs (to survive as a marginal player or sustain their position as a dominant player). To determine its right path, the firm must consider two dimensions: its own technological capability and the market's or industry's profit reservoir, i.e., whether the market, albeit mature, has the potential to support the firm at least with a minimal profit.

Figure 10.9 systematically shows the four possible scenarios for the company facing market maturity or even decline. When the company's globalization capability is strong but the current market lacks further potential for profitability, the company doesn't have any other choice but to move to a new market or a new product life cycle, capitalizing on its capability (**regenerating, renewing**). If the company's capability is weak and also the market potential is limited, i.e., declining rapidly, the company cannot move to a new

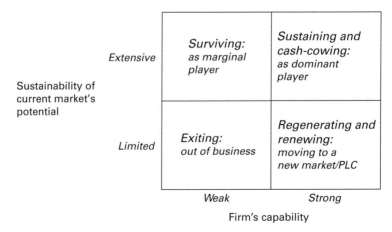

Figure 10.9 Strategic Choices in the Face of Global Market Maturity

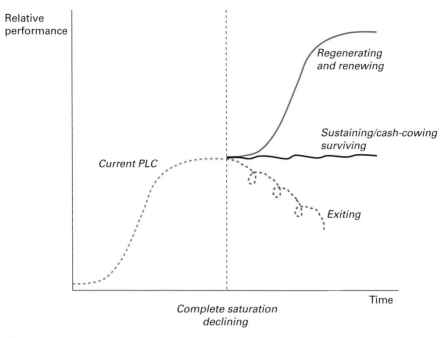

Figure 10.10 Alternative Paths amid Global Market Maturity

market: in this case, **exiting** from the market completely, i.e., being out of business, is probably the most logical choice. If the market still has a strong potential for profit generation, then surviving or sustaining the company's position in the market can be possible, depending on the company's capability. That is, if the company has a weak capability, it cannot regenerate itself to move to another opportunity, but perhaps it can be "**surviving**" in the market as a minor or marginal player. On the contrary, if the company has a strong capability, it may opportunistically stay in the market, while searching for better opportunities, i.e., it can be **sustaining** its position in the market as a major player and **cash-cowing** to accumulate resources that can fund its future strategic initiatives. Figure 10.10 graphically depicts the possible paths from which the company can choose when it faces the market's maturity and eventual decline. In effect, while contemplating the issue of market exit, the company has to make a decision on strategic trade-offs, which are largely affected by the relative advantages and also opportunity costs of the company's resources.

10.2.5   Flexibility in Globalization

There is no such thing as a perfect strategy which can be valid under any circumstances. This dictum applies to globalization, too. Therefore, it is futile for the company to try to design a perfect strategy at the beginning of its globalization process and assume it to be valid for the long term. Instead, it should develop flexibility to enable itself to adjust its globalization strategy as the global circumstances vary further down the road. We propose that such flexibility requires two strategic mechanisms, i.e., dynamic learning and continuous environmental surveillance. **Dynamic learning** consists of two elements: (1) since the company cannot know everything that might happen during the process of globalization, it should not try to learn everything a priori, but design a fast feedback process, i.e., fast **learning and updating process**, through which it learns a little about the market and technology, implements its strategy based on this learning, and updates and improves its current state of learning; and (2) in doing so, the company must pursue the balance between short-term and long-term learning, as well as performance. The company's **continuous environmental surveillance** can provide it with the capability vital to support its dynamic learning. The company can carry out continuous environmental surveillance through negotiation and continuous monitoring of cultural, administrative, economic, and technological changes in the global market. Of course, these two processes, i.e., dynamic learning and continuous environmental surveillance, must be derived from the company's global management capability.

10.3   Overarching Foundations

As previously explained, the framework categorizes key issues in global manufacturing according to two dimensions: *time* and *scale/scope/speed*. At a more fundamental level, the principles of dynamic learning theory underlie the framework. In fact, the learning propensity model (LPM) encompasses these learning principles. Based on the LPM, we develop two additional concepts, *market-based learning* and *risk containment analysis*.

10.3.1   Learning Propensity Model (LPM)

The learning propensity model was originally developed after studying the Korean shipbuilding industry. It enabled us to explain why two shipbuilding companies sharing much in common in terms of structural factors had developed completely different problem-solving mechanisms.[1] We successfully applied this model to analyzing the global capacity expansion strategies of two Korean carmakers:[2] the two carmakers pursued very different strategies for their global manufacturing capacity expansion, and thus experienced quite different globalization paths. The LPM turned out to be effective in explaining such intriguing phenomena, which previous theories had been unable to elucidate fully.

Figure 10.11 depicts the learning propensity model which was applied to the automobile industry in Korea. Determining factors effected by the top management's will, organizational capability, and endowed resources played a key role in deciding the firms' relative competitive advantage in the domestic market. The determining factors, along with the result of relative competitive advantage, influenced each firm's initial global strategy, which each firm's management implemented consistently with the context (condition) shaped by the determining factors and current competitive position.

[1] B. Kim, "Manufacturing Learning Propensity in Operations Improvement" (1998) 8(1) *Human Factors and Ergonomics in Manufacturing* 79–104.

[2] B. Kim and Y. Lee, "Global Capacity Expansion Strategies: Lessons Learned from Two Korean Carmakers" (2001) 34(3) *Long Range Planning* 309–333.

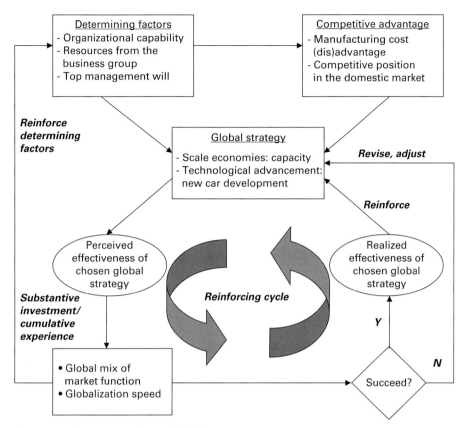

Figure 10.11 "Global" Learning Propensity Model

Depending on the fit between each firm's global strategy and the specific characteristics of the global market environment, each firm's strategy resulted in success or failure. With the result, the firm's management had to decide whether to reinforce or revise their initial strategy, thus starting a dynamic learning cycle.

There are two feedback loops working in the LPM. The smaller cycle consists of: global strategy → perceived effectiveness → specific strategic implementation → evaluation → realized effectiveness → reinforced or revised global strategy. This cycle repeats frequently, perhaps on a weekly or monthly basis, and compares to the **single-loop learning**. The other larger cycle consists of determining factors, competitive advantage, the smaller cycle (i.e., the single-loop learning cycle), and the interaction between strategic implementation and global market environment. These forces in the larger cycle can redirect or reinforce the determining factors in the long run. This cycle repeats on an annual or longer basis, and compares to Argyris's **double-loop learning**.[3]

---

[3] C. Argyris, *Reasoning, Learning and Action: Individual and Organizational* (San Francisco, CA: Jossey-Bass, 1982).

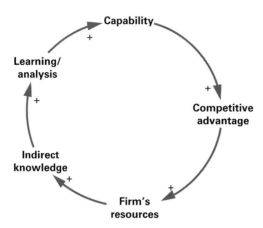

Figure 10.12 Monotonous Learning

10.3.2   Market-Based Learning

As a corollary of the LPM, we refined the dynamic concept of market-based learning. Consider the following question: *How should the decision-maker make a decision when the decision problem arises in a unique environment, where no prior information and/or data are available?* For the decision-maker facing such a problem, we suggest the market-based learning process, through which she gets initial market information/data quickly and rapidly updates her strategy by incorporating the information/data gathered from the market into the next round of strategy formulation.

We can think of two different learning processes: one is internally focused and the other is dynamically engaged in the market. Figure 10.12 shows the internally focused learning cycle, which we call "**monotonous learning**." A firm can learn through a somewhat abstract and conceptual process which is internally designed and managed. Although this kind of monotonous learning is useful, it is certainly not enough, especially when the firm faces a very unique and innovative environment. When the firm finds itself in such an uncertain competitive terrain, it has to reinforce its learning by engaging itself in the market at an early stage.

Since there is no reliable prior information/data available when the firm faces a highly new and innovative environment, it has to find out its own information/data to shape its long-term strategy. In fact, the market itself is where the firm can get the most relevant information/data about the market.

For instance, suppose your company wants to enter the Chinese market with a very innovative product, which has not yet been tested in that market. In this case, you probably do not have sufficient information/data about the Chinese market *directly relevant* to your innovative product. In this situation, it will prove futile for you to try to design your strategy using only very general, abstract, and sometimes conceptual information and/or statistical data provided by outside organizations. Even if you can afford just a small-scale test, you have to enter the Chinese market and engage yourself with the Chinese customers in order to obtain first-hand, direct, and the most relevant

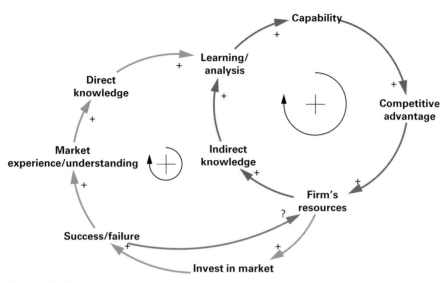

Figure 10.13 Market-Based Learning

information, and to incorporate these "live data" into your next round of strategy formulation (Figure 10.13).

In order to support the logic underlying the **market-based learning** process, let's consider the Korean government's experience in building the new internet infrastructure. Korea is one of the most advanced countries in the world in terms of using the highly sophisticated and efficient internet infrastructure. Regarding this enormous development in a relatively short period of time, we propose that the success of Korea as an internet powerhouse has much to do with the government's shrewd choice of ADSL as the next-generation internet technology, replacing ISDN in the early period of internet technology.[4] The choice of ADSL was made possible through the government's initial market-based learning process, which sent an unambiguous signal to the market so that the private sector could afford to make a long-term resource commitment to the then relatively unknown technology, ADSL.

Understanding and utilizing the market-based learning process should be very important to business managers and government policymakers alike, especially those who should direct their organizations in the global arena.

Facing a changing and complex competitive environment, managers and policymakers can't rely on indirect learning only. When they have to deal with utmost uncertainty and innovation, they have to engage themselves in the market where the real competition is being played out, albeit they might have to do it on a relatively small scale at the outset. In this situation, what counts is not scale or scope, but speed – *speed of getting the relevant information and updating the strategy appropriately.*

---

[4] B. Kim, "Managing the Transition of Technology Life Cycle" (2003) 23(5) *Technovation* 371–381.

10.3.3   Risk Containment Analysis

The market-based learning concept advocates the firm's early involvement in the global market as a way to gather more relevant market intelligence. However, the initial thrust should not be a haphazard, irrational entry into the new market. In effect, the market-based learning requires a deep analysis, or calculus, before actually engaging in the market. The risk containment analysis is one such deep analysis to support the market-based learning strategy. The basic concept of risk containment analysis is that the decision-maker or manager should know the full range of consequences due to her decision to engage the firm in the market before an actual decision is made.

The full range implies an entire gamut of decision outcomes, from the worst to the best outcome. The risk containment analysis should enable the manager to make an intelligent decision on the market-based learning strategy by providing her with probabilistically adjusted and sorted decision consequences. Only when the decision-maker understands the full range of what it means to engage in the global market can she make the decision in an unbiased and confident manner.

One example of risk containment analysis is to utilize the decision tree methodology as in Figure 10.14. This approach needs to be supported by more sophisticated tools, such as simulation. In effect, the risk containment analysis helps the decision-maker to understand what it takes to globalize by simulating potential upside and downside scenarios. In the example, we underscore the evolutionary development of supply chain coverage over time. A global company doesn't have to move its entire supply

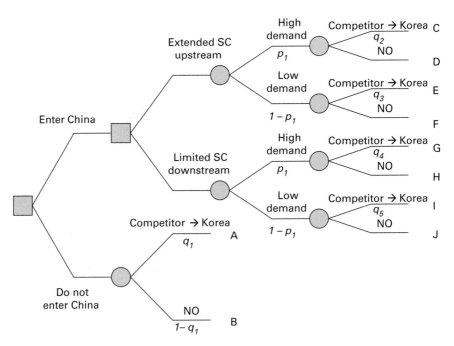

Competitor → Korea: competitors enter the Korean market

Figure 10.14 An Example of Risk Containment Analysis, Using the Decision Tree

chain or production process to foreign markets at the same time: it can adopt a gradual or measured approach so that it extends its supply chain coverage as it gathers more knowledge about the market.

Discussion Questions

1. Define global supply chain management. What are the key elements of globalization defined from the SCM perspective?
2. What are the important factors the company should consider before entering the global market, i.e., during the pre-entry period?
3. What are the important factors the company should consider at the entry point?
4. What are the important factors the company should consider after the entry point, i.e., the post-entry period?
5. As a going concern, the company has to think about its growth in the global market. What factors will affect the company's growth speed, i.e., how fast can the company grow, in the global market?
6. What are the three possible paths the company can choose when faced with possible exit from the global market? How should the company choose one of the three?
7. What are the overarching principles underlying the process model for global supply chain management?
8. What is the primary benefit of applying the risk containment analysis?

案例 CASE STUDY 10.1
LG Display's First Module Plant in Europe

In January 2012, Champ Shin, Senior Vice-President at LG Display (LGD, www.lgdisplay.com/), was evaluating one of the most important long-term strategic choices he had helped LGD to undertake in 2004. It was the company's decision to build its first module plant in Europe, i.e., the first plant LGD had ever built outside of Korea and China. In a week, Mr. Shin had to report the overall evaluation result about the Poland plant to the company's executive committee. He decided to prepare the report in two parts: one about the decision-making processes his team had gone through in 2004 to decide to build the European plant in Poland; and the other about the plant's performance since its construction, which was completed in 2007.

LG Display. In 2004, LG Display was one of the largest LCD manufacturers in the world. Being headquartered in Seoul, Korea, LGD had one R&D center, twelve LCD panel plants, and nine LCD module plants in Korea and China. In a relatively short period of time, LGD had grown to be a major LCD manufacturer and has since been continuously making new records of success, not only from the sales volume perspective, but also from a technological point of view. In 2004, LGD recorded revenues of US$8.0 billion, with operating incomes of US$1.7 billion, and enjoyed nearly a 20 percent share of the global LCD market. LGD continued to retain its leadership in the global LCD industry after 2004. In 2010, LGD recorded revenues of US$22.5 billion, operating incomes of US$1.2 billion, and over a 25 percent global market share. While investing aggressively to improve its technological competency, LGD has also built additional panel and module plants since 2004.

Liquid crystal display (LCD). In the early 2000s, LCD along with FPD (flat panel display) was a leading product in the display industry. An LCD consisted of two glass substrates, combined with a TFT (thin film transistor) array and color filter respectively, with liquid crystal sandwiched in between. A TFT array glass substrate, made by depositing thin films of semiconductor and electrodes over a glass substrate, controlled the pixel – the basic unit of image. A color filter glass substrate, a mosaic of color filters placed over a glass substrate, provided color information.

The LCD manufacturing process at LG Display was conducted in two types of plants (Figure 10.15): a panel plant and a module plant. In a panel plant, a high degree of technical skills was required throughout the entire process because of its complexity, which was conducive to risks of technology leakage and immense investment cost. Therefore, panel plants were mainly located in Korea. Unlike the process in the panel plant, the process in the module plant was seen as a simple fabrication process from a technological point of view, and there were almost no critical concerns about the leakage of core technology. Moreover, the shipping rate for an LCD module was several times higher than that of an LCD panel, and the shipping cost increased significantly since LCD TV sizes recently became even larger. Because of all these factors, it was often considered reasonable to have module plants near major client sites.

Source: Revised from, B. Kim, H. Kim, J. Shim, and C. Shin, "LG Display's First Module Plant in Europe" (2014) 18(2) *Asia Case Research Journal* 339–370. © 2014 World Scientific Publishing.

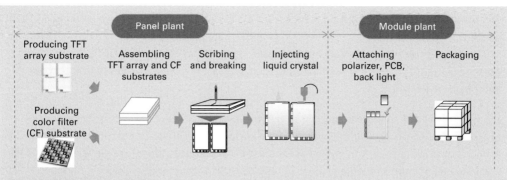

Figure 10.15 LCD Production Process

The global LCD TV market in 2004. Until the early 1990s, Japan dominated the global LCD market. However, Japan's grip on the market rapidly dwindled as Korean companies entered the market in the late 1990s and then Taiwanese counterparts grew quickly in the early 2000s. More recently, the two countries, Korea and Taiwan, were fiercely competing for a global hegemony in the industry. Amid the competition between Korea and Taiwan, Chinese companies geared up investments in manufacturing LCD to enter the global arena. Nevertheless, it was too early to count out the Japanese. In fact, Japan was still playing a leading role in R&D, while Korea was trying to improve its technology level by increasing the patents, leveraging its expertise and experience in mass production. As such, there was fierce competition among rival countries to be the first mover in the HDTV market.

In general, there were three groups of LCD products: the IT group for PC monitors and notebooks, the small LCD group for mobile phones, and the TV group. Since most countries didn't impose any import duty on complete sets of notebook computers and computer monitors, many IT companies manufactured those products in mainland China or Taiwan and exported them across the world. Similarly, most of the LGD's direct customers, who manufactured IT set products, were concentrated in China or Taiwan. Moreover, LCDs for IT products were small and light so as to make it economical for LGD to air-ship them from Korea to its customers in China or Taiwan. To support its customers in China more efficiently, however, LGD set up a module plant in Nanjing, which was the only module plant outside Korea as of 2004.

The situation was completely different for LCD TV. The smallest size of an LCD TV was 15 inches, which would be one of the largest sizes for a computer monitor. Moreover, the TV size was expected to get increasingly larger. As such, if the current air-shipment would continue for the LCD TV, LG Display would suffer from the exponentially increasing transportation costs. Unlike the IT set products such as notebook computers and computer monitors, most countries imposed heavy import duties on complete TV sets and therefore all of the global TV manufacturers, LGD's key customers, located their production plants close to their end-consumer markets. Many market analysts also believed that the EU countries would impose import duty on LCD TVs in the near future. It would be a devastating situation for LGD, since more than 50 percent of its sales were made in Europe and the company expected the European market size to be the largest and fastest-growing in the world.

Therefore, in order to capitalize on the fast-growing global demand for LCD TV, LGD had to quickly and significantly increase the capacity of its module plants. The question was where to build the new capacity.

Decision processes to build a module plant in Europe. For several weeks in January 2004, Mr. Shin was intensively working with his team. After lengthy analysis and heated discussion, his team finally chose Wroclaw in Poland as the site for the European module plant: they decided that it was crucial to build a module plant in Europe because of the market's strategic importance and the need for operational efficiency; they chose Poland as the most desirable country based on the country's economic performance, government efficiency, business efficiency, and infrastructure (Figure 10.16); finally, they selected Wroclaw as the final location of the plant after assessing such strategic aspects as the possibility of forming alliance/collaboration with the set manufacturing companies, strategic congruence with LGD, and the site's investment environment, and also such operational aspects as human resources, natural environment, land and utility, logistics, and SCM (Table 10.3). However, Mr. Shin realized that the most important thing should be to organize the issues related to the capacity expansion and the decision processes in great detail.

Table 10.3 Weights and Scores for Site Selection

Category	Weight	Criteria	Weight	Poland Wroclaw	C	A	B
Strategy	50%	Alliance/collaboration with set manufacturers	30%	13.5	11.7	12.0	8.7
		Strategic conditions congruent with LGD business	50%	23.5	20.5	21.0	14.5
		Site's investment environment	20%	8.6	8.0	5.4	7.0
		Subtotal		45.6	40.2	38.4	30.2
Operations	50%	Human resources	30%	13.1	11.8	10.5	10.5
		Environment	5%	1.9	2.0	1.9	1.9
		Land and utility	20%	9.0	9.6	9.1	8.6
		Logistics	35%	10.5	10.6	10.8	10.4
		SCM	10%	3.6	3.0	2.7	3.0
		Subtotal		38.1	37.0	35.0	34.4
		Total		83.7	77.1	73.4	64.6

Note: Wroclaw, Poland was determined as the best candidate site for module plant based on overall assessment. The team planned to use Lodz, located in central Poland, as a bargaining chip for negotiation. Also, the team considered country C, a big player in FDI (foreign direct investment), as another bargaining chip to maximize negotiation power.
Source: LG Display document (2004).

(a) Country competitiveness*

Country competitiveness	A	B	Poland (PL)	C	D	E
Economic performance	◑	◔	●	◕	◕	◔
Government efficiency	◕	◕	◕	●	◕	◔
Business efficiency	●	◕	●	◔	◔	◔
Infrastructure	●	◕	◑	◑	◑	◑
Total	●	◕	●	◕	◑	◔

◔ Very bad   ◑ Bad   ◕ Good   ● Very good

* Country D and E failed to be short-listed.

(b) Country attractiveness

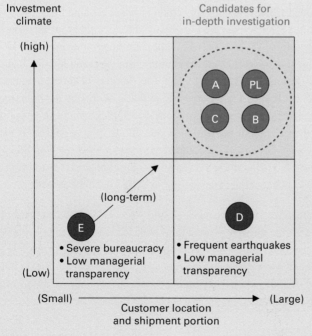

Figure 10.16 Initial Criteria for Country Selection

Strategic importance: The first issue which his team struggled to define was whether it was really necessary to build a new module plant. This required an extremely careful analysis, since total investment in building a new module plant would be enormous: it was expected that at least US$500 million would be required to build a new module plant in Europe. After lengthy and intensive brainstorming, the team finally identified two primary justifications for building a new plant in Europe. The first was concerned with the potential for market growth. The market for LCD TVs had grown rapidly and was expected to surpass the traditional CRT TV market in the near future. For instance, the annual growth rate was expected to be 123, 131, and 76 percent in 2004, 2005, and 2006, respectively. Although the industry experts predicted slower growth rates in later years, they would be still 47, 33, and 19 percent in 2007, 2008, and 2009, respectively. In terms of the volume, about 83 million units of LCD TV would be sold worldwide in 2009, compared to only 8.7 million units in 2004. Although LGD's capacity plan for TFT glasses showed continuous growth from 547,000 in 2004 to 953,000 in 2009, it was expected to be necessary to build a new module plant so as to capitalize on the growing demand in the market.

There was another justification. Geographically speaking, the Japanese market accounted for about 30 percent of the global LCD TV market in 2003. But, since the European market was expanding fast, it was estimated to be the largest market sometime soon after 2004. Moreover, Europe had been a strategic market to LG Display, whose sales in that region accounted for almost 50 percent of the company's global sales. As such, LGD desperately needed to have the presence in Europe so as to enjoy flexibility to make and deliver LCD panels to its customers and to become the unquestionable number one player in the market.

Operational efficiency: In addition to the strategic importance, LGD needed a European module plant for an efficiency imperative. In 2003, the company could afford to air-ship LCD TVs to Europe since the volume was not yet large. However, as the European market would grow ten times and the popular size of an LCD TV grew from 15–20 to 32–42 inches, air-shipping from Korea to Europe could become almost impossible due to soaring transportation costs. According to the team's simulation, the total module cost to make a 32-inch LCD TV in Europe, including raw materials, production, and delivery costs, would be 6.1 percent less than that in Korea, mainly due to lower logistical costs. Moreover, it was expected that the European government would soon impose an import duty on LCD. Without the LCD module plant in Europe, LG Display would be in a severely uncompetitive position since it would be unable to compete with the competitors that had plants in Europe if it had to pay the import duty in addition to higher transportation costs. In addition, further investment in the module plant was inevitable, considering its future business growth.

Product types: Once Shin's team agreed upon the need to build a new LCD module plant in Europe, they discussed what sizes of LCD TV the new plant should make. It was important because the plant's production lines and capacity all depended on the product types. Although currently 20- and 23-inch LCDs were selling more, it was expected that larger sizes like 32- and 42-inch LCDs would dominate the market from 2006 or 2007, when the operations at the new plant would start in earnest. As a result, the team decided to recommend larger LCD sizes for the new plant.

Plant site selection: Although it was decided to build a module plant, the team had to determine in exactly which country in Europe the plant would be built. First, they defined four initial criteria with which to select the country, i.e., the country's economic performance, government efficiency, business efficiency, and infrastructure. For the initial evaluation, the team considered six countries in Eastern Europe. Using both publicly available information and in-house research, the team shortlisted four countries; some countries failed to be shortlisted due to severe bureaucracy, lack of managerial transparency, and/or natural disasters such as frequent earthquakes.

In order to select the final destination, the team visited the prospective sites in the shortlisted four countries. Unlike the four criteria used to decide the shortlisted countries, the team used more managerial criteria to select the final site.

There were two categories of criteria: strategy and operations. For strategy, the team adopted three specific criteria, i.e., the possibility of alliance/collaboration with the set manufacturing companies (e.g., TV manufacturers), strategic conditions congruent with LGD business, and the site's investment environment. To assess the possibility of collaboration, they considered such factors as strategic importance, location, infrastructure, and supply chain capability of the set manufacturers. Regarding the strategic conditions, they evaluated how much each country's government was willing to support LGD's plant construction. Also, they checked whether there were other competitors that had already built strong ties with the local government or strong market recognition in the country. Airport accessibility of each country was also important. In terms of the site's investment environment, they evaluated the level of economic development – for instance, they employed such indicators as unemployment rates, annual growth rates, and the country's GDP. Each country's labor culture was also examined.

Regarding operations, they used five criteria, i.e., human resources, environment, land and utility, logistics, and SCM. For human resources, the general wage level and benefit packages as well as the working conditions in each country were reviewed. In evaluating the environment, the team gathered information on each country's climate, such as temperature, precipitation, and humidity. Conditions like air quality and noise level were also evaluated for workers' health and safety. Concerning the land and utility, they evaluated factors such as geography, real estate price, electricity, water, and communication networks, along with inbound and outbound logistics infrastructure and government policies on customs clearance. In terms of SCM, the possibility of local sourcing was primarily examined. Working with consulting companies and using the company's internal data, the team finally determined the weights to use and also the final scores for the four potential sites. Eventually, they chose Wroclaw in Poland as the site for the new LCD module plant in Europe. In fact, LGD expected its major suppliers and a TV set maker to set up their own plants nearby to form a cluster in the area of about 0.8 million m^2. In addition to the formal criteria, Poland had extra advantages. For instance, geographically, Poland was close to the largest market in Europe, i.e., Germany. As the fourth largest city in Poland, Wroclaw would be able to provide highly competent workers at relatively low wages: the city had about ten colleges and universities and Wroclaw University alone boasted ten Nobel Prize winners among its alumni and faculty.

Entry mode: With the site chosen for the new plant, the team had to decide the entry mode the new plant should take. Although LGD wanted to play the major role, it was a little worried because of the large investment required to build the plant. Thus, the team searched for an investment partner and succeeded in persuading a Japanese company to contribute 20 percent of the total investment in the project. The Japanese partner was mostly interested in the investment's profitability and therefore would not actively participate in management.

Supply chain management: As the LCD panel was a part for the finished product, i.e., TV, computer monitor, and notebook computer, it in turn required many parts and raw materials. Since it would be very expensive to transport those required parts and materials from Korea to Europe, local sourcing would be extremely critical to the success of LGD's operations in Europe. Unfortunately, however, the local suppliers were not cost-competitive, i.e., working with the local suppliers would put LGD in a seriously uncompetitive position in the market. As the first step to resolve this issue, the team tried to categorize parts so as to identify those that had to be supplied by capable Korean suppliers. In fact, LGD had to ask some of them to build their own plants close to LGD's LCD module plant. For the categorization, the team employed two dimensions, i.e., the need for strategic partnership and the logistic risk. The need for strategic partnership would increase if the parts were strategically and technologically important to LCD manufacturing. When the need for strategic partnership was high, the company should invest in developing its suppliers' core capability from a long-term perspective. As more parts were expected to be customized and the market demand volatility intensified more severely, the company should face a higher logistical risk if it tried to supply the parts from Korea to Europe, taking more than 30 days by ship.

Using the framework, the team categorized parts into three groups: group A, which required Korean suppliers to build their own plants near LGD's module plant in Europe; group B, which would be OK with local sourcing; and group C, which would be supplied by Korean suppliers without any additional construction in Europe, meaning parts would be supplied from Korea. Group A consisted of such parts as polarizer, backlight assembly, top case, and inverter, which the company believed could require five to eight Korean suppliers to build their plants close to that of LGD in Europe. Actually, the parts classified as group A were the core and most important parts for manufacturing LCDs. Thus, intensive coordination between part suppliers and LGD was critical to the stable operation. For instance, if there were any changes in the product design or quality problems arose, suppliers and LGD needed to communicate immediately and have face-to-face meetings frequently until the issues could be resolved satisfactorily. Furthermore, the parts were often customized for each major customer of LGD rather than standardized, thus planning and managing inventory of customized parts at an appropriate level would be quite challenging. Securing high quality of these parts was also crucial to overall LCD quality. Since LGD had developed a long-term relationship with many Korean suppliers of group A parts, they often had extensive knowledge about LGD's product and retained sufficient technology and knowhow to meet LGD's requirements. Thus, from LGD's perspective, effective utilization of existing suppliers was one of the key factors for starting operations smoothly in Europe. For local sourcing of group B parts, the team estimated that about five local suppliers were needed. Many of the group B parts were not as critical as the group A parts, but often required high flexibility and prompt delivery during manufacturing. As such, establishing a supply network in Europe for local sourcing would provide substantial advantages compared to sourcing from Korea. The group C parts were mostly standardized, i.e., it was not necessary to maintain extensive coordination with the suppliers as long as there were many alternative suppliers willing to supply those parts at competitive prices.

Now the team had to plan for developing the parts supply infrastructure in two ways simultaneously: on the one hand, it had to identify competent Korean suppliers for the group A parts and work with them to build their supply plants in Europe; on the other hand, it needed to identify competent local suppliers for the group B parts and train them to improve their quality to meet the standards set by LGD. The team developed a tentative time schedule for developing the supply infrastructure. After determining potential partners of group A based on the overall assessment of their supply capability as well as financial status, LGD suggested that they set up new plants near LGD's module plant in Europe. While that was a big decision for the suppliers, there were two major reasons that partners decided to build plants in Europe. First, they expected the investment to be profitable. LGD guaranteed sufficient sales volumes for the suppliers and furthermore they could jointly receive substantial benefits from the Polish government's support for the infrastructuref investment, which LGD had obtained via negotiation with said government. Also, they had built up trust in LGD over the years and desired to maintain a close relationship with the company for future business.

Human resource management: Finally, the team realized it was necessary to suggest a well-designed HRM (human resource management) plan for the European plant. They listed four key areas for which they had to prepare well before constructing the plant. First, in order to secure highly capable employees, it would be necessary to build a good relationship network with local universities. The team suggested conducting regular promotional activities in the local universities, offering scholarships, and sponsoring educational programs between local universities and R&D centers in Korea. Second, it would be critical to fully understand local labor laws and labor-management relationships. LGD observed that other companies experienced difficulties when globalizing due to their failure to understand these issues thoroughly. The team decided to recommend hiring local experts in such areas as labor laws and related rules and regulations in the country. Third, it would be important to study the national characteristics of the people in the foreign country and their work ethics, i.e., general attitudes toward working, since whether LGD would be successful in drawing wholehearted cooperation from the local employees could determine whether the company's foreign operations would eventually succeed or fail. They knew if the company controlled the local employees solely from its own "Korean" perspective, it would most likely fail. The key to success was how to motivate the local workers to work responsibly and eventually to have loyalty to the company. The first step was to find ways to reduce the turnover rates and the rates of absenteeism among the local employees: LGD needed to do so before starting actual operations there. Finally, LGD had to design the workforce composition to utilize the local employees effectively. Depending on the levels of skills and expertise required by different tasks and jobs, the company needed to define different employee categories such as regular full-time workers, part-time workers, and contactors. For instance, tasks requiring simple and repetitive activities like cleaning and logistics could be outsourced to outside contractors. The team also suggested hiring part-time workers and paying them more generously for the initial period before hiring regular full-time workers, in order to give more time to LGD to find highly competent and well-qualified workers for the full-time positions.

Performance evaluation of the European plant. In January 2004, Shin's recommendation to build the plant in Poland got the final approval. Now, with full support from the top, LGD immediately embarked on construction and the new plant in Poland started churning out LCD TVs in 2007.

When opened in 2007, the new plant was not without a few serious problems. As somehow anticipated during the decision-making process, there was an issue in managing human resources. Korean managers from LGD in Seoul tried to manage the plant operations in a Korean way, which put too much emphasis on improving performance at any cost, respecting a strict hierarchy, and top-down communicating. Unfamiliar with these demanding management styles, Polish employees were not embracing the management wholeheartedly and worked rather passively. Shin noticed the lower-than-expected productivity at the plant and also many complaints from the local workers. Although it was too early to say, nonetheless, Shin became very concerned about the initial poor performance at the plant. He appointed a plant manager and gave him an urgent mission to fix problems in HRM. Upon arriving at the plant, the plant manager launched several initiatives to boost the morale among the Polish employees. First, he implemented the employee exchange program, under which Polish employees visited LGD in Korea to learn more advanced technology and skills from Korean employees and managers, and also experience Korean culture, which would help them to better understand the corporate culture at LGD. Second, the manager launched a company project, called "Joyful Company," which organized training sessions for learning new skills, sponsored various social and sport events for socializing among Polish employees, and opened forums where the local employees expressed their opinions and suggested ideas to build trust with the management and to improve their capabilities to enhance performance and problem-solving skills. Shin delivered a clear message that the company's effort to improve the working conditions was not a single isolated event, but a sustaining, long-term endeavor.

Thanks to these ongoing consistent efforts, the employee satisfaction index improved: it was 3.4 out of 5 in January 2009, 3.8 in October 2009, and 4.3 in December 2010. Other plant performance indices were also improving significantly: compared with the performance in 2007, the plant productivity improved by 286 percent, the module defect rate decreased by 85 percent, and the return rate decreased by 69 percent in 2010.

Questions

1. Assess the entire decision-making and implementation process by the company. Observing the performance measures, do you believe that overall the decision was right?
2. Did Mr. Shin and his team fully take into account other possible limitations or constraints? What might have been possible loopholes or weaknesses in the analyses?
3. Assess whether the company implemented the strategy effectively, i.e., whether the company should have done something differently, once the strategy had been approved by the top management.
4. Is it possible for other companies to apply LGD's globalization strategy? Explain why or why not.

CHAPTER 11

Sustainability and Supply Chain Management

We define sustainability from a value chain perspective,[1] which we term **"value system sustainability."** Value system sustainability emphasizes a firm's effort to make decisions so as to be sustainable not just from the firm's own perspective, but from the perspectives of the entire value chain participants, including internal stakeholders like managers and employees and external stakeholders like suppliers, vendors, distributors, customers, communities, governments, and non-governmental organizations, and even those in other countries, i.e., in the global market. In a sense, it looks into the sustainability issue in a holistic manner, and therefore is sublimated to a highly comprehensive level. Sustainable action or behavior means that value is created in such a way that the output is more valuable than the input so that the surplus, i.e., output minus input, can be preserved for future value creation. Here, the concept of value is not just monetary, but encompasses various tangible and intangible elements. We develop a framework to define and assess a firm's corporate sustainability, i.e., value system sustainability. It consists of three dimensions. First, there are three areas of sustainability, i.e., economic, social, and natural (environmental). Second, there are stakeholders for whom the firm should pursue sustainability, i.e., the firm's effort for sustainability must be assessed not only by the firm's own internal perspective, but also by that of the external stakeholders. Finally, the level of sustainability should be measured. Our model uses seven levels determined by strategic and operational priorities: ignorant, passive, reactive, receptive, constructive, proactive, and, finally, transcendental.

Key Learning Points

- Value chain sustainability comprises three dimensions: sustainability area, sustainability stakeholder, and sustainability level.
- Consistent with the "triple-bottom-line" concept, there are three areas of sustainability: economic, social, and environmental (or natural).
- Sustainability strategy must be viewed from the perspective of both internal and external stakeholders, i.e., the entire value chain stakeholders.

---

[1] B. Kim and C. Kim, "Defining and Measuring Value System Sustainability: Initial Concepts and Blueprints," KAIST Business School Working Paper Series No. 2012–007 (September 1, 2012), available at: http://ssrn.com/abstract=2151705.

- A company's sustainability level is measured by its strategic and operational priority placed on sustainability activities.
- An ideal decision-maker for sustainability must have ethical, qualitative, and quantitative capabilities.
- An ideal decision-making process calls for three elements, i.e., calculus, creativity, and commitment.
- Supply chain strategy is dynamic in that its scope and scale evolve over time in response to changes in the environment, both economic and technological.
- To ensure sustainability in supply chain management, it is quintessential for the consumer to play an active and leading role in various economic and social activities. That is, consumer awareness should be a key factor or variable in studying sustainable supply chain management.

學 WISDOM BOX 11.1
Wisdom and Insights

Do Good Companies Thrive?

Sustainability comprises three dimensions: economic, environmental, and social. The social dimension, in turn, is related with ethics and also justice to a great extent. As such, sustainability cannot be properly fathomed unless ethics is taken into account. When considering ethics, we are always inclined to ask a question, *Do good companies thrive?* In effect, the question is about whether being good is also profitable. If someone had asked us this question, say, even just a few years ago, we could have found it difficult to say "Yes" unambiguously. It was mainly due to a general lack of empirical evidence. Over the years, however, fortunately or unfortunately, we have been able to observe relevant cases.

The first great shock came to us in 2010, when Toyota had to recall millions of its cars due to a problem causing the vehicles' gas pedals to stick.[2] Before this incident, Toyota had been an icon of quality for a long time. The company had been an unbeatable role model of quality. There were many who tried to explain how the quality beacon had failed so helplessly. We ourselves developed our own theory about why from the perspective of value chain sustainability. At the turn of the century, Toyota seemed to shift its strategic focus from quality to growth in the global market: it took thirteen years to increase its overseas output from 0.45 to 1.62 million units per year, but only three years from 1.62 to 2.17 million units in 2002.[3] We

Box continues

[2] See http://money.cnn.com/2009/09/29/news/companies/toyota_lexus_floor_mats/; and http://money.cnn.com/2010/01/21/autos/toyota_recall/.
[3] See www.toyota-global.com/investors/presentation/2003/pdf/041603.pdf.

suspect that in order to grow that fast, Toyota compromised its commitment to value chain sustainability and probably failed to work properly with its global suppliers (e.g., in a way its famous Toyota Production System should have recommended). Even before the shock of the Toyota recalls faded away or stabilized, we experienced another ethical failure by a Japanese company in the automobile industry. Now it was Takada that did not act honestly by trying to cover up the deadly malfunctioning of its airbags installed in millions of Japanese-made cars.[4] These two huge incidents of failure in sustainability and ethics shattered the belief about Japanese quality and its management principles as a whole.

Although it was very painful to lose quality icons such as Toyota and other Japanese companies, we still felt safe because there remained German companies that symbolized quality and integrity. But our last resort abruptly came to an end when the truly disappointing Volkswagen scandal surfaced in 2015.[5] We couldn't grasp how a company from Germany, which had always been the ultimate role model for engineering perfection and economic conscience, had been deceiving customers for such a long time regarding its diesel engines emitting pollutions beyond the set guidelines. But, a more fundamental question we should ask is, *How long did the managers at the company hope they could make the market go on not noticing the scam?* By any chance, did they hope that nobody would be able to find out a few "manipulated" lines among several thousands of programming codes, which were developed by such geniuses as themselves after all?

Let's go back to the original question, *Do good companies thrive?* In the present world we are all part of, we often feel that good people do not always get rewarded or even worse they sometimes fall victim to bad people. We have a similar feeling for business as well, wondering why bad companies thrive, while good ones fail. Is it true that being good is bad for business? We cannot answer the question definitely. Rather, we need to refer to one of Laozi's sayings:[6] "Although the heaven's net looks loose, it is fine enough to allow nothing to slip out." The closest proverb in English (Figure 11.1) might be "Heaven's vengeance is slow but sure."

天網恢恢 疏而不失
Heaven's vengeance is slow but sure.

Figure 11.1 Laozi's Saying

In Chapter 1, we defined value as a function of responsiveness and efficiency. In light of the ethics in business, we would like to refine the definition to include "sustainability" as an integral part of the equation (Figure 11.2). That is, to create the true value, the company must make an effort to improve and innovate in three dimensions simultaneously: efficiency, responsiveness, and sustainability.

Box continues

---

[4] See www.nytimes.com/2015/10/22/business/takata-and-honda-kept-quiet-on-study-that-questioned-airbag-propellant.html?_r=0; and www.cnbc.com/2015/10/23/us-inquiry-into-defective-takata-airbag-widens.html.
[5] See www.bbc.com/news/business-34324772.   [6] See https://en.wikipedia.org/wiki/Laozi.

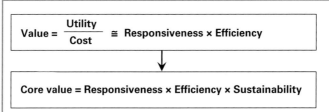

Figure 11.2 Core Value with Sustainability

Questions

1. What do you think are the main reasons for the Toyota recalls in 2010? What do you believe are the main causes that drove such a fiasco?
2. What about the case of the Takada airbag scandal? Is the case similar to that of Toyota? Why or why not?
3. Regarding the Volkswagen scandal, some people blamed the US government for divulging the company's scam. Others criticized the high emission standards set by the US government in the first place. Do you agree with these people who place the blame on the US government divulging the scam? Why or why not?
4. Are there any actions that the market or consumers should take in preventing companies from turning unethical or unsustainable? What do you think you can do as a consumer?

學 WISDOM BOX 11.2
Wisdom and Insights

Who Am I?

When you are faced with a dilemma involving a social or economic injustice, what should you do? We suggest that in such a situation, everybody should ask, *"Who am I?"* The question is essentially *"Why do I exist?"* Here, we develop a framework to define who the decision-maker is from an ethical perspective. It comprises two dimensions, i.e., **critical mind to recognize problems** and **action to change**. We believe it is important for the decision-maker or a human being to be able to recognize and understand an ethical problem when it actually exists in the world. It is the kind of problem that is involved with moral, ethical, or social dilemmas. That is, the first dimension of the framework is concerned with whether the person has a critical mind to fathom why a certain event or issue is problematic and should be corrected. The other is the decision-maker's commitment to taking an action to rectify the problem. It is true that justice is not served until an action to uphold it is actually taken. We all know that even if a person finds a problem, it takes more than just "thinking or believing" to actually correct the problem. That is, an action must be taken and it is true bravery to take an action to fix the wrongdoing. Using these two dimensions,

Box continues

critical mind and action, we define four different types of decision-maker from an ethical standpoint (Figure 11.3).

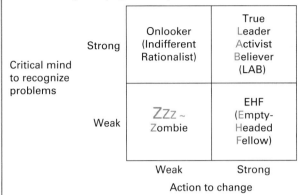

Figure 11.3 Typology of Decision-Makers from an Ethical Standpoint

When the decision-maker has a critical mind to recognize the ethical failure and is able and willing to rectify it by taking a strong action, she is a true **leader, activist, and believer (LAB)**. A LAB is the most ideal individual who can make the world a better place. Unfortunately, however, there are very few of them in this world. There is a kind of decision-maker who has the critical mind, but is unable or unwilling to take a concrete action to tackle the problem. This is a typical onlooker, who takes no action, and just talks all the time. At the other extreme, there is an individual who is always hasty in taking an action without proper understanding or knowledge about the issue, i.e., lacking any decent ability. This is an **empty-headed fellow (EHF)**. Unlike its amusing image, an EHF is a dangerous figure who can make the world degrade or deteriorate. When an EHF falls victim to its own greed, it becomes truly vicious one, and often destroys its own organization or the very foundation of human society. Finally, some in the society or organizations are individuals who neither have a critical mind nor are capable of taking a decisive action to rectify an ethical or moral failure. Although we hate to use the word "**zombie**" to define this kind of person, we couldn't find a more appropriate word. This kind of person is always looking for his own myopic self-interest without paying any attention to ethics or justice, willing to bend any principle so as to maximize his own profit, and without any shame in flattering a corrupt man of power (e.g., often an EHF) if doing so helps him achieve what he wants. It is usually assumed that these kinds of people are at least harmless or even benign small citizens. Regrettably, however, we must warn that sometimes or under certain dangerously concocted circumstances, they might become a powerful mob manipulated by an EHF, which in turn enables the EHF to achieve his own wicked goal of injustice.

Is this typology valid only for individuals as human beings? No, we believe it can be equally applicable to businesses and managers. We need managers who are LABs. If we trust that good companies thrive, we should also have confidence in the roles played by LABs. Only the manager who is a true leader, activist, and believer can be

Box continues

the one who can attest "good companies thrive" and "being good is profitable." Otherwise, we have no hope. We as humankind need and raise many LAB managers. *Which side are you on?*

Questions

1. Do you agree that some of the ordinary managers are those with a lack of critical mind and concrete action? What do you think is the greatest motivation of these kinds of managers? Why do you think they believe they should exist?
2. What do you estimate is the proportion of each manager type in the world? What is the percentage for LABs or EHFs?
3. Which type of manager do you think is the most dangerous to the business world?
4. Can you categorize customers using the same framework? Why or why not?
5. We would most cordially like to ask about your true thought. Do you truly believe that a LAB manager can make "good companies thrive" happen? What do you think are the possible obstacles that could make it fail?

11.1   Value Chain Sustainability

We now develop a framework of value chain sustainability, which is comprised of three dimensions, i.e., sustainability area, sustainability stakeholder, and sustainability level (Figure 11.4).

11.1.1   Sustainability Area

A firm's efforts to ensure sustainability can be grouped into three categories (Figure 11.5), i.e., the "triple-bottom-line" concept consisting of economic, social,

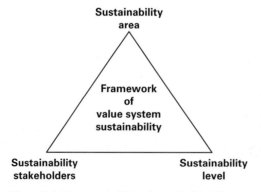

Figure 11.4 A Framework of Value System Sustainability

Table 11.1 Characteristics of Sustainability Area

Sustainability Area	Elements of Defining Characteristics
Economic Sustainability	Economic cost and benefit analysis
	Economic efficiency
	Output larger than input
	Current profit with reserved resources for future economic activities
	Self-financing as a going concern
Social sustainability	Social stability and development
	Improving human conditions such as education, job skills, quality of life
	Self-actualization
	Justice, fairness, moral, ethics, and trust
	Preservation and improvement of culture
Environmental sustainability	Earth carrying capacity
	Environmental friendliness
	Reduction of CO_2 emission
	Carbon footprint
	Greenhouse gas effect, ozone

Figure 11.5 Sustainability Area

and environmental (or natural) aspects.[7] Table 11.1 summarizes the elements of defining characteristics for each dimension.

Economic sustainability. The firm must make sure that it satisfies economic sustainability. That is, the firm should not consume economic resources more than the economic value it creates by making products and services for the market. Economic efficiency is a primary factor in judging the firm's effort for economic sustainability.

---

[7] J. Elkington, *Cannibals with Forks: The Triple Bottom Line of 21st Century Business* (Oxford: Capstone, 1997).

Social sustainability. While carrying out its economic activities, the firm must make decisions in a way to ensure social sustainability. In order for society to be sustainable, its members should adhere to basic moral or ethical principles, sometimes embedded in its cultural systems. Justice, fairness, morality, and ethics constitute criteria to assess the firm's effort for social sustainability.

Environmental (natural) sustainability. While conducting its economic activities, the firm must preserve the environment or the natural **ecosystem**. For instance, it should not emit excessive CO_2, which could exacerbate the greenhouse effect and contribute to destroying the natural climate balance. The firm should not abuse natural resources such as trees, water, minerals, and so forth to the extent that the **earth capacity** of those resources is irrevocably diminished so that the future generations cannot enjoy a quality of life greater than or equal to the current level.

11.1.2   Sustainability Stakeholder

Internal stakeholders. There are stakeholders inside the firm, i.e., managers, employees, and all those working for the firm within its legal boundary. When it makes an effort to ensure sustainability, the firm views this issue from the perspectives of its internal stakeholders.

External stakeholders. While pursuing sustainability, the firm has to take into account its value chain as a whole, i.e., the perspectives of the stakeholders throughout its value chain. There are value chain stakeholders such as vendors, suppliers, distributors, and customers. In addition, as a member of the broader society, the firm must also consider general stakeholders such as communities, non-governmental organizations, the general public, and governments. Finally, the firm is also a member of the global market, and thus it must take into account the perspectives of the stakeholders in other countries, albeit in varying degrees.

Accordingly, we group these stakeholders as follows:

(a) internal stakeholders: managers, employees inside the company
(b) external stakeholders
    A. value chain stakeholders
        i. indirect upstream
       ii. direct upstream
      iii. direct downstream
      iv. indirect downstream
       v. customers

    B. national stakeholders (not directly involved in the focal value chain)
        i. general public
       ii. communities (including NGOs)
      iii. other competing value chains
      iv. other non-competing value chains

         v. governments

      C. global stakeholders

         i. comprehensive stakeholders in the global market, i.e., counterpart stakeholder groups like those within the national boundary

Figures 11.6 and 11.7 depict the stakeholders within the national boundary and in the global context. Table 11.2 shows detailed definitions and descriptions of the value chain stakeholders.

Table 11.2 Characteristics of a Sustainability Stakeholder

	Stakeholders	Characteristics
Internal (to the focal firm)		- Firm's top management - Firm's employees, including managers and workers
Value chain	Indirect upstream	- Upstream participants indirectly transacting with the focal company, usually through direct upstream participants - Example: 2nd or lower tier suppliers, vendors, cooperating companies in the upstream
	Direct upstream	- Upstream participants immediately linked with the focal firm - Upstream value chain participants directly transacting with or controlled by the focal company - Example: 1st tier suppliers, vendors, cooperating companies in the upstream
	Direct downstream	- Downstream participants immediately linked with the focal firm - Downstream value chain participants directly transacting with or controlled by the focal company - Example: 1st tier distributors, sales and logistical channels, cooperating companies in the downstream
	Indirect downstream	- Downstream participants indirectly transacting with the focal company, usually through direct downstream participants - Example: 2nd or more remote tier distributors, sales and logistical channels, cooperating companies in the downstream
	Customers	- Buyers or consumers of the products and services provided by the focal firm - Possible to include final or ultimate buyers/consumers of the product/services that are made of products and services provided by the focal firm

Table 11.2 (cont.)

	Stakeholders	Characteristics
National boundary	General public	- People in the country where the focal company is operating
	Communities (NGOs, others)	- Communities either directly or indirectly connected with the company - Non-governmental organizations (NGOs), social groups, interest groups
	Competing value chains	- Other value chains that are competing with the company's own value chain (e.g., Samsung Electronics' value chain is competing with that of LG Electronics in Korea)
	Non-competing value chains	- Other value chains that are not *directly* competing with the company's own value chain (e.g., Samsung Electronics' value chain is not directly competing with that of Hyundai Motors in Korea, at least currently)
	Governmental	- Governments at both local and national levels
Global market stakeholders	General public	- People in foreign countries where the focal company is not directly operating
	Communities (NGOs, others)	- Communities in the foreign countries - NGOs, social groups, interest groups in the foreign countries
	Competing value chains	- Other value chains in the foreign countries that are directly competing with the company's own value chain (e.g., Samsung Electronics' value chain in Korea is competing with that of Apple in the United States)
	Non-competing value chains	- Other value chains that are not *directly* competing with the company's own value chain (e.g., Samsung Electronics' value chain in Korea is not directly competing with that of GM in the United States, at least currently)
	Governmental	- Governments at both local and national levels in the foreign countries

11.1.3   Sustainability Level

We develop a framework to measure the firm's sustainability level. The framework is defined by two dimensions: strategic priority and operational priority. This enables us to identify seven levels of a firm's sustainability for each pair of sustainability area and stakeholder, i.e., ignorant, passive, reactive, receptive, constructive, proactive, and finally transcendental.

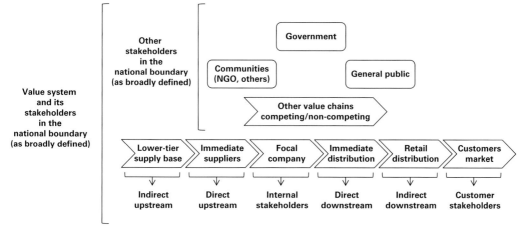

Figure 11.6 Stakeholders within the National Boundary

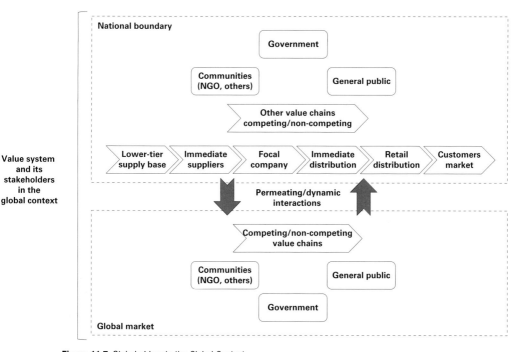

Figure 11.7 Stakeholders in the Global Context

Strategic priority. This is concerned with how much "**strategic commitment**," i.e., strategic significance, the company has attached to its sustainability effort. There are five strategic priorities, i.e., liability, neutrality, relevance, asset, and enabler. Table 11.3 discusses the detailed characteristics of these strategic priorities.

Table 11.3 Characteristics of Strategic Priorities

Strategic Priority	Characteristics
Liability	It is viewed as a burden to the company. It doesn't help the company to have more competitive advantage. On the contrary, it actually hampers the firm's competitive advantage. As such, the company wants to avoid the strategic liability as much as possible. Sometimes the company believes the best strategy to deal with the strategic liability is to ignore it.
Neutrality	It is neutral to the company's competitive advantage. That is, it doesn't help the company to enhance its competitive advantage, nor it does exacerbate the company's competitive advantage.
Relevance	Now the company starts to recognize that the issue of sustainability is relevant to its competitive advantage, albeit not quite sure about how to deal with it so as to make it positive for enhancing competitive advantage.
Asset	The company views the issue from a strategic perspective and believes it can understand clearly how to utilize it so as to enhance its own market position significantly. That is, resolving the issues becomes the company's key asset to improve its competitive advantage.
Enabler	Finally, the company masters how to deal with the issue most effectively so that its impact on the company goes beyond the current competitive advantage. The company's capability of sustainability enables it to improve its organizational competence that can transform the entire strategy and process to the extent that the company can enjoy much stronger competitive advantage in the global market, not just currently, but also in the future.

Operational priority. This is concerned with how much implementation (operational) priority the company has devoted to its sustainability activity. There are three types of activities the company can implement for sustainability, i.e., corrective, preventive, and innovating activities. More detailed definitions of operational priorities are listed in Table 11.4.

Using the two attributes, *strategic priority* and *operational priority*, we can define seven levels of sustainability:

(1) ignorant;
(2) passive;
(3) reactive;
(4) receptive;
(5) constructive;
(6) proactive; and
(7) transcendental.

Each of these sustainability levels is characterized by strategic and operational priorities as shown in Table 11.5.

Table 11.4 Characteristics of Operational Priorities

Operational Priority	Characteristics
Corrective activities	The company takes actions only when it identifies problems (e.g., system breakdowns) due to its failure to attend to sustainability. For example, abiding by the charges imposed by the government agency for environment protection, the company is forced to repair its manufacturing process that is generating excessive CO_2.
Preventive activities	The company takes actions in order to prevent the imminent problems due to its failure to attend to sustainability. For example, even though the current CO_2 emission is well under the legal limit, the company takes a preventive action to fix the manufacturing process, which the company estimates could start emitting excessive CO_2 in a few months.
Innovating activities	The company invests in research and development to find out more innovative ways to reduce future harms to sustainability. For example, although its manufacturing process is in good shape and not generating any substances harmful to sustainability, the company invests actively in research to develop newer processes to be more consistent with and supportive of its sustainability effort.

Table 11.5 Characteristics of Sustainability Levels

Sustainability Level	Attribute Dimensions	
	Strategic Priority	Operational Priority
Ignorant	– Sustainability is regarded as a liability, something to avoid as much as possible. – The best way to deal with it is to ignore it.	– Usually not to take any concrete actions to deal with the sustainability issue. – To take a corrective action only in a very limited sense.
Passive	– To deal with only the aspects that are clearly violating governmental regulations.	– To take an action only ex post. – To try to meet the minimum standards set by the government.
Reactive	– Still sustainability is regarded as a liability, albeit in a limited sense.	– The company tries to be more active in taking actions to fix problems that violate the government's regulations.
Receptive	– Now sustainability is treated as neutral to the company's competitive advantage, i.e., neither contributing to nor harming its competitive advantage.	– The company becomes more willing to take actions to correct obvious sustainability failures. – The company begins taking actions to prevent potential sustainability failures.

Table 11.5 (cont.)

Sustainability Level	Attribute Dimensions	
	Strategic Priority	Operational Priority
Constructive	– The company realizes sustainability is real and relevant to the company's competitive advantage. But, still the company doesn't firmly trust that sustainability can contribute to strengthening its competitive advantage significantly.	– The company becomes increasingly active and aggressive in taking preventive measures even without clear and visible failures.
Proactive	– The company views sustainability as an important asset for its competitive advantage. As such, it embarks on defining ways to leverage sustainability for enhancing its competitive advantage significantly.	– The company increasingly pays more attention to finding innovative ways to prevent sustainability failures as a pre-emptive measure.
Transcendental	– The company sees sustainability as one of the most important capabilities it can nurture not only for current competitive advantage, but also for future competitive advantages. – It designs/develops every strategy by taking into account sustainability issues and considerations.	– The company fully integrates across its various strategic and operational functions in its efforts to deal with present and future (potential) sustainability failures. – It has developed an extensive capability to find out innovative ways to pre-empt sustainability failures.

Figure 11.8 shows how these seven sustainability levels are mapped on the space defined by the two types of priorities. As in the figure, we expect there is in general a positive relationship between a company's strategic priority and operational priority regarding its sustainability efforts. In the real world, however, companies might show different patterns. For instance, some companies might assign very high strategic priorities with very low operational priorities to their sustainability efforts, showing a pattern deviating from the curve in Figure 11.8. There could be an opposite pattern as well, e.g., very high operational priorities with very low strategic priorities. When measuring the companies' sustainability levels, we must take into account these irregular patterns.

Sustainability is an almost noble concept in the modern society. Despite its perceived importance, however, it still remains poorly defined and understood. In the early days,

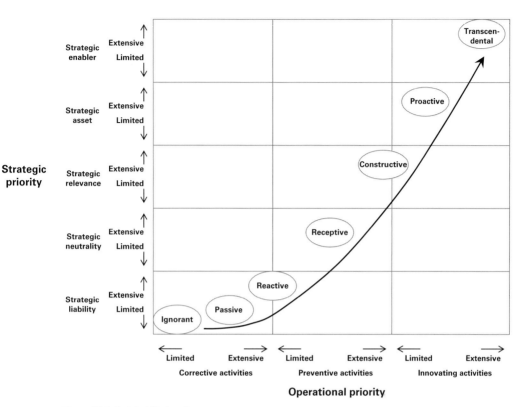

Figure 11.8 Sustainability Level

most efforts for sustainability were made by governments, local and national. Primary enforcement tools adopted by governments were legalistic approaches like decrees and regulations. For the most part in the past, business was slow or passive in embracing the principles of sustainability, focusing on responding to the governmental regulations ex post. More recently, things have changed as the market's demand as well as awareness of sustainable development has become stronger. New concepts more relevant to business have rapidly emerged, e.g., **corporate sustainability**. An increasing number of firms are now accommodating the new concepts, albeit in varying degrees.

In this section, we have approached sustainability from a value chain perspective, i.e., sustainability that must be defined and assessed from the viewpoints of various stakeholders sharing the same value chain. In effect, the value chain perspective is an integrating standpoint rooted on broader literature, which amalgamates **green management**, **social responsibility**, **corporate sustainability**, and **business ethics**. The most important premise we espouse in this discourse is that unless the firm understands and wholeheartedly accepts the value chain sustainability, it is impossible to expect any significant or meaningful improvement in terms of sustainability in a true sense; that is, any governmental regulation alone is doomed to fail unless it is supported by the behavioral and strategic changes on the part of the firm, consistent with the value chain sustainability.

11.2   Fundamental Characteristics and Roles of the Capable Decision-Maker

Supply chain management and competitive advantage. In order to have competitive advantage vis-à-vis competitors in the market, the firm should excel in at least one of three strategic choices: overall **cost leadership**, **differentiation**, and **focus**.[8] There is a simplified categorization of supply chains into efficient and responsive ones.[9] **Competitive priorities** of the **efficient supply chain** include low cost, consistent quality, and on-time delivery. These are the operations principles that must support the firm's competitive strategy to accomplish low-cost leadership and differentiation.

On the other hand, the primary motivation for the **responsive supply chain** is to enable the firm to improve such capabilities as development speed, fast delivery times, customization, volume flexibility, high-performance design quality, and learning/integrating ability. In fact, all of these capabilities should underlie the firm's focus strategy, which requires extraordinarily advanced competencies in both technology and management. It clearly shows that effective supply chain management has to be one of the most important strategic levers the firm needs to master to maneuver in order to achieve competitive advantage and sustainability in the market. Effective SCM must be part of the firm's core competence. By coordinating and integrating connected activities in the supply chain, the firm becomes more capable of designing a winning competitive strategy and sustainability that optimally combine the strategic choices, i.e., low-cost leadership, differentiation, and focus.

Supply chain capability for sustainability and globalization. In order to enable her company to be competitive in the global market and sustainability, the decision-maker should have enduring characteristics. In this section, we discuss such characteristics and roles of a capable decision-maker, i.e., one construct consisting of "qualitative-quantitative-ethical" dimensions and the other of "calculus-creativity-commitment" dynamics.

There is one caveat. Although it is the top manager that has been regarded as the key decision-maker in the company, we have to emphasize that all of the members of the company, including the workers (i.e., labor), should participate in the decision-making process in varying degrees. That is, in order to achieve sustainability in the global market, it is essential for all of the company's own stakeholders (managers and workers alike) to make an effort to design and implement the company's strategic activities albeit at varying levels. As an example, we already presented a case where a Korean carmaker was struggling to reach a world-class quality level through administrative efforts without the active participation from the workers on the production lines.[10] The managers invented a concept of "**administrative quality**" which could be achieved at a relatively high level through the management's commitment only (without involving the labor's

---

[8] M. E. Porter, *Competitive Strategy: Techniques for Analyzing Industries and Competitors* (New York: The Free Press, 1980).

[9] M. L. Fisher, "What Is the Right Supply Chain for Your Product?" (1997) *Harvard Business Review* (March–April), 105–116.

[10] See Case Study 1.2, "Administrative Quality at an Automobile Company."

effort). While the administrative quality could help the company to compete against major players in the market for a limited time, in order to *consistently* win against the truly top carmakers in the global market it has to acquire the ultimate **world-class quality**, which will be hard to achieve without an active role played by the labor. To compete and win against world-class companies, the firm should attain the **integrated quality**, which requires both labor and management to actively participate in the quality improvement process. In sum, attaining competitiveness and sustainability in global supply chain management requires wholehearted efforts and support from each and every one of the stakeholders (both managers and workers) in the firm.

11.2.1   EQ$_2$: Ethical, Qualitative, and Quantitative Capabilities

There are many competencies a capable manager must have. For instance, one can think of key managerial competencies such as communication, planning and administration, teamwork, strategic action, global awareness, and self-management.[11] The first five competencies require both qualitative consideration and quantitative analysis. A qualitative consideration involves organizational as well as behavioral factors such as teamwork building, motivation, perceptions, fairness, human emotions and feelings, and other non-quantifiable or subjective elements in decision-making. On the other hand, a quantitative analysis utilizes formal, sometimes mathematical, methods to find objective evidence to help managers reach robust decisions. This involves extensive data analysis that takes into account such elements as cost-and-benefit economics, uncertainty and risk factors, forecasting, resource allocation, simulation, sensitivity analysis, and the like. It is not always possible to distinguish between qualitative and quantitative areas of decision-making, however, and it is even futile to try to make a sharp distinction between them. What is important is that a capable decision-maker should be able to utilize both qualitative and quantitative approaches optimally in order to make a decision, which can support the firm's competitive advantage in the global market.

But mastering both qualitative and quantitative capacities does not automatically make the manager a capable one. The sixth competency is another must – a truly capable decision-maker must be a human being with higher standards for integrity and ethical conduct. Without these, the manager cannot be trusted by the stakeholders of the firm, including shareholders, employees, customers, and the market as a whole. Enron's collapse[12] in the early 2000s is a vivid testimony to the essential need for the capable decision-maker to have higher ethical standards.

In Figure 11.9, we visualize the crucial interrelationship among the three fundamental characteristics of a capable decision-maker: qualitative, quantitative, and ethical capability. We denote the three capabilities combined as EQ$_2$. The manager must continuously pursue the ultimate state where EQ$_2$ is integrated and balanced in an optimal manner as much as possible.

---

[11] D. Hellriegel, S. E. Jackson, and J. W. Slocum, Jr., *Management*, 8th edn. (Cincinnati, OH: South-Western College Publishing, 1999).

[12] S. Hamilton and I. Francis, "The Enron Collapse," IMD Case No. IMD-1–0195 (2003).

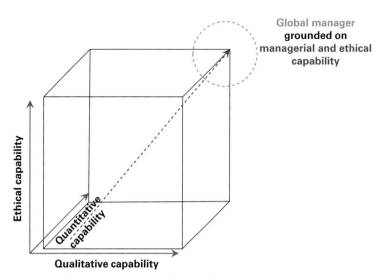

Figure 11.9 Characteristics of a Capable Decision-Maker

11.2.2   The 3Cs: Calculus, Creativity, and Commitment

Albeit closely related to the EQ_2 model, we suggest another conceptual model for the dynamic processes of decision-making that the capable decision-maker should understand and implement. In a bid to generalize the learning propensity model, we develop the 3C model – 3C stands for calculus, creativity, and commitment. As in Figure 11.10, its overall structure is similar to that of the LPM (learning propensity model).

Calculus represents the in-depth fundamental analysis before making any resource and strategic commitment to particular choices or actions. It is a constrained calculation based on a deep and logical analysis (Figure 11.11). The level of calculus, i.e., whether the analysis is logical, robust, and thorough enough, will affect the firm's **creativity** in relation to its competitive strategy. Creativity can be stimulated by **communication**, **controversy**, and **concurrency** among the members of an organization. Communication also implies **connectivity** and **collaboration**. Managers of the firm should design their own global competitive strategy consistent with their level of calculus and resulting creativity, and employ resources accordingly. That is, they have to decide their level of **commitment** in a way consistent with their calculus and creativity attributes. It is materialized via the decision-maker's **choice**, **concentration**, and **consistency**. The remaining dynamics resemble those of the LPM. Note Figure 11.12 shows that effective SCM should integrate the value chain activities both horizontally (within an organization/function) and vertically (across different organizations/functions). SCC (supply chain coordination) underscores that effective SCM needs to be supported by the integrating technology in facilitating the horizontal and vertical integration of the value chain activities.

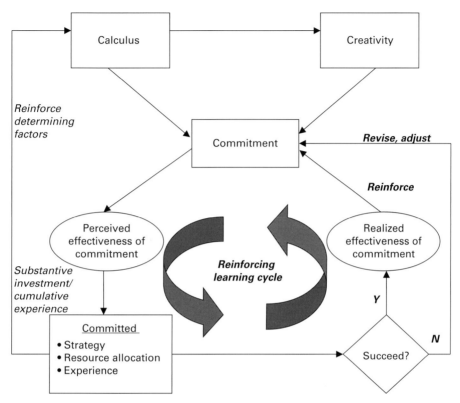

Figure 11.10 The 3C Model

- Calculus
  - constrained calculation (deep and logical analysis)
- Creativity
  - communication (connectivity, collaboration), controversy, concurrency
- Commitment
  - choice, concentration, consistency

Figure 11.11 3Cs for Effective SCM

Calculus. As briefly defined in Figure 11.11, calculus means the analysis of factors related to managerial decision problems. Such an analysis can be done at two levels (Figure 11.13). At the first level, the firm has to conduct both an internal and external analysis. The primary goal of an internal analysis is to enable the manager to identify the most effective and efficient ways for integrating intra-firm functions, activities, and communications. On the contrary, an external analysis is focused on integrating with the firm's suppliers, customers, partners, and the market in general. At the second, higher level, the firm needs to conduct an **ecosystem analysis** involving macroeconomic investigations: although it overlaps partly with the

• Carrying out value-creating activities using the integration technology

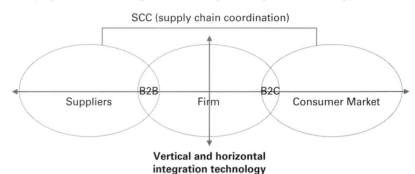

Figure 11.12 SCC and Integration Technology

■ Internal and external analysis
 ▪ Internal integration – integrating intra-firm functions, activities, and communications
 ▪ External integration – integrating with suppliers, customers, partners, and the market in general
■ Ecosystem analysis
 ▪ What are the players in point?
  ▫ Competitors, partners, suppliers, customers?
 ▪ Where are we?
  ▫ How to relate to others?
 ▪ Where is the value?

Figure 11.13 Calculus Level

external analysis, it is more oriented toward macro-environmental issues. Relevant questions include, *What are the major players in our ecosystem or market in point?*, *Where exactly are we in the ecosystem?*, and *Where is the value we can create?* The ecosystem analysis examines who are the major constituencies in the market, what relationship we have or should have with them, how we can create value in the competitive environment, where all these players are dynamically interacting with each other, and the like.

In essence, calculus should help the decision-maker define the firm's **value proposition**. The value should be viewed and defined from the customer's perspective, not by internal stakeholders only. In a very simplistic way, the customers perceive more value as the product's utility increases or as the effective cost (price) of the product decreases. The firm should try to find the most effective and efficient measures to improve its product's utility at the least cost possible. Calculus should help the decision-maker here.

Creativity. As Figure 11.10 indicates, deep and logical analysis is the prerequisite for creativity. Whereas calculus is more related to the quantitative dimension of the EQ_2 model, creativity is closer to the qualitative dimension, involving important behavioral as well as organizational factors. Creativity must be nurtured by communication, controversy, and concurrency.

Without frequent communication among the relevant members of an organization and between members of different organizations like suppliers, partners, and customers, creativity cannot be engendered. Hence, connectivity and collaboration between managers, between relevant decision-makers, between partners in the supply chain, and between the firm and its ecosystem as a whole are key to cultivating creativity in the firm and also among its members.

In effect, there is a close relationship between **competition** and **collaboration** in managing technological innovation. Figures 11.14 to 11.16 present example dynamics. If we don't consider complicated dynamics for the time being, we can draw a chain of relationships as follows: technological innovation → (enables the firm to reduce) price → (reduced price shortens) product life cycle → (shortened PLC instigates more) competition. Thus, technological innovation intensifies competition. As the competition grows, sooner or later the firm finds it necessary to introduce more new products in the market at an accelerating speed. There are two ways for the firm to enhance its new product development capability, through its own internal, independent effort and through collaborating with other partners (or even competitors) in the value chain. These dynamics show that technological innovation eventually reinforces the firm's effort to collaborate with its partners and/or competitors in the value chain – collaboration is a crucial element of creativity. Figure 11.16 describes a more complex dynamic interaction, which includes macro-environmental forces. As technological innovation accelerates, it could happen that people are lagging behind it – the gap between technology potential and human acceptability of technology might increase. As the gap widens, it could depress the innovation speed – elongate the PLC. On the other hand, technological innovation will also contribute to developing techniques and mechanisms that help collaboration between people or organizations, and thus make the collaboration effort more effective. For effective SCM, the firm has to closely monitor and understand the complex dynamics concerning technological innovation, competition, and collaboration.

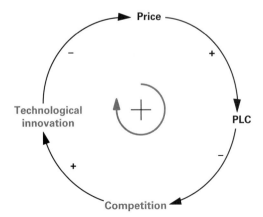

Figure 11.14 Creativity – Competition and Innovation

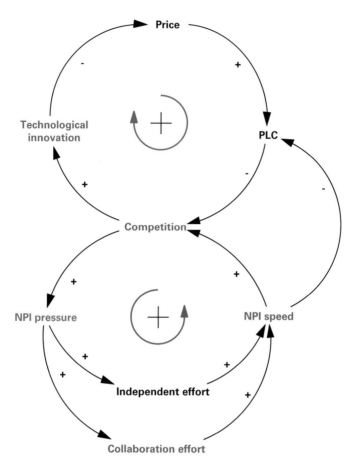

Figure 11.15 Creativity – NPI (New Product Innovation) Dynamics

Why and how does controversy enhance the firm's creativity? We observe that when there is always consensus in the firm – no debate, argument, or lively discussion – it is a symptom of ineffective and inefficient communication between important players involved in the decision-making. In fact, we even put forth that no communication is real without controversy. Therefore, controversy is a vital factor to engender creativity. But, it should be noted that controversy is not the same as irreconcilable division or difference in the organization. Healthy controversy should eventually lead to consensus, but it occurs through spirited debate and argument among the members of the decision-making entity.

Concurrency is also an element of creativity. Concurrency enables the decision-maker to take into account multiple factors and/or variables when making a decision. Since every decision-making problem involves many factors and variables simultaneously, it is crucial for the decision-maker to be able to consider the complex **cause-and-effect relationships** among critical factors/variables at the same time. Otherwise, the decision outcomes can be incomplete at best, or even false ones that lead the firm to erroneous

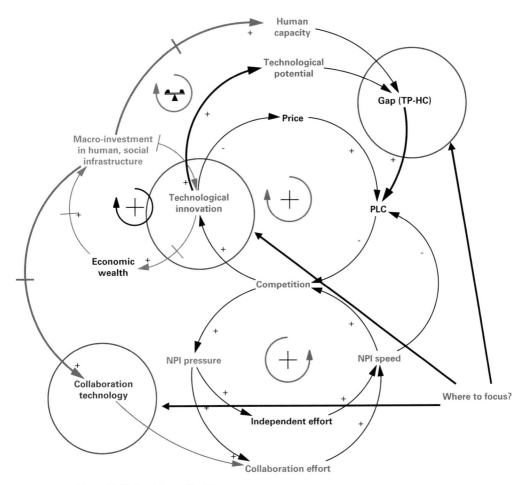

Figure 11.16 Creativity – a Big Picture

strategic choices. But, true concurrency should help the manager to pay appropriate attention to important issues of decision-making, and yet avoid excessive redundancy or duplication. As such, it is related to the principle of sufficiency and parsimony as discussed in Chapter 2 (Figure 2.6).

Before considering commitment, we want to think about the "being smart and nimble" part of creativity (Figure 11.17). Before industrial convergence was realized by the internet technology, the generally accepted dogma of competition was a **head-to-head competition**, where the **scale economy** supported by heavy capacity was the most powerful mantra. Under the head-to-head competition, the enemy was clear and straightforward, and strategy was simple: just to build up your size. With the new technological innovation centered on the coordination technology, however, the rule of competition has changed. Some compare it to the "Judo strategy," as opposed to the "Sumo strategy" that symbolizes the old mantra of competition. In developing a Judo strategy, the firm should play smart: one example is to focus on **strategic alliances** and **collaborative**

- Sumo
  - Head-to-head competition
- Judo
  - Make your own disadvantage into your very advantage
  - Use your competitor's weight in your favor (as your own force)

Figure 11.17 Creativity – Sumo versus Judo Strategy

- Choice – concentration – consistency
- Commitment – The Persistence of Strategies
  - Ghemawat (1991)
    - As the tendency of strategies to persist over time → caused by lock-in, lock-out, lags, and inertia
    - The irreversibility implicit in commitment necessitates a deep look into the future
  - To be lasting, should be formed after calculus and creativity → dynamic commitment

Figure 11.18 Definition of Commitment

strategies with not only partners in the supply chain, but also competitors on a case-by-case basis if that ultimately enhances the firm's competitive advantage and is consistent with its long-term strategic direction. Creativity is also the firm's capability to design and implement its competitive strategy in a smart and nimble manner, and utilize the vast potential of technological innovation within the firm and also in the market as a whole.

Commitment. Commitment can be defined as the tendency of strategies to persist over time (Figure 11.18). Why should we be concerned with commitment? It was suggested that commitment is the only general explanation for sustained differences in the performance of organizations.[13] One can tell why an organization performs better than others by analyzing the organization's commitment to implementing its strategic choices. Commitment, by its very nature, is irreversible, long-term, and strategic. This nature requires the firm to look into the future based on a thorough analysis and innovative ideas, which can help the firm to have a stronger competitive advantage vis-à-vis its competitors. Here we can see the connection between commitment and creativity, and at the same time between commitment and calculus.

Commitment consists of three steps: choice, concentration, and consistency. The firm must make a choice among alternative strategic options. As mentioned previously, these options have to be developed through the two stages: calculus and creativity. During the calculus stage, the firm analyzes various factors, both strategic and environmental, using analytical approaches to come up with alternative plans. During the creativity stage, it enriches the plans put forth from the calculus stage by taking into account its own behavioral and organizational factors. Also, it sometimes screens out some of the plans on the ground that they are not compatible with the firm's propensity toward a particular direction for creativity. At the choice step (the first part of commitment), the firm has to prioritize the strategic options endorsed and enriched through the two stages, so as to

---

[13] P. Ghemawat, *Commitment: The Dynamics of Strategy* (New York: The Free Press, 1991).

- Simultaneous focus on 3C
  - prioritization
    - short-term objectives
    - long-term objectives
- Making flexibility as part of commitment
  - dynamic commitment
  - learning capability in place

Figure 11.19 Managerial Insights

design a strategy map that shows the firm's short-term as well as long-term strategic activities – in other words, to make a strategic choice. Once the choice is made, the firm has to concentrate its available resources on implementing the strategic choice with utmost intensity. As we learned from the learning propensity model, the calculated and intentional resource concentration on a chosen strategy is the essential force that realizes the **self-reinforcing** "virtuous" cycle. In addition to an immediate **concentration** of resources right after the choice is made, the firm has to be ready to live with its strategic choice in the long run – it must stick to its strategic plan until it comes to fruition. This is the third step of commitment, i.e., **consistency**.

11.2.3   Managerial Implications

From the two dynamic decision-making models, EQ_2 and 3C, we learn a few common lessons. First, a capable decision-maker should be able to integrate various capabilities, dimensions, factors, and perspectives simultaneously and effectively. For instance, it is important to combine both qualitative and quantitative analyses, involve the managers across the board (i.e., all organizational ranks), coordinate with the supply chain partners such as suppliers and customers, and so forth.

In addition, it is crucial for the decision-maker to be able to pay keen attention to various decision factors at the same time. In reality, however, it is not always feasible for the decision-maker to deal with numerous alternatives simultaneously and effectively. One way to circumvent this fallacy is to systematize or prioritize the goals or objectives of the firm so that the decision-maker can progressively readjust her attention allocation pattern as the decision environment evolves (Figure 11.19). This is the **dynamic commitment**, which provides the firm with both decisiveness and flexibility at the same time. To accomplish the dynamic commitment is not an easy task. At the heart of this commitment should be the firm's **learning capability**.

11.3   Evolution of Supply Chain Strategy

Dynamics of SCM. Globalization is the process through which the firm expands its supply chain in the global market. As such, it is closely related to the evolution of SCM itself. That is, the firm must redesign its supply chain constantly as the market condition

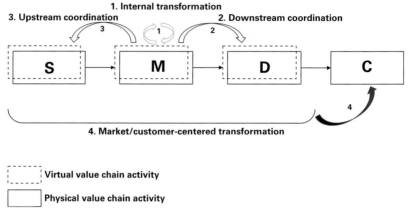

Figure 11.20 Stages of SCM Evolution

changes or the firm reformulates its own strategy. In effect, it is part of the firm's effort to be sustainable.

Here, we propose a general pattern of **supply chain evolution**, presenting the stages through which the firm advances its supply chain. We by no means intend to assert that every company must follow the path. In fact, for some companies, supply chain evolution may be neither necessary nor desirable. Our model is expected to shed light on understanding the dynamics of SCM.

Consider the model in Figure 11.20. There are two different value chains, i.e., physical value chain and virtual value chain. The **physical value chain** is the usual supply chain most managers are familiar with: it consists of participants such as suppliers, manufacturers, distributors, and customers; it is the channel through which physical objects such as products and materials flow upstream and downstream. The **virtual value chain** is mirroring the physical value chain: rather than physical products or materials, however, intangibles like information and communication (also, ideas, standards, and the like) flow through the virtual value chain. Under normal conditions, managers don't pay much attention to the two different value chains separately. That is, the two value chains are generally integrated and managed as one, not separately.

We postulate five stages of SCM evolution: goals and initiatives for each stage are summarized in Table 11.6. Note that the focal company is the manufacturer, i.e., M.

Stage 1 – internal transformation. As the initial step, the firm first tries to improve its own internal operations. For instance, the firm rationalizes or economizes its production processes, resource allocation, and various operations policies; it also makes an effort to form or restructure its manufacturing networks, e.g., adding and closing plants. In a bid to be more responsive to the market, the firm attempts to reorganize its processes to implement the "**make-to-order**" process strategy.

Table 11.6 Goals and Initiatives of SCM Evolution

Stage	Goals	Initiatives and Changes
1	Internal transformation	– Improving/rationalizing internal operations – Setting up manufacturing network – Transforming into a "make-to-order" system
2	Downstream coordination	– Enhancing/refining coordination with downstream partners or activities – Setting up a VMI relationship
3	Upstream coordination	– Enhancing/refining coordination with upstream partners or activities – Consolidating suppliers to set up a supply hub
4	Market-centered transformation	– Optimally coordinating or integrating all SC activities to maximize value for the customers – Offering an extended product mix – Upgrading customer services
5	Value chain transformation	– Separating the virtual value chain from the physical value chain – Cultivating a strategic partnership with an "integrated contract manufacturer" for the physical value chain activities – Focusing on virtual core competences, e.g., design, R&D, marketing, brand, quality assurance, global management, and the like – Seamless integration between virtual and physical value chain is key to sustainable value creation

Stage 2 – downstream coordination. Once the firm completes its internal transformation at least partially (in fact, the firm probably has to sustain its effort to continuously improve its internal operations), it can search for external ways to carry on improving its performance. The company usually finds improving its downstream coordination to be an ideal opportunity. For instance, the firm needs to have better information about the end market so that it can plan its production effectively. Setting up a VMI arrangement with its downstream partner can be a good strategy for rationalizing its downstream connection.

Stage 3 – upstream coordination. The next step is to enhance or refine its coordination with upstream partners or activities. For instance, the firm makes an effort to consolidate its suppliers by forming a **supply hub**, in a bid to reduce the upstream uncertainty.

Stage 4 – market-centered transformation. Once it rationalizes its own supply chain system, i.e., internal, downstream, and upstream coordination, the firm can embark on an audacious plan to serve the entire target market, i.e., satisfying changing and diverse requirements of the customers in the target market. For instance, it probably makes an effort to expand its **product offering** so as to meet the demand diversity or upgrade its

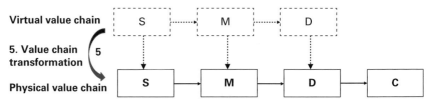

Figure 11.21 Value Chain Separation

services in a bid to maximize the utility experienced by the customers. That is, the firm should be a superb player in creating both efficiency-driven and responsiveness-driven value at the same time.

Stage 5 – value chain transformation. The final stage of supply chain evolution calls for the firm to focus on its strongest core competences (Figure 11.21). It usually involves the separation of the virtual value chain from the physical value chain. Of course, before even considering this stage, the firm must have a highly competent "integrated contract manufacturer" as its trustworthy partner. An **integrated contract manufacturer** differs from a usual contract manufacturer in that it can creatively perform manufacturing for the client (i.e., the focal company) by relieving the client company from most of the complexity due to the tasks or activities involved with manufacturing. For instance, the integrated contract manufacturer identifies the best raw material suppliers, sets up the necessary manufacturing facilities, and performs quality control activities according to the quality assurance standards set by the client. On the contrary, a **traditional contract manufacturer** performs simple manufacturing only, passively following the instructions from the client.

Once it delegates the physical value chain management, i.e., actual manufacturing, to its **strategic outsourcing partner** (i.e., the integrated contract manufacturer), the focal company can focus on its virtual value chain, which consists of the company's strongest core competences such as product design, creative R&D, marketing, brand management, quality assurance, global strategy, and the like. In order to be able to continue maximizing value creation, however, the firm must *continuously* work and coordinate with its strategic outsourcing partner in building a seamless integration between the virtual and physical supply chains.

So far, we've put forth a general pattern of SCM evolution. Although we defined it using stages, we by no means imply that the higher stage is better than the lower ones. That is, not every company should progress through the stages monotonously or unilaterally. For instance, we cannot say that Stage 5 is better than Stage 4 and thus every company has to pursue the value chain transformation, i.e., value chain separation. In fact, for some companies, Stage 5 never becomes an ideal choice. Compare Samsung's strategy with Apple's. Although both companies are great and strong in the same industry, they pursue very different supply chain strategies, i.e., they are currently at different stages of SC evolution as of early 2016. That is, Samsung is still in Stage 4, whereas Apple has almost moved to Stage 5. Nevertheless, one cannot say Apple is more competitive than Samsung in every aspect. We must re-emphasize that which stage is best for the firm depends on the unique competitive environments and conditions, internal and external, faced by the firm.

11.4 Consumer's Role for Sustainable Value Chain

Environmental sustainability is important both economically and managerially.[14] That is, it is an essential issue not only for the economy, but also for the firm, since a large portion of **pollution** is emitted during the firm's production process. Some stakeholders are concerned about pollution in the environment. To curtail the **economic disutility** due to the pollution, the government imposes a penalty on the polluting firm. Pollution can directly reduce the consumer's utility. Therefore, if the consumer is sensitive to the pollution, she is willing to adjust her demand for the product produced by the "pollution-emitting" firm: one of the effective ways for the consumer to penalize the "pollution-emitting" firm is to reduce her demand for the firm's product.

Regarding the government's environmental policy, some found that emission taxes facilitate a firm's technological innovation in pollution abatement more than other regulatory policy instruments. On the contrary, some suggested that the effect of a government policy such as an environmental tax to reduce a firm's emissions is rather complex, i.e., not always effective. There is another perspective focused on the consumer's role in reducing the pollution or at least facilitating such a process. Some postulated that the subsidy to the firm adopting a cleaner process reduces the total pollution in the presence of environmentally conscious consumers. In a similar vein, others observed that the firm's environmental practice increases the firm's "financial" performance by improving customer satisfaction and loyalty, highlighting the role of **consumer awareness** in intensifying corporate environmental responsibility.

Nevertheless, it has been generally perceived that the government must take a leading role in fighting pollution. To a great extent, that has been the case as well. Then, the question is, *How effective has government policy been in reducing the pollution?* Unfortunately, however, our answer to the question may not be favorable unanimously. That's the reason why we focus on the role of consumers. In the free, democratic, capitalist economy, the company is motivated by positive incentives more than discouraged by negative penalties. Facing government regulations and penalties, the company is likely to try to avoid those negative disincentives rather than "proactively" solve problems, probably by searching for loopholes. On the contrary, the company is likely to make more effort to meet the consumer's requirement in order to reap the benefit if the consumer is sensitive to the pollution's harmful effect and willing to take an action to improve the environment. One such action, which is probably the easiest and the most direct, is to take into account the pollution level when determining the consumer's own buying decision. We put forth that the consumer's role in curbing the pollution is more

---

[14] B. Kim and J. E. Sim, "Impacts of Government and Market on Firm's Efforts to Reduce Pollution" (2015) 3 (1) *Cogent Economics & Finance* 1062634, available at https://doi.org/10.1080/23322039.2015.1062634.

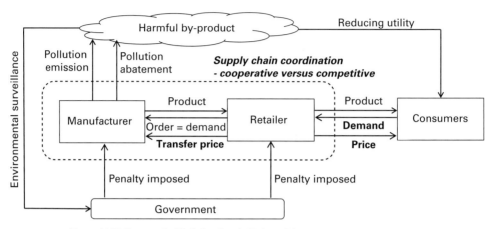

Figure 11.22 Framework of Pollution, Supply Chain, and Consumer

consistent with the market mechanism and more powerful than the government enforcement. It further implies that the government needs to shift its focus on environmental policy from "**enforcing regulations only**" to "**educating consumer** to be more aware of the issue and more active in participating in the problem-solving process."

In this section, we approach the issue from the supply chain perspective. The consumer is an integral part of the supply or value chain. As such, it is important to highlight the role played by the consumer in ensuring sustainability. Two fundamental questions we would like to ask are: *Is it possible for the consumer to play an important role in reducing the pollution or inducing the supply chain partners to behave ethically? How does the supply chain coordination structure (i.e., cooperative versus competitive) interact with the consumer's awareness of sustainability so as to affect the pollution emission or ethical behavior?*

Figure 11.22 depicts the general structure of a value chain in the context of environmental sustainability. The key dynamics and sequence of events assumed in this particular framework are as follows:

(1) There is a supply chain consisting of manufacturer, retailer, and consumer.
(2) Facing the consumer's demand, the retailer decides two things: the sales price, which controls the demand; and the **transfer price**, which affects the manufacturer's decision-making.
(3) It is assumed that due to the bargaining power balance, the manufacturer accepts the transfer price offered by the retailer. Although unfortunate or unacceptable in a society of perfect justice, it reflects the current reality in the supply chain, e.g., in general, it is the retailer that has stronger bargaining power and therefore wields more decision-making power in the supply chain relationship.
(4) It is further assumed that the supply chain partners, the retailer and the manufacturer, agree that they operate as a make-to-order system, i.e., the consumer's demand should always be satisfied. Then, the questions are, *What is the leverage*

the retailer can use to optimize its profit? What is the leverage the manufacturer can use to optimize its own profit? We return to these questions after explaining the framework in more detail.

(5)   While producing its product, the manufacturer emits **pollution**, which deteriorates the consumer's **quality of life**. Due to this harmful effect of pollution, the government imposes a penalty on both the retailer and the manufacturer. In fact, the government sets the total amount of penalty and then divides it between the retailer and the manufacturer appropriately, e.g., in a way to encourage both to behave so as to maximize the pollution reduction.

(6)   There are two different types of consumers. One consists of consumers who are aware of the pollution's harmful effect and active in responding to the accumulated pollution so as to improve their quality of life. They are changing their demand function as the accumulated pollution level changes. For instance, the more pollution due to the retailer's (or, the manufacturer's) product, the less product demanded by the consumers. That is, the demand is negatively affected by the pollution level associated with the product in point. The other type consists of consumers who are neither sensitive to the pollution emission nor active in reducing the pollution's harmful effect. They usually do not change their purchase behavior according to the pollution level, i.e., their demand function is not affected by the pollution level. The fundamental question is, *How important is it for the consumer to be aware or alert in reducing the pollution?*

(7)   Let's return to the questions raised in (4). The manufacturer should produce the amount of the product requested by the retailer. It also accepts the transfer price set by the retailer. Then, it seems like that there is little room for the manufacturer in decision-making. But, the manufacturer doesn't have to be passive. It decides how much to invest in reducing the pollution.

(8)   As the manufacturer makes more effort to cut the pollution and thus the pollution level is indeed reduced, there will be more demand for the product, of course, if the consumers are aware of and sensitive to the pollution. The increased demand benefits the retailer as well. Therefore, the retailer would like to encourage the manufacturer to make more effort to reduce the pollution. But, what incentivizes the manufacturer to do so? Yes, profit! After taking into account its profit primarily determined by the transfer price, the manufacturer decides its effort level to reduce the pollution, which in turn affects the market demand and eventually the retailer's profit itself. Consequently, the retailer has to decide the transfer price very cautiously. If the transfer price is too low, it might look good for the retailer since it increases its short-term profit, but it would discourage the manufacturer from making an effort to reduce the pollution and thus dampen ultimate demand (of course, if the consumers are aware of and sensitive to the pollution's harmful effect). On the other hand, if the transfer price is too high, it might cause the retailer's profit to decrease and possibly lead to the sales price increase, which in turn would reduce the market demand sooner or later.

(9)   Is there no incentive to make an effort to reduce the pollution if the consumers are not aware of or sensitive to the pollution? Yes, there is. The government imposes a

penalty on the retailer and the manufacturer if they collectively cause pollution. Therefore, even when the consumers are not very active, the manufacturer and the retailer are still concerned about pollution and try to minimize it as much as possible, of course, at a far lower level compared to the case where consumers are alert to the problem.

(10) As we have considered two different types of consumers, we now examine two different supply chain coordination modes, *cooperative* versus *competitive*. Under the **cooperative coordination**, the supply chain partners, i.e., the retailer and the manufacturer, coordinate with each other when making a decision regarding production, pricing, and resource allocation. To model such a case, we often define a single objective function for the supply chain partners as a whole, i.e., a single **decision-making entity** is assumed. On the contrary, in the **competitive supply chain**, the supply chain partners compete against each other, e.g., when making a decision, each tries to maximize its own profit, irrespective of the other's. In general, we model this case by setting up separate objective functions for the supply chain participants, e.g., the retailer's objective function is separate from and independent of the manufacturer's.

Using the two dimensions, i.e., **supply chain coordination** and **consumer awareness**, we consider four models as shown in Figure 11.23. Model 1 is a **consumer-ignorant competitive supply chain**, where the consumers are ignorant of and insensitive to the pollution's harmful effect and the supply chain partners are competing with each other, i.e., the retailer tries to maximize its own profit at the cost of the manufacturer, and vice versa. Model 2 (**consumer-aware competitive supply chain**) is different from Model 1 in that now the consumers are aware of and sensitive to the pollution. Model 3 is a **consumer-aware cooperative supply chain**, where the consumers are aware and the supply chain partners are cooperative with each other. Finally, Model 4 is a

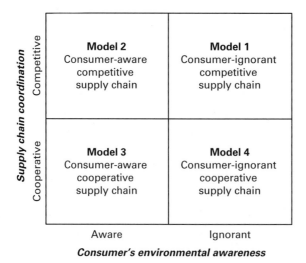

Figure 11.23 Framework of Supply Chain Coordination and Consumer Awareness

consumer-ignorant cooperative supply chain, where the consumers are ignorant and the supply chain partners are cooperative.

With the four cases in the framework (Figure 11.23), we ask questions like, *Which model is better from the economic perspective? Which model is better from the sustainability perspective? How should the retailer or the manufacturer make a decision from the economic or sustainability perspective? Can we determine the best model from a perspective of society or the economy as a whole? What is the primary trade-off relationship in answering the question?*

There are several methodologies we can use to answer these questions. Case studies can be employed to answer some of them. Survey is also a possible approach to answer a few questions. Game theory can be a strong analytical tool to model and analyze the four cases. It should be noted, however, that no single research method can generate perfect answers to all of the questions. That is, whatever methodology we choose we can only hope to find a set of reasonable explanations within certain boundaries or constraints, i.e., generalizability can be limited and the specific context should always be factored in. Nevertheless, applying the **differential games theory**, we model the four cases and find solutions which enable us to derive a few preliminary managerial implications.[15]

(1) We should highlight the importance of **consumer awareness** in reducing the pollution emitted by the manufacturer. It is well known that from a purely economic (profitability) perspective, whether the supply chain participants are competing or cooperating with each other affects the consequences of supply chain strategy to a great extent. However, unless the consumers are aware of and sensitive to the pollution, i.e., taking into account the pollution when making their purchasing decision, there is no difference between the two supply chain strategies in influencing the manufacturer to reduce its emission of pollutants.

(2) We should also emphasize the **role of the retailer** in reducing the pollution. In general, the retailer occupies a very influential position as an information integrator in the supply chain, connecting the manufacturer and the market, i.e., consumers. The primary tool the retailer can adopt in influencing the manufacturer is the price it pays to the manufacturer. For instance, if the transfer price is excessively low, it gives the manufacturer little incentive to make an effort to reduce the pollution, leading to less investment in pollution abatement effort and therefore more accumulated pollution stock. Therefore, an excessively low transfer price turns out to be detrimental to the retailer itself. That's why it is very difficult for the retailer to determine the optimal transfer price: in fact, it requires the retailer to take into account many factors throughout the supply chain.

(3) It can usually be demonstrated that the government penalty is effective for each of the four cases, implying that, when executed properly, the government penalty can play an important and effective role in curbing the environmental degradation due to the pollutant emission in the supply chain. Nevertheless, this observation does not necessarily mean that the government penalty is a tool more effective than the

---

[15] B. Kim and J. E. Sim, "Supply Chain Coordination and Consumer Awareness for Pollution Reduction" (2016) 8(4) *Sustainability* 365; doi:10.3390/su8040365.

consumer's environmental awareness. Some studies show that depending on the market size and the current level of government penalty, consumer awareness can complement or be a substitute for government penalty.

(4) In our specific setting (Figure 11.22), which we believe reasonably reflects the reality, the government has another important policy tool. That is, it can adjust the proportion of the total penalty attributed to each supply chain player by taking into account relevant factors (e.g., each player's sensitivity to the government penalty, i.e., how much it takes to change its behavior) optimally. The government can directly control the manufacturer's behavior by imposing its penalty on the manufacturer or indirectly influence it via the retailer by imposing the penalty on the retailer.

As we already pointed out, there is a very important caveat here: no research methodology can answer the questions perfectly. At the same time, every methodology helps us find a few solutions which can be meaningful at least for certain cases. As such, what is important is how to interpret the solutions within a reasonable boundary or context. Bearing in mind this caveat, we put forth that the managerial implications shed light on understanding the critical interaction between SCM and sustainability. Effective SCM is the key to sustainability.

Discussion Questions

1. Do you think good companies will thrive?
2. Define value chain sustainability.
3. Explain the framework to assess the firm's sustainability level using two dimensions, i.e., strategic priority and operational priority.
4. Explain the 3C model, consisting of calculus, creativity, and commitment.
5. Explain the evolution steps through which a supply chain develops over time. In addition, discuss the forces that drive such a progression.
6. Should every company reach the final stage of SCM evolution? Why or why not?
7. Why should the consumer play a more conspicuous role in reducing the pollution? What is the mechanism through which the consumer influences the firm's behavior and contributes to reducing pollution?

案例 Case Study 11.1
Ford's Sustainability Initiatives

In 1913, Ford Motor Company secured its place as a pioneer in automobile production with its introduction of the integrated moving assembly line. This allowed the Model T, a durable and affordable automobile, to be manufactured in 6 instead of 12.5 hours. This greatly helped Ford to sell the car at a much lower price, and revolutionized manufacturing in all industries.

Ford is still striving to give access to affordable and good quality vehicles to people around the world. However, the twenty-first century brings an additional goal for them: being even more sustainable from environmental, social, and economic points of view. As Executive Chairman Bill Ford puts it, "Improved sustainable performance is not just a requirement, but a tremendous business opportunity." When Ford researches and implements new sustainable technologies, the company always looks for the one that can bring more sustainability not only on one front, but in as many ways as possible. Also, using the fact that growth is a good opportunity for standardization, Ford has been combining this goal with new sustainable technologies in order to effectively reduce their impact on the environment while improving their manufacturing process.

For example, Ford has implemented minimum quantity lubrication (MQL) in several of its powertrain production plants. Usually, during the manufacturing process of an engine or transmission, a significant amount of metal machining is required. In order to cool down the part during or after machining, a large amount of a mix of water and coolant is repeatedly sprayed onto the piece. MQL, however, involves spraying a fine mist over the exact part that needs to be cooled down. The water and coolant savings resulting from the implementation of MQL is significant: for a typical 450,000-unit line, they amount to savings of 28,000 gallons of coolant and 282,000 gallons of water per year.

Another technology that Ford has implemented is the 3-Wet Paint Process. This new technique eliminates the need for a primer spray booth and the subsequent baking process to bake the primer, resulting in both energy savings and 15 to 25 percent less CO_2 emissions and 10 percent less volatile organic compound (VOC) emissions. Also, because this process applies three coats of paint (primer, base coat, and clear coat), each before the prior coat has dried, unlike the traditional method, this technique also allows the painting step to be processed 25 percent faster. This is a great example of a technology that is beneficial from both an environmental sustainability perspective and a manufacturing efficiency perspective.

Ford is also currently developing and testing a new technology that would allow it to reuse VOC emissions resulting from painting car parts. Since car parts are sprayed in a spray booth, the company is working on a way to collect and further concentrate those emissions so as to economically recover the value of this raw material. Previously, VOC would be concentrated 10:1 and then burned by using large amounts of natural gas, producing NOx and CO_2. However, with the new concentrator, VOC will be concentrated by as much as 1,500:1, allowing for innovative opportunities to work with the recovered solvents, ultimately decreasing CO_2 emissions by 70 to 80 percent and decreasing NOx emissions.

Source: This case is developed by B. Kim. ©

With the help of these technologies implemented in some production plants, as well as other environmentally friendly initiatives, Ford has already accomplished progress when it comes to the environment. Since 2000, the company was able to reduce water use by 62 percent and reduce CO_2 emissions by 53 percent. It has also reduced waste to landfill by 36 percent from 2011 to 2014.

However, planning is required to implement all these new sustainable technologies. First, the idea is tested in one or a few plants, then it is slowly implemented in plants around the globe. This presents challenges: changing the way people performed their work up until that point and overcoming the varying levels of environmental engineering experience of their employees in different locations. The key to solving these problems is to form good global teams that can build a sense of trust with each other, making them more accepting of new ideas than what they have been doing so far, and also letting their input be heard and taken into consideration. By overcoming these challenges, successful global operations can be conducted.

Ford is not the only automobile manufacturer to be aware of and actively trying to solve sustainability issues within its supply chain. The worldwide trend for car manufacturers is to reduce their environmental footprint. The fact that virtually all car manufacturers are currently working on sustainability issues, with more or less emphasis depending on the individual company, shows a level of awareness that resources are limited in the long term and that it is necessary to think about these issues now before they become a really serious problem. Even if a particular implemented technology does not offer immediate cost savings, Ford knows that if it improves sustainability by a reasonable amount, it is worthwhile for itself in the long run. For example, Ford is very well aware that the manufacturing of cars and the raw material it buys to build cars use a large amount of water, and this has played an important role in the direction of its sustainability goals. According to Bill Ford, "We believe that business has a key role to play in finding sustainable solutions to current and future global water challenges." It is this way of thinking that has also led the company to create the Partnership for a Cleaner Environment (PACE), through which it shares best practices with selected suppliers on sustainability issues. By doing this, Ford is showing that the company is increasingly taking steps in order to build cars in the most sustainable way possible, all the way to the parts and raw materials that it purchases. That is, Ford is demonstrating a great leadership for sustainability, which can have a lasting impact on the automobile industry for years to come.

Questions

1. Do you agree with Bill Ford's saying "Improved sustainable performance is not just a requirement, but a tremendous business opportunity"? Explain why or why not.
2. What are the specific projects undertaken by Ford to make an effort to enhance sustainability?
3. Why are many automobile companies trying to pay more attention to sustainability issues? What do you think will happen to the automobile industry regarding environmental sustainability in the future?
4. Using some of the frameworks developed in this chapter, evaluate the level of Ford's sustainability strategy.
5. What extra steps do you suggest Ford should take in order to keep its leadership position in the automobile industry?

案例 Case Study 11.2
Building a Sustainable Supply Chain: IKEA

It is easy to think about the present without considering the future. Consumers want more goods and services to improve their standard of living. The problem is that they make choices about goods and services that have long-term consequences for the environment. In our modern world, organizations need to show responsibility. This means that they use resources efficiently, do not harm the environment, and consider how what they do affects the ability of future generations to meet their needs.

IKEA aims to be a responsible organization. It sells low-price home furnishing products around the world. These include furniture and accessories for kitchens, bedrooms, living rooms, bathrooms, and children's rooms. IKEA now has stores in thirty-six countries around the world. It has come a long way in its sixty years of business.

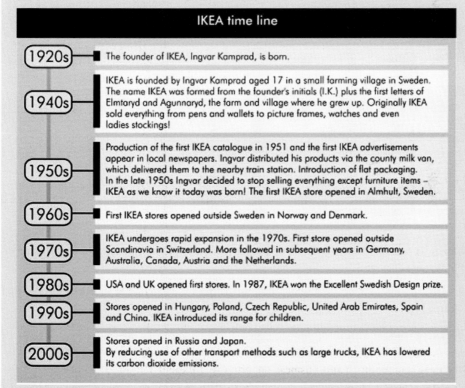

IKEA time line

1920s — The founder of IKEA, Ingvar Kamprad, is born.

1940s — IKEA is founded by Ingvar Kamprad aged 17 in a small farming village in Sweden. The name IKEA was formed from the founder's initials (I.K.) plus the first letters of Elmtaryd and Agunnaryd, the farm and village where he grew up. Originally IKEA sold everything from pens and wallets to picture frames, watches and even ladies stockings!

1950s — Production of the first IKEA catalogue in 1951 and the first IKEA advertisements appear in local newspapers. Ingvar distributed his products via the county milk van, which delivered them to the nearby train station. Introduction of flat packaging. In the late 1950s Ingvar decided to stop selling everything except furniture items – IKEA as we know it today was born! The first IKEA store opened in Almhult, Sweden.

1960s — First IKEA stores opened outside Sweden in Norway and Denmark.

1970s — IKEA undergoes rapid expansion in the 1970s. First store opened outside Scandinavia in Switzerland. More followed in subsequent years in Germany, Australia, Canada, Austria and the Netherlands.

1980s — USA and UK opened first stores. In 1987, IKEA won the Excellent Swedish Design prize.

1990s — Stores opened in Hungary, Poland, Czech Republic, United Arab Emirates, Spain and China. IKEA introduced its range for children.

2000s — Stores opened in Russia and Japan. By reducing use of other transport methods such as large trucks, IKEA has lowered its carbon dioxide emissions.

Figure 11.24 IKEA Time Line

IKEA vision. The direction for the organization is provided by its vision. This acts as a guide for everyone within and outside the organization about what IKEA wants to achieve.

IKEA's vision is "To create a better everyday life for the many people."

To meet its vision, IKEA provides many well-designed, functional products for the home. It prices its products low so that as many people as possible can afford to buy them.

Source: Reprinted with permission from Business Case Studies LLP.

However, in creating low prices, IKEA is unwilling to sacrifice its principles. "Low price, but not at any price" is what IKEA says. This means it wants its business to be sustainable. IKEA supplies goods and services to individuals in a way that has an overall beneficial effect on people and the environment. Customers all over the world have responded positively to IKEA's approach. This is evident in its increasing sales. In 2006, IKEA had a group turnover of nearly €18 billion.

Sectors of industry and sustainable supply chains. When consumers go to a retailer like IKEA, they will be looking at the different ranges of products and how they are presented. They may also look for quality customer service. However, consumers may not be aware that, before products reach them, they must move from being raw materials through a variety of stages to become finished products suitable for sale. This is known as the supply chain.

The supply chain involves a flow of production and processes through each of the three industrial sectors, as shown in Figure 11.25.

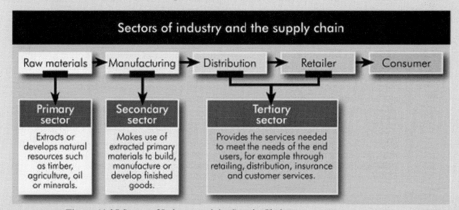

Figure 11.25 Sector of Industry and the Supply Chain

IKEA takes its responsibilities seriously and organizes its operations in order to have a positive effect upon the environment:

- It aims that all the products and materials it takes from the primary sector do not harm the environment.
- Its products are manufactured in a responsible way.

This case study looks in detail at how IKEA has achieved its aim to be a responsible business in each of the three sectors of the supply chain.

The primary sector. IKEA is not a primary sector organization, but it needs raw materials to develop its products. It therefore works closely with primary sector suppliers to ensure a sustainable impact on the people and the environment in which it operates. The primary sector involves the development of the raw materials. IKEA designs its own products. At the design stage, IKEA checks that products meet strict requirements for function, efficient distribution, quality, and impact on the environment. Low price is one of the main factors that IKEA considers in producing well-designed, functional home furnishings available to everyone.

IKEA buys products from more than 1,300 suppliers in fifty countries. It uses a number of trading service offices across the world. They negotiate prices with suppliers, check the quality of materials, and analyze the environmental impacts that occur through the supply chain. They also keep an eye on the suppliers' social and working conditions.

Environmental impact: IKEA uses a tool – the "e-Wheel" – to evaluate the environmental impact of its products. The e-Wheel helps IKEA to analyze the four stages within the life of a product. This also helps suppliers to improve their understanding of the environmental impact of the products they are supplying.

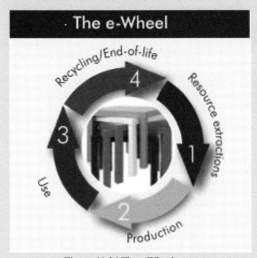

Figure 11.26 The e-Wheel

Approximately 50 percent of IKEA's 9,500 products are made from wood or wood fibers. This is a good resource as long as it comes from sustainable sources. It can be **recycled** and is a **renewable** resource.

IKEA creates many design solutions to minimize the use of materials. For example:

- some tables are made out of recycled plastic;
- some rugs are made of material clippings that would otherwise be wasted; and
- products such as water cans are designed to be stacked. This means that more can be transported in each load, reducing the number of lorry journeys and therefore lowering fuel costs.

Each of these ideas helps IKEA's products to be more sustainable and reduce the impact on the environment.

Supplier codes of conduct: A key part of IKEA's success is due to its communications with suppliers of materials and with manufacturers. During manufacturing, IKEA specifies to its producers that waste should be avoided. Where waste does occur, IKEA encourages suppliers to try to use it in the manufacture of other products. IKEA has a code of conduct called the IKEA Way of Purchasing Home Furnishing Products (IWAY). This contains minimum rules and guidelines that help manufacturers to reduce the impact of their activities on the environment. The IWAY code complies with international legislation.

A product in use should not have a harmful effect upon consumers or their environment – for example, it should not cause allergies. If it uses energy, it should do so efficiently. When a product comes to the end of its useful life, it should be possible to reclaim or recycle the materials that make up the product. Such materials can then be reused for making other products.

The secondary sector. Manufacturers within the secondary sector create IKEA products from raw materials. As products move through the supply chain, the process of value-added takes place.

IKEA designs many of its products so that the smallest amount of resources can make the best products. For example, IKEA saves on resources by using hollow legs in furniture (e.g., the OGLA dining chair). Another example is by using a honeycomb-paper filling material instead of solid wood for the inside of table tops (e.g., the LACK series).

As manufacturers or suppliers add value to products, the IWAY code of practice identifies IKEA's minimum requirements.

The IWAY code of practice expects suppliers to:

- follow national and international laws;
- not use child labor;
- not use woods and glues from non-sustainable forests;
- reduce their waste and emissions;
- contribute to recycling;
- follow health and safety requirements;
- care for the environment; and
- take care of their employees.

The application of the code raises standards. Each of the requirements within the code of conduct helps to develop sustainable business activities. They have a positive impact on the business environment in which the suppliers operate. They also improve the experience of people working for those businesses. To monitor suppliers, IKEA regularly carries out an IWAY audit. This involves talking to employees and inspecting documents and records. IKEA visits suppliers on site on a number of occasions to ensure that they are following the code of conduct.

The code of conduct for suppliers and the work with other organizations underlines IKEA's commitment to "low price, but not at any price." Although IKEA wants its customers to enjoy low prices, this should not happen at the expense of its business principles.

Sustainable partnerships: In 2000, IKEA formed a partnership with UNICEF to work on a community program in Northern India. The aim of the work was to prevent child labor by raising awareness and addressing the root causes.

IKEA has also formed a partnership with the World Wildlife Fund (WWF). IKEA and WWF have committed themselves to promoting the sustainable use of natural resources. This helps to ensure that forests can be used both now and in the future.

To support sustainable partnerships with suppliers, IKEA works with other organizations. For example, IKEA and WWF actions have led to:

- a series of training courses for people in Russia, Bulgaria, Romania, and China on responsible forest management;
- the development of forestry plans in China; and
- demonstrations to managers in Latvia on the benefits of responsible forestry.

All of these projects show IKEA's commitment to supporting sustainable practices.

The tertiary sector. Businesses in the tertiary sector provide a service, such as banking, transportation or retailing. They do not extract the raw materials or make products themselves. Retailers make up 11 percent of businesses within the United Kingdom.

In the tertiary sector, IKEA's retail stores add value to manufactured goods by providing a form of shopping different from the usual high-street experience. IKEA has more than 260 stores in over thirty-six countries. These meet the needs of consumers in a number of different ways:

- Retailing turnover in the United Kingdom was more than £250 billion in 2006.
- Each IKEA store is large and holds more than 9,500 products, giving a wide variety of choice.
- Within each store, there are a number of realistic room settings that enable customers to see what the products would look like in their own homes.
- The IKEA store is built on a concept of "you do half, we do half; together we save money." This refers to, for example, the customer assembling furniture at home.
- Customers handpick products themselves using trolleys.
- IKEA provides catalogues and home delivery to save customers time.
- IKEA stores have restaurants that provide Swedish dishes alongside local food choices.

To make its activities more sustainable, IKEA has set up many local UK initiatives:

- In 2006, IKEA UK recycled more than 70 percent of its waste products. Its goal is to recycle 90 percent of materials.
- To reduce environmental impact, in 2006, IKEA UK started to charge for carrier bags. This reduced the use of carrier bags by 95 percent. In June 2007, IKEA UK removed carrier bags from its stores completely.
- In December 2006, IKEA UK gave a brand-new folding bike to each of its 9,000 employees. It also gave subsidized travel tickets to encourage them to travel to and from work on public transport.
- IKEA UK has provided low-energy light bulbs to its entire UK workforce and switched its fleet of company cars to low-emission hybrid models.

Conclusion. IKEA's long-term ambition is to become the leading home furnishing company. However, for IKEA, getting there is not simply about developing profitability and market share.

As a global organization, IKEA has chosen to undertake a leadership role in creating a sustainable way of working. It has educated suppliers to understand how and why sustainable production is vital. This has helped IKEA differentiate itself from its competitors.

Consumers are made aware of IKEA's commitment to sustainability through its involvement with many other organizations such as WWF and UNICEF. IKEA is now considered by both suppliers and consumers to be a responsible company that they can trust.

Questions
1. Using the case study, provide two examples of sustainable activities.
2. Explain how each sector of industry is linked together within a supply chain.
3. Describe how IKEA influences all elements of its supply chain to adopt sustainable practices.
4. Evaluate and discuss the effect that IKEA's sustainable practices are likely to have upon the furnishing industry over the longer term.

References

Argyris, C. (1982). *Reasoning, Learning and Action: Individual and Organizational* (San Francisco: Jossey-Bass).

Arino, A. and J. de la Torre (1998). "Learning from Failure: Towards an Evolutionary Model of Collaborative Ventures" 9(3) *Organization Science* 306–325.

Aronow, S. (2012). "Case study: Award Highlights Success of Verizon Wireless-Samsung CPFR Journey," Gartner Operation Excellence Series, Case ID: G00224201, available at www .gartner.com/doc/2126419/award-highlights-success-verizon-wirelesssamsung.

Bianco, A. and W. Zellner (2003). "Is Wal-Mart Too Powerful?" *Business Week*, October 6, cover story.

Crosby, P. B. (1980). *Quality Is Free: The Art of Making Quality Certain* (New York: McGraw-Hill).

Edmondson, A. C. and D. Lane (2012). *Global Knowledge Management at Danone (A) (Abridged)*, Harvard Business School, Case No. 613003-PDF-ENG.

Elkington, J. (1997). *Cannibals with Forks: The Triple Bottom Line of 21st Century Business* (Oxford: Capstone).

Fisher, M. L. (1997). "What Is the Right Supply Chain for Your Product?" *Harvard Business Review* (March–April), pp. 105–116.

Fisher, M., J. Hammond, W. Obermeyer, and A. Raman (1997). "Configuring a Supply Chain to Reduce the Cost of Demand Uncertainty" 6(3) *Production and Operations Management* 211–225.

Garvin, D. A. (1988). *Managing Quality: The Strategic and Competitive Edge* (New York: The Free Press).

Ghemawat, P. (1991). *Commitment: The Dynamics of Strategy* (New York: The Free Press).

Hamilton, S. and I. Francis (2003). "The Enron Collapse," IMD Case No. IMD-1–0195.

Henderson, R. M. and K. B. Clark (1990). "Architectural Innovation: The Reconfiguration of Existing Product Technologies and the Failure of Established Firms" 35(1) *Administrative Science Quarterly* 9–30.

Hellriegel, D., S. E. Jackson, and J. W. Slocum, Jr. (1999). *Management*, 8th edn. (Cincinnati, OH: South-Western College Publishing).

Jaikumar, R. and R. E. Bohn (1992). "A Dynamic Approach to Operations Management: An Alternative to Static Optimization" 27(3) *International Journal of Production Economics* 265–282.

Jordan, W. C. and S. C. Graves (1995). "Principles on the Benefits of Manufacturing Process Flexibility" 41(4) *Management Science* 577–594.

Kaplan, R. S. and D. P. Norton (2005). "Balanced Scorecard: Measures that Drive Performance," *Harvard Business Review*, July–August.

Kim, B. (1996). "An Integrating Perspective on Intelligent Production Systems" 2(3–4) *Information and Systems Engineering* 205–227.

    (1998)."Manufacturing Learning Propensity in Operations Improvement" 8(1) *Human Factors and Ergonomics in Manufacturing* 79–104.

(2003). "Managing the Transition of Technology Life Cycle" 23(5) *Technovation* 371–381.

(2013). "Quality Goals and Supply Chain Strategy in the Fashion Industry" 16(2) *Qualitative Market Research: An International Journal* 214–242.

Kim, B. and C. Kim (2012). "Defining and Measuring Value System Sustainability: Initial Concepts and Blueprints," KAIST Business School Working Paper Series No. 2012–007, September 1, available at SSRN: http://ssrn.com/abstract=2151705.

Kim, B., H. Kim, J. Shim, and C. Shin (2014). "LG Display's First Module Plant in Europe" 18(2) *Asian Case Research Journal* 339–370.

Kim, B. and S. Kim (2016). "Inventory Types and Their Effects on Sales" 3(2) *International Journal of Inventory Research* 115–133.

Kim, B. and Y. Lee (2001). "Global Capacity Expansion Strategies; Lessons Learned from Two Korean Carmakers" 34(3) *Long Range Planning* 309–333.

Kim, B. and C. Park (2013). "Firms' Integrating Efforts to Mitigate the Trade-Off between Controllability and Flexibility" 51(4) *International Journal of Production Research* 1258–78.

Kim, B., K. Park, and T. Kim (1999). "The Perception Gap among Buyer and Suppliers in the Semiconductor Industry" 4(5) *Supply Chain Management: An International Journal* 231–241.

Kim, B. and J. E. Sim (2015). "Impacts of Government and Market on Firm's Efforts to Reduce Pollution" 3(1) *Cogent Economics & Finance* 1062634, available at https://doi.org/10.1080/23322039.2015.1062634.

(2015). "The War for Rechargeable Electric-Vehicle Batteries," Asia Case Research Centre, The University of Hong Kong, Case No. 14/547C.

(2016). "Impact of Technological Innovation on Operations: A Korean Shipbuilder's Strategic Shift from Shipbuilding to Offshore Projects," unpublished case.

(2016). "Supply Chain Coordination and Consumer Awareness for Pollution Reduction" 8(4) *Sustainability* 365; doi:10.3390/su8040365.

Leonard-Barton, D. (1988). "Implementation as Mutual Adaptation of Technology and Organization" 17(5) *Research Policy* 251–267.

Malnight, T. W. (1995). "Globalization of an Ethnocentric Firm: An Evolutionary Perspective" 16(2) *Strategic Management Journal* 119–141.

Narus, J. A. and J. C. Anderson (1996). "Rethinking Distribution: Adaptive Channels," *Harvard Business Review*, July–August, pp. 112–120.

Perlmutter, H. V. (1969). "The Tortuous Evolution of Multinational Corporation," *Columbia Journal of World Business*, January–February, pp. 8–18.

Porter, M. E. (1980). *Competitive Strategy: Techniques for Analyzing Industries and Competitors* (New York: The Free Press).

(1985). *The Competitive Advantage: Creating and Sustaining Superior Performance* (New York: The Free Press).

Simon, H. (2009). *Hidden Champions of the 21st Century: Success Strategies of Unknown World Market Leaders* (London: Springer).

Skinner, W. (1978). *Manufacturing in the Corporate Strategy* (New York: John Wiley).

Wikipedia, n.d., "Laozi," available at https://en.wikipedia.org/wiki/Laozi.

Wood, D. and N. Gao (2013). *Elizabeth Arden: Executing Global Supply Chain Re-Engineering*, Ivey Publishing, Case No. 9B13D017.

Zaheer, A., B. McEvily, and V. Perrone (1998). "Does Trust Matter? Exploring the Effects of Interorganizational and Interpersonal Trust on Performance" 9(2) *Organization Science* 141–159.

Index